The Humble Story of Don Quixote

Cesáreo Bandera

The Humble Story of Don Quixote

Reflections on the Birth of the Modern Novel

The Catholic University of America Press
Washington, D.C.

Another, somewhat longer, version of this book has been published in Spanish under the title "*Monda y desnuda*": *La humilde historia de Don Quijote. Reflexiones sobre el origen de la novela moderna* (Madrid: Iberoamericana, 2005).

The paper used in this publication meets the minimum requirements of American National Standards for Information Science—Permanence of Paper for Printed Library Materials, ANSI Z39.48-1984.
∞

LIBRARY OF CONGRESS CATALOGING-IN-PUBLICATION DATA
Bandera, Cesáreo.
The humble story of Don Quixote : reflections on the birth of the modern novel / Cesáreo Bandera.
p. cm.
Includes bibliographical references and index.
ISBN-13: 978-0-8132-1452-8 (cloth : alk. paper)
ISBN-10: 0-8132-1452-1 (cloth : alk. paper) 1. Cervantes Saavedra, Miguel de, 1547–1616. Don Quixote. 2. Cervantes Saavedra, Miguel de, 1547–1616—Influence. 3. Literature—History and criticism. I. Title.
PQ6352.B19 2006
863'.3—dc22
2005021681

To Veronica, Vicky, and Mateo

Contents

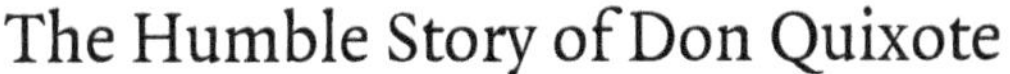

The Humble Story of Don Quixote

Introduction

In the whole world there is no deeper, no mightier literary work. This is, so far, the last and greatest expression of human thought. . . . And if the world were to come to an end, and people were asked there, somewhere: "Did you understand your life on earth, and what conclusions have you drawn from it?"—man could silently hand over Don Quijote.

(Dostoyevsky, *The Diary of a Writer*, cited in Gilman, 76)

In any genre it may happen that the first great example contains the whole potentiality of the genre. It has been said that all philosophy is a footnote to Plato. It can be said that all prose fiction is a variation on the theme of Don Quixote.

(Lionel Trilling, 209)

Great and Humble

Citations expressing similar feelings and opinions to those just quoted could be multiplied.[1] *Don Quixote* is clearly not just another good novel, not even just one among the greatest; it is more than that, if for no other reason

1. In the jacket to the new translation of *Don Quixote* by Edith Grossman (New York: HarperCollins, 2003), in addition to Lionel Trilling's praise, similar testimonies are included from Carlos Fuentes, Milan Kundera, Vladimir Nabokov, V. S. Pritchett, and Thomas Mann. We could add still others—for example, Thomas Macauly and Ortega y Gasset.

than it was the first among the greatest. It did something that no other novel had done before. And that, in itself, was extraordinary. It is therefore generally admitted today that *Don Quixote* inaugurates the modern novel and becomes its archetype. In some sense, every modern novel worthy of its name is written, as Henry Fielding said of his *Joseph Andrews*, "in imitation of the manner of Cervantes, author of *Don Quixote*."

Critics have also reacted on occasion to this general consensus by pointing out that, although Cervantes was a pioneer, he was not alone in creating the new kind of novel.[2] Studies abound showing, for example, that Cervantes's novel, and the modern novel in general, is linked, sometimes in rather subterranean ways, to medieval romance narrative,[3] or that Cervantes's view of his own work was well within the cultural parameters and the limitations of his own time.[4] All of this is, of course, true up to a point, and one can certainly profit from the mountains of erudition that have been produced in this regard. But it is not what Cervantes's *Don Quixote* owes to the past that is important here, but what is new in it, that is to say, the way it is oriented toward the future, the way it announces the historical arrival of the modern novel and is related to it like no other narrative before or during its own time. In this sense, in its seminal and fruitful orientation toward the future, *Don Quixote* is something of a breakthrough, a moment of revelation that opens up a new horizon. But precisely because the full extent of its fruitfulness lies in the future, the breakthrough may not be recognized as such immediately. *Don Quixote*'s novelty arrives without fanfare, in the form of a new horizon that opens up gradually, and that, once it is revealed, looks perfectly logical, the most natural thing in the world, as if it had been there all the time. Such novelty does not destroy anything directly or immediately; it simply puts everything in a new light. But in this new light it becomes increasingly difficult to do things that everybody was still doing only the day before.

Cervantes was not a revolutionary, nor is his *Don Quixote* imbued with a revolutionary spirit. Quite the opposite: one of the most amazing things about this extraordinary novel is that it is also incredibly humble. The story it tells is almost trivial, and it knows it. As Marthe Robert observed: "Dante, Goethe, and Shakespeare treat serious subjects touching upon universal

2. See Riley, 1994, 73.
3. See Dudley, passim, and Jewers, passim.
4. See Russell, passim.

. . . human problems. The pitifully improbable story of *Don Quixote*, by contrast, consists of a trivial plot that is anecdotal, scant, and rather foolish. . . . [There is an] unusual disproportion between the stature of the work and the triviality of its subject" (47). Not only that, but, as if to ratify the fact that this inauguration of the modern novel is not conceived as a triumphant, trampling, entry of the novel on the historical stage, the "trivial plot" of this "pitifully improbable story" speaks of a man who became crazy, a laughingstock, a fool, by reading novels. The first great modern novel is a warning against the reading and the writing of novels—which, at first sight, is indeed a most unlikely inauguration.

But what if the humility of the story, on the one hand, and the greatness of the novel, on the other, rather than being contradictory or paradoxical, are intimately related? In other words, one must explore the possibility that the conjunction of these two things, humility and greatness, is more than a mere accident, that the greatness of the first modern novel may be inseparable from the humble character of its material. This will be the subject of this book. I would like to explore and, I hope, to demonstrate the fundamental connection between such greatness and such humility. I would like to show that the horizon that *Don Quixote* opens up for the development of a new kind of literary fiction is truly new and truly open to the same extent to which it is humble, that is, the horizon where the fruitfulness, the creative power, of such humble material, explicitly recognized as such, is revealed.

We are not talking about rhetorical humility, however. The meaning of such humble greatness goes well beyond the limits of rhetoric and the poetic art (*ars poetica*). *Don Quixote* is indeed a masterpiece of literary ingenuity, and that truth cannot be ignored. But no amount of literary ingenuity alone could ever produce the kind of greatness and historical relevance that *Don Quixote* has achieved through the centuries, that *Don Quixote* opened up into the future. What might be called the prophetic character of Cervantes's novel is only the literary expression of an epochal phenomenon. It could be said of Cervantes what was said of his contemporary Francis Bacon: that he was *buccinator novi temporis*, the trumpeter, the herald, of a new time, the one who announces that a new era has arrived—a new era that had been gestating, as it were, in Christian Europe for centuries, the dawn of which constitutes the transition from the Middle Ages to the modern era. As a result of that transition, Christian Europe separated itself radically from every other society on the face of the earth. A historical phenomenon such as the modern novel did not happen anywhere else. That is the kind of novelty of which I think *Don Quixote* is a particularly striking example.

The Historical Perspective

In *The Sacred Game* I tried to show that the profound change that occurred in the very conception of literary fiction during that historical transition cannot be properly understood outside the context of an equally profound historical process of Christian desacralization, that is to say, a desacralization, or, as it has also been called, a disenchantment, of worldview effected under the powerful influence of the nonsacrificial, or nonvictimizing (since there is no sacrifice without a victim), inspiration of the Christian text, about which some general observations should still be made here.

It has been repeated time and again that the transition of which we are speaking is characterized by a change in emphasis from a God-centered to a man-centered view of the world. I believe that is substantially correct not in the sense that God becomes less important or that people became less religious (the Reformation, on the one hand, and the protracted wars of religion throughout much of Europe, on the other, amply testify to the contrary), but in the sense that man acquires an increasingly greater responsibility for what goes on in the world of human society and history. At the same time man faces a physical world outside, which, as it becomes rapidly disenchanted or desacralized, also becomes far less threatening and far more predictable than it used to be—a world that reflects not God's unconcern, but God's innocence, or the fact that He, as Descartes would say, is not capricious, does not play tricks on humans. Only humans play tricks on humans.

This gradually discovered world outside, the world of nature, had always been, in the Judeo-Christian tradition, a manifestation of the power and glory of God. It was His signature, His book. Now, in addition to that, it is being discovered as a manifestation of the innocence of God, and as a result, as safe and open for exploration. There is no hidden intention to be feared behind it, no taboos, no forbidden knowledge, no truth that must be kept from sight. As Unamuno would say, "[L]o que hace más grande a la Naturaleza es el ser desintencionada" (*Obras completas*, 3.241). Truth itself is innocent. Its discovery may actually hurt human beings, but it is not Truth's fault, it is the fault of whoever is not ready to accept it. As we read in that immediate precursor of the modern era, the *Imitatio Christi*:

> If you were good and pure inwardly in your soul, you would be able to see and understand all things without impediment and understand them aright. (Thomas à Kempis, 2.4.2)

Desacralization of Violence

All of this has been said in one way or another many times before. What is not always sufficiently realized is that, in this new world, the responsibility for social violence, not only the violence that may threaten social stability, but defensive violence as well, without which human society has never been able to exist, also becomes increasingly human and nothing but human. In other words, just as everything becomes desacralized, so does violence, both the good and the bad. It becomes comparatively more difficult for historical Christian society to justify its own violence directly on sacred, transcendent grounds. (This situation may in fact exacerbate the violence, make it even more dangerous, like the violence of an animal fatally wounded.) The old sacrificial unanimity around the sacred victim begins to crack and disintegrate. A new realization gains ground by the day: the traditional victims of social violence may not be quite as unique, sacred, untouchable, demonic, intimately associated with, and calling for, expulsion or elimination as they used to be. The powerful association of the new sacred with a victim, Christ, who is totally and transcendentally innocent, inevitably hangs dangerously (from a societal point of view) over all victims, introducing hesitation, making their expulsion less compelling. And the possibility of an utterly unprecedented meaning of the old sacred, obligatory act of victimization emerges: the meaning that our society today attaches to the word *victimize*. The immediate association we automatically establish today between "victimization" and the innocence of the victim is a direct heir to the historical process to which we are referring, a new meaning that runs counter to the old meaning attached to the sacred act of the killing or expulsion of the victim.

The desacralization of violence could not fail to have a profound impact in the history of literature. Its most visible and dramatic result was the historical exhaustion of the traditional epic model.[5] It was a truly amazing phenomenon. For at no time had the prestige of classical epic, the epic of Homer and Virgil, been higher than at the time when it was no longer possible to reproduce such revered models. Cervantes himself still believed in the possibility of a new, modern, Christian epic. There were numerous attempts to carry on the epic tradition. But, ironically, it was the best practitioners of the epic, Camoens, for example, and Tasso, who best understood that they were attempting the impossible. The Christian muse, in the words of Tasso, had nothing to do with the old classical muse on Mount Helicon:

> O Muse, that do not wreath your brow on Helicon with fading bays, but among the blessed choirs in Heaven above possess a golden crown of deathless stars . . . grant me pardon if with the truth I interweave [fictional] embroiderings, if partly with pleasures other than yours I ornament my pages. (1.2)[6]

Having lost his attachment to the sacred, what might be called his "sacrificial character," the traditional epic warrior lost his very soul, his roots. In the most fundamental sense the old hero, having undergone a process of historical disintegration, to which the popular books of chivalry testify, was out of place in modern Christian Europe. It is not so much that the publication of Cervantes's *Don Quixote* dealt a fatal blow to the chivalric genre. Rather, *Don Quixote* reveals, makes explicit, what had already happened. It is in this sense that Cervantes was, as we just said, a herald of the new time.

The End of the Traditional Antihero

But what about the antihero? For, since time immemorial, in the shadow of an Achilles always lurked, in a more or less visible way, the anti-Achilles, the deformed, ridiculous, despicable, and hateful figure of a Thersites of some sort. Would the traditional antihero now replace the fallen, or dysfunctional, old hero? Would the old hero now simply become a fool? Within the nonsacrificial, nonvictimizing logic of Christian desacralization, obviously such a substitution or transformation would have changed nothing at all. It would have been a repetition of the old sacrificial model. For

5. See chapter 4, "Beyond the Epic Model," in *The Sacred Game*.

6. Torquato Tasso, *Jerusalem Delivered*, trans. Ralph Nash (Detroit, Mich.: Wayne State University Press, 1987).

hero and antihero are simply the two aspects, the good and the bad, the remedy and the poison, of the old sacred victim, the victim who embodied the irreducible ambivalence of the old sacred itself.

It is nevertheless important to notice that the historical exhaustion of the epic model, its failure to live up to contemporary expectations, coincides with a renewed interest in the antihero as a literary character. This is the moment when the picaresque novel is also born in Spain. And I believe it is no historical accident that the *Quixote* was born within the context of the emergence of the picaresque. It is precisely in such a context that its originality and most profound meaning can be appreciated. Literary critics are, of course, fully familiar with the formal similarities and differences between the *Quixote* and its picaresque siblings, as well as between Cervantes himself and the two major authors of picaresque novels, Alemán and Quevedo. Our own approach recognizes this critical awareness and tries to deepen it through our analysis of the two major picaresque novels, the *Guzmán de Alfarache* and the *Buscón*, within the same theoretical parameters in which we are considering the modernity of *Don Quixote*.

The picaresque novel, as a genre, devotes an unprecedented degree of attention to a type of character, an antihero, a rogue, who had never been considered worthy of serious consideration. Referring in particular to the first picaresque novel, *Lazarillo de Tormes* (1554), F. Rico observes that "literary convention was not yet on very good terms with the low-born. . . . Narrative prose in particular had no close precedents to offer in which such continuous and exclusive attention was devoted to a character of so lowly a station" (2). This is an accurate observation that should be extended to include other types of antiheroic characters not necessarily of a roguish and lowly station. Cervantes's story of the fool Don Quixote was as unprecedented as the *Lazarillo*. Who had ever devoted so much attention to a fool, a "figura de entremés," a typical character for a theatrical interlude or farce? Who would have ever thought that the story of a fool could acquire such an extraordinary significance?

The Genius of the Story

Don Quixote, however, is not just foolish. The type of foolishness he exemplifies is also important. This fool is a fool because he thinks he is a hero, a hero like the heroes of old of which one reads in the works of the poets. It is this specific kind of foolishness that gives *Don Quixote* the possibility of being read as a historical symbol of what was actually happening well beyond the level of the merely anecdotal, namely, the historical exhaustion of the epic model.

But such a symbolic possibility would remain purely abstract and disconnected from the text of the story itself unless the parodic story of this fool could be raised above the level of mere parody. Parody alone would not make *Don Quixote* the first great modern novel. Something positive and new, something unprecedented, had to happen within the parodic intention of the story that could transform the parody from inside, that could raise something trivial and lowly into something for which I can find no better word than prophetic. What is it, therefore, that Cervantes did with this particular fool who thought he was a hero? What did he do with his fool that nobody else had done with the conventional fool before?

Or perhaps we should rephrase the question. What is it that everybody else, that is to say, literary convention, had always done with fools, madmen, and other marginal figures, with whom "it was not on very good terms"? And the answer is very simple: what literary convention, or its folkloric antecedents, expressions of collective behavior, had always done with its fools and madmen was to expel them, either literally or by treating them in one way or another as scapegoats, victims, figures of public scorn and derision. The fool, like the *bobo*, the old Roman *stupidus*, had always been the object of *burlas*, deceptions, practical jokes, at the hands of a trickster, for example, carried out to the laughter and applause of the community. These victims of public ridicule, as Anthony Close has observed in his book on the comic mind of the period, were treated "as in primitive ritual, . . . as scapegoat: the butt of injurious derision, which is essentially of a communal nature" (330). That is what had always been done with the antihero, while everybody cried at the death or the sufferings of the hero, a most beautiful and noble death or suffering for the benefit of everybody. These were the two sides of the same coin.

Cervantes begins with such a public antiheroic figure, but will gradually distance himself from the jeering crowd not by taking the side of the fool against the crowd—this is of crucial importance—but by rescuing the fool from his own foolishness. He rescues the fool from the crowd by rescuing him from himself. That was truly unprecedented. The story of Cervantes's fool is not structured as the story of an expulsion, but as the story of a prolonged and compassionate rescue.[7]

This is the formidable, the extraordinary, thing about Cervantes's Don Quixote: he unites within himself, he embodies, both aspects of the desacralizing process, the historical collapse of the old epic figure and the rescuing of the outcast, because both are aspects of the same historical event: the growing erosion of the sacrificial (sacred-making)—victimizing—mechanism, the mechanism that structures and channels social violence. The modern novel does not begin with the ridiculous, antiheroic collapse of the hero, it begins when that fallen hero, broken down and pitiful, laughable, is rescued from the self-destructive foolishness of his impossible dream, and discovered to be human and nothing but human. It was a combination, on the one hand, of the artistic genius of Cervantes guided at all times by a profound sense of Christian compassion, and on the other, the genius of the story itself.

We could say about the happy historical coincidence of Cervantes with his subject matter, the story of the madman who thought he was a hero, what Kierkegaard said about Homer and the Trojan War, and about the category of the classic in general. It was not a random accident, it was "good fortune":

7. I must disagree with what the distinguished critic Peter E. Russell said in his *Cervantes* (1985): "It was [Samuel] Johnson himself who first signalled unambiguously that new ways of interpreting the work were in the making. He made the good point that, although the knight was a ridiculous figure, he was never a contemptible one and, writing in 1750, he even allowed pity as well as mirth to be a possible reader's response to him. . . . Johnson . . . gets near to inviting readers of *Don Quixote* to identify themselves with the mad knight on the grounds that his madness was no more than the works of human imagination writ large. This represented a radical change in traditional attitudes to the book. . . . Whether Cervantes himself could have understood Johnson's interpretation of his book must . . . be rated unlikely" (93). While Johnson's attitude may have indeed represented a radical change in "traditional attitudes," that is most certainly not the case with regard to Cervantes himself. Pity for the mad knight is something that appears explicitly and repeatedly in *Don Quixote*. Let me anticipate here just one example in the words of Bachelor Sampson Carrasco to Don Antonio Moreno in Barcelona, to which we will have to return in a later chapter: "My name, sir, is Bachelor Sampson Carrasco, and I come from the same village as Don Quixote de la Mancha, whose madness and folly have excited the pity of all who know him" (2.65.891). And a little later the narrator will repeat the same idea as he tells us about the bachelor's explanation to the Duke and the Duchess: "It was that in fact which had caused him to assume his disguise, for it was a pitiful thing that a gentleman of Don Quixote's intelligence should remain a lunatic" (2.70.916). All those "who know him," the people in his town, feel pity for him. And, of course, so does Cervantes, who, against the advice of all the Antonio Morenos of the world, will finally rescue Don Quixote from his madness.

"Good fortune has two factors: It is fortunate that this most remarkable epic subject matter came into the hands of Homer. Here the emphasis is just as much on Homer as on the subject matter. Here is the deep harmony that pervades every production we call classic" (*Either Or*, 1.48).

The fool rescued from the crowd and from his own foolishness by Cervantes is neither a hero nor an antihero. For we must insist on the fact that the historical fate of the traditional epic figure runs parallel to, is essentially the same as, the historical fate of the marginal antihero. As we will also see when we speak about Quevedo's *Buscón*, it was by no means the case that the old epic hero was eventually overtaken by and displaced by new forms of its traditional opposite, the antihero; or that such a displacement of the hero by the antihero made possible the birth of the modern novel, as Bakhtin may have thought. That was not at all the case. In reference to the development of the modern novel, the traditional antihero became as historically obsolete as the epic hero himself, and precisely at the same time, and for the same nonsacrificial, nonvictimizing reason.

Cervantes's intuitive genius, his compassion and tolerance, and the profound historical understanding he had of what he was doing as an artist, made it possible. Obviously he could not know that he was writing the first great novel of the modern era, that he was inaugurating a genre (or antigenre) with such an extraordinary and fruitful future. We know that now, more than four hundred years later. More than four hundred years later we must marvel at the extraordinary potential that lay hidden in such an apparently insignificant and foolish story. It was clearly the work of Cervantes's genius, but it was also undoubtedly the genius of the story itself. The story of a fool who thought he was a hero is a trivial story. The story of a fool who not only thought he was a hero, but went out into the real world of sixteenth- or seventeenth-century Spain determined to resurrect the heroic age, and was gradually rescued from his own foolishness in an act of compassion, instead of being laughed into irrelevance, was not a trivial story, it was *the story of the birth of the modern novel.*

The Cervantine *story of Don Quixote* inaugurates the modern novel not only because it was the first and probably the best, something that could have been purely accidental, but because it is *something like a literal allegory that narrates the birth of the modern novel*. It tells us how the modernity of the novel came to be. It narrates the end of one era and the beginning of a new one. This new era is truly new because in it an old distinction, a distinction as old as human society itself, namely, the immemorial poetic distinction between the heroic and its opposite, the antiheroic, is rendered irrelevant.

Cervantes's Compassion

Neither of these two poles in a perfectly symmetrical polarity has anything to do with what gradually becomes, as Cervantes's novel advances, the guiding principle of its development, which is nothing more mysterious, or more complicated, than a simple act of compassion, the act of a good Samaritan who rescues the old fool from the immemorial crowd; who believes that behind the foolishness of the fool there is still the dignity of a basically good and decent human being—a human being who does not quite know what he is doing. It is truly amazing to see what such a simple, childlike act of compassion can do. It reduces to utter irrelevance a frame of mind that had never been able to understand poetic characters except within the framework of the heroic-antiheroic polarity. Cervantes could not have written, in its sheer simplicity, a more profoundly Christian novel.

What makes this artistic act of compassion and understanding even more remarkable is the fact that the *Quixote*, which has turned out to be the historical signpost of the exhaustion of the traditional epic model, was written by a man who still had faith in such a model, who was convinced, or at the very least wanted to believe, that the epic had a future, if only it were properly modernized, perhaps along the lines sketched by Tasso in the *Discorsi del poema eroico*, but in prose; a man who actually tried to do just that in the *Persiles*, an admirable novel, and of great interest to specialists today, but which, as a novel, ceased to be historically relevant a long time ago.

In fact, I think it is safe to assume that what must have drawn Cervantes's attention to this particular kind of fool was not of a kind to stir his sympathy. For in his foolishness this fool made a mockery of things deeply held by Cervantes, in particular his cherished Tassian belief in the fundamental nobility and truth of the epic, features that made it, at its most essential, an excellent candidate for Christian modernization, and therefore for long survival into the future. While, on the other hand, this foolish quixotic imitator of those late descendants of the epic, books of chivalry, was particularly attracted to a caricature of the epic, to the epic at its worst, at its furthest remove from the truth, at its most fictitious. One can only imagine what a Quevedo would have done in such a situation. For the underlying scenario was all ready for a merciless victimization of the fool, Quevedo-style. Fortunately for the entire history of the modern novel, it did not happen that way. At the beginning of that history, therefore, what we find is an extraordinary act of generosity where one might have expected the very opposite[8]: a generosity that saves the outcast from his traditional fate, not in order to turn him into a hero once more, but to take him out of the sacrificial equation altogether.

Don Quixote's Old Understanding

We should remember at this point that famous passage in chapter 3 of Part 2 of the novel, when Don Quixote meditates on the astonishing news that Sancho has just brought him: the story of his deeds is already in print.

> He could not persuade himself that such a history existed, for the blood of the enemies he had slain was scarcely dry on his own sword-blade. . . . Nevertheless he imagined that some sage, either friendly or hostile, had given [his deeds] to the Press by magic art; if a friend, to magnify and extol them above the most renowned actions of any knight errant; and if an enemy, to annihilate them and place them below the basest ever written of any mean squire—although, he admitted to himself, the deeds of squires were never written of. But if it were true that there was such a history, since it was about a knight errant it must perforce be grandiloquent, lofty, remarkable, magnificent and true. (485)[9]

In his foolishness, Cervantes's fool cannot conceive of a literary narrative except in terms of the heroic versus the antiheroic. As Giuseppe Toffanin pointed out in his classic study *La fine dell'umanesimo*, it is remarkable that the thought never crosses Don Quixote's mind that the author may have narrated his deeds the way they actually happened. Don Quixote clearly adheres to

8. It is no surprise that Walter L. Reed, a perceptive historian of the novel, finds that "[t]he ethos of the picaresque novel [in particular the pioneering Spanish examples] . . . is one of exclusion: the exclusion of literature as a cultural institution, the exclusion of social codes as definitions of the individual *vida*, the exclusion of other points of view. . . . The ethos of *Don Quixote*, on the other hand, is ironically inclusive" (73). The critic, however, does not appear to be aware of the sociohistorical mechanism of "exclusion" that grounds the literary manifestations that he does perceive.

9. *The Adventures of Don Quixote*, trans. J. M. Cohen (London: Penguin Books, 1950). I will be using Cohen's translation throughout this book, but I will occasionally alter it to bring the meaning closer to the original Spanish.

the old view of literature as a vehicle for the expression of praise or blame, an idea that is already present in Aristotle's *Poetics*, for he tells us that in the beginning poetry was of two kinds, either celebratory of noble deeds, like hymns and encomiums, or accusatory, like lampooning invectives or satires (1448b25). In Averroes's commentary on the *Poetics* this remark by Aristotle on the origin of poetry becomes central. In the words of "the great commentator" of Aristotle, as Dante calls Averroes, "Every poem and all poetry are either blame or praise" (Preminger, 349).[10]

Toffanin was right: Cervantes's *Don Quixote* is the most profound answer given by a poet to the questions raised by Aristotle's treatise, in particular this question pertaining to the most basic character of poetry in the Aristotelian sense:

Ora che cos'é il Don Chisciotte? Credo che sia la risposta più profunda data da un poeta, ed in poesia, al questionario aristotelico. . . . Il significato letterario mi pare . . . evidente e punto oscuro. Vi è sfatato il pregiudizio che le regole aristoteliche debbano condur la poesia a diventare astrazione di bene o di male, parenetica descrizione di santi e di eroi o di dannati e, quindi, inevitabile esagerazione della realtá. (218)

(Now, what is the *Quixote*? I believe it is the most profound answer given by a poet and in poetry, to Aristotle's questions. . . . The literary meaning seems evident to me and not at all obscure. There the preconception is destroyed that sees poetry becoming, as a consequence of the Aristotelian rules, an abstraction of either good or evil, an exhortary description of saints and heroes, or of the damned, thereby becoming an exaggeration of reality.[11])

But from the perspective afforded by the desacralizing process, it is clear that this old view of poetry refers to a social reality that goes much deeper and farther than the words and the authority of Aristotle. The process that, ignoring reality in all its particular circumstances, "exaggerates" the good and the bad, praising the one to the heavens and condemning the other without appeal, resonates with sacrificial echoes that link the most basic conventions of literary form to social practices of the most elemental and universal kind, which is to say, the collective victimizing mechanism.

10. Preminger writes: "Averroes could understand this theory much better than the complex theory of imitation developed in the first three chapters of the *Poetics*. Better still, it seemed consistent with what he knew of Arab poetry, whose early forms tend heavily to invective and encomiastic verse" (343).

11. Unless otherwise indicated, all translations are my own.

Everything we have said so far can be contained within the limits of a reflection on the genius of the story itself, that is to say, the story at its literal level, the level of the action, the intrigue, the plot.

In his seminal work *Christ and Apollo: The Dimensions of the Literary Imagination*, Father William F. Lynch calls "action . . . the soul of the literary imagination" (155). And he comments as follows on Francis Fergusson's "insistence that the distinction between plot and the deep human action of a play is fundamental":

> It is true enough that "plot" is only the literal level of a drama, and that it may be looked upon as a mere external level of movement, to be deepened by the insight proceeding from other and deeper levels of action. Yet it is also necessary to remember that, when all these other levels have been gained or added, it is the literal itself, that is to say, the plot, that has been deepened and illuminated for the content it always had, at least in potency. (155)

I believe that Cervantes's *Don Quixote* is a perfect illustration of the truth of that statement. Everything here is contained *in nuce* at the level of the plot. That is to say, the humble plot—the story of a fool who thought he was a hero, went about acting like one to make a name for himself and destroy all evil, was gradually purged from his indignity, revealed to be worthy of admiration for his basic goodness, and finally restored to his sanity, his people, and his God—when situated at the dawn of the modern era in Christian Spain, acquires a meaning that far transcends its immediate literal function *without leaving it behind, without changing its letter*. It is still a humble plot. But it is also as if its humility were rewarded with a superabundance of meaning. Its letter means exactly what it says, but it also simultaneously tells a much deeper story, a story without words—not a different story or one alien in any way, but precisely the story that makes the humble plot possible, that supports it, although not directly but from a distance, like a spirit, the distant spirit of the letter.

Comparison with Sophocles' *Oedipus*, Symbol of a Genre

Perhaps it will be worthwhile to illustrate what I just said by comparing the case of *Don Quixote* with another case in the pre-Christian past where this superabundance of meaning at the most immediate level, the level of the plot, also occurs: the case of Sophocles' tragedy *Oedipus the King*. The story line of *Oedipus the King* is indeed very simple. The city, the community, is undergoing a terrible crisis: people are dying; the plague, the anger of the gods, is upon it; and nothing seems to work. They plead with their king, their savior, to save them again. He has already made arrangements to consult the sacred oracle. The divine answer is clear: there is "a defiling thing" among them who is polluting the city. The crisis will persist until that one source of all their ills is found and expelled. "By what rite shall we cleanse us?" asks Oedipus. "By banishing a man, or by bloodshed in quittance of bloodshed" is the answer. But the investigation itself proves to be a very dangerous affair, threatening to make matters even worse, to add fuel to the fire instead of putting it down. In the end, the king himself, the investigator, the hero and former savior of the city, turns out to be the guilty one. He has committed, unwittingly, the most terrible crimes: parricide and incest. Horrified at his own unsightly image, he himself demands to be removed from everybody's sight, to be expelled: "Hurry, for the gods' love, hide me somewhere beyond the land, or slay me, or cast me into the sea, where you shall never more behold me!"

We should remember that this is the tragedy that Aristotle considered the best, the model for all tragedies. In it subject matter and form are perfectly matched. It is no wonder. It can only take a moment of reflection to realize that the plot of *Oedipus* is not just the plot of a particular tragedy, it gives form to the very spirit of Athenian tragedy, which is in turn the theatrical expression of the sacrificial spirit in general. It is always the victim that saves the city, the "one head [that] must be given up for the sake of many," as we read in Virgil (*Aeneid*, 5.815). The city structures itself around the sacred victim, who gathers unto himself the pollution that spreads throughout the entire community, destroying everything. This is why the sacred victim is not only the guilty one but also the savior. The real problem, however, in this universal sacrificial scenario is finding that saving victim, the final and definitive guilty one, the one touched by the gods (and thus godlike), whose elimination will put a stop to the plague, to the crisis. Because every attempt at finding the saving victim, at pinning the sign of god on the one and only, immediately runs the risk of spreading the violence even further. The internal conflicts that are generated as soon as Oedipus starts the unavoidable investigation are a realistic sample of the mysterious and mythical plague that is devastating the city. Oedipus, the investigator, has brought the city to the brink of disaster, on the verge of a civil war. He, therefore, the king, the savior, is the guilty one. He bears himself the unsightly and unspeakable horror of the sacred curse. He himself gouges out his own eyes not to see the horror. At that point there is no higher or more sacred a duty than to get rid of him. In other words, Sophocles has managed to concentrate in an incredibly powerful nutshell, at the level of the plot, all the fundamental ingredients of sacrificial humanity. And it looks so simple!

Cervantes's *Don Quixote* also looks disarmingly simple. And just as I would rank the poet Sophocles as the clearest and most dramatic representative (and representer) of the sacrificial mind, I would rank the poet Cervantes as the clearest poetic, that is, novelistic, representative of the nonsacrificial Christian mind. In fact, our unlikely modern Oedipus, Don Quixote, also sets out to rid the human city of all its destructive ills. And as the novel progresses it becomes increasingly clear that the nature of those ills has a lot to do with the nature of the process that made him go insane in the first place, that turned him into a fool, the laughingstock of the entire city, the one traditionally marked for expulsion. Gradually we begin to see that he is not only carrying on his shoulders his own disease but everybody else's as well. At that point old Zeus would have certainly nodded in the direction of the fool, and he would have been quickly eliminated, thus cleansing the city, at least for the moment, of its ills. But this time there was a different god in town. It was he who told Cervantes at that point that the moment had come not to expel the fool, but to save him, by making him repent and ask for God's mercy, for he had come not to save the city as such but each and every one of its inhabitants.

The tragedy *Oedipus the King*, which was performed next to the sacrificial altar, imitates the sacrificial rite, which is itself a form of imitation. The tragedy is a new sacrificial form, one that actually connects with the inner logic of the sacrificial operation at a more reflexive and deliberate level than any particular ritual practice, which is inevitably tied to very specific ritual prescriptions. The tragedy is a more self-conscious form of sacrifice than the sacrificial rite *stricto sensu*. Sophocles, therefore, had a freedom of movement or freedom of thought that the sacrificer approaching the victim at the altar did not have. But that could be something far from reassuring, it could actually be rather frightening, even the more so the better he understands what he is doing. And this is the reason why: as Sophocles masterly represents and motivates the violence that Oedipus introduces into the city through his investigation and suspicions, antagonizing everybody and making everybody react violently to his violence, there is an obvious danger that the violence of Oedipus will become increasingly similar, undifferentiated, from the violence of his antagonists, in the typical tit for tat of the tragic dialogue. As a matter of fact, Sophocles is playing a very dangerous game with the sacred mythical material, which he is molding in his hands. As Sandor Goodhart has insightfully pointed out,[12] the text of the tragedy suggests insistently that the guilty party, the one who murdered Laius, may not have been one but many. And if that were the case, then Oedipus would not be guilty, as the sacrificial myth invariably asserts. In which case, the sacrificial operation in which Sophocles, the maker of tragedies, is engaged will miscarry. If the victim about to be sacrificed is not guilty, is not responsible for the ills that devastate the city, then the very sacred character of the victim becomes a sham, and the tragic perfomance some sort of sacrilege or horrible blasphemy, which is precisely Plato's accusation against the tragic poets. You cannot play around with the sacred uniqueness, the sacred isolation, of the victim. In the end, of course, the sacrificial crisis, the crisis of the most sacred institution of sacrifice, will be resolved, and the violence of Oedipus, the pollution that adheres to him like an infection, will turn out to be uniquely horrible, more horrible than anybody else's.

The tragedian senses the danger attaching to a too realistic portrayal of tragic violence. For if he knows what he is doing, he must know what the consequences are of going too far with the idea that the victim may not be uniquely guilty, and therefore not sacred, and therefore that the expulsion may be arbitrary. As I have just said, the very thought horrified Plato.[13] And it must have horrified the tragedian himself. As René Girard has pointed out in reference to Sophocles and Euripides, they both stopped just short of becoming too realistic in their portrayal of intersubjective human violence. In the case of Euripides, this retreat into the safety of the sacrificial mechanism appears to be explicit:

12. *Sacrificing Commentary: Reading the End of Literature* (Baltimore: Johns Hopkins University Press, 1996), chapter 1.

13. See *The Sacred Game*, 50ff.

His tragedies contain numerous passages whose emphatic tone and repetition of theme clearly mark them as expressions of the poet's decision to retreat and his attempts to justify himself:

> Human wisdom is not wisdom, and to aspire to more than man's due is to shorten life, is to sacrifice the fruit at hand for what is out of reach. I think it is sheer madness or plain stupidity to act in such a manner. . . .
>
> Keep heart and mind aloof from overreaching intellects.
>
> The beliefs and practices common to the common man are good enough for me. (*Violence and the Sacred*, 129)

Behind such words lies the fear and the knowledge of a reciprocally, mimetically, spreading human violence, an open-ended violence, where the final mechanism of defense, the sacrificial mechanism, would fail to function, would fail to gather the required unanimity around the victim. On the other hand, the tragedian owes his artistic greatness, his first prize, if you will, precisely to his daring proximity to the truth, a truth that he knows he must prevent from complete disclosure. For that would mean facing up to the maddening representation of the total unrestrained breakdown of everything.

Between Truth and Concealment

Cervantes also had a problem, but it went in exactly the opposite direction. In the end, the old fool will be saved because his foolishness will be shown to be fundamentally no different from anybody else's. The disease he carries is indeed extremely contagious. But while the disease is contagious, the individual guilt, the individual responsibility, is not, in the sense that there can be no transfer of guilt from one guilty party to another, and therefore no collective transfer onto the victim. In fact, all such collective transfers of guilt are now revealed to be unjust, because a uniquely innocent and divine victim has taken the immemorial place of *the* victim. Now any transfer of guilt falls on the shoulders of the one and only innocent victim—the victim, that is, whose innocence exposes the arbitrariness and injustice of all such transfers. Now everybody is forced to look inward in order to find the one to blame.

The problem is that if the fool is revealed to be no different from anybody else, there is no novel. The interest of the novel, its success as a novel, rests on the difference of the fool qua fool, on his separation from everybody else.

Cervantes cannot fully disclose the truth that underlies the salvation of the fool, he cannot bring it too obviously to the surface, without ruining the novel qua novel. As a novelist, Cervantes is facing a situation similar to that of Sophocles as a tragedian. They both have a problem with the truth. The radical difference between them is in the consequences of a full disclosure of the truth: it would be far more serious and socially destructive in the case of Sophocles than in the case of Cervantes, because, among other things, tragedy was far more important to the old sacred order and the society structured by it than the modern novel ever was to its own sacred and social environment. Whether the novel was faithful or not to the truth, succeeded or not as novel and at what cost, could be something of great personal importance to the novelist, but only of minor relevance at the social level. Knowledge of the truth about human violence had become far less threatening. And that gave Cervantes, in return, a degree of freedom that Sophocles could not have had.

Nevertheless, in order to succeed artistically, the novel has to isolate the madman from everybody else. It has to maintain and promote a kind of human singularity or uniqueness that does not reflect the truth, but is only a reflection of its own novelistic need, that thrives on visibility, on attracting attention toward itself and away from everybody else; in other words, a kind of ad hoc, made-up singularity, that inevitably looks like, and is in fact a direct heir to, the one needed for the proper operation of the old sacrificial mechanism. But in the eyes of the new god, who saves victims, and of the new nonsacrificial mentality, such a singularity is only a way to cover up the truth at the expense of the victim; it is the singularity of the victim qua victim, the victim dressed up in either heroic or antiheroic attire ready to be sacrificed. Clearly the victim who has been saved cannot look in the eyes of the new savior like the old victim in the eyes of the sacrificers. The singularity, the uniqueness, of the victim saved, granted to it by the Christian salvation event itself, cannot be of the same kind as before. For the new singularity is the way the victim looks after he has shed the old sacrificial appearance, the sacrificial appearance that made him look different from everybody else, aesthetically satisfying, but marked for elimination. Saving the human individual is one thing, saving the novel is quite a different one. But Cervantes has to move, has to navigate, between these two opposites, if he wants his novel to tell the truth without ceasing to be a novel.

Thus both Sophocles and Cervantes are confronted by a similar problem in the face of the truth. Neither one of them can reveal it completely. But while Sophocles must hide the truth sufficiently to allow for the proper tragic performance of the expulsion of Oedipus, Cervantes must reveal the truth sufficiently to be able to save Don Quixote in a convincing Christian way. In Sophocles the mimetic performance must ultimately triumph over the truth, while in Cervantes the truth must ultimately triumph over and beyond the mimetic performance, or else there will be no difference with the old way, nothing new will be created at all. Besides, a repetition of the old way would not have worked either. Nobody could repeat in sixteenth- and seventeenth-century Christian Europe what Sophocles did in pre-Christian Athens (just as nobody could do what Homer or Virgil did). The greatness of Shakespeare's tragedies, for example, consists in large measure in showing how difficult it was for the old tragedy to work, to be effective, in the new, thoroughly "gospelled" environment.

What this means is that both Sophocles and Cervantes are handling fundamentally the same kind of mimetic and sacrificial instrument (tragedy, narrative fiction). But they are handling it for two radically different purposes: Sophocles is doing it to justify the expulsion of the victim, which is what his god demands; Cervantes is doing it to save the victim, which is also what his god demands. Of course, by doing that, Cervantes is subverting the inherently sacrificial form of the novelistic fiction, tricking narrative fiction, as it were, into serving the opposite purpose of that for which formal, conventional fiction had always been meant. Furthermore, this very subversion of the old fictional form is recognized explicitly at the level of the theme: Don Quixote is mad because he has fallen victim to the old fiction. The disease that he is carrying, which is so contagious and so protean, so capable of metamorphosing into all kinds of appearances, bears the unmistakeable mark of the old fiction. What is new about Cervantes is that he is transforming the old poison into a vehicle for the remedy. He is using the fictional form in which mad Don Quixote is trapped to free him, to save him from his madness. But, at the deepest possible level, is that not a reflection of what the new victim, Christ, did with the old sacrificial mechanism? He submitted to it in order to free human beings from it. It is a very old Christian idea that Christ tricked the devil. At the very moment when it appeared that the devil—the spirit of the old victimizing mechanism—had triumphed over him, he had in fact triumphed over the devil. And by doing that, he gave an entirely new meaning to the notion of sacrifice, which in him became an instrument of salvation instead of condemnation. I think that is the spirit that inspires the first and greatest modern novel: the story of a man who almost destroyed himself by believing in novels too much.

By Way of Contrast: Avellaneda's *Quixote*

A brief analysis of what Avellaneda did in his spurious continuation of Cervantes's Part 1 may help us understand better what Cervantes did in his *Quixote*.

In Avellaneda's second part (1614), we see the Manchegan knight at a ring-lancing pageant and contest in Zaragoza by the side of Don Alvaro Tarfe, the character who planted in Don Quixote the idea to take up arms again (beautiful arms provided by Tarfe himself) and go on his third knightly sally with the intention of participating in a tournament at that city, where Tarfe was also going.

> The crowd was much astonished to see that man in armor ready to take part in the ring-lancing contest. . . . This sight did not cause such wonder in the people of quality because everybody in this class had learned from don Alvaro Tarfe . . . who Don Quixote was, about the strange mania, and the objective of having him appear in the plaza, which was to add to the fun with an absurd adventure. It is not unusual on such festive occasions for the knights to bring lunatics into the plaza, dressed up and adorned, wearing fanciful headdresses, and have them do tricks, tilt, joust, and carry off prizes, as has been seen sometimes in big cities and in Zaragoza itself. (11.95)[14]

This public exposure of lunatics, "dressed up and adorned, wearing fanciful headresses," has obvious links with other public spectacles at the center of which we also see dressed-up figures exposed to public ridicule or shame, such as would happen in countless manifestations of Carnival and the Feast of Fools, and also in the parading of criminals as part of the spectacle of judicial executions.[15]

14. Alonso Fernández de Avellaneda, *Don Quixote de La Mancha (Part II). Being the Spurious Continuation of Miguel de Cervantes' Part I*, trans. and ed. Alberta Wilson Server and John Esten Keller (Newark, Del.: Juan de la Cuesta, 1980). Citations are by chapter and page.

15. Cf. E. Cros: "Nous voudrions insister sur l'homologie structural qu'il est donc possible d'établir entre la description d'une fête carnavalesque . . . et celle de l'exécution d'un jugement de justice" (43; We would like to insist on the structural homology that can be established between the description of a Carnival feast . . . and that of a judicial execution).

We will address the carnivalesque dimension of the novel as a genre at a later time. What I would like to point out now is that it is not only "the people of quality" at Zaragoza who are dressing up the lunatic Don Quixote and bringing him out into the public square so that everybody can have some fun at his expense. This action also describes the underlying structure of Avellaneda's novel. For this is exactly what he intends to do with his fictional hero: to publicly expose his folly for entertaining purposes with some didactic possibilities to boot.

In its bare bones the internal logic of such a working structure is flagrantly dehumanizing. And Avellaneda, a Christian man, must have felt some qualms about it, even as Don Alvaro Tarfe felt them toward the end of the novel, when he decided to cover all expenses for the care of Don Quixote in the Casa del Nuncio, the famous insane asylum of Toledo: "[He] felt obligated to do this because of his qualms about being responsible for Don Quixote's leaving Argamesilla for Zaragoza, since he had informed him about the jousts being held there and had left his armor with him and praised his courage" (34.317).

There were indeed good reasons for Don Alvaro Tarfe to feel responsible for luring Don Quixote out of his home and town. He had not simply "informed him about the jousts," he had done so in a language carefully calculated to produce an immediate and irresistible response in Don Quixote's mind, full as it was with the archaic rhetoric of fictional knight-errantry: "We are knights from Granada and we are going to the illustrious city of Zaragoza to some tournaments being held there. Having learned that the tournament's president is a valiant knight, we have resolved to undertake this task in order to gain some renown, impossible to attain otherwise" (1.13). How could the poor lunatic not react to such a tempting piece of "information"?

But Don Alvaro Tarfe was by no means the only one. Practically everybody contributes to push the good hidalgo once more over the edge. Sancho is the first one, by providing the initial temptation. He turns Don Quixote's attention from the wholesome and devout reading of the *Flos Sanctorum* (the book he has in his hands when Sancho first appears) toward the dangerous adventures narrated in *Don Florisbrán de Candaria*. In fact, he promises Don Quixote, at the latter's urging, to bring him the book "this very night, if I can, [and] I'll surely manage to bring it to you under my cloak," so that "neither the priest nor anyone else will know."

But the priest himself contributes to Don Quixote's relapse with a very strong push of his own. Here is the situation: almost immediately after Sancho has left "the good hidalgo . . . with his pate boiling with the new refreshment of his vanquished knightly exploits revived in his memory . . . they saw entering the square from the main street four people of quality, on horseback, with servants and pages and twelve lackeys leading twelve richly saddled horses" (1.12). This sight is clearly calculated to add to the process of Don Quixote's incipient relapse. And if we had any doubt about the authorial intention of such a timely arrival, here is what "the Priest said to Don Quixote": "By the sign of the cross, Señor Quijada, if these people had come here six months ago, you would have thought it one of the strangest and most dangerous adventures you had ever seen or heard in your books of chivalry. You would have imagined that these gentlemen were probably kidnapping some princess of high rank. . . ." This is really incredible. And to make matters even worse, such words at such a time are those of a man who—we have just been told—had counseled everybody "[not to dare] say a word to [Señor Quijada] about the things that had happened because of him," that is, about his past adventures, in order not to put him in danger of a relapse.

The final stroke, however, in this collective driving of the poor hidalgo out of his mind and his home is reserved for Don Alvaro Tarfe:

> The priest told him what Don Quixote was and what had happened to him the previous year, which astonished Don Alvaro very much. . . . [Then] he drew Don Quixote aside and said, "My dear sir, in a big trunk I have some armor engraved in Milan, which you will be good enough to keep carefully for me in your house until I return. I think I'll not need it in Zaragoza, for I'm sure to have friends there who will supply me with less elegant armor, because this is so elegant that it serves only to draw attention and make me very conspicuous when I wear it." (3.28)

This is either diabolical or stupid, that is, a sign of incompetence on the part of the author. I'm inclined to think the latter, for, as Cervantes had said of the author of *Tirante the White* in the famous scrutiny of Don Quixote's library, "he did not do it on purpose," that is to say, knowingly, fully aware not only of what he was doing but of how he was doing it. A clear sign of such incompetence is the fact that he proceeds immediately to tell us (without a tinge of irony) that "Don Alvaro answered all [of Don Quixote's questions], not realizing that there was passing through Don Quixote's mind the idea of going to Zaragoza and doing what he did, which will be related in due time." Nevertheless, in spite of this unbelievable claim of innocence for Don Alvaro at this point, the gentleman, as we have seen, will recognize at the end that he was quite instrumental in taking Don Quixote out of Argamesilla to make a fool of himself, literally, at Zaragoza and elsewhere.

Avellaneda's novelistic fool has no will of his own. He is conceived as a puppet on strings, reacting to the pull from the outside. He does not go out on his own, as the genuine Don Quixote does. He is tricked into going out. Underneath the outer looks of social respectability both the priest and Tarfe (i.e., Avellaneda) are dangling before the poor lunatic the glitter of the novelistic fiction. The author is literally playing with his character, pushing him out into public view to do his thing, that is, to do what is expected of the fool, and the fool will perform exactly on cue. This is why the occasional admonitions to Don Quixote to quit his dangerous nonsense and go back home must sound hollow and profoundly contradictory.

Such is, for example, the case with the admonition given by Mosén Valentín, a charitable clergyman who puts Don Quixote and Sancho up in his house for a few days, and who delivers a completely useless speech to "Señor Quijada" for the purpose, he says, of "advising you about what is relevant to the situation and warning you, while we are alone and in my house, that you are in mortal sin when you leave your house and estate . . . to go roaming about these roads like a crazy man, making yourself conspicuous and doing so many nonsensical things. . . . I know very well that you have acted as you do, as you say, in imitation of those ancient knights . . . invented by books of chivalry . . . which you consider authentic and true, knowing, in all truth, that never in the world were there such knights, nor is there any Spanish, French or Italian history—at least an authentic one—which mentions them" (7.65).

Of course Avellaneda's fool knows no such thing "in all truth." The speech is completely out of touch with the situation at hand, as is made obvious by the knight's insane reply: "Don Quixote had been pensive while Mosen Valentín [was] talking, but now, as one who awakens, he began to speak in this way: 'Put aside inaction, Señor Archbishop Turpin! I am most astonished that you, belonging to that illustrious house of Emperor Charlemagne . . . should be so faint-hearted and cowardly. . . .'" In other words, he might as well not have heard the speech at all. This is not a real conversation, not even with a madman. There is no communication between the two. What a difference there is between this situation and the genuine Don Quixote's answer to the Canon of Toledo toward the end of Part 1:

> Don Quixote listened most attentively to the canon's arguments, gazed at him for some time when he saw that he had finished and said: "Sir, your discourse was intended, I think, to persuade me that there have never been knights errant in the world. . . .
>
> You were pleased to add also that such books have done me much harm, that they have turned my brain. . . ."
>
> "Just so," answered the canon.
>
> "Why then, in my opinion it is you," replied Don Quixote, "that are deranged and enchanted, for daring to blaspheme against an institution so universally acknowledged and so authenticated. . . ." (1.49.437)

This is a real conversation, even though there is no realistic chance that Don Quixote will be convinced by the canon. By contrast, the utter lack of communication between the two characters in Avellaneda's novel, their blindness before each other's reality, is such that one gets the impression they are not really talking to each other but making statements for the benefit of the reader, the public at large. In other words, Mosen Valentin's advice is just something he has to say to prove his good intentions before the public, a way of washing his hands from any guilt associated with the exposure of the lunatic to public ridicule. Having delivered it, he can go back to enjoying the laughable string of incoherent nonsense coming out of the madman's mouth: "The good clergyman, seeing that Don Quixote was so resolute and stubborn, did not try to reason any further; rather, he continued listening to all that he said as Sancho put on each piece of the coat of mail. He made most amusing remarks, stringing together a thousand beginnings of old ballads in a confused and disconnected manner."

To some extent, the madness of Avellaneda's fool is symptomatically closer to that of wild Cardenio in the Sierra Morena mountains than it is to Cervantes's Don Quixote. We frequently find in him the same kind of fixed-eye stupor and total disconnection from surrounding reality that came over Cardenio when his story was interrupted. The fundamental difference is, of course, that such a mental breakdown, in and of itself, offers no novelistic interest to Cervantes. Nonsense all by itself is just nonsense.

But in Avellaneda's book the mental breakdown itself becomes the centerpiece. He has no interest in the process that led to it. Mental breakdown is just something that happens if you are foolish enough to do foolish things. Because Avellaneda's purpose is precisely to exhibit foolishness, irrationality, as such, as foolishness, as irrationality, things that also carry with them a heavy load of moral condemnation. As Mosén Valentín would say, it is a mortal sin to make a fool of yourself in front of everybody. Of course, this is the sort of sin that carries with it its own punishment because, by sinning that way, well, you truly make a fool of yourself, you become a scandal; so you should not complain if scandalized people laugh or throw insults at you, you deserve it. If you are the victim of the people, don't blame anybody but yourself. The entire book becomes a self-feeding victimizing circle with the foolishness of the fool at its center. Avellaneda's view of Don Quixote's madness is a much better example of that equation between "folie" and "déraison" of which M. Foucault speaks in his *Histoire de la folie à l'âge classique* than Cervantes's is, as we will see in due time. Not surprisingly, the destiny of Avellaneda's "unreasonable" fool is the insane asylum, or, as Foucault put it, "the great confinement," the historical heir to an earlier expulsion of the fool from the city. We will have to see that Foucault remained blind to the novelty of Cervantes's approach to Don Quixote's madness.

Long before he is actually sent to the insane asylum Avellaneda's Quixote is totally isolated from the human reality around him. And that brings about another result: the complete disconnection of the central story, Don Quixote's story, from the interpolated ones included by Avellaneda in his book. While the story of Cervantes's Don Quixote overflows with meaning and resonates in each and every one of the interpolated stories of the novel (How could it be otherwise in a story that keeps resonating in so many novelistic masterpieces through the centuries?), the story of Avellaneda's Don Quixote has absolutely nothing to do with the stories that happen next to it. As Cervantes himself tells us in the Prologue to Part 2, this poor fellow Avellaneda must have thought that adding to a novel is like blowing air into a dog.

Nevertheless, we can learn from Avellaneda's failure. First of all, it provides a good illustration of how the story of a fool who thought he was a hero could still be perceived in seventeenth-century Spain. If you took away from it everything that was new and unprecedented in Cervantes's version, what you would have is what we see in Avellaneda's "corrected," streamlined version, that is, hardly anything other than the public exposure of a lunatic, painted over with Christian moralizings.

The second thing we can learn from Avellaneda is that it was, indeed, a failure. His novel is very mediocre and very boring. He could not combine successfully a basic victimizing structure with his Christian scruples. It did not work. He wanted to play it safe, which meant giving the fool as little leeway as possible, while keeping his authorial voice solidly on the side of public morality and respectability. And that meant keeping the fool isolated from everybody else—in other words, keeping in place the old victimizing structure.

In the case of Cervantes, on the other hand, both his compassion and his literary instinct must have told him from the beginning that he could not just laugh at the fool from a distance, he had to make the fool interesting as a human being, bring him closer to the people, make him at least a little like them, break his isolation. In other words, he had to relax the victimizing structure, give it some flexibility, do with it what even Sophocles had to do in order to win the tragic contest, especially since he, Cervantes, had a lot more freedom to do it. And that meant giving the fool a voice of his own, which had to be much more than the senseless sound of a chaotic mind or of a mental breakdown. The fool had to be able to make sense and communicate, even though he would still prove to be mad.

But if the fool's mind was sound enough to make rational sense, to communicate with the sane, how could he still be mad? Where would his madness reside? There could only be one explanation: if there was nothing basically wrong with the fool's capacity to reason, it had to be a defect of the will, or to be more precise, his mad behavior would be not the expression of mental chaos but of intense desire, a desire that went beyond the bounds of reason, or a reason entirely subservient to the force of desire. And since desire attracts desire, the intensity of the fool's desire, together with his rational capacity to fabricate a justification for it, would certainly make him attractive to us, to our own desire as readers of poetic fiction. But was that not precisely the kind of desire that drove Don Quixote mad in the first place? In other words, our own desire, our being attracted to him, becomes a form of contagion. Not only can he communicate rationally with us, but as he does so we also catch a little bit of his madness. There is an implicit message to us, the readers, in *Don Quixote* that becomes clearer as the novel progresses: *de te fabula narratur*. Our enthusiasm for the lifelike figure of the Manchegan knight and his singularity is by no means without danger of self-deception. We will see how even powerful critical insights into the nature of that singularity can be self-deceiving.

For we may fool ourselves concerning the question of what really constitutes in our eyes the uniqueness of Cervantes's Don Quixote. Is it his realism, the fact that he is so much like us? Or is it precisely the opposite, the fact that he is mad, that he is distinctly different from us? Probably the safest way to answer this question would be to say that it is a well-calculated combination of those two things. Which also amounts to saying that his uniqueness is a combination of the old and the new—the "old" being that which isolates the madman from us (or insulates us from the madman), and the "new" being that which brings us together, revealing that we are far from immune to his madness, that he is ultimately no different from us. Now, if we put this in the terms of the novel itself, we come up with a rather unexpected discovery: the new is not mad Don Quixote, completely insane, but Alonso Quijano, or what is still left of him in Don Quixote, Alonso Quijano "el bueno," an intelligent, cultivated, judicious human being who never meant harm to anybody, but who would have never attracted the poetic imagination of anybody either. The surprise is that it is precisely this unpoetic individuality or personality that saves Don Quixote from being a madman like Avellaneda's madman or any other traditional madman being paraded in public for everybody's amusement. It is that which lies basically beyond the pale of literary interest (although by no means without interest altogether) that gives the literary personality of Don Quixote its depth, its lifelike quality, and brings him closer to us. If Don Quixote, as a character, is the precursor of the modern novel and the modern novelistic character, it is not insofar as he left behind, broke with, the nonpoetic personality of Alonso Quijano, but precisely because he didn't. Cervantes's modern discovery was not the madman, but the ordinary unpoetic man behind the madman. If Don Quixote appears in the eyes of Cervantes as neither a hero nor an antihero, it is because Cervantes continues to see beyond his madness, beyond his literary singularity, the nonliterary but valuable personality of Alonso Quijano "the good." Of course, once he discovered the nonliterary goodness and the equally nonliterary value of the ordinary human being behind the madman, he could also see the threat of the quixotic madness lurking behind the ordinary human being just as clearly. If it happened to Alonso Quijano, it could happen to anybody.

Deceiving Singularity or the Desire of the Crowd

The quixotification of Alonso Quijano turned him into a literary figure, gave him a distinct poetic singularity, but such a singularity was just that, poetic, strictly confined to the limits of poetic fiction. It did nothing to clarify the unpoetic individuality of Alonso Quijano as an ordinary human being, to make us see it better, or in a new light. Rather, what it did was to hide or to blur the view of human individuality and uniqueness as something existing beyond fiction. A quixotified Alonso Quijano is not an improved Alonso Quijano, but one who is ashamed of that ordinary individual and who does not want to be him any longer. But apart from this unpoetic individuality, which now remains in the background, and is without interest to the quixotic individual, the quixotic individuality itself is nothing but a form of fiction, a mirage kept in place by the intensity of desire. The problem is that such a desire is fundamentally contagious, mimetic, imitative. It comes into being through imitation and then spreads through imitation. And this being the case, what individuality, what uniqueness, can there be on the basis of a desire that is never its own master, that is always an imitation of some other equally mimetic expression of desire? This is why it must be said that the quixotic, literary individuality does not really exist, it is a mirage. If it did not have behind it the nonliterary individuality of the ordinary human being, it could not sustain itself, it would disintegrate. What the quixotified individual expels from his field of vision, from the scope of his desire, keeps sustaining him in the shadows.

Without the unpoetic (in the sense of that which is of no interest to literary desire), the poetic individuality disintegrates. What does that mean? It does not just vanish into thin air. As the mirage disintegrates, it reveals its true nature. It was not the unique thing it appeared to be. All by itself that uniqueness was pure appearance, a decoy. In reality it was a crowd. Its name was not radiant Amadís, as the quixotified individual believed, but legion, or the multitude, or the crowd. Because that is precisely what mimetic, contagious desire creates: the crowd. Radiant, singular Amadís, the desired one, was the object of the crowd's desire. It is how the crowd escapes from itself, hides itself as crowd. Amadís, the object of the crowd's desire, is also the one expelled by the crowd from within itself. For that is how the crowd fabricates both heroes and antiheroes.

Is Don Quixote's desire, then, the crowd's desire? There is one towering figure in the history of the reading of Cervantes's great novel to whom such an idea would have sounded like an outrageous blasphemy. I am speaking, of course, about Don Miguel de Unamuno, for whom Don Quixote was the very symbol of the anticrowd singularity. It may also sound outrageous to many other critics. But Unamuno's case is different not only because of his passionate defense of Don Quixote's quasi-sacred individuality, not only because Unamuno's *quijotismo* had profound religious overtones,[16] but above all because he knew that that was not the way Cervantes meant it, which is why he either despised Cervantes openly or had very ambivalent feelings toward him. And that is also why we will encounter Unamuno repeatedly in the course of this investigation. Indirectly, sometimes in a negative way, he can still be an accurate and profound guide to fundamental aspects of *Don Quixote.*

Unamuno believed that Don Quixote went mad trying desperately to be himself. And that was, in Unamuno's eyes, a glorious undertaking. Anything in Cervantes's novel that deviates from that, or casts doubts on that, was utterly unimportant (like all the interpolated stories) or downright malicious on the part of Cervantes. Cervantes, on the other hand—I will maintain—does not have much faith in the spontaneity of human desire. Not only is intensity of desire no guarantee at all of originality or individual authenticity, but it is exactly the opposite. In Cervantes, far more often than not, the intensification of desire is associated with the presence and influence of literary fiction: as desire intensifies, the person becomes increasingly like a character in a fictional story. And to become a character in a fictional story is to stop being oneself. That went completely against Unamuno's grain, so to speak. And yet, in his own novelistic creations, Unamuno, more or less unwittingly (it is hard to judge), confirms Cervantes's fundamental intuition. That intuition, which speaks of the mimetic character of human desire, will be at the center of this book.

16. In a recent collection of essays edited by Danielle Perrot, *Don Quichotte au XXe siècle* (2003), no less than three contributions are devoted to different aspects of Unamuno's *quijotismo*.

CHAPTER I

A Story "Naked and Unadorned"

The Prologue to Part I

The creative process we have just sketched cannot be easily reduced to a subjective experience of self-satisfaction and reassuring feelings of accomplishment. For Cervantes it must have been something rather ambivalent, a mixture of satisfaction at his artistic feat, and a sense of uneasiness, not so much about the fate of his novel after publication, but more deeply about the very meaning and significance of what his own story had taught him about himself and about the making of it. As we pointed out, in a novel so prophetic and defining of the new spirit of the novel, the fact that its protagonist becomes mad reading novels cannot possibly be considered an accident.

In the Prologue to Part I Cervantes tells us that the creation of *Don Quixote* took place away from "the pleasantness of the fields, the serenity of the skies, the murmuring of streams and the tranquility of the spirit." It felt "much like one engendered in prison, where every discomfort has its seat and every dismal sound its habitation." Apart from any possible extraliterary autobiographical reference, the statement is both revealing and intriguing. It may help in the understanding of such a statement to keep in mind the rather unique status of the *Quixote* in the context of Cervantes's narrative production in general. The story of Don Quixote, as we have said, was not of a kind to sooth the spirit of the author who, at the time he wrote the words just quoted, may have already had in mind the project for which he would have liked to be remembered, his magnum opus, his great Christian romance, *The Travails of Persiles and Segismunda*. For it is hard to imagine a greater formal contrast between these two stories and their respective protagonists.

I think it is safe to say that the artistic genesis of the *Persiles*, for example, must have been a very different experience from that of the *Quixote*. If *Persiles* describes the Christian journey to final redemption and therefore, in a sense, to paradise, the artistic genesis and development of the *Quixote* must have felt somewhat like purgatory, some sort of ascetic experience, a purging or cleansing of the artistic spirit of its author.[1] For there was a lot that Cervantes, who wanted to believe in the possibility of a Christian epic, had to overcome and accept in order to bring himself to the compassionate and sustained understanding of such a fool, to the only kind of profound understanding that could turn an old madman into the Knight of La Mancha that he created. Saving the old madman from his madness could only be the other side of an effort on the part of Cervantes to rid himself of his own demons.

It is remarkable to see how different Cervantes's attitude is in the presentation of Part 1 of the *Quixote* from the way he presents or announces his other narrative works, in particular those closest in time to the composition of his famous novel: *The Exemplary Stories* and the *Persiles*, the latter published posthumously.

In the Prologue to the *Exemplary Stories* (1913) he clearly feels proud because he considers himself to be the first to have written that kind of short story or novela in the Castilian language, "because the many *novelas* printed in that language are all translated from foreign languages, while these are my own, not imitated or stolen." He also feels confident about their "exemplary" character, and invites the reader to look closely at and to find moral profit in them. Furthermore, since he has been "bold enough to dedicate them to the great Count of Lemos, they [must] have some mystery hidden in

1. From a rather different perspective, Henry W. Sullivan describes Part 2 of the *Quixote* as a "grotesque purgatory." See Bibliography.

them to raise them to that higher level." In fact, in the Dedication he tells the count that the twelve short stories he is sending him "could aspire to a position next to the best."

In this same Prologue he also announces the forthcoming "*Travails of Persiles*, a book which dares to compete with Heliodoro," the prestigious Hellenistic author of the *Ethiopian Story*, considered at the time throughout Europe as one of the classics. (This announcement, by the way, is followed by another, on the continuation of *Don Quixote*, made without further comment.) Two years later, in his Dedication of Part 2 of the *Quixote* to the same Count of Lemos, he again announces the imminent completion of *The Travails of Persiles and Sigismunda*, a book "which ought to be either the worst or the best ever composed in our language, among those meant for entertainment. Although, I regret having said *the worst*, because in the opinion of my friends, it will reach the top of goodness." Finally, at the end of the Prologue to Part 2 of the *Quixote*, once again he reminds the reader to wait for the soon-to-appear *Persiles* ("I forgot to tell you to wait for the *Persiles*, which I am finishing now"). He seems to be saying, "Wait for it, you will not be disappointed."

The difference with the attitude expressed in the Prologue to Part 1 of the *Quixote* is striking. He presents the *Quixote* as "the story of a lean, shrivelled, whimsical child [of my brain], full of varied fancies that no one else has ever imagined." In fact, he wants to keep his distance from such a whimsical child: "I, though in appearance Don Quixote's father, am really his stepfather, and so will not drift with the current of custom, nor implore you, almost with tears in my eyes, as others do, dearest reader, to pardon or ignore the faults you see in this child of mine. For you are no relation or friend of his . . . , and so you can say anything you think fit about this story, without fear of being abused for a bad opinion, or rewarded for a good one."

What does this attitude mean? How are we to read this authorial detachment? Perhaps Cervantes senses that this is a rather unusual story, one that does not fit any traditional category. Perhaps he does not quite know what to make of it.[2] Of one thing he seems to be certain: none of the conventional ways of presenting a literary work to the public suits the occasion. He is at a

2. A. Castro also sees Cervantes's doubts and hesitations in this Prologue, but he interprets them as Cervantes's doubts about himself before the others, his contemporaries, the society that, according to Castro, had marginalized him. Needless to say, in Castro's view, Cervantes triumphs inwardly against all such doubts, and the words just quoted, "you can say anything . . . ,"

loss about how to proceed: "I would have wished to present it to you naked and unadorned, without the ornament of a prologue. . . . For I can tell you that, much toil though it cost me to compose, I found none greater than the making of the preface you are reading."

If he senses the radical novelty of the story he has just finished, such a novelty does not appear to be something reassuring to him. He does not feel confident or particularly proud of it, in the manner, for example, in which he feels proud to be the first to write novelas in Castilian. Why not? Why the cautious detachment? Is there something to fear? We will have to explore these questions in some detail.

There is, of course, a lot of irony and deliberate parody in this peculiar nonprologue. He is clearly making fun of those "other works, never mind how fabulous and profane, [that are] so full of sentences from Aristotle, Plato and the whole herd of philosophers, as to impress their readers and get their authors a reputation for wide reading, erudition and eloquence." In fact, he may have had someone specific in mind: Lope de Vega, for example, whose recently published *Peregrino en su patria* would certainly fit the parodic description.

However, as is usually the case in Cervantes, there is much more to it than that. If he had been looking for an occasion to parody such pompous or extravagant displays of unnecessary erudition, the *Quixote* would indeed provide the perfect one. He could not have found a better opportunity. Because it is true that, as his rhetorical friend tells him, "this book has no need of any of the things that you say it lacks." But we must still ask why, because the reason given by the rhetorical friend is far from convincing:

---

are interpreted as an indication of such a triumph, something like "I no longer care what you may think about it. I know it's good." In Castro's words, "La fe en su libro era ya absoluta" ("Los prólogos del Quijote," *Hacia Cervantes*, 265). I, on the other hand, would like to explore those doubts as grounded not in Cervantes's personal confrontation with anything, but in the literary task in which he was engaged, a task, of course, whose implications went far beyond the literary. Cervantes's doubts are a witness to the clarity and depth of his vision. And if this is so, it should be of great interest to find out what it was that he saw in what he was doing that so troubled him.

Two recent works have also taken up the subject of the first Prologue: Diana Alvarez Amell, *El discurso de los prólogos del Siglo de Oro* (Potomac, Md.: Scripta Humanistica, 1999); and Charles D. Presberg, *Adventures in Paradox: "Don Quixote" and the Western Tradition* (University Park: Pennsylvania State University Press, 2001), in particular Chapter 3, "This Is Not a Prologue."

The whole of [your book] is an invective against books of chivalry, which Aristotle never dreamed of, Saint Basil never mentioned, and Cicero never ran across. Nor do the precisions of truth or the calculations of astrology come within the scope of their fabulous nonsense [*ni caen debajo de la cuenta de sus fabulosos disparates las puntualidades de la verdad, ni las observaciones de la astrología*]; nor are geometrical measurements important to it; or the confutation of arguments, which is the province of rhetoric; nor does it set out to preach to anyone, mingling the human with the divine; which is a kind of motley in which no Christian understanding should be dressed [*ni tiene para qué predicar a ninguno, mezclando lo humano con lo divino, que es un género de mezcla de quien no se ha de vestir ningún cristano entendimiento*]. . . . And since this book of yours aims at no more than destroying the authority and influence which books of chivalry have in the world and among the common people, you have no reason to go begging sentences from philosophers, counsel from Holy Writ, fables from poets, speeches from orators, or miracles from saints. . . . In short, keep your aim steadily fixed on overthrowing the ill-based fabric of these books of chivalry, abhorred by so many yet praised by so many more; for if you achieve that, you will have achieved no small thing.

A moment's reflection should make it clear that the reason given by the friend for the *Quixote* to be in no need of help from philosophy and other disciplines is at the least a little perplexing. It would seem that if the principal and explicit aim of the book is the overthrowing of the nonsensical fiction of novels of chivalry, the book should offer plenty of opportunity for a display of the "precisions of truth," and, at the very least, the arguments of philosophers and moralists, all of which could be marshalled against the evils of such ill-founded books. How could such a didactic and moral purpose, in and of itself, not be an occasion precisely "to go begging sentences from philosophers, counsel from Holy Writ," and the like?

The friend's explanation is not convincing. It is, in fact, counterproductive, even self-defeating. I think it is a feeble attempt on the part of Cervantes to still give his novel some didactic respectability, in spite of the central point of his Prologue, which is that he wants to present the story of Don Quixote "naked and unadorned," without the help of philosophy, theology, the science of rhetoric, or any other science or discipline having to do with rigorous fidelity to the truth of the real world. Because the story of Don Quixote is a work of fiction, and Cervantes is telling us that he does not like "works fabulous and profane" to be full of sentences from philosophers or quotes from Holy Scripture. In fact, his dislike of the explicit mixture of philosophical and religious truth with fiction appears to be stronger by far in the particular case of the *Quixote* than in the case of his other works. There is no explicit declaration of his "allergic" reaction to such a mixture either in the *Exemplary Stories* or in the *Persiles*.

In principle, a work of fiction could still be a thing of beauty, elegance, eloquence, and even learning, and as such not entirely inimical to a judicious use of theology, philosophy, or science. However, in Cervantes's own perception, none of these qualities apply to this "child of [his] brain . . . lean, shrivelled, whimsical, and full of varied fancies." Which means that the story he has just finished, bears, as a story, the unmistakable imprint of its protagonist, a fool, a madman. Furthermore, if "the whole [book] is an invective against books of chivalry," if the author has kept his aim "steadily fixed on overthrowing [them]," without any help from outside the story itself, then everything rests on showing the ill effects of books of chivalry on the protagonist, the one who went insane reading them. In other words, the author must keep "[his] aim steadily fixed" on the madness of the madman and its connection with those dangerous books.

But can the father of such a literary creature keep his eyes fixed on its foolishness and still pretend to be a loving father? For "it may happen that a father has an ugly and ill-favored child, and that his love for it so blinds his eyes that he cannot see its faults." Of course, that is what a loving father is supposed to do with an ugly and ill-favored child. It would be cruel to do otherwise. A loving father does not expose his ugly or foolish child in its ugliness or foolishness. A loving father does not abandon his child to whatever the public may want to do with it, without even trying to come to its defense. But this is precisely what Cervantes says that he wants to do with this child of his brain. This is also why he tells us he is more like a stepfather than a father.

In other words, from the historical, nonfictional, perspective afforded by the Prologue on the literary, fictional character of Don Quixote and his story, both the dereliction of the character and the nakedness of the story, that is, its lack of rhetorical ornamentation and other respectable and reassuring attire, are inseparable from the fact that we are dealing with a traditionally marginal character: a fool. What else—Cervantes seems to be telling us—but such a kind of marginal, unprotected character would fit into a literary form equally unprotected, that is, cut off from the protection of philosophy, theology, traditional rhetorical tropes, and the like—in other words, we may add, a desacralized literary form, the literary form of a fiction that saw itself for the first time, out of the ruins of the epic, as nothing but fiction? And vice versa, what else but a "naked," unprotected literary form could be more appropriate to introduce such a character? Character and form are really made for each other: they communicate to each other their respective nakedness and dereliction.

And that was really lucky for the fool. Can we imagine what the poor devil would have looked like against a traditional backdrop fabricated with the help of theology, philosophy, rhetorical eloquence, and so on, that is to say, in the context of a reassuring and confident rationality? Well, we got a strong hint of what he might have looked like from our analysis of Avellaneda's fool. The poor devil would not have gotten much of a chance to speak his mind and try to defend himself. But a literary form that sees in the dereliction and nakedness of the outcast an image of its own dereliction and estrangement from philosophy, theology, science, and so on is a literary form far more hesitant to carry out the traditional expulsion, a literary form on its way to seeing the expulsion for what it really is: a collectively reassuring event at the expense of a victim who is far less unique and differentiated than the reassured members of society imagine.

Critics have paid little or no attention to this literary "nakedness" of the *Quixote*. Although indirectly acknowledged and misunderstood, it may have actually given rise to or supported the old notion that Cervantes was an "*ingenio lego*," an uncultivated genius. But the "nakedness," the vulnerability, of the form, its being deprived of help from philosophy, theology, and so forth, is clearly the flip side, so to speak, of a profound awareness of its fictional character, of its being, in the final analysis, nothing but fiction. In fact, this profound and constant awareness becomes throughout the course of the novel the basis for a devastating parody of the nonfictional pretensions of books of chivalry, that is, of their feigned historical character.

The "Hermetic" or "Intranscendental" Character of the Modern Novel

In the awareness of this "nakedness," this isolation, of the literary form, we see, perhaps for the first time in the realm of narrative fiction, what centuries later Ortega y Gasset would refer to as "la intrascendencia del arte," the nontranscendental, or intranscendental, character of art in general, and of the modern novel in particular, whose "intrascendencia" is closely tied to its typical "hermetic" quality: "Una necesidad puramente estética impone a la novela el hermetismo, la fuerza a ser un orbe obturado a toda realidad eficiente. Y esta condición engendra entre otras muchas, la consecuencia de que no puede aspirar directamente a ser filosofía, panfleto político, estudio sociológico o prédica moral. No puede ser más que novela, *no puede su interior trascender por sí mismo a nada exterior*" (203; A purely aesthetic need forces the novel to be hermetic, a world closed up to all efficient reality. And this condition produces, among many others, the consequence that [the novel] cannot aspire directly to be philosophy, political pamphlet, sociological study, or moral preaching. It cannot be anything more than a novel. *Its inside cannot transcend itself to anything outside*; original emphasis).

The only comment I would like to make on Ortega's words is that such a "purely aesthetic need" cannot be understood as referring to some timeless essence of the novel because the modern novel is a historical phenomenon with a clear beginning in the historical environment of sixteenth- and seventeenth-century Christian Europe. Things were not always like that in the history of literary or poetic fiction. The literay forms, both narrative and dramatic, that precede the modern novel are much less "hermetic," and, therefore much less "intranscendental," that is, more tied to all other important social activities, because there is something that ties them all: religion (from *religare*, "to tie, to bundle together"). For example, as we have already indicated, the religious, partly ritual, character of the tragic performance placed it, both symbolically and physically, next to the sacrificial altar.

To Cervantes the "hermetic" quality of the novel was much more than a "purely aesthetic need" because it was part and parcel of the historical process of Christian desacralization, to which he was profoundly sensitive; that same process, we now know, brought about the demise of the traditional epic hero, and therefore of the traditional epic form. The "hermetic" form of which Ortega speaks was for Cervantes a desacralized form, which is the reason why it appeared to him as something naked, vulnerable, a form of dereliction. And this is also why the Quixotic figure, "lean, shrivelled," a pathetic fallen hero, becomes the archetypal, paradigmatic protagonist of the modern novel.

The new form of the novel, the one who could say, like Cide Hamete's pen after Don Quixote's death, "For me alone Don Quixote was born and I for him," the novelistic form that found itself by finding Don Quixote, which saw itself in the form of the old fool, and saved itself by saving him, could not see itself as a heroic conqueror. The new form of the novel was not a conquest of the aesthetic spirit over previous forms supposedly shackled to an oppressive, intolerant sacred. It was much more like a humbling discovery of what it meant, in novelistic terms, to be in the service of the sacred, of the old, sacrificial, victimizing sacred. It was not an act of rebellion against anything. In Cervantes, the father of the modern novel, it was a profound realization of how intimately connected, and intrinsically well suited, traditional poetic fiction was to the demands of the sacrificial mechanisms of the human mind and of society, including the defensive mechanisms of a society from which the old sacrificial institutions *stricto sensu* had long disappeared. In Cervantes what the new form of the novel discovered was the innocence of the victim, the very victim that the novel itself demanded in order to be itself, to structure itself as a form of fiction.

Roberto Calasso has said that "what speaks in art is the voice of the victim who escaped the killing *in extremis*—and forever—when the ritual had already caused all the sacred to flow back into that victim" (199). True, but such an escape did not just happen on its own and of itself. It took a wrenching act of Christian compassion that saved not only the victim but the artistic form itself, granting it a new lease on life, so to speak. As far as the modern novel is concerned, that creative act of compassion was the work of Cervantes. A literary form "naked and unadorned," an entertaining and profitable fiction, which is nevertheless nothing but fiction, is, or is meant to be, also a literary form liberated from its victimizing roots and propensities.

Literature Desacralized

It could be said that Cervantes's *Don Quixote* is the first modern novel because it is the first full-length desacralized narrative of a conventional antiheroic figure.[3] But such a statement can be more than a little misleading.

3. Cf. Fredric Jameson: "[As] any number of 'definitions' of realism assert, and as the totemic ancestor of the novel, *Don Quixote*, emblematically demonstrates, that processing opera-

Desacralization is not in itself a literary process or a literary form. It is more like a dynamic and flexible attitude on the part of the author vis-à-vis his or her own work. One does not write a "desacralized" work without "desacralizing" oneself in the process—a rather ascetic process, we might add. Desacralization begins and ends anew with every work.

It would be nonsensical to imagine Cervantes, or anybody, setting out to write a "desacralized novel," as if we were talking about a particular type of novel. There is no such thing as a desacralized genre in a formal sense, because no formal feature can ever be, all by itself, a guarantee of desacralization. Contrary to what Marxist criticism believes, it is not the form (the result of the mode of production) that desacralizes, but the author every time he sets out to write. Even if we could imagine such an explicit literary purpose or goal, it would provide no warranty at all of literary quality or genius. Desacralization cannot substitute for artistic criteria in general or literary criteria in particular. It is not directly concerned with literature as such. It only concerns directly the fate of the structuring victim who lies at the deepest level of human society, at its foundational—sacred—core, and, indirectly, everything that reflects or echoes in any way, literary or not, that victimizing core. Only literary criteria can decide what is or is not literature at any given time. Desacralization is not a literary or artistic criterion.

On the other hand, no literary criterion, by itself, has ever been sufficient to define what is or is not great in literature. Literary greatness transcends literary criteria. It even transcends its own historical moment, in the sense that such greatness must be recognized as such, must be meaningful, be-

tion [i.e., 'the novel as process rather than as form'] variously called narrative mimesis or realistic representation has as its historic function the systematic undermining and demystification, the secular 'decoding,' of those preexisting inherited traditional or sacred paradigms which are its initial givens. In this sense, the novel plays a significant role in what can be called a properly bourgeois cultural revolution—that immense process of transformation whereby populations whose life habits were formed by other, now archaic, modes of production are effectively reprogrammed for life and work in the new world of market capitalism" (152). Of course, this tells us absolutely nothing about the process whereby those "inherited traditional or sacred paradigms" get demystified or desacralized. In the end, that process governs the making of the novel not only from outside the novel completely, but from beyond anything that Cervantes could even remotely imagine that he was doing when he was writing it. The overriding influence and centrality of the "modes of production," the secret of human history, in Marx's terminology, had not yet been revealed to proletarian humanity. On the other hand, Jameson, like Marxist critics in general, is well aware of the "immense process of transformation" that was taking place through the process of demystification or desacralization.

yond that moment, even when it is no longer repeatable. As far as the relationship between the historical process of Christian desacralization, on the one hand, and literary fiction, on the other, is concerned, I think there can be little doubt that the authorial desacralization of the old forms saved literary fiction from historical exhaustion and collapse. And there is no doubt that such desacralization, the careful separation of "the human and the divine," was a profoundly Christian occurrence that, in some way, reconciled literary fiction with the spirit of the Christian text. However, we must keep in mind that the reconciliation was also something like an act of contrition on the part of literary fiction, a renunciation to any claim to be the herald, the authoritative speaker of the new sacred, of the God of the Gospels. This is crucial. To desacralize the old forms did not mean directly to Christianize them. It was simply a way of saying that the God of the Gospels was not there, that it was an error to look for him in the house of fiction. This was a most important discovery, one that-implied that literary fiction could not and should not formally become a preaching instrument for the Christian word.

The very meaning and spirit of the Christian text became a formidable obstacle to any attempt to Christianize the old mimetic forms of literary fiction, that is to say, to pass them on in Christian attire. But not everybody sensed as deeply as Cervantes did in the *Quixote* that the only Christian way to deal with such forms was to disconnect them completely from the sacred, because, in themselves, as forms of fiction, the only sacred that suited them, that was, as it were, natural to them, because they had been born from it historically, was the old victimizing sacred. To try to turn those forms into instruments of the Christian revelation was really an impossible task, "a kind of motley in which no Christian understanding should be dressed."

And that was Mateo Alemán's basic mistake in his picaresque *Guzmán de Alfarache*. He wanted to Christianize the picaresque novel. He thought he had found the perfect formula by having the picaro write his autobiography after repenting from his life as a picaro and undergoing a profound conversion. But the autobiography that Guzmán ends up writing is like any other picaresque autobiography. The only difference is the enormous amount of moralizing commentary that it contains. In other words, the novel we read in no way reflects the spirit of a Christian conversion. In fact, Alemán uses the conversion of the picaro, an outcast, another traditional victim, like a merciless weapon against the society that expels him, castigating its vices and corruption. It is even possible that Cervantes could specifically have had in mind Alemán's "mixture" of the human and the divine when he penned his famous phrase.

The answer to Alemán's failed attempt was not long in coming. Quevedo's picaresque *Buscón* can be considered as a sort of anti-*Guzmán*. He swung the pendulum all the way in the opposite direction. It was as if Quevedo wanted to show Alemán what a "real" picaresque novel, that is, one without any pretensions of being Christian, was capable of doing with a "real" picaro, that is, one without any saving features. And such a "real" picaresque novel, a faithful expression of the victimizing mechanism of society, will be mercilessly cruel with its picaro, who will appear to deserve everything he gets. Quevedo saw what apparently Alemán did not, the intimate connection between the victim and the traditional novelistic victimizing artifact, but did not move a finger to save either one or the other.

Alemán and Quevedo represent the two opposite and symmetrical dangers between which Cervantes had to navigate; they are his Scylla and Charybdis. They serve as points of reference to better understand the meaning and the importance of what Cervantes achieved in the *Quixote*, and therefore what was involved in the birth of the modern novel, that is to say, why it happened with the *Quixote*, and not with either the *Guzmán* or the *Buscón*.

CHAPTER II

The Picaresque Point of Reference 1

Guzmán de Alfarache

From Folklore to Literature

In reference to the first picaresque novel (or the immediate precursor of the picaresque novel, in the view of some), *Lazarillo de Tormes*, it has been said that

[e]l personaje del pícaro . . . en su primera encarnación emerge, por supuesto, de un fondo de historietas populares. . . . Pero, a partir del momento en que Lázaro de Tormes dice "yo," es decir, en el momento mismo en que nace a la literatura, cesa de pertenecer al folklore: rompiendo con su anterior existencia de personaje de chascarrillo, se convierte en el portavoz de una forma de pensar seria que se encarna en él . . . en sus palabras y gestos burlones, aun siendo los mismos de la marioneta folklórica de antaño. (Molho, 11)

(To be sure, the picaro character . . . emerges initially from a background of popular tales. . . . But from the moment when Lázaro de Tormes says "I," that is to say, from the very moment he is born to literature, he ceases to belong to folklore: breaking away from his earlier existence as a joke character, he becomes the spokesman for a serious mode of thinking that becomes embodied in him . . . in his words and joking gestures, even though they are still those of the old folkloric puppet.)

I think this is a perceptive observation, which may, of course, be extended to all traditional folkloric antiheroes, such as the madman or the fool. But what the critic describes as an automatic and sudden transformation would be more accurately described as an encounter, indeed, as a rather problematic and difficult encounter of the old and laughable folkloric puppet with an emerging form of literature that aspires to treat him seriously. How does one deal with the low-born or marginal character, the traditional object of collective ridicule, in a sustained serious way? To judge by what we saw in Avellaneda's *Quixote*, the encounter of the old with the new was by no means an easy one. It was an uncertain process, full of tension, and capable of threatening the newly emerging literary forms with internal collapse. And not every author was equally aware of the problem or equally successful in dealing with it.

What we find when we compare the three major representatives of the picaresque, the *Lazarillo*, the *Guzmán de Alfarache*, and the *Buscón*, is an increasing authorial awareness, and a progressive deepening, of the problem itself. In the *Lazarillo*, the uneasy coexistence of the old victimizing structure with the new seriousness leads to a rather ambivalent situation. Peter N. Dunn, who has written one of the most perceptive books on the Spanish picaresque, interprets the ambivalence as follows:

The book is titled *La vida de Lazarillo de Tormes, y de sus fortunas y adversidades*, and it has been shown that the only literary genre that regularly appeared with such a title (*The life of* . . .) since the thirteenth century was the saint's life. . . . The surname de Tormes, as has often been noted, is a trivializing parody of the chivalric nomenclature (Amadís de Gaula, Palmerín de Inglaterra, etc.). Lazaro's life is therefore set up in a parodic relation to two exemplary traditional models: the real-life saint and the traditional hero. Given these generic coordinates . . . the reader would have the delicate task of deciding whether the career of Lázaro was being ridiculed by contrast with the exemplary models or whether the models were being satirized by contamination with Lázaro's squalid life. . . . If this novel makes us conscious of some of the cant that adheres to noble heroes and to models of virtue, it continually ironizes itself in the process. (41–42)

We could put it somewhat differently: in the *Lazarillo* it is not clear whether the object of the ridicule is the antiheroic picaro or the seamy side, the hidden face, of the hero. This is a rather ironic dilemma because, in fact, the antihero has always been the hidden side of the hero. Ultimately hero and antihero are the two sides of the same sacrificial entity, the victim. It seems to me, therefore, quite telling that in its first literary manifestation the antihero may appear as a parody of the hero, which is probably a sign of primitivism rather than of modernity. What is rather modern, however, is the sympathetic understanding the author displays in presenting the child Lazarillo, as opposed to his handling of the shameless adult Lázaro. The contrast between the old and the new, and the authorial awareness of it, does not seem to be fully developed in the *Lazarillo*. But this awareness is quite high when we get to the masterpieces of the genre, the *Guzmán* (Part 1, 1599; Part 2, 1604), and the *Buscón* (1626, but written much earlier, probably between 1604 and 1620).

As we have just indicated in the case of Cervantes, the author who comes out to meet the traditional laughable antihero armed with seriousness and respectability may not help at all with the fate of the poor devil. In order to be truly new, to have a future, the new form of literature had to meet its new character, the old folkloric outcast, humbly, sympathetically, on its own ground, "naked and unadorned." In other words, it had to examine itself seriously in the image of that laughable lowly character. Such a serious self-examination could, nevertheless, become a profound source of irony. In other words, the literary transformation that is supposed to happen as the old folkloric character encounters literature will not happen unless it works both ways.

How did it happen in the first fully developed picaresque novel, the *Guzmán de Alfarache*? One thing is clear from the beginning: the *Guzmán* is not meant to be something "naked and unadorned" in the sense meant by Cervantes in the *Quixote*. If Cervantes found it difficult to write a prologue to his novel, Alemán obviously did not, for he wrote two, one for the vulgar and malicious crowd ("Al vulgo") and one for the wise reader ("Al discreto lector"), in addition to a "Declaration for the understanding of this book." And he "picked a lot from learned and saintly men": "No todo es de mi aljaba; mucho escogí de doctos varones y santos: eso te alabo y vendo" (94). If we find something less than grave and well composed, we must blame it on the fact that its subject matter is a picaro: "Lo que hallares no grave ni compuesto, eso es el ser de un pícaro el sujeto deste libro" (94).

Clearly Alemán conceives his novel as something more serious and on a much grander scale than its predecessor, the anonymous *Lazarillo*. The subtitle to its second part is that of *Atalaya de la vida humana*, an elevated "watchtower" offering a view on human life. By its size and the literal complexity of its adventures it brings to mind the epic, or the so-called Byzantine novel (cf. Dunn, 51). Its picaro, Guzmán, roams over much of Spain and Italy. In contrast to his predecessor, the child Lazarillo, he is not forced out of his home, or given away; nor were the conditions at home so precarious that he could not have stayed with his mother, a woman, as is to be expected in most picaresque novels, of more than dubious reputation, but by no means unresourceful. It was *his* decision to leave home, as it is often *his* decision to move from one place or one master to another. Alemán goes to great lengths to point out that Guzmán is fundamentally a free agent, and therefore ultimately responsible for his own fate. "El enemigo mayor que tuve fue a mí mismo. Con mis propias manos llamé a mis daños. . . . Mis obras mismas me persiguieron" (778; The worst enemy I had was myself. With my own hands I brought my own damage. . . . My own works pursued me). This is very important because the novel itself, Guzmán's autobiography, his "confesión general," is motivated—we are told—by a profound act of religious conversion.

Guzmán's Conversion

The conversion happens toward the end of the novel, while Guzmán is serving as a prisoner in the galleys. He is at the lowest point of his career, or, as he puts it, "at the summit of the mountain of my miseries," from which he can either "jump into the depths of hell or, easily, by lifting my hand, reach heaven" (889). His conversion is conceived in a perfectly orthodox manner. He is confronted with the realization that he must make a decisive and fundamental choice, while also realizing that he cannot count on his own merits or strength to reach out to heaven and be saved. He must rely on Christ, "who became our brother, [for] what brother is there who would abandon his good brother?" And he must depend on Christ's infinite merit, without which nothing is of any avail, not even "the accumulated merits of all the saints" (890). But with the help of the Lord, he made it, even though it was not easy to keep on the straight path, because "I was made of flesh. I stumbled at every step, and many times I fell; however . . . I remained much renewed from that moment on" (890).

It must be this powerful experience of conversion that gave him the strength to endure. For, as Professor Dunn has noted, "After his moment of 'conversion,' of lucidity and decision, Guzmán is tested to the utmost: his fellow convicts intend to murder him if their plan to mutiny succeeds. The officers believe him to be guilty of a theft he did not commit, so he is totally isolated, abandoned, and subjected to the most extreme torture. Nothing in his earlier life leads us to suppose that he will remain firm in the face of excruciating adversity; his story until now has been one of endless failure, in much easier circumstances, to stay whatever course he has chosen. But he does remain firm, and this is an emphatic sign that Alemán underwrites his protagonist's reform" (60).

Some critics, however, have expressed doubts about the sincerity of Guzmán's conversion. Within the fictional parameters of the novel itself, I see no reason to doubt Alemán's sincerity in presenting the act of conversion itself as genuine. He clearly means it to be read that way. As we have just seen, it is, in its own terms, both psychologically and doctrinally coherent, in other words, a verisimilar representation of the real thing. It is meant to function in the novel as genuine. There does not seem to be anything dubious about it. The only alternative I can think of to accepting in good faith the intentional genuineness of the conversion would be to accept the letter of it, but to deny that it corresponds to any kind of Christian sincerity on the part of the author, Mateo Alemán. In other words, we would have to accept its genuine appearance as deliberately faked, thus turning Mateo Alemán into a hypocrite. This is an idea that would have to be based on all kinds of extratextual reasons impossible to prove with only the text in hand. And just as there once was a myth about the hypocritical Cervantes, we would end up with another myth of the hypocritical Alemán.

I not only believe that Guzmán's conversion is sincerely meant to be genuine, I think that literary historians have not paid it all the attention it deserves. The author's use of conversion was a truly unique and, in a sense, daring and radical attempt to ground the seriousness of his work. I do not think it is either inappropriate or exaggerated to place Alemán's effort regarding the picaresque or, in general, the narrative fate of the antihero on a level with what epic writers of the stature of Tasso, for example, were attempting to do with the old epic form, that is to say, to Christianize it, and thereby give it a new historical relevance. It was an effort that would only reveal the fundamental reason for the demise of the epic, as it will also reveal Alemán's ultimate failure to open the future to a new kind of fictional narrative with the traditional antihero at its center. But nobody can take from him the glory of being the only author of a picaresque novel in seventeenth-century Spain to have really tried.

Today, of course, we may bracket, as it were, the Christian dimension of the work and simply look at it as human experience in the making. But if we ask whether or not the novel that we read today would be what it is, would even exist, without the specifically Christian intention that accompanied its author as he wrote it, the answer can only be negative. So the problem we are about to examine is not exactly whether Mateo Alemán made the wrong choice by Christianizing the picaresque novel in order to raise it to the level of serious literature. What else could he have done? Historically speaking, he had no other choice. Furthermore, even from a doctrinal point of view, the choice was far from arbitrary. To see the despised, roguish picaro as a persecuted figure, the object of public violence, and then to see through it the image of the persecuted Christ is something not only perfectly logical for a Christian, but also the most profound transformation that a Christian can envision.

We do not know exactly at what point in the writing of his novel the idea came to Mateo Alemán to anchor the story of Guzmán in an act of Christian conversion.[1] But it is perfectly clear that the Christian dimension or meaning of his protagonist is directly linked to a perception of him as a victimized outcast. This is how Guzmán explains what motivated him to write the story of his life, to offer "this public display of my things" (484):

[Mi intención] ya te dije que sólo era de tu aprovechamiento, de tal manera que puedas con gusto y seguridad pasar por el peligroso golfo del mar que navegas. Yo aquí recibo los palos y tú los consejos de ellos. . . . Yo sufro las afrentas de que nacen tus honras. (483)

([My intention,] as I told you, was aimed at your profit, so that you can navigate the dangerous waters in which you find yourself, pleasantly and in safety. I get the beatings, you get the advice. . . . I suffer the insults from which you derive your merits.)

1. Recently Edward H. Friedman (1987) has suggested that Alemán "fabricated" Guzmán's conversion as part of his defensive strategy against the author of a spurious second part of the novel (1602). The suggestion seems plausible. I find no reason to deny this additional motivation.

A mi costa y con trabajos propios descubro los peligros y sirtes para que no embistas y te despedaces ni encalles a donde te falte remedio a la salida. (485)

(At my expense and with my own toil I reveal the sand banks and dangers so that you do not break apart or run aground hopelessly.)

He is willing to take all the beatings, suffer all the affronts, and undertake all dangers alone so that all of us, we readers, can grow in honor, and can avoid those hidden dangers that the story of his life reveals. In other words, he willingly accepts his role as expiatory victim for our salvation. But we, the readers, must also look upon this public spectacle of the rogue being beaten and affronted with the right kind of attitude. We must be willing to learn from it, which means that we cannot look at it and feel exhilarated, cruelly applauding the beatings and the affronts. In other words, the reader will not learn anything "[i]f I am for him like the bull in the ring, the lancing of which, and the wounds and the beatings, exhilarate those who look at it, an inhuman act in my opinion" (490). This is another way for Alemán to say that it is possible to transform the traditional victimizing representation of the low-life or antiheroic character—picaresque or otherwise—into a nonvictimizing one, which for him could only mean looking at the victim with Christian eyes, seeing in that traditional object of public scorn and blame the suggestion of a Christ-like figure, if only he would repent and accept the public's blame and scorn.[2] It was obvious, simple, and truly unprecedented. This is why it is also important to realize that Guzmán's explanation of his intention is much more than a rehashing of the typically medieval notion of teaching by contrary example, even though such a notion is also explicitly propounded by Guzmán himself:

2. The profound change in Christian spirituality that takes place in the transition from the Middle Ages to the Modern Era is reflected in the religious poetry of the period, as noticed, for example, by Michel Darbord: "Si l'on ne peut parler vraiment d'une révolution dans la poésie religieuse traditionnelle, lépoque des Rois Catholiques apporte cependant une innovation frappante. . . . [Tout] est centré désormais sur le texte évangelique: . . . évangile de la Passion surtout. . . . Il s'agit de mettre au premier plan, avant tout, l'économie du salut et de provoquer la conversion du pécheur par la contemplation de la sainte Agonie et des mystères de la Rédemption" (15; Although we really cannot speak of a "revolution" in traditional religious poetry, we can nevertheless speak of a striking innovation at the time of the Catholic Monarchs. . . . From then on everything is centered on the Gospel text: . . . the Gospel of the Passion above all. . . . It is a matter primarily of bringing to the foreground the process of salvation and of triggering the conversion of the sinner by the contemplation of the holy Agony and the mysteries of the Redemption). Alemán's spirituality belongs in this historical context.

Digo—si quieres oirlo—que aquesta confesión general que hago, este alarde público que de mis cosas te presento, no es para que me imites a mí; antes para que, sabidas, corrijas las tuyas en tí. (484)

(I say—if you want to hear it—that this general confession that I am making, this public exhibition of my things that I present to you, is not so that you may imitate me; rather it is so that, once you know them, you can correct those things in yourself.)

The Fundamental Contradiction

But there was a fundamental flaw in Alemán's implementation of his Christianizing solution. It is this: from a Christian perspective, the existential and religious meaning of Christ's sacrifice, the sacrifice to end all blood sacrifices, the antidote to the old way of sacrificial thinking itself, clashes with the structuring form of the picaresque autobiography, a form conceived as the public spectacle of a rogue who is pushed around, victimized, for the benefit of the crowd, which will either laugh at him or moralize about him. There is no problem with the meaning of Christ's sacrifice serving as the inspiration for Guzmán's individual, personal conversion, but there is a huge and inevitable incompatibility between Christ's sacrifice and the traditional form of presentation for the picaro. The individual could be saved but not the literary form anchored in that kind of presentation, at least not without the latter undergoing such a major transformation that it would render the old form practically unrecognizable. The genuineness of Guzmán's conversion clashes with the form of the novel that he tells us he decided to write as a result of the conversion itself. Quite simply, Alemán cannot have it both ways. If Guzmán's conversion is meant to be genuine, as I think it is, then he is definitely in the wrong kind of novel.

Actually we can take this reasoning one step further. In Christian terms, the meaning of Christ's sacrifice is immediately compromised as soon as we look at it as a public, socially sanctioned spectacle. If one appreciates or in any way enjoys the spectacle as such, that is, as a spectacle, the meaning of Christ's Passion is lost, or utterly devalued. Christ on the cross is not a cathartic tragedy, a mimetic spectacle for the masses. He is not there for the benefit of the crowd as such, but quite the opposite. He is there to break up the power of the crowd by addressing each of its members apart from the crowd, individually. Therefore, precisely to the extent that a fictional form is, inevitably, a public mask, a rhetorical way of standing before the other, a staging of oneself before the crowd, its primary or most immediate allegiance is to the sacrificers, to the persecutors, not to Christ. No author can claim the fictional literary form for Christ without understanding this profound incompatibility, and then only to the extent that he or she is capable of overcoming the inherent sacrificial, persecutorial proclivities of the fictional form itself. This is to say that in sixteenth- and seventeenth-century Christian Europe the old forms of narrative fiction had no future except through a radical process of what might be called "repentant self-analysis." That is precisely what Cervantes did in the *Quixote*. Clearly Alemán fell much too short of this goal. Guzmán de Alfarache is just not believable when he tells us that he was moved to write his picaresque autobiography, or "poética historia," as a result of his remorseful Christian conversion.

To repeat: although I have no doubt that Alemán meant his picaro's conversion to be genuine, the fact is that there is an insurmountable conflict between this conversion and the form of the novel that is meant to emerge from it. That, I think, is the fundamental reason behind the various reasons adduced by a significant number of modern critics who have found the conversion insincere, a fraud,[3] a finding which has, in turn, led some of them on a rather futile search for the reasons Alemán may have had to be so devious. I do not think he was devious at all. He simply made a historical mistake, and a very common one at the time, the beginnings of the modern era—a mistake, in a certain sense, far more easily detected today, after four hundred years of literary and religious history, than it could be at the time.

After a genuine experience of Christian conversion, the only autobiography that seems appropriate is something like Saint Augustin's *Confessions*, a baring of one's soul before God, even if it is done for the benefit of others, as was the case with the saint—a baring of the soul to God, which is indeed a form of storytelling, for one's story is what one is: the self is not some sort of metaphysical essence, but a story in the making. Yet this telling of one's story before God cannot be a literary or poetic genre in any traditional sense of the word, that is to say, subject to social conventions or mimetic fashion. In this particular sense, in its loneliness, if you will, in its nakedness and vulnerability, the baring of one's story before God ressembles, by no means accidental-

3. See Arias, Brancaforte, Rodríguez Matos, and Whitenack.

ly, the modern "naked and unadorned" story of Don Quixote. In other words, such an autobiographical story of one's own conversion, if true to itself, cannot be a rhetorical mask. For one does not address the Christian God as one addresses a primitive idol. One cannot communicate with Him through a mask, while, on the other hand, the use of a mask or of a disguise, the sacrificial substitution of one identity for another, is *the only safe way* to communicate with the primitive sacred, the idol. The Christian God is either the one before whom all masks are useless, or He is nothing at all, just another idol.

Implicitly Alemán, a good Christian who must have been familiar with the *Confessions*, knew that. This is why his protagonist never addresses his "confession" to God, as one would expect from a repentant Christian sinner who has been saved from himself by the grace and mercy of Christ. Guzmán always speaks like a typical picaro, and nobody can pretend to speak like a typical picaro, or any other fictional type, to the Christian God. Such an exercise, as we have just suggested, could only be either absurdly grotesque or deliberately blasphemous. As a literary mask, as a disguise, Guzmán can only "confess" to "the reader," the human other, to one who is no better or worse than himself, which inevitably makes the confession a very ambiguous affair.

Benito Brancaforte is quite right in detecting "[un] movimiento de atracción y repulsión [que] corresponde al modo de reaccionar de los lectores y estriba en el papel del narrador, quien toma una doble postura, la del juez y la del penitente. A veces el narrador-protagonista . . . se sitúa en un plano de superioridad y fustiga al lector y los vicios del mundo. Otras veces se sitúa en un plano de inferioridad, y adoptando la actitud del penitente, busca conmiseración para sí mismo . . ." (21; a movement of attraction and repulsion corresponding to the reactions of the readers, and based on the role of the narrator, who adopts a double posture, that of judge and that of penitent. Sometimes the narrator-protagonist . . . places himself on a superior level and castigates the reader and the vices of the world. Some other times he places himself on an inferior level, adopting the attitude of the penitent, and looking for pity for himself). Judith Whitenack's perceptive analysis of Alemán's novel comes even closer to what I am trying to explain. Her observations about the differences between secular and religious confessions are particularly relevant:

In most cases a confessant cannot forget his motives of excuse and self-justification and concentrate upon confession, penance, and absolution, unless his interlocutor is God or his representative. This is because the secular confessant is almost inevitably trying to mold his interlocutor's opinion of him, whereas for a believer, God cannot be deceived, and there can be no absolution for anyone who lies to his confessor. (29–30)

This is another way of saying that it is very difficult "to confess" to the other, the human other, without putting on a show, without competing, without wearing a mask, without becoming self-conscious in the ordinary negative sense of the word, without becoming defensive, hostile, or its opposite, excessively submissive or servile. In other words, "confessing" to the human other immediately runs the risk of lapsing into the very sins, weaknesses, and problems that brought about the need for "confessing" to begin with, for such problems and such a psychological need are all generated within the same intersubjective, interindividual matrix. The sincerity of such confessions is unavoidably problematic.

The incompatibility between Guzmán's conversion and the fictional form in which it is presented is also indirectly acknowledged by modern criticism when it feels obligated to dilute and minimize the Christian specificity of the *Guzmán* in its defense of the book's novelistic qualities. Peter Dunn, for example, in spite of his strong defense of Alemán's emphatic underwriting of "his protagonist's reform" (notice the choice of words: "reform," not "conversion"), as we saw above, sees "nothing specifically Christian in a narrative that assumes, on the one hand, that we can seldom control our nature as we wish, and on the other, that we may experience a moment when we suddenly 'find ourselves' and are able, we know not how, to break free, to turn our lives around. Magazines and television shows supply a steady stream of such upbeat stories of addicts, jailed criminals, and the like who have touched bottom and then emerge to become new people in their community" (59).

Of course, we do not know what happened inwardly, to the individual human being as such, in those upbeat stories. But we do know that those magazines and television shows would have very little interest in the kind of circumstances that Alemán considered essential to test the sincerity or authenticity of his picaro's conversion: "totally isolated, abandoned, and subjected to the most extreme torture." These circumstances are clearly intended to reflect those of the Passion of Christ, who was despised, tortured, and abandoned, or those of the suffering servant in the Old Testament. These are the paradigmatic circumstances that will not only test inner resolve but will also define and guarantee the Christian character of the conversion. That is to say, this is not just a possible test among many. These are the circumstances of the only test that was ultimately meaningful to Alemán: Christ's test. The details may vary, of course, but the new man will not really be a new man in a Christian sense unless he is ready to accept, for Christ's sake, the sufferings of the one who is persecuted, tortured, isolated, and abandoned by everybody.

But Professor Dunn is right. If, on the one hand, we want to read Alemán's novel as a modern novel (which it is not), we would do well to substitute a nonspecifically Christian story of reform, a story that could have happened almost anywhere at almost any time, for Alemán's radically Christian view of what real reform entails. If, on the other hand, we want to learn about Alemán's noble effort but ultimate failure to produce a modern novel, then we cannot lose sight of the intended Christian character of Guzmán's conversion.

There is no point in minimizing the flagrant contradiction at the center of Alemán's novel. Our goal is not to save the novel from itself, but to try to understand what happens in it. Everybody knows that even though Guzmán's conversion and the description of its circumstances is probably the highest, the most intense, moment in the novel, the voice who speaks throughout the novel is not the voice of a man who found Christ in the depths of suffering, violence, and injustice, but either the typical voice of a picaro or that of a moralizing prosecutor scourging society for all its vices. Two very attentive readers of the novel, Michel and Cécile Cavillac, have summarized what they see as follows:

> Tout au long de son existence misérable, le *picaro* s'est efforcé de transgresser les interdits pesant sur l'infamie de ses origines . . . ; cette transgression impossible s'accomplit alors que tout semble perdu . . . par la voie transcendante de la grâce qui le place, face à la collectivité, non en position de repli, mais en position de force. . . . Non content des confesser ses erreurs, il se retourne contrer les fausses valeurs d'une societé "bloquée" et, en premier lieu, contre l'imposture de l'honneur aristocratique qui est à l'origine de sa perte. Son discours où l'humilité se distingue mal de la superbe . . . met en cause, compromet et accuse. Celui qui semblait devoir s'offrir en victime expiatoire se révèle le plus intransigeant des censeurs. (118–19)

> (All along his miserable existence the picaro has been trying to break through prohibitions weighing on the infamy of his origins . . . ; this impossible breakthrough is

[finally] accomplished when everything seems to be lost . . . by the transcendant way of grace, which places him, in the face of society, not in a retreating position, but in a position of power. . . . Not content with confessing his errors, he turns against the false values of an immobile society and, first of all, against the imposture of aristocratic honor, which is at the root of his handicap. His discourse, in which it is difficult to separate humility from pride . . . denounces, exposes, and accuses. The one who, it seemed, should have offered himself as an expiatory victim, turns out to be the most intransigent of censors.)

Trying to hear the merciful voice of a God who has just rescued a dejected sinner from damnation in the autobiographical words of Guzmán would put too much of a strain on our suspension of disbelief. Here is one example that occurs shortly after Guzmán has told the reader that he hopes his travails will be of profit to him. He goes on to wish that the telling of his troubles will also help the "republic" by eliminating certain categories of particularly obnoxious people, the "poisonous vermin":

How beautiful they would look, if they would all perish! For not even Brussels [famous for its tapestries] can boast of tapestries so fine, so ornamental, and so becoming in the house of a prince as those which executioners hang alongside the roads. (485)

He is referring, of course, to the dismembered bodies of criminals that public executioners hang, or simply throw, outside the city walls, alongside roads leading to town. Fine tapestries, indeed! But such a gruesome metaphor does not sound very Christ-like, does it? In fact, it sounds like the language that Quevedo, Alemán's opposite, uses in the *Buscón*, as we will see in the next chapter.

The harsh moralizing tone of the *Guzmán*, its lack of humility, is a byproduct of Alemán's lack of awareness of, or insensitivity to, that inconsistency at the center of his novel, which Cervantes described as an unchristian mixing of "the human and the divine" because, in Cervantes's view, this is not a separation between two things of equal rank and importance. The separation was also a value judgment: a recognition that the literary object, whose aesthetic integrity had to be preserved by keeping it within the sphere of the human, was of a lower rank and value than sacred Christian objects. In the judgment of Cervantes, there was something irreverent and thus blameworthy in any attempt "to mix" the two, to put them on the same level. Therefore, acknowledging, submitting to, the separation between literary form and the Christian sacred was also an act of humility, whether explicit or implicit, whether deliberate or not. It was precisely in that artistically wise spirit of humility that Cervantes was able to achieve his extraordinary novelistic feat, the compassionate saving of the old fool from his conventional fate as the victim of society's violent defensive mechanism.

The incompatibility between traditional forms of fictional representation and the Christian word was not something that came into being full blown and for the first time in sixteenth-century Europe. It had always been there latently, in a somewhat dormant state, throughout much of the Middle Ages. As all Christian moralists in the sixteenth century knew quite well, the Fathers of the Church had already pointed that out insistently. What was new was not the incompatibility itself but the degree to which it became impossible to ignore and, as a consequence, the need to approach and conceive literary fiction in the light of it, without trying to bypass it, soften it, or look for excuses. The humble status of poetic fiction acquired a new and deeper meaning.

A Point of Reference: Saint Augustine's *Confessions*

Since we are dealing with a fictional autobiography supposedly anchored in a Christian conversion, it seems only appropriate that we make reference to Saint Augustine's *Confessions*, which have on occasion been mentioned by critics as a formal precedent to *Guzmán*, although these same critics generally overlook the fact that the *Confessions* is one of the most profound indictments of literary fiction ever written.

As is well known, there were two things that Augustine's conversion required of him: he had to renounce the flesh, specifically, fornication, on the one hand, and poetry or rhetoric, or what might be referred to as "fornication of the spirit," on the other:[4]

> For what could be more miserable than a wretch that pities not himself; one bemoaning Dido's death, caused by loving of Aeneas, and yet not lamenting his own [spiritual] death. . . . I did not love thee, and I committed fornication against thee, while in the meantime everyone applauded me with Well done, well done! But the love of this

4. See Leupin, 83ff.

world is fornication against God. . . . But I bemoaned not all this; but dead Dido I bewailed. . . . (1.13, p. 39)

He is driven by a passion for truth. He wants to make sure that people understand that he is not making things up, that he is telling the truth. He worries about the effect of his confession on his readers. Will they, "a curious people to pry into another man's life, but slothful enough to amend their own" (10.3, p. 77), believe him? They will believe him if they join him in the spirit of charity, because then they will be hearing not so much what he has to say, but the voice of Truth itself in their inner spirit:

And how do they know when they hear myself confessing of myself, whether I say true or no; seeing none knows what is in man, but the spirit of man which is in himself? But if they hear from thee anything concerning themselves, they cannot say, The Lord lieth. For what else is it from thee to hear of themselves, but to know themselves? And who is he that knowing himself, can say, It is false, unless himself lies? But because charity believeth all things. . . . I therefore, O Lord, do also confess unto thee, as that men may hear: to whom though I am not able to prove that what I confess is true; yet those believe me whose ears have been opened by charity. (10.3, p. 77)

Everything rests on the fact that in order for people to profit from what he is telling them, they must believe him, they must know that he is not making it up, that he is telling the truth. They must know that God is his witness, or rather, that he is confessing before God. But nobody can be sure of that unless they listen in the spirit of charity, in other words, unless they also hear in themselves the voice that cannot lie, the voice of Truth. "Because that charity, by which they are made good, tells them, that I would never belie myself in my Confessions."

His whole autobiographical exploration is driven, therefore, by a passionate desire to find out and confess the Truth, first about himself and then about everything else, the entire universe, because—he argues—everything that is, insofar as it really is, is in God. In other words, the Truth is the Truth, there are not different kinds of truth. The Truth, wherever it is, is always identical to itself. And something else is also of crucial importance when we compare Saint Augustine's and Guzmán's autobiographies: the subject of the saint's book is not what he was or had been before he saw the light, but what he is *now at the moment of his confession*, including what he still is of what he had been, because it is not he who judges himself:

> This is the fruit of my Confessions, not of what I have been, but of what I am: namely, to confess this not before thee only, in a secret rejoicing mixed with trembling . . . but in the ears also of the believing sons of men, sharers of my joy. . . . To such therefore, will I discover myself, whom thou commandest me to serve: not discovering what I have been, but what I now am, and what I still am [*non quis fuerim, sed quis iam sim et quis adhuc sim*]. But I do not judge myself. (10.4, p. 83)

Whereas, if we follow the logic of Alemán's fiction, what Guzmán decided to do after his conversion was to give us a detailed account of everything he was and did *before* his conversion, to lay out for our entertainment and moral profit his picaresque life, profusely interspersed with moralizing commentaries about himself and almost everything else around him. The protagonist of those events who appears before our eyes is not the converted Guzmán but the old picaro. The picaro, not the *converted* picaro, is definitely the main literary attraction. Nothing could be more contrary to the Christian spirit of Saint Augustine's autobiography than Guzmán's picaresque adventures.

Alemán wanted to make the figure of Christ the victim, the persecuted, the abandoned one, the guarantor of the seriousness of his novel. But there is enmity between literary fiction qua fiction and the sacrifice of Christ, whereas there is no enmity whatsoever between literary fiction and the exposure, the sacrificial treatment, of any other victim, be it tragic or antiheroic. Or, in a more general sense, while literary fiction has always thrived and prospered on the sufferings of its characters, it has never been able to properly digest, as it were, the sufferings of Christ, a literary difficulty that became particularly aggravated at the dawn of the modern era, a profoundly Christological period.

Aristotle found it perfectly natural that we delight in unpleasant things when we see them imitated: "For we look with delight on pictures that accurately represent things that in themselves are painful for us to behold, such as forms of the most unpleasing animals and dead bodies. The cause of this is that to learn is very pleasant [man first learns by means of imitation] not only to philosophers but also . . . to men generally, even though they partake of this pleasure but to a slight extent" (*Poetics* 1448b4). Curiously, however, philosophers, those lovers of learning, have not, by and large, been great admirers of poetic imitation, beginning with Plato; this fact suggests that perhaps Aristotle was not telling us everything about poetic imitation. If our poetic delight is rooted in our thirst for learning, what exactly do we learn when we delight in the imitated sufferings of heroes, and if we delight in them, why do we cry and weep with "pity and fear"? Plato did not think that such "pity and fear" were justified at all. In fact, he called them blasphemous (*Laws* 7.800b–801c).[5] Why should we cry and be fearful, he said, when we see parricides and murderers receiving the punishment they so justly deserve? Plato strongly disagreed with his best-known disciple on the value of poetic imitation not because he considered the imitated suffering illegitimate or because he wanted to stop it. Quite the contrary, what he did not like was the devious way the poets did it. They inflicted the punishment, but at the same time they apologized for it. They did it and also tried to hide it, claiming innocence, washing their hands of what they were doing, weeping and crying the whole while. Poetic imitation, in Plato's penetrating eyes, was the ideal vehicle for a despicable and blasphemous attitude, the attitude that says "This that I am doing I am not really doing." He abhorred such poetic ambiguity, as he repeated in a hundred different ways that poets are not to be trusted because they do not know how to clearly differentiate between good and evil.

Saint Augustine also meditated on this strange delight that we feel in our own pain as we imitate within ourselves the fictitious pain of the poetic character, but his motivation and his conclusion were exactly the opposite of Plato's:

> Stage plays also at that time drew me away; sights full of images of my own miseries, and the fuel to my own fire. What is the reason now that a spectator desires to be made sad when he beholds doleful and tragic passages, which he himself could not endure to suffer? Yet for all that he desires to feel pain [*dolor*], and his pain becomes his pleasure too. What is all this but a miserable madness? . . . So when one suffers those pains in his own person it is usually called misery, when one has a sympathetic feeling of another's pain it is called compassion. But what compassion can there be in things feigned and scenic? *For the auditors here are not provoked to help the sufferer, but invited only to be sorry for him.* (3.2, p. 101; my emphasis)

The Victimizing Character of Aristotelian or Poetic Catharsis

Fiction-motivated compassion is certainly not a Christian kind of compassion. When there is true compassion, says Augustine, "grief does not give delight. For though he that condoles with the miserable by reason of

5. See *The Sacred Game*, 50ff.

charity deserves approbation, yet he is most brotherly compassionate who would prefer there were no occasion for him to condole" (3.2, p. 105). Thus, while Plato condemns the poets for introducing dangerous ambiguity in the punishment or expulsion of their victims, Saint Augustine accuses them of not doing anything to save those victims, of developing a spurious, fictitious kind of condolence, which instead of saving the victim becomes an accomplice in the process of victimization and uses it for its own selfish gratification. It would be difficult indeed to find a clearer indictment of the devious and shifty character of the famous Aristotelian catharsis.

There is no catharsis whatsoever in the passion and death of Christ. "Do not weep for me, weep for yourselves and your children," says Christ to the women of Jerusalem. This is an extraordinary thing to say, a thing that forever sets the Christian victim apart from the literary victim par excellence, the tragic hero, as Reinhold Niebuhr saw: "[The tragic hero] is always crying 'weep for me.' . . . What would the hero of tragedy do without these weeping, appreciating and revering spectators?" (164–65). Christ rejects any sort of Aristotelian "pity and fear." "Do not pity me, pity and fear yourselves," he seems to be saying. The salvation Christ offers is definitely not of the literary variety. "Where in the Gospel," asked Reinhold Schneider, "in the whole of Sacred Sripture, is there one, single, even roughly adequate sentence that would provide a basis for art?" (quoted in Balthasar, 12).

But if the suffering and victimization of Christ, or the spirit of the text in which it is narrated, resists poetic fictionalization, it is not because Christ is a special kind of human being or that his suffering is somehow different from human suffering. He is simply the witness to a new kind of revelation that says that make-believe human suffering, manipulated suffering for collective purposes, whether or not such purposes may in themselves be laudable, or for entertainment, is not only an affront to real human suffering, but much worse, an act of complicity, a coverup of the real thing. Even in a society like ours, so thoroughly driven by an appetite for everything that the "unreality industry" turns out, there are little gestures that acknowledge the new revelation, as when a grieving person is shielded from the public eye of the camera "out of respect" for his or her suffering. This respect, this recognition of a fundamental dignity at the core of human suffering, which would be sullied or distorted if it were turned into a mimetic representation for public consumption, is unprecedented. There is nothing "natural" about it.

The "natural" thing (in the sense of something universally widespread) has always gone in the opposite direction, in the direction of the public ritual or the public expression of human suffering, in the direction of turning it into a public affair to be handled carefully through proper conventional channels. What today may be viewed as the dignified object of our respect had traditionally been regarded with apprehension and fear, as something dangerous requiring inmmediate public attention. As we go back in time, the difference between mimetically, "cathartically" induced grief and the real thing tends to disappear. But that difference is crucial for the spirit of the Christian word.

Like the Greek chorus, who laments the impending doom of the heroic victim, thus echoing the ritual laments of the sacrificers as they prepare to kill the victim, we too, readers of literary fiction, while we are absorbed by narrated sufferings, feed on those sufferings and become sacrificing accomplices. Something along these lines is clearly implied in Saint Augustine's words at the end of his recollection of how successful he was as a youth in declaiming "upon the words of Juno, expressing her anger and sorrow . . . words I had never heard Juno had uttered; yet were we enforced to imitate the passsages of these poetical fictions," when he wrote "by more ways than one is there sacrifice offered to the transgressing angels" (1.17, p. 53), that is to say, to the devil. Because we know what the ultimate, the paradigmatic, sacrifice to the devil was, the sacrifice of the human victim, since that is precisely the sacrifice to which Christ submits in order to free humans from it. To suggest that being mentally and emotionally seduced by literary fiction is to participate in the sacrifice demanded by Satan is to suggest that literary fiction itself is a form of complicity with such a satanic sacrifice.

CHAPTER III

The Picaresque Point of Reference 2

The Buscón

Aesthetic Detachment or Cruelty?

Opinions about Quevedo's *Buscon* tend to be extreme.[1] Michael Holquist, editor of Bakhtin's *The Dialogic Imagination*, calls it "one of the most heartlessly cruel books ever written" (Bakhtin, 163, note). On the other hand, Fernando Lázaro Carreter, a leading Quevedo scholar, speaks of Quevedo's artistic intention as one of sheer linguistic virtuosity and ingenious, clever manipulation of literary language for its own sake. His emotion is purely aesthetic:

Quevedo experimenta un sentimiento puro de creador; digámoslo sin rodeos: un sentimiento estético. El *Buscón* es una novela estetizante. Un ajusticiamiento, una profanación, un adulterio, son hechos que nos conmueven si nuestro corazón se va tras la mirada. Pero si podemos refrenarlo, si acertamos a mirar aquello como un acontec-

1. This chapter is a revised and updated version of "Satan Expelling Satan: Reflections on Quevado's Buscón," which appeared in *Homenajes* 19, in honor of Peter N. Dunn (Newark, Del.: Juan de la Cuesta Hispanic Monographs, 2002).

> imiento de otro planeta, nuestra versión de los hechos será sólo material virgen para el intelecto. En este punto lo recoge Quevedo, aquí comienza su portentosa elaboración artística. (1974, 97)
>
> (Quevedo's feeling is strictly creative. Let's put it plainly: it is an aesthetic feeling. The *Buscón* is an aesthete's novel. An execution, a profanation, an adultery are things that move us if we put our heart in what we see. But if we hold it back, if we manage to look at such things as an event on a different planet, our version of those events will only be subject matter for our intellect. This is the point at which Quevedo picks it up, it is here that his prodigious artistic elaboration begins.)

Of course, these two opinions do not necessarily contradict each other. To view such things as an "execution" or a "profanation" as purely aesthetic objects, an occasion for the aesthetic display of ingenious word games, can in itself be something "heartlessly cruel." In fact, I think that both critics are right. One of the reasons why Quevedo's treatment of his picaro protagonist appears to be so much more cruel than is the case with other picaresque novels is precisely his "aesthetic detachment" from, or "aesthetic insensitivity" to, the picaro's misfortunes. Not only is his heart not "moved" at all by such misfortunes, he actually makes their description an occasion for the literary display of brilliant jocular virtuosity. Everything is a joke. We are supposed to roll with laughter as we see the miserable creature being pushed around, pelted with garbage, spat upon, smeared with human excrement, exposed to public shame, and beaten up. While Guzmán de Alfarache advised his readers—if they wanted some moral profit—not to look at the story of his life in the way cheering and exhilarated spectators look at the bull in the ring being lanced, wounded, and beaten, there is no such advice in Quevedo's novel. On the contrary, through its brilliant artistry we are constantly invited to go in the opposite direction. If mediocre Avellaneda could not hide his qualms about exposing his lunatic Don Quixote to public ridicule, there are no such qualms in the *Buscón*.

The tendency of those critics who, in the manner of Fernando Lázaro Carreter, concentrate on the stylistic virtuosity of the work is to deny that there is any serious intention underlying the virtuosity. They see Quevedo as only interested in displaying his *ingenio*, his linguistically acrobatic ingeniousness (a quality of his novel that is practically impossible to retain in translation). I suspect most readers would find this critical attitude more convincing if the occasion for such ingeniousness were not so dehumanizing, frequently gruesome, or downright disgusting.[2]

Whatever Quevedo's intention may be, it can be safely stated that no

2. Here is a telling example. The following is part of the letter that Pablos's uncle, the official executioner in the city of Segovia, sent him with the news of the execution of Pablos's father, a convicted thief, and of the imprisonment of his mother, who is scheduled to be burnt at the stake for sorcery:

> My dear Son Pablos—he loved me so much, you see, that he always addressed me as "son":
>
> . . . I am deeply grieved to have to inform you of something you will not be pleased to hear. Your father died a week ago—and with the greatest courage ever shown by any man in all this world. I tell you this because I am the one who hanged him. . . . [With] the crosses before him, he bore himself with such dignity that no one could doubt he was a man about to be hanged. He rode along completely at ease, looking up at the windows, and bowing to those who had left their work to watch him. He even twirled his mustachios a couple of times. He would ask his confessors to take a break once in a while, and applauded when they said something good. When he came to the gallows, he did not crawl up on all fours or did it slowly either, but went right up the steps. When he saw that one board was cracked, he asked the official in charge to have it repaired before the next victim came along, for not all had his guts. I cannot possibly stress sufficiently how well your father looked to everyone there. When he reached the top, he sat down and pulled the wrinkles on his frock back. He himself placed the rope around his neck . . . He asked me to move his pointed hood a little to one side, and freshen up his beard and put it in order. This I gladly did, and then down he dropped—without bending his legs or performing any of those usual ugly actions people engage in at such times. He maintained such a grave composure that no one could have asked for a better performance. I afterward cut him up and scattered his pieces along the highway. God knows how sad I feel to see them being served for free at vultures' tables. But pastry makers will console us by putting him in their pies.
>
> About your mother, although she is still alive, I can almost tell you a similar story. She is a prisoner of the Inquisition in Toledo, for, whereas scandalmongers cause the dead to turn over in their graves, your mother, who never had a mean tongue, preferred to dig them up in person. It is further said that she had cultivated a habit of kissing the old he-goat of a devil every night—on the eye that has no pupil. At her house they found more legs, arms, and hands than in a chapel commemorating miracles. And besides, she was always producing counterfeit maidens and renovated virgins. They tell me she is to appear in an auto-da-fe on Trinity Sunday. I am deeply affected by the dishonor she has brought upon us all—indeed, I have more of a right to feel that way than any of you, for, after all, am I not the King's good servant? Relatives like your mother are not the sort of people who lend luster to someone who has such a position as mine. ("The Life and Adventures of Don Pablos the Sharper," in *Masterpieces of the Spanish Golden Age*, 85–233; quoted passage from 127–29).

It should also be noted at this point that when Pablos goes to Segovia to collect his inheritance and has dinner at his uncle's house, the gruesome notion of the human flesh of executed criminals being baked into meat pies comes up again:

> Five meat pies appeared on the table of the four-real variety. They removed the crust, and taking up an aspergillum they said a prayer for the dead, with a *requiem aeternam* for the victim who had furnished the meat for the pie. My uncle said:
>
> "You no doubt recall, Nephew, what I wrote you about your father."
>
> I no doubt did.

amount of stylistic wordplay can ultimately hide the tremendous violence that permeates his novel. Peter Dunn has probably said it best:

> *El buscón* has a plot that is minimally sufficient: Pablos tries to rise socially and efface his family origin, and is defeated by his own self-destructive strategies and by the defensive violence of the society. What strikes the reader most forcibly and immediately, however, is the surface; it is from the very first a display of parodic virtuosity, a violent joke that seems designed to absorb and dissipate the political and social violence of the story by dissolving it in "mere" words. This feint on Quevedo's part to mask the . . . violence, either by displacing [it] from the center of the narrative or by dissolving [it] in the aggressively facetious discourse, demystifies itself, however. The lexical and rhetorical violence with which Quevedo constitutes his fictive world does not succeed in displacing the political and social violence of the story; it confronts [it], but yields under [its] pressure and turns against itself to become, in the discourse of the narrator, a linguistic self-laceration (to be read as comedy), and on the authorial plane a vindication of the action (to be read as poetic justice). (77)

I am not even sure that Quevedo is the least bit worried by questions of poetic justice, to which he only pays a very tepid lip service in the final words of the novel, when Pablos, fleeing from justice, decides to move to the Indies "to see whether I might, by changing worlds and countries, perhaps better my plight. But it turned out worse than ever for me. . . . For a man may change his lifelong habitat, but it will do him no earthly good unless he likewise changes his lifelong habits" (233). This is the only moralizing comment in the entire novel, and it comes at the very end. One cannot help but think that such a comment is just pro forma. At any rate, it does not change anything, least of all the moral fiber of the protagonist, who, for all practical purposes, has been shown consistently to have none. So much so, indeed, that Dunn feels justified in stating that Pablos is "far from being an autonomous character with a soul to be saved" (81), that he is more like "a trajectory . . . a Proppian function" (85). Or, in the words of Edmond Cros, "Par rapport à ces deux antécédents [*Lazarillo*, *Guzmán*], l'indigence [de vie intérieure] du *Buscón* est d'une evidence incontestable . . . on constate que sa vie intérieure est nulle, sa vie imaginative réduite au minimum, sa vie spirituelle très superficielle, pratiquement inexistente" (*L'aristocrate*, 97; Compared with

---

> Well, they all ate, but I contented myself with the crust. I have since then always maintained that custom, and whenever I have meat pie I always say an Ave Maria for the soul of the departed. (157–58)

its two predecessors, the lack [of an inner life] in the *Buscón* is strikingly obvious . . . , his inner life is nil, his imaginative life is reduced to a minimum, his spiritual life very superficial, practically nonexistent).

Pablos is something like a living human void moving along a perfectly predictable trajectory—a terribly violent trajectory, that is to say, driven by a clearly victimizing intention. And it is important to point out that there is an intimate connection between such a human void and the violent predictability of the trajectory. In other words, the absence of inner freedom and the external violence mirror each other. Pablos has no personality other than that granted to him by the violence that expels him. The novel defines Pablos simply as the one to be expelled, the victim in the old sense of the word, the one whom everybody without exception *ought to* expel, the object of a public violence in which everybody is urged to participate. No wonder that Cros has seen a basic similarity between the structure of the *Buscón*, which he defines as "a fiction centered around a festive calendar" (*Historia*, 11), and the structure of a public execution.[3] Furthermore, it is the victim himself who lends his voice to the expelling violence.

Dehumanizing and the Spirit of Carnival

It is somewhat shocking to see such a character in what is formally a novel, a book that devotes a lot of attention to him, that is supposed to be his autobiography. But it was not Quevedo who invented such a living human void. He picks it up from an immemorial tradition. What we see in Pablos is the old folkloric puppet, which we mentioned at the beginning of the last chapter. While it is generally admitted today that the picaresque novel as a whole is rooted historically in the folkloric past, particularly that of a carnavalesque type, of none can this be said more accurately than of Quevedo's *Buscón*. Quevedo simply exploited or carried to its logical consequences the inherently dehumanizing public view of the old laughingstock, the antiheroic puppet.

But if our theory is correct, if the old antihero has no more of a future in the modern era than the old hero, then Quevedo's narrative feat is certainly not an encouraging sign for the future development of the modern novel. If

3. "Nous voudrions insister sur l'homologie structurale . . . entre la description d'une fête carnavalesque (la fiesta del rey de gallos) et celle de l'exécution d'un jugement de justice" (*L'aristocrate*, 43).

we are correct, Quevedo's novel should rather be called something like an antinovel, a deliberate denial of the possibility of transforming the old folkloric puppet into a modern novelistic character, which is what Mateo Alemán had intended to do. And, indeed, some critics have already noticed something peculiar about Quevedo's picaresque novel. They notice that the violence, whose object is, of course, the picaro, seems to spread to the narrative medium itself. "Il s'agit d'un véritable déni d'autorité et de dignité qui atteint, á travers le personnage de Pablos, la fiction picaresque elle-même," says Cavillac (122; It is truly a denial of authority and dignity, which, through the character Pablos, extends to the picaresque fiction itself). Or, in the words of B. W. Ife, "Quevedo made use of the picaresque in a way which suggests that . . . he intended to destroy the genre along with the society it depicts" (150); "It is as if the moral and social misrule that the book documents has spread to the medium itself" (148).

This is what I think we should understand. Quevedo's "rejuvenation" of the carnival forms (the word has been applied to his farcical interludes [*entremeses*] by E. Asensio [228]), on the one hand, and his contemptuous disrespect for the novelistic form of the picaresque, on the other, are the two sides of the same phenomenon. The victimizing violence that openly structures his novel, depriving it of a future, is the same violence that links it to the festive folkloric past, to that collective effervescence (Carnival, Feast of Fools, *Festum asinorum*, etc.) that usually structures itself around a victim, whether individual or collective, such as certain ethnic or religious groups. But this will be difficult to understand as long as we maintain the prevailing glamorized view of the carnival as a carefree, joyful letting go of normal inhibitions, or even as a psychologically useful outlet for pent-up frustrations and aggressive tendencies.

I have no interest in denying that such psychological effects may in fact occur, although things in this regard are far less simplistic than it is generally believed.[4] Nevertheless, the historical and social significance of the

4. Cf. Ernst Kris: "The progress of psychoanalytic knowledge has opened the way for a better understanding of the cathartic effect; we are no longer satisfied with the notion that repressed emotions lose their hold on our mental life when an outlet for them has been found. We believe rather that what Aristotle describes as the purging enables the ego to reestablish the control which is threatened by dammed-up instinctual demands. The search for outlets acts as an aid to assuring or reestablishing this control, and the pleasure is a double one, in both discharge and control" (45).

carnival is not primarily psychological. I would like to repeat here E. Cros's accurate observation regarding "l'homologie structurale qu'il est . . . possible d'établir entre la description d'une fête carnavalesque . . . et celle de l'exécution d'un jugement de justice" (43), and the fact that in the *Buscón* "la promenade des 'criminels' dans les rues des villes se présente avec toutes les caractéristiques d'un défilé de fête populaire dont les héros seraient déguisés" (44; The walking of criminals on the streets of cities has all the characteristic features of a parade during a popular festivity, in which the heroes would be disguised).

This structural similarity between public feast and public execution is by no means accidental. The carnival or carnival-like feast is commonly structured around a victim, be it an animal (cock, goat, bull, etc.); a person in effigy, like Guy Fawkes in Great Britain or the Judases so popular in many towns throughout the Spanish-speaking world; or real people disguised in various ways, who are paraded through town and pelted with eggs and vegetables, in a scene clearly reminiscent of the old ritual of the Athenian *pharmakos*, who, chosen from the lowest strata of society and kept at the city's expense for the occasion, was paraded and then expelled or even killed as a ritual way of purifying the city.[5] "En última instancia," says Caro Baroja, "el Carnaval parece una reelaboración de viejos rituales que tienen un carácter sistemático y que sobrepasa en significado a lo que se llamaban 'ritos de fertilidad'" (146; "Ultimately," says Caro Baroja, "the Carnival appears to be a reelaboration of old rituals that have a systematic character, and whose meaning goes beyond what were known as 'fertility rites'").

It is also important to notice that, in case after case, it becomes clear that

5. Here are a few examples found in the classic study of the carnival by Julio Caro Baroja: "Hasta la primera mitad del siglo XIX existió en Reus la bárbara costumbre de que el Domingo de Carnaval por la tarde salieran unos hombres cubiertos a la plaza [los 'geps' o jorobados], a los que los chicos podían echar tronchos y nabos recogidos antes, constituyéndose una verdadera batalla" (87); "En Oviedo . . . un pobre hombre era paseado por las calles . . . la cara pintarrajeada y enorme sombrero, sobre unas angarillas, y la canalla le arrojaba huevos, tronchos de verdura, etc., y cuando estaba hecho una especie de tortilla lo precipitaban en una alberca de la plaza" (87); "En la provincia de Burgos, el juicio y muerte de Judas constituyen una verdadera representación teatral. A veces, la representación se ha hecho tan a lo vivo que ha resultado trágica y se ha suprimido. En 1944 decía don José de la Fuente, refiriéndose a Guadilla de Villamar: 'También había antes la costumbre de disfrazarse un mozo de Judas y perseguirle todos los demás, habiendo llegado la farsa en el vecino pueblo de Villanueva de Odra, no hace muchos años, a costarle la vida al mozo que hacía de Judas, a quien soltaron una perdigonada'" (132).

the violence of the crowd almost instinctively gravitates toward the poor, the weak, the physically handicapped, or the stranger—in other words, toward the traditional victims of low-comedy scapegoating. According to Caro Baroja, "Las bromas, los agravios con frecuencia se dirigían a personas determinadas, desvalidas. Un costumbrista del siglo XVII, Francisco Santos, describe una broma terrible de Carnaval, y comienza así su descripción: 'Aquí conocí que era fiesta de Carnestolendas porque luego vimos mojigangas y soldadescas, notando algunas burlas harto pesadas, hechas de ordinario con gente pobre y desvalida'" (87; The tricks, the insults, were frequently directed specifically toward helpless persons. A seventeenth-century writer about local customs, Francisco Santos, describes a terrible trick of Carnaval, and he begins his description as follows: "Here I realized it was a Carnaval feast because we then saw mummers and unruly soldiers playing cruel tricks on poor and helpless people."). This next comment comes from an eyewitness to the carnival in Madrid in the seventeenth century: "Pasaba un pobre hombre por la calle y desde alguna casa le insultaban o le echaban en cara su flaca condición, guardando, en cambio, respeto a los que parecían mejor situados en la vida" (83; A poor man would pass by the street, and from some houses people would hurl insults at him and blame him for his infirmity, while, on the other hand, they showed respect to those who appeared to be better situated in life). Of course, such things also occurred elsewhere: "Au carnaval de Nuremberg, des fous, les *laüfer*, couraient et dansaient dans la foule autour du cortège du Schembart. Partout, les masques avaient des seringues d'apothicaires et ils projettaient de l'eau bouese à la figure des ceux qui ne se gardaient pas assez vite, les filles et les étrangers étant leur cibles preferés" (Bercé, 33; At the Nuremberg carnival, fools, *laüfers*, would run and dance in the crowd surrounding the pageant of Schembart. Everywhere the maskers carried syringes and squirted dirty water on the faces of those who did not protect themselves enough, young girls and foreigners being their preferred targets).

Amid boisterous laughter there was real violence in those festive crowds: "Con máscara o sin ella, las gentes realizaban una serie de actos violentos y de aire brutal" (Caro Baroja, 83). In his *Letters from Spain*, Blanco White describes the fear and sense of insecurity of the visitor to popular districts in Seville or Madrid during Carnaval time: "El acercarse a un barrio popular durante los tres días clásicos de Carnaval . . . producía una sensación de inseguridad desagradable, pues hombres y mujeres estaban dispuestos, bajo el menor pretexto, a armar broncas e incluso agredir. . . ." (146; Approaching a lower class suburb during the three classical days of carnival . . . produced an unpleasant feeling of insecurity because men and women were prone, on the smallest pretext, to become verbally abusive and even aggressive).

By reference to a public execution, the mock executions, chases, or expulsions of the carnival have all the appearance of a popular lynching at the hands of an overexcited crowd. Apart from its make-believe character, one could say that the only difference between those carnival executions and a real one is the presence or absence of a constituted legal authority in charge of the execution. In the real one, it is the legal authority who executes; in the carnival, it is the crowd itself—the lynch mob, we would call it today. But the fact is that such a lynch mob represents a much older and primitive version of the administration of "justice" in human society, at a time when the only important or even conceivable form of "justice" was to maintain or regain the internal cohesion of the group, to expel violence and dissension from within, to purge or purify the city, the group, as the old Athenians might say. Prior to all forms of differentiated legal authority, and perhaps as their ultimate anthropological foundation, lies the power of the crowd. For even in the absence of such legal authority, the crowd still has its own violent way of achieving cohesion, of constituting itself as a group. All it needs is a victim.[6]

The prevailing uncritical view of the carnival focuses its attention on the traditional breakdown of social conventions ("traditional" means that even the breakdown itself is subject to rules; in England, for example, there was a Lord of Misrule), the upturning of hierarchies, the pauper turned king for a day, and so forth. It does not see that this breakdown is only a first step, the step that turns the structured social group into a crowd, an effervescent, excited crowd, which sets itself the immediate goal of finding an outlet for its own violent excitement, and finds it by victimizing, for example, the pauper it has just dressed as a king, who will be paid mock homage, and will be ridiculed and abused for "pretending" to be a king (just as the Roman soldiers paid homage to and ridiculed Christ, "King of the Jews"); but it could be any

6. Cf. E. Adamson Hoebel: "Lynch law among primitives . . . is not a backsliding from, or detouring around, established formal law as it is with us. It is a first fitful step towards the emergence of criminal law in a situation in which the exercise of legal power has not yet been refined and allocated to specific persons" (277).

other person the crowd happens to meet on its way, a cripple, for example, or a hunchback, or a foreigner, or a bashful young girl, in sum, any easy, low-risk target who looks different enough from the crowd itself to attract its attention.

Mesmerized by the breakdown of conventional social differences and barriers, and blind to everything else, the prevailing view interprets the breakdown as a movement toward greater freedom and inclusiveness, a rejection of social exclusions, a rebellion of the masses against oppressive power. But this is, at best, a Marxist fairy tale. Because all that the breakdown does, as we have just said, is to turn the social group into an agitated crowd, a lynch mob in germ, and the behavior of the group-turned-crowd is anything but "inclusive." The irresistible, the overriding, animal-like movement of the violent crowd is directed toward its own self-preservation as a crowd, and that means inevitably diverting its own violence from itself by channeling it toward the outside, toward that which is perceived as different.[7] The "liberation" offered by the violent crowd requires the worst kind of servitude, the undeviating submission of the will to the human other, whether it be a faceless crowd or a divinized leader, a false god. Pablos of Segovia fits perfectly within such a crowd. No wonder some readers have found him to be "remarkably gregarious."[8]

Turning the crowd, or the spirit of the crowd, against him, which is what

7. The intolerance of the carnival crowd vis-à-vis any kind of deviant behavior has, on occasion, been greatly appreciated by official defenders of public morality. Here is a case involving the famous "charivaris" (the equivalent of the Spanish "cencerrada," still practiced today in rural Spain): "Sous la Restauration, un sous-préfet de Marmande n'hésitait pas à écrire au ministre de l'Intérieur que, 'au fond de ces justices populaires, on rencontre peut-être une certaine moralité. Les jeunes gens de la ville . . . se réunissent chaque soir, rendent témoignage de la censure publique et accomplissent l'usage invariablement établi.' Le romancier nivernais Claude Tillier . . . abondait dans le même sens. 'C'est une des grandes joies du Carnaval, c'est la comédie du peuple et, tout en le faisant rire, il lui donne des bonnes leçons. C'est d'ailleurs, un moyen de répression très efficace de ces petits scandales que la loi ne peut atteindre et le charivari est un auxiliaire utile, en bien des occasions, du procureur du roi'" (Bercé, 43; During the Restoration a deputy commissioner in Marmande did not hesitate to write to the minister of the interior that "at the bottom of these popular forms of justice one finds a certain kind of morality. The young people in town gather each evening, give expression to public censure, and carry out established customs without deviation." Claude Tillier, the novelist from Nevers, was even more explicit. "[The *charivari*] is one of the great pleasures of the carnival, it is the people's comedy, which, while making them laugh, gives them good lessons. Furthermore, it is a very effective means of repression of those little scandals that the law cannot reach. On many occasions the *charivari* are a useful auxiliary to the royal prosecutor").

8. "[Pablos] revela un gregarismo notable" (Vaíllo, 264).

Quevedo does with his hopeless protagonist, does not truly change anything from the old attitude. It amounts to turning the spirit of the crowd against itself. And that was a historical dead end. Nothing truly new could be created out of that. But we must make absolutely clear that Quevedo reached such an intentional novelistic dead end not by "perverting" the spirit of the carnival, but, quite the contrary, by wholeheartedly joining the ancient festive crowd. So his critics are right when they call him conservative. But in regard to his antinovelistic stance, his conservatism was not particularly "aristocratic" in spirit. It was never the aristocracy who chased poor devils or criminals down the streets of the city: that was always the enthusiastic work of a carnival-like crowd—although we can be sure that the "people of quality" were also looking on complacently. Quevedo is a clear historical witness to the fact that the modern novel did not flow naturally, without insurmountable internal contradictions, from the old folkloric, Saturnalian forms, as Mikhail Bakhtin believed.

A Critique of Bakhtin's Theory

Bakhtin knew, of course, the significant formal differences between the modern novel and the old folkloric forms. Such formal differences were important to him because they were expressions of radically different socioeconomic conditions. Nevertheless, in his view, the primitive intentions and ultimate social purposes that animated the old forms continued to be valid with the new forms of the novel. There is no fundamental incompatibility between the old and the new. There is, indeed, something of a suprahistorical affinity between the modern novelist and the old folkloric characters, "the rogue, the clown, and the fool," typically victimized, marginalized characters, precisely because the modern novelist also places himself or herself outside the epic discourse, the discourse or "monoglossia" of the dominant power:

> The novelist stands in need of some essential formal and generic mask that could serve to define the position from which he views life, as well as the position from which he makes that life public.
>
> And it is precisely here, of course, that the masks of the clown and fool (transformed in various ways) come to the aid of the novelist. These masks are not invented: they are rooted deep in the folk. . . . All of this is of the highest importance to the novel. At last a form was found to portray the mode of existence of a man who is in life, but not of it, life's perpetual spy and reflector. (161)

"A man who is in life, but not of it." That could easily be construed as a definition of the sacrificial victim. And I have indeed no objection to placing the modern novelist on the side of the victim, on the side of "the rogue, the clown, and the fool." But I think Bakhtin has interpreted this situation in reverse. It is not the modern novelist who is in need of the old folkloric masks to find his voice. If anything, it is the other way around: it is the modern novelist who must come to the aid of the old folkloric characters, masks, puppets, in order to give them a voice, which of course they never had, because if they did have a voice they would not have been the masks, the puppets, that they actually were in the eyes of the folk. The modern novelist is indeed very much in need of giving those puppets an individualized voice, for, without it, they could not become modern characters, and the modern novel could not have happened; but giving them such a voice and rescuing them from the folk is one and the same thing. The modern novelist cannot be on the side of the "rogue, the clown, and the fool" and also be on the side of the folk who collectively created those characters.

Let us apply this to the case of Quevedo. Bakhtin could point to the *Buscón* as a clear example of what he is saying: the rogue, embodied in Pablos of Segovia, came to the aid of Quevedo. That is to say, Quevedo found his novelistic voice when he encountered the old folkloric character, which is, of course, formally correct. Without such a ready-made character, without this mask, Quevedo could not have written the novel that he wrote. But does that mean that the *Buscón* is a modern novel in the same sense that the *Quixote* is one? Is there no difference between the modernity of the one and of the other? I do not think that Bakhtin's theory can account for such a difference. But that is a fundamental difference in the theory we are developing here. In my view, to ignore such a difference is to ignore something crucial about the historical genesis of the modern novel. The modern novel was not born automatically, as part of the superstructure that emerged out of the new modes of material production. It required the will and the capacity of individual novelists to rescue the old antihero from his traditional fate, to answer the call of the desacralizing logos. Cervantes had both the capacity and the will to do it; Quevedo may have had the capacity—we will never know—but he certainly did not have the will.

In Bakhtin's theory the individual intention of the novelist is irrelevant. Alemán, Cervantes, and Quevedo equally confirm his theory about the debt of the modern novel to the oldest forms created by processes of social marginalization. In fact, for Bakhtin, the historical announcement of the modern novel is there practically from the beginning of human society, or, to be more precise, from the very moment when a human voice was heard that was not part of the dominant discourse, the discourse—we are told—of heroic myth and epic; a human voice that spoke from the outside, that, by its very existence, questioned the pretension of the dominant discourse to speak for the totality of the real; a human voice, therefore, that exposed the hidden side, the seamy side, of the dominant discourse, revealing its weakness, its incompleteness, and which made possible poliglossia, the coexistence of more than one language, which would become the fundamental characteristic of the modern novel.[9]

From the beginning, therefore, it was announced that the development of the novel would eventually mean the end of the epic. In this sense, the *Quixote* was announced from the beginning. But, while I fully agree with Bakhtin's view that the beginning of the modern novel is intimately tied to the historical disintegration of the epic, there are problems with situating the sociohistorical mechanism that would eventually produce the modern novel right at the beginning—indeed, even in the prehistory—of human society.

As Bakhtin goes back in time he reaches the earliest known forms of parody or clowning, in other words, the earliest voices to be heard outside the mythical sacred forms of the dominant discourse. But these earliest voices of resistance or rebellion—he realizes—are themselves sacred. They are "such phenomena as *ritualistic violations* . . . and, later, *ritualistic laughter, ritualistic parody* and *clownishness*" (212; emphasis in original). In fact the two forms of discourse, dominant and otherwise, are strictly contemporaneous and are, by no means, felt to exclude each other:

It is our conviction that there never was a single strictly straightfoward genre . . . that did not have its own parodying and travestying double, its own comic-ironic

9. "Thus we see that alongside the great and significant models of straightforward genres and direct discourses . . . there was created in ancient times a rich world of the most varied forms and variations of parodic-travestying, indirect, conditional discourse. . . . I imagine this whole [world] to be something like an immense novel, multi-generic, multi-styled, mercilessly critical . . . reflecting in all its fullness the heteroglossia and multiple voices of a given culture, people and epoch. . . . These parodic-travestying forms prepared the ground for the novel in one very important, in fact decisive, respect. They liberated the object from the power of language in

contre-partie. What is more, these parodic doubles and laughing reflections of the direct word were, in some cases, just as sanctioned by tradition and just as canonized as their elevated models. (53)

This is why, for example, "the literary consciousness of the Greeks did not view the parodic-travestying reworkings of national myth as any particular profanation or blasphemy" (55). However, if these two languages are strictly contemporaneous, equally "original," and both are sacred, where do we get the idea that one of them is some sort of an impious rebellion against the other, a liberation from the confinement of the other? How do we privilege one as closer to reality, more "authentic," than the other? When and how did this usurpation of power by the dominant discourse take place? How did the usurper plot against reality and authenticity? For beyond the originally sacred character of language itself, we know absolutely nothing about anything we could call human with any degree of confidence. The original "matrix" of which Bakhtin speaks seems to be prior to human self-consciousness, something similar to what Marx called "herd consciousness":

We stress again: the matrix under discussion was experienced by primitive man not as a function of his abstract thought-processes or consciousness, but as an aspect of life itself—in a *collective laboring* with nature, in the *collective consuming* of the fruits of his labor and in the *collective task of fostering the growth and renewal of the social whole*. (211; my emphasis)

Within this matrix, "the life of nature and the life of man are fused together . . . : the sun is part of the earth, as a kind of consumer good, it is eaten and drunk. The events of human life are just as grand as the events of nature's life (the same words, the same tones are used for both, and in no sense metaphorically)" (211).

But then something arbitrary, something unpredictable, must have happened, something that deviated from the perfect communion of the human herd with nature: "the first ideologues, priests," in Marx's own words, come upon the scene. Or in Bakhtin's words, "cultic activity separates itself from undifferentiated production" (211). In other words, for the first time we can

which it had become entangled as if in a net; they destroyed the homogenizing power of myth over language . . . destroyed the thick walls that had imprisoned consciousness within its own discourse, within its own language" (Bakhtin, 59–60).

speak with confidence of true human consciousness because now for the first time we can speak of a true division of labor—mental labor as opposed to material labor. Marx—Bakhtin's ideological guide—continues:

> From this moment onwards consciousness can really flatter itself that it is something other than consciousness of existing practice, that it really represents something without representing something real; from now on consciousness is in a position to emancipate itself from the world and to proceed to the formation of "pure" theory, theology, philosophy, ethics, etc. (Marx and Engels, *The German Ideology*, 51–52)

In other words, from the very first moment when the human possibility arises of conceiving or conceptualizing, no matter how crudely, something like an emancipation, a detachment from totality, a liberation from material labor and the consciousness of the herd, from that very moment we also see the sacred at work. And if we are to believe Marx—the ideological foundation of Bakhtin—the sacred is entirely (at least at the beginning) on the side of the liberating movement, because it is there as a witness to the transition from human (or prehuman) herd to human society.

Therefore, if we still insisted in talking about two different kinds of language or discourse from the beginning, the dominant sacred one, stilted, rigid, removed from the solid materiality of everyday life, and the other one, antidominant, authentic, flexible, in touch with reality, and so on, we would have to ground such "authenticity" or "reality," psychologically, in the undifferentiating consciousness of the herd. The "liberation" offered by the second language would in reality be a profound regression toward animality.

But we do not have to. The idea of a human society prior to the sacred, in direct, unmediated contact with nature, exclusively concerned with producing enough to survive, and therefore pristinely clean of any "ideological" contamination, is an untenable Marxist assumption, a mythical construct from which all internal fratricidal violence has been conveniently eliminated, and for which, of course, there is no evidence whatsoever. This means that right from the start what we find is not two different kinds of discourse, one "mythical" and "ideological," and the other transgressive, "realistic," "liberating," and so forth. What we find is the typical, well known by now, irreducible ambivalence of the primitive sacred. What we have is a system of taboos and prohibitions, on the one hand, and ritualized transgressions of those same taboos and prohibitions, on the other hand. What we have is a ritually prescribed sacrificial crisis, a violent crisis of the sacred, and its sacrificial victimizing resolution. What we have is disorder leading to order—not an order based on immutable transcendental principles, but an order generated out of disorder, collective violence collectively evacuated through the unanimous elimination of a victim, on whose head is placed, literally and physically, the violence of all.

Historically speaking, prior to all "ideological" renderings of origins (including the Marxist one), lies the fundamental structure and internal logic of the sacred itself. And this structure, the sacrificial (sacred-making) structure, as we have stated elsewhere, "has remained basically unchanged since time immemorial across all kinds of forms of 'material production and material intercourse.' . . . [It] has operated at all levels of hunting, nomadic, or agricultural societies; in rural or urban communities" (*Sacred Game*, 278).

This fundamental sacrificial structure has to do with violence. Most sacred myths of origin tell us in one way or another that in the beginning of human society there was violence, a violence that in some sacred way became the foundation of everything, including all sacred institutions, customs, and conventions. This is the sacred violence that must be ritually reenacted not because it reveals a "richer" reality than the orderly one, but because it is at the very origin of order. Order came out of that which could also destroy it. That foundational violence could, in fact, go either way. So it must be handled with extreme care. It is sacred, and every primitive human being knows that nobody can really be certain which way the old sacred is going to reveal itself.

These are the basic anthropological facts of which Bakhtin shows no awareness. As a result, he reads the entire Saturnalian phenomenon and its carnivalesque derivations entirely in the wrong key. He attributes to the heroic and its institutions a sense of self-sufficiency, a lack of awareness of its limitations, that it never had; and he places such awareness elsewhere, with the people of the street, as it were, with a mythically separate realm he calls "everyday reality." It was left to this supposedly separate awareness to remind the heroic of its unavoidable limitations, to ridicule the confining straitjacket of its language, very much like the the Roman soldiers in the legions who ritually ridiculed their victorious commander.

What Bakhtin apparently did not understand, or did not care to take into consideration, was the ancestral fear that motivated all such ritual ridicules.

Self-sufficiency was much more than epistemologically mistaken, it was dangerous. Too much of it would inevitably attract the jealousy or anger of the gods, not to speak of the envy of your neighbor; although, in the final analysis these two dangers would be indistinguishable from one another, for they are both aspects of the foundational or sacrificial crisis. In other words, what Marxist Bakhtin rejoices in describing as multifaceted, inexhaustible everyday reality would translate in the language of the primitive sacred as radical insecurity, a deep awareness of the fact that nothing can ultimately shelter you from the irreducible instability, the profound ambivalence, of the sacred.

Bakhtin is right, of course, when he points out that behind every heroic Odysseus or Hercules there is a comic laughable one. The ambivalence of the sacred in general expresses the ambivalence of the sacrificial victim, both savior and outcast, king and slave. He could rightly see the transformation of god into outcast, of hero into victim or antihero, but he failed to see that if a god can become an outcast, an outcast can also become a god, because all victims, whether tragic or comic, are ultimately sacred. The victim who is sacrificed to the god participates in the nature of the god, is made godlike, in fact, becomes a substitute for the god.[10] In its origin—an origin never com-

10. A particularly striking example of this assimilation of the victim to the god is the case of Achilles, who is destined to die at the hands of Apollo (the god will guide the arrow shot by Paris). His resemblance to the god who will kill him, and to his anger, *menis*, has been noticed and analyzed by modern critics like Gregory Nagy (see, e.g., Nagy, 73). Nagy tells us that "Walter Burkert is so struck by the physical resemblance in the traditional representations of the god and the hero . . . that he is moved to describe Achilles as a *Doppelganger* of Apollo" (143). The death of Achilles is not narrated in the *Iliad*, although it is anticipated and the hero is fully aware of the fact that he will not return home. The death that happens in the poem, the death that diverts the terrible anger, *menis*, of Achilles away from the Greeks and toward the Trojans, is the death of Patroclus, the *therapon*, close friend of, and substitute for, Achilles, at the hands, not surprisingly, of Apollo himself, who stuns the hero with a terrible blow in the back that shakes off the armor of Achilles that he is wearing, leaving him fatally vulnerable. Nagy notes that this word *therapon* "had actually meant something like 'ritual substitute' at the time it was borrowed into Greek from Anatolia. . . . [The] Hittite word [equivalent] designates an entity's *alter ego* . . . , a projection upon whom the impurities of this entity may be transferred" (292). The death of Patroclus is widely recognized today as a substitute for and an anticipation within the poem of the death of Achilles outside the poem. Gentle Patroclus becomes Achilles-like as he dons his friend's armor and goes to his death as a substitute for the terrible hero. In the words of Cedric Whitman, "The gentlest man in the army becomes a demon-warrior, who drives the Trojans headlong from the ships. . . . He even is given new epithets at the climactic moments: elsewhere his name is modified only by his patronymic or by *hippeus*, 'knight'; but when he tussles with Apollo, he is 'equal to a god,' and the epithet is repeated just before Apollo destroys him" (200).

pletely left behind—the hero-antihero relationship, rooted in the sacred, is profoundly unstable and fully reversible.

In sum, there are not two types of discourse, one heroic, dominant, direct, and the other parodic, indirect. There is but one discourse in both cases, the sacred discourse, the discourse of the old sacred. And as long as this violently ambivalent sacred discourse maintains its grip on human society, it prevents the full development of the kind of "polyglossia," the coexistence or comingling of different human voices or languages, that Bakhtin rightly considers the fundamental characteristic of the modern novel. And that means that before the modern novel could fully unfold historically, a deep process of desacralization of literary forms must have taken place, a process that is completely ignored by the Marxist critic, for whom the sacred, if he is in agreement with Marxist theory, could only be "ideological muck," having no real history of its own, for it is supposed to be a by-product of the forces of production, in spite of the fact that, as we have already said, it can survive unchanged despite all kinds of changes in the forces of production.

The historical demise of the epic that is relevant to the development of the modern novel is a direct result of the process of desacralization, not a triumph of the Saturnalian spirit of carnival over heroic myth. There is no such triumph, just the opposite. The carnivalesque antihero, the old mask, is as much on its way to historical obsolescence as the epic hero is— neither one of them is open to the future, as we have seen already. It was precisely this lack of a future of the folkloric antihero that the author of the *Buscón* understood probably better than anybody else.

Since the voice that is heard through the heroic mask as well as through the antiheroic mask is the old voice of the sacred, it is ultimately the multitude, the crowd, that is talking. *Vox populi, vox Dei*, according to the old saying—a most unchristian old saying. Only the process of desacralization is capable of granting the individual a voice of his or her own, rescuing him or her from the absorbing power of the crowd. But this, to quote another old saying, is easier said than done. The new novelist is precisely the one who is going to discover, or to rediscover with an interest without precedent, how difficult it is to find and keep one's own voice, not to surrender to the extraordinary power of the crowd. The new novelist typically will become interested in the countless and twisted ways in which the individual surrenders his or her own inner freedom to the other in a conflictual, contradictory, and anguished way. The great subject matter of the modern novel will be the incredibly complex network of intersubjective relationships, and, among these, in particular, those strategies whereby a human being brings upon himself or herself his or her own misfortune. Although these will not only be of interest to the novelist, as Calderón illustrates:

> El ser uno desdichado
> todos han dicho que es fácil,
> mas yo digo que es difícil;
> que es tan industrioso arte
> que, aunque le platiquen todos,
> no le ha penetrado nadie.
> (*El mayor monstruo del mundo*, 1.1)

(Everybody has been saying it is easy for a man to be unhappy, but I say it is difficult, because it is such a complex art that, even though everybody practices it, nobody has penetrated it.)

The Paradox of the *Buscón*

Quevedo apparently did not have the slightest interest in exploring the "complex art" of human misfortunes in the psychology of his pícaro. He was only interested in exposing his character to public shame and laughter. Nevertheless, even in order to do that he still had to create a character who would look consistently laughable and shameful in the eyes of everybody. I say "consistently" because he was, after all, writing a novel, not a short theatrical interlude. How does a puppet or stock character, devoid of inner life, become a character in a novel? We know what happened with Avellaneda's Quixote. It was a failure. His novel is without interest. But that is not the case with Quevedo's *Buscón*. It is certainly not a modern novel, it is regressive, it undermines the very presuppositions of the genre, but the fact is that Pablos is far from being without psychological interest. Indeed, the critic Walter L. Reed has called the *Buscón* "the most brilliant of all the successors of the original *Lazarillo de Tormes* and *Guzmán de Alfarache*" (65). And I think he is right.

The key to this apparent paradox, a psychologically interesting character who has been described as empty, lies precisely in the nature of that emptiness because the protagonist's inner void is still an existential space. He lives it, and he reacts to it. Furthermore, it has a logic of its own. There is a reason why Pablos de Segovia does not have an inner life of his own: he is totally dependent on others. As Richard Bjornson has noticed, "Pablos is an 'other-directed' man" (54), to use the phrase coined by David Riesman in his study of *The Lonely Crowd*, which is actually a bit of an understament. Bjornson also notes that "[Pablos's] decisions always reflect . . . a nearly absolute dependence upon the approval of others" (60). But even that is still too general a statement. He is not equally dependent on all others. He is particularly, preferentially, dependent on those who despise him, on those who insult him, push him around, laugh at him—in other words, on those who see him as nobody, as empty. Pablos's self is not his own: it belongs to the crowd that points at him in derision and expels him in one way or another. His greatest desire is to be one of them precisely because they deride him and expel him. He is ashamed of himself because they are ashamed of him. Apart from the most elementary needs, there is nothing in him other than this obsessive desire to escape from himself toward the jeering crowd, as long as they are jeering. And the crowd, that is to say, the novel that he inhabits, is more than happy to oblige, by creating plenty of opportunities to shame him, in which he will predictably show himself fully deserving of the shame, thereby creating a hellish vicious circle.

The radically anti-Christian nature of this shameful complicity, of this complete surrender to the power of the crowd, of the other, of the condemning idol, was perfectly obvious to Quevedo. In a famous passage in the novel—the subject, years ago, of a critical debate among illustrious *quevedistas*[11]—Pablos, who has just been covered with spit from and chased by a group of university students in Alcalá, tells his landlord, who is looking at him and is tempted to spit on him too, "I am not *Ecce Homo*," in other words, "I am not Christ, don't look at me as if I were the Christ on whom the Roman soldiers or the Jews spat." This is something both literally and symbolically correct. Pablos is definitely not Christ, nor does he want to be Christ, for he is trying to escape Christ's fate. If his choice is between Christ and the crowd, there is no doubt at all that he will choose the crowd.

Thus the story of the *buscón* Pablos is not exactly the story of a young picaro who is trying "to rise socially" and is defeated by his own mistakes and

11. See T. E. May and Alexander Parker.

"by the defensive violence of society." It is really much more than that. In the eyes of Quevedo Pablos represents something far more dangerous and universal than social climbing. By reference to Quevedo's Christian horizon, the merciless treatment of Pablos cannot be sufficiently explained as an obsessive, anxious defense of class privileges or even, in general, of established social distinctions for their own sake, as something sacred, inherently untouchable. Nothing in his seventeenth-century Christian culture of *desengaño*, pervaded by the notion of the world as a stage, for example, would support such a view. He could only have engaged in such a fanatical defense of social class barriers, as he supposedly did, in full knowledge that his deep-seated Christian convictions, which he so vigorously upholds elsewhere, radically undermined such a defense.

In one of his best known *Sueños*, or "Dreams," *El sueño del infierno* (The dream of hell), also known as *Las zahurdas de Plutón* (Pluto's pigsties), the narrator travels through different areas of hell, where he sees different kinds of condemned people, and learns about them through explanations given by devils. At one point he sees an "hidalgo," or nobleman, who cannot understand why he, his lineage being what it is, has been condemned. One of the devils explains:

> Acabaos de desengañar que el que desciende del Cid, de Bernardo y de Godofredo, y no es como ellos, sino vicioso, como vos, ese tal más destruye el linaje que lo hereda. *Toda la sangre*, hidalguillo, *es colorada*; y parecedlo en las costumbres, y entonces creeré que descendeis del docto cuando lo fuéredes o procuráredes serlo; y si no, vuestra nobleza será mentira breve en cuanto durare la vida . . . ; la virtud es la ejecutoria que acá respetamos, pues aunque decienda de hombres viles y bajos, como él con divinas costumbres se haga digno de imitación se hace noble a sí y hace linaje para otros. Reímonos acá de ver lo que ultrajais a los villanos, moros y judíos, como si en éstos no cupieran las virtudes que vosotros despreciais. . . .
>
> —Desvaneceos, pues, bien, mortales—dije yo entre mí—¡y cómo se echa de ver que esto es el infierno, donde por atormentar a los hombres con amarguras les dicen las verdades! (165–66; my emphasis)

(Get it right once and for all. The descendant of El Cid, of Bernardo, or of Godfrey, if he is not like them, but corrupt, like you, he destroys, rather than inherits, his lineage. *All blood*—you little hidalgo—*is red*. Show it in your behavior. I will believe you descend from the wise when you are or try to be wise. Otherwise your nobility will be a brief lie while you are still alive. . . . Virtue is the [only] proof of nobility we respect down here. For even though a man may descend from plebeian and low origin, if he, with divine behavior, becomes worthy of imitation, he makes himself and his own lineage noble in the eyes of others. Down here we laugh when we see how you insult peasants, Moors, and Jews, as if they were not capable of those virtues that you despise. . . .

Disabuse yourselves, you mortals—I said to myself—how clear it is that this is hell! They torture men with bitterness by telling them the truth.)

"The atrabilious blueblooded conservative," as Dunn called him, knew perfectly well that "toda la sangre es colorada," everybody's blood is just red. Social blue blood is not going to make any difference in the afterlife, that is to say, in the eyes of God. The supposedly rabid anti-Semite also knew perfectly well that all those virtues scorned by Christian bluebloods who go to hell may be found in "Moors and Jews," and to pretend otherwise is utterly ludicrous, as the devils in hell tell us when they laugh at those stupid bluebloods who despise "peasants, Moors, and Jews," but it's they, the despisers, who find themselves in hell. Could it be that in Quevedo's mind such a laughable belief in the incapacity for virtue of "peasants, Moors, and Jews" is part of the reason why they, the stupid bluebloods, go to hell?

Quevedo is not a social and political fanatic. His merciless treatment of Pablos goes far beyond political and social considerations. It has to do with the picaro's abject surrender to the other, to the crowd. Pablos does not just fawn on the rich and noble. He fawns on anybody who happens to be in authority at the moment, or simply happens to be "in," that is to say, admired, or fashionable, anybody who attracts the eyes of the crowd. He will fawn on the teacher and the teacher's wife in grammar school, as much as he fawns on the children of the noble attending school. And he will try anything and risk everything in an effort to be accepted by the crowd of mischievous students at the University of Alcalá, the same students who spat on him and smeared him with human excrement.

Unamuno said that "[e]l más hondo sondaje que se haya hecho en España de la envidia hispánica—o ibérica—. . . lo hizo nuestro gran Quevedo en su *Virtud militante contra las cuatro pestes del mundo: invidia, ingratitud, soberbia, avaricia*" (Quevedo, *Obras completas*,[12] 5.172; the deepest exploration that has been made in Spain about Spanish or Iberian envy . . . was made by our great

12. Hereafter the *Obras completas* will be abbreviated as *O. C.*

Quevedo in his *Militant Virtue against the Four Plagues of the World: Envy, Ingratitude, Pride, and Avarice*). In this work by Quevedo we read the following:

> La invidia fue vientre de los pecados, el pecado fue parto primogénito de la invidia. . . . Ella derribó al ángel, sedujo a Adán, hizo a Caín fratricida, y dio la muerte a Abel, cuya sangre fue la primera mancha de la tierra. (Quevedo, *O. C.*, 1366)

> (Envy was the womb of [all] sins, sin was the firstborn of envy. . . . She brought down the angel, seduced Adam, turned Cain into a fratricide, and killed Abel, whose blood was the first stain on the earth.)

I think that the *Buscón* could also be considered an exploration, or rather an illustration, of the workings of envy. The *Buscón* could also be called *The Envious One*. In his abject and envious dependence on the other, Pablos anticipates the existential pathology of much later novelistic characters, such as those portrayed by Dostoyevski in *The Devils* (also known as *The Possessed*) in whom Pablos's disease has intensified and reached a truly infernal depth. It may be instructive to listen to one of them. This is Shatov speaking to diabolical Stavrogin:

> "Stavrogin, why am I condemned to believe in you for ever? . . . I have modesty, but I was not ashamed of my nakedness because I was speaking to Stavrogin. I was not afraid of caricaturing a great idea by my touch because Stavrogin was listening to me. . . . Don't you know that I shall kiss your footprints after you have gone? I can't tear you out of my heart, Nicholas Stavrogin!"
>
> "I'm sorry I cannot bring myself to like you, Shatov," said Stavrogin coldly. (261–62)

A little before this scene, Stavrogin, "looking really surprised," had said to Shatov:

> "You seem to regard me as a sort of a sun and yourself as a sort of insignificant insect compared with me." (249)

Satan Expelling Satan

However, that does not mean at all that Quevedo's novel anticipates that of Dostoyevski, or that his treatment of the diabolical character resembles that of the Russian author. The comparison with Dostoyevski highlights the difference that separates the two novelists. It is highly significant that in Dostoyevski the "devils" are many, "legion" to be exact, which is the name used in the passage from the Gospel of Luke used by Dostoyevski as a heading for his novel. In the *Buscón* the universal disease, the envy of the devil, is drained of its universality and concentrated in one individual, who is made more shameful, more laughable, more abject than anybody else. Everybody's envy is ignored while everybody turns their violence against this one ridiculous and despicable poor devil who would do anything to be like everybody else. Quevedo knows exactly the nature of the disease that corrodes human society from inside, but in the *Buscón* he chooses the old victimizing mechanism to expose and attack the disease. When he makes his picaro say, "I am not Christ," that is, "Do not treat me like you would treat Christ," he is not only defining the personality of his picaresque character, he is also, indirectly, but just as clearly, defining the novel that has created such a character. It is not only Pablos, it is the novel that expels Pablos that is also saying "Do not see Christ here." This is what, in the language of the Gospels, could be called Satan expelling Satan:

> All in the crowd were astonished. "Might this not be David's son?" they asked. When the Pharisees heard this, they charged, "This man can expel demons only with the help of Beelzebul, the prince of demons." Knowing their thoughts, he said to them . . . "If Satan is expelling Satan, he must be torn by dissension. How, then, can his dominion last? . . . But if it is by the Spirit of God that I expel demons, then the reign of God has overtaken you." (Matthew 12.23–28)

It is definitely not the Spirit of God that expels Pablos of Segovia. In all likelihood, he was Quevedo's answer to Alemán's picaro, Guzmán, who wanted us to look at him precisely as Christ's brother. In other words, it was Quevedo's radical answer to Alemán's attempt to turn the picaresque novel into a Christian exercise, an attempt that ultimately failed. As we saw, Alemán could not successfully combine the Christian image of his converted picaro with the spirit and form of the picaresque novel, heir to the old folkloric forms. Quevedo's answer, on the other hand, shows a perfect integration of character and novelistic form. Pablos of Segovia embodies the very spirit of the novel that treats him as a human void, as a man without inner substance. This is why when the novel expels him, it expels itself, that is to say, it rejects hope, it denies itself the possibility of having a future. One must wonder if Quevedo ever understood the fundamental difference between Alemán's attempt and Cervantes's effort. For we must remember that the *Quixote* is also an answer to the *Guzmán*.

CHAPTER IV

Don Quixote's Madness and Modernity

Old Madness and the Sacred

The traditional fate of the fool in general, and the madman in particular, was no better than that of the rogue. In fact, it could be argued that it was much worse. Madness has usually been seen as a more radical form of marginal existence (in the sense of differentiation or distance from the social norm) than roguery. And in premodern society this deeper marginality automatically meant a deeper association with the old sacred. The process of desacralization that brings about modernity had to operate at an even deeper level.

In other words, if it was difficult enough to rescue the literary rogue, the picaro, from its traditional victimizing representation, as we have just seen with the aid of the two contrary approaches of Alemán and Quevedo, it should have been even more difficult to do it with a madman. Cervantes did not have it any easier than either one of the two masters of the picaresque. But he succeeded where they failed. And I would also like to suggest that the fact that he succeeded with a madman rather than with a rogue (that he was dealing with madness rather than with delinquency or criminality) may itself have meaningful implications worth exploring.

I think that even today it is easier to admit that a rogue is not always, inevitably, a rogue than it is to admit that a madman is not always, inevitably, a madman. Even today, the general view seems to be that madness encompasses the totality of the individual human being more tenaciously, more radically, than roguery or even criminality. In fact, when criminal behavior reaches a certain degree of violent inevitability, we associate it with madness: then we call the criminal a psychopath or a sociopath. In premodern, tradition-bound society, this totalizing character of madness is inseparable from its association with the sacred (indeed, social historians have addressed this association for over a century now). Madness was conceived as something that struck from above or from outside and turned the individual into a special, different kind of human being, a very ambivalent human being. On the one hand, the madman was too dangerous to approach, not only dangerous to individuals, but dangerous to the social body; the madman was a witness to the possibility of a total collapse of the community, a complete breakdown of all cultural differences. On the other hand, the madman was also the carrier of the antidote to that same disease. He held the secret of the defense against that collapsing danger. In other words, the madman was clearly a sacrificial figure. His erratic behavior bore the mark of "the sacrificial crisis," in Girardian terms.

To the best of my knowledge, Anton Zijderveld, a sociologist, has the deepest understanding of the sacrificial character of folly or madness in a primitive community. This is how he describes it:

> [In] his myths and rituals "primitive" man transfers himself to the primeval time prior to history in which he becomes the contemporary of the gods and shares their work of creation. This again throws light on the eerie behaviour of the ceremonial fool: he is the representative of the primeval chaos, the "tohowabohu" which existed prior to the creation of the cosmos. The anarchic behaviour of these ritual clowns demonstrates in a lively manner what the raw material has been, out of which the gods once created the cosmos, the present order—nature, society, culture. It is indeed a regression—a mythic "mimesis" of "illud tempus". . . . Ceremonial folly . . . is a dangerous activity, which can only be executed anonymously [i.e., with masks] and ritually. But it is also a necessary activity. . . . The behaviour of these revolting fools . . . demonstrates, in a vivid and very concrete manner, what would happen to the participants in soci-

ety should they decide to abandon their culture . . . : they would change into cultural protoplasm [i.e., complete undifferentiation], into witless and revolting monsters. (148–49)

Fools and madmen have also been perceived as possessing a particularly penetrating kind of knowledge, even prophetic powers. It is this ambivalent sacred status that keeps the madman, an object of public scorn and derision, a scapegoat figure, also at the center of political and social power, in the role, for example, of the court jester, the double of the prince, a double who, in more primitive times, was literally a sacrificial substitute.

In the history of the Christian world this primitive sacred ambivalence of the madman undergoes a rather peculiar transformation or adaptation; it may become grafted, as it were, onto the idea that the wisdom of God is folly to the world, that the Incarnation is "folly to the Greeks," and more specifically on the Pauline description of the apostles as "fools for Christ's sake":

As I see it, God has put us apostles at the end of the line, like men doomed to die in the arena. We have become a spectacle to the universe, to angels and men alike. We are fools on Christ's account. . . . Up to this very hour we go hungry and thirsty, poorly clad, roughly treated, wandering about homeless. . . . We have become the world's refuse, the scum of all; that is the present state of affairs. (1 Corinthians 4.10–13)

This state of affairs is, of course, not something that Saint Paul appreciates for its own sake. He is not deliberately seeking to be roughly treated or to become "the world's refuse, the scum of all," although he would gladly suffer all of that and more for Christ's sake. But historically, this foolishness for Christ's sake becomes something like a vocation, a special calling, leading to a deliberate decision to become a fool, a madman—something which, in practice, becomes easily confused with the real thing. Reading the accounts of holy fools, it is by no means always easy to separate real madness from its simulated counterpart, for, simulated or not, madness was perceived as a sign of the sacred. The phenomenon was particularly prevalent in those areas where Eastern Christianity flourished, but it was also present in other parts of the Christian world, like Ireland. In Russia these holy fools occur as late as the sixteenth century. In the words of John Saward,

The greatest era of the *yurodivye*—fools for Christ—in Russia is the sixteenth century. Nearly all travellers to Muscovy at this time mention them, including the Englishman, Giles Fletcher, who wrote as follows:

> They have certain hermits, whom they call holy men, that are like gymnosophists for their life and behaviour. . . . They use to go stark naked save a clout about the middle, with their hair hanging long and wildly about their shoulders, and many of them with an iron collar or chain around their necks or midst, even in the very extreme of winter. These they take as prophets and men of great holiness, giving them a liberty to speak what they list without any controlment, though it be of the very highest himself. So that if he reprove any openly, in what sort soever, they answer nothing, but that it is *po graecum*, that is, for their sins. (23)

"*Giving them a liberty to speak what they list without any controlment.*" What reader familiar with Cervantes's *Exemplary Novels* would not think of *El licenciado vidriera* when reading this passage about the Russian fools? And yet there is a fundamental difference. Tomás Rodaja, the Licenciado Vidriera, is not presented to us as a holy man. Even though people flock to him to hear his wise and witty pronouncements, there is nothing sacred about him or his wisdom. The ironic narrator makes us ponder why nobody pays attention to this wise man once he has been cured of his madness. The reader is left wondering about the reason why people would listen to a madman and not to a sane person. Clearly, the sacred halo has worn out, or lost its meaning, for the question remains hanging in the air without an answer.

But the fact that the question comes up is in itself significant. It means that, historically speaking, Cervantes is still close to a very old view of madness, but one that is rapidly changing into something else, something new, as it loses its old association with the sacred and increasingly portrays its object, madness, as strictly human.[1] The case of the Licenciado Vidriera is by no means the only one in which we clearly see the new as it emerges from the old. Think, for example, of the image of mad Cardenio as we first meet him in the wild reaches of the Sierra Morena mountains. He is "half-naked," "his

1. Is Erasmus's *Praise of Folly* not indebted as well to the old ambivalence? According to Willeford, "Erasmus's notion of madness as folly, and as a blessing, is crucial to his whole enterprise of ironic praise. The notion entails a rhetorical trick that complements that by which he has banished the dangers of madness: having convinced us of the blessing of madness, he plays with the various senses in which this blessing may be understood. Sometimes, for example, he regards such madness, satirically, as equivalent to vanity and self-delusion; and at other times he regards it as analogous to a transformation of consciousness that would allow us to see things more truly. And, quite generally, he is at pains to keep us from knowing for certain in what sense he is, at a given moment, praising folly. As a result of these pains, and despite the subtle logic of his ironies, we feel that in the *Praise of Folly* madness is a unitary and contagious force, as it was in folk belief" (25).

legs and feet bare; . . . his thighs . . . clad in a pair of breeches . . . so tattered that in many places his skin showed through"; he is very swift, "leaping from rock to rock and from bush to bush with extraordinary agility"; "his hair long and tangled." Shortly thereafter the old goatherd will tell Don Quixote and Sancho how the wild young man took the goatherds' food by force and "ran into the mountains at an amazing speed," and how "several of our herdsmen spent almost two days looking for him in the roughest part of this mountain, and finally found him hiding in the hollow of a huge cork-tree."

The different elements that form this image of mad Cardenio have all been identified by Ó Riain as typical structural components of madness in the sagas of the *gelta*, or Irish holy mad- or wild men. Saward, who wants to show the similarity between the Irish holy madmen and their Eastern counterparts, quotes Ó Riain as follows:

> In order to facilitate our comparison with the Eastern evidence it will be useful to reproduce Professor Ó Riain's list of the structural components of madness in the sagas of the *gelta*.
>
> (A) THE OCCASIONS OF MADNESS: (i) the curse of a sacerdos; (ii) a battlefield experience; (iii) *consumption of contaminated food or drink* [applicable to the Licenciado Vidriera]; (iv) *the loss of a lover.*
>
> (B) THE STATE OF MADNESS: The madman (i) *takes to the wilderness*; (ii) *perches on trees*; (iii) collects firewood; (iv) is *naked, hairy*, covered with feathers or *clothed with rags*; (v) *leaps* and/or levitates; (vi) *is very swift*; (vii) *is restless and travels great distances*; (viii) *experiences hallucinations*; (ix) has a special diet.
>
> (C) THE OCCASIONS OF RESTORATION TO SANITY: (i) *intervention of a sacerdos* [I do not think the intervention of the priest qualifies, in the case of Cardenio, but it does, up to a point, in the case of the Licenciado]; (ii) consumption of blessed food or drink; (iii) the act of coition. (40–41)

Saward adds the following comment after quoting Ó Riain: "In section (A), while madness in the East does not follow a curse, it usually follows self-accusation or conviction of sin; folly for Christ's sake has a strong penitential aspect." Here I can do no better than to repeat Cardenio's explanation to the herdsmen when he met them during one of his tranquil periods: "He greeted us courteously, and in a few polite words begged us not to be surprised to see him wandering about in that state; for he had to do so to fulfill a certain penance which had been laid on him for his many sins." And, of course, we should not forget that this is the occasion for Don Quixote's sudden decision to do penance for his lady Dulcinea in imitation of Amadís, and also to turn mad in imitation of Roland.

Desacralization of Madness

But, once again, in spite of the formal similarities, there is nothing sacred or holy about mad Cardenio. He does not inspire awe or reverence, only pity and compassion. The herdsmen are only trying to do something for his own good, to help him, and, if they can, to take him to the nearest town where someone can try to cure him. It would be absurd to imagine that, for example, he could perform miracles. Cardenio's madness is a sad and strictly human affair.

This desacralization of madness is happening almost everywhere in the Christian West by the second half of the sixteenth century. It would take a little longer in the East. According to Saward, "[T]he last Russian fool for Christ's sake was canonized in the seventeenth century. After this period the fool became suspect not only during his lifetime but also after his death; not even the cultus of the *yurodivye* was sufficient for the Church to admit another subversive to the ranks of the blessed" (23).

It is important to realize that the old view of madness became suspect to Christian minds of all persuasions (Catholic and Protestant alike, as well as Eastern Orthodox) specifically and explicitly because of its underlying and profound association with the pre-Christian or non-Christian sacred. The Christian Church knew that "throughout the Middle Ages, folly functioned as a disguise for ancient forms of magical paganism" (Zijderveld, 40). But the Church could not just ban madness, or declare it a dangerous fiction, as the Church tried to do in the case of the theater, which was also accused of having pagan sacrificial origins.

What happens, then, to the old view when it becomes desacralized? The threat of a catastrophically contagious spread and violent collapse is still there. What has disappeared is the good, or, rather, the remedial, side of the violence, the foundational function and meaning of the catastrophic crisis. That violence, that crisis, is now bad and only bad. It does not have God's approval. Therefore, it is no longer sacred. The Christian God does not emerge from, and thereby sanctify, such violence. But if God is not behind the crisis, the crisis itself loses its ultimate inevitability. It is no longer the last word.

Furthermore, if it does not have God's approval, the crisis does not have to be—or, at the very least, there has to be some way to avoid it, or to minimize it, or to get out of it. In this sense, the fact that such catastrophic violence has no redeeming qualities whatsoever (because God is not in it) must have produced an extraordinary sense of relief.

In other words, desacralization in no way minimizes or hides the danger posed by madness. Quite the opposite, it allows its evil and destructive power to come into view like never before. And the danger, as we just saw, is not only to the individual human mind, but to society as a whole. The final collective crisis, which had always lurked behind the old view of madness, is still there, although now transformed into a purely man-made catastrophe. The spectacle of the individual madman is not only still capable of triggering the fear of an apocalyptic breakdown, it can do it now with unprecedented clarity, because the veil of the sacred has been removed from it.

Michel Foucault has noticed this apocalyptic conception of madness in the transition from the Middle Ages to what he calls the "Classical Age." He describes it as "tragic" or "cosmic":

> Le thème de la fin du monde, de la grande violence finale n'est pas étranger à l'expérience critique de la folie telle qu'elle est formulée dans la litterature. Ronsard évoque ces temps ultimes qui se débattent dans le grand vide de la raison:
>
> Au ciel est revolée et Justice et Raison,
> et en leur place, hélas, règne le brigandage,
> la haine, la rancoeur, le sang et le carnage.
>
> Vers la fin du poème de Brant [*Das Narrenschiff*, or *The Ship of Fools*, 1494], un chapitre tout entier est consacré au thème apocaliptique de l'Antechrist: une immense tempête emporte le navire des fous dans une course insensée qui s'identifie à la catastrophe des mondes. (32–33)
>
> (The theme of the end of the world, of the great final violence, is not alien to the critical experience of folly such as it is formulated in literature. Ronsard evokes those final times that rage inside a great void of reason:
>
> Justice and Reason have flown back to heaven,
> And in their place, alas, there reign brigandage,
> Hatred, rancor, blood, and carnage.
>
> Toward the end of Brant's poem an entire chapter is devoted to the apocalyptic theme of the Antichrist: an immense storm carries the ship of fools on a senseless course, which is identified as a universal collapse.)

Indeed, Foucault thinks that both Cervantes and Shakespeare are still witnesses to this cosmic conception of madness:

> Et sans doute, sont ils, l'un et l'autre [Cervantes et Shakespeare], plus encore les témoins d'une expérience tragique de la Folie née au XVe siècle, que ceux d'une expérience critique et morale de la Déraison qui se développe pourtant à leur propre époque. Par-déla le temps, il renouent avec un sens qui est en train de disparaître, et dont la continuité ne se poursuivra plus que dans la nuit. (47)
>
> (Doubtless, both [Cervantes and Shakespeare] testify more to a tragic experience of madness appearing in the fifteenth century, than to a critical and moral experience of Unreason developing in their own epoch. Outside of time, they establish a link with a meaning about to be lost, and whose continuity will no longer survive except in darkness.)

I think he is basically right, even though there is nothing "fascinating" about this "cosmic" experience of madness in Cervantes or Shakespeare, in the sense in which Foucault also says that, in the fifteenth century "la folie fascine l'homme." If this fascination may have been true in the fifteenth century, that is no longer the case for Cervantes or Shakespeare. But in reading Ronsard's verses, one cannot help but think of Cardenio's sonnet in Sierra Morena:

> Santa amistad, que con ligeras alas,
> tu apariencia quedándose en el suelo,
> entre benditas almas en el cielo
> subiste alegre a las impíreas salas:
> . . . .
> Deja el cielo, ¡oh amistad!, o no permitas
> que el engaño se vista tu librea,
> con que destruye la intención sincera;
>
> que si tus apariencias no le quitas,
> presto ha de verse el mundo en la pelea
> de la discorde confusión primera.
>
> (1.27.303)
>
> (O holy friendship that with nimble wing,
> thy semblance leaving here on earth below,
> with blessed souls in heaven communing,
> up to the empyrean halls dost go,
> . . . .

> Leave heaven, friendship, or do not permit
> deceit to wear thy robes,
> with which it destroys an earnest will,
>
> For if you do not take your semblance from deceit,
> the world will soon return to the violence
> of its primeval chaotic confusion.)

As "holy friendship" ascends to its blessed place in heaven, it leaves below only its appearance, a fraudulent friendship that looks like the real one. It is this deceiving appearance, rather than an absence of friendship—an empty space that could be easily detected—that causes, in the words of Cervantes, "la pelea de la discorde confusión primera." But, clearly, the living sign of such violent confusion, through which the world would regress to its primeval chaos, is the dark and violent madness of Cardenio, at the root of which is something all too human, the story of a deceitful friendship. And let us keep in mind the explicit and deliberate connection Cervantes establishes between the furious madness of Cardenio and the laughable, imitative madness of Don Quixote. We laugh at Don Quixote, but beyond the literary madness of the Manchegan knight, the figure of furious Cardenio looms like an ultimate and devastating horizon, an apocalyptic possibility.

What Cervantes sees in the madman, therefore, is an anticipation, an individual sample, of what can easily spread, like a public scandal, to the entire community and threaten its very existence. There is no fundamental difference here between the nature of the threat posed by madness to the individual mind and to the community, between individual insanity and collective insanity. From this "tragic" or "cosmic" perspective, it could be said that individual insanity is fundamentally the individual experience of a collective crisis.

The Modernity of the Newly Desacralized View

As it turns out, this desacralized "cosmic" view may actually be, in some respects, more modern or anticipatory than we might have imagined. "Emergent madness is a collective event lived in solitude," says Henri Grivois (1999, 120), head of psychiatry at Paris Municipal Hospital (Hôtel-Dieu); "to be mad is not only the feeling of being uniquely in contact with all humanity, whether as alienated from it or as uniting all of it in oneself. . . . It is [also] to infer that one occupies a unique place in the human world. It is the feeling of being encircled by everyone" (1999, 105). No wonder he calls emergent or nascent psychosis elsewhere "un mythe sacrificiel" (a sacrificial myth) (2001, 177).

Today there can be no doubt about the interindividual roots of madness. "The place where madness is born . . . is also the place where we all live together" (Grivois, 1999, 117):

> Patients admit the interpersonal origin of their travail. It is even the single point they never question. They feel a tacit participation of others in the most secret part of themselves . . . they hesitate to attribute to themselves alone what they do and think, while what happens around them seems to be entirely dependent on themselves. While at the same time being dictated by others, guided, carried, curbed by the movement of the world, patients have also the feeling of directing it, in a spiral without end or beginning. (Grivois, 1999, 107)

Of course, it is madness to see oneself as the center of a world in which everybody conspires against one, and in which everything also depends on one; a world in which one's self is both annihilated and placed at the center of everything. But, as Grivois suggests, that does not mean that such an individual maddening experience is totally devoid of all referential value, that it refers to nothing at all beyond itself, or to nothing that makes any sense whatsoever. For the structure of this maddening experience of the individual appears to reproduce the basic structure of the collective insanity that moves the victimizing crowd to transfer onto its random victim the responsibility for everything. If these observations of modern psychiatry are correct, then the voice of the madman echoes the collective, undifferentiated voice of the victimizing crowd.[2] He sees himself just as that uniform and unanimous crowd sees him. And his experience includes the anguished feeling of not having a voice of his own, of not being able to say "I" with enough confidence that it is he indeed who says it. Perhaps this, or an anticipation of this, is what Quevedo might have discovered in his picaro, so lacking in selfhood, as we have just seen, so desperate to join the crowd, if Quevedo had first discovered the

2. "[L]a foule de la psychose . . . 'est tout sauf une société, ne serait-ce que du fait de son illimitation et de son absence totale de différenciation'" (Grivois, *Le fou et la mouvement du monde*, 129). The quote within the quote is from *Mécanismes mentaux, mécanismes sociaux. De la psychose à la panique*, ed. H. Grivois et J. P. Dupuy, 9–10.

madness of that victimizing and folkloric crowd that he so willingly joined. The point is that there seems to be enough clinical evidence to suggest that the desacralized, though "tragic" or "cosmic," view of madness that contemplates the possibility of a catastrophic expansion of madness beyond the individual is far from arbitrary, is more than purely poetic hyperbole.

Maybe now we can understand better what it meant for Cervantes to break with the crowd, to save the madman from his immemorial fate. It was not only an act of compassion—which indeed it was—but also a revolutionary change in perspective, in focus: from public danger to individualized danger. Madness, that old threat of veiled and disturbing origin, capable of driving human society to a state of violent "primeval confusion," became more directly, more urgently, focused now on the individual human being, the one to be saved; the one, that is to say, seen precisely at the center of that "primeval confusion," toward whom all fingers used to point as the carrier of the threat—that same one toward which all eyes also turned in awe, in reverential fear. If Cervantes could see the "primeval confusion," the victimizing crowd in panic, through the individual madness of Cardenio, he could also see the situation in reverse: he could see the individual breakdown beyond the "primeval confusion." Such confusion, the sway of the crowd in panic, was not enough to block his view of the individual human being, the individual madman, who was both a victim of the crowd and a member of it. The violence of the "primeval chaotic confusion" became more than the collective image of the immemorial fear of an origin lost in time. It became present as an individual state of mind: the state of mind of the madman. And by turning his attention to the cure of the individual, Cervantes also made a first step toward curing the community of its old sacred fear, the cause of its own sacrificial madness, the collective violent confusion that demanded the expulsion of the mad victim.

Inevitably the madman, desacralized, ceased to be a monolithic embodiment of madness, all mad and nothing but mad, and therefore with nothing to be saved in him. Genuine compassion (not prescribed, not ritual, not cathartic) for the victim of the multitude does not see the madman as all mad, as all of one piece. Instead, it sees him as worth saving. Furthermore, that which is worth saving in him is precisely what the violent "confusion" of madness threatens with destruction: his individuality, his singular self. That is to say, compassion grants him distinctness, singularity, selfhood, while madness threatens to turn him, from inside himself, into what the multitude, driven by the sacred fear of collective madness, sees when it looks at him, namely, a sacrificial projection, an embodiment, of its own collective insanity. Therefore, from the point of view of genuine compassion, the old sacrificial equation was turned around: the carrier of the threat of madness was not the individual human being as such, as a singular self, but the multitude, the mimetic crowd, insofar as it is constituted of and driven by the old fear of the collective crisis, the apocalyptic breakdown. The madman, in his madness, succumbs to that old and sacred fear, to the spirit of the sacrificial multitude, the spirit of Satan. He joins the crowd against himself.

Don Quixote, "Mad in Patches," *Un Entreverado Loco*

At the beginning of the novel Cervantes tells us that Alonso Quijano "had utterly wrecked his reason" (*rematado ya su juicio*). But very soon we find out that that is certainly not the case. Had that been the case, the novel *Don Quixote* would have been impossible to write. A Don Quixote who was conceived as already completely mad when the book began would have only produced something like Avellaneda's novel, as we saw already, or nothing at all, if his madness were something like the furious madness that took hold of Cardenio. You cannot build a work of art on the basis of such madness. We should remember that, after a while, Cervantes had to drop the all-embracing fury of Cardenio's madness in order to be able to keep him in the novel as a meaningful character. Likewise he will simply ignore that initial statement about Don Quixote, who will, in fact, turn out to be *un entreverado loco*, a madman in patches or streaks, with many lucid intervals, as Don Diego de Miranda's son told his father.

Don Quixote is mad, but not totally so, and therefore not hopelessly or inevitably mad. It was undoubtedly a stroke of artistic genius on Cervantes's part to conceive him in this manner. As I just said, total madness would have meant the complete miscarriage of *Don Quixote*'s literary modernity. But it is equally doubtless that the idea of a partial or incomplete madness is essential to a desacralized and compassionate view of the madman, a view fundamentally interested in the possibility of saving him from his madness—a view, that is, fostered by the desacralizing process that rescues the social victim from his immemorial fate.

Thus if these two things go together, the artistic genius of the novelist and his interest in saving the madman from his madness, it should come as no surprise to learn that a similar change in the historical view of madness, from total to partial, should characterize the first scientific efforts to study madness with a view to cure it. Modern literature and modern psychiatry are not the same thing. But I believe it is most revealing to see that the same historical process that was at work in the development of one was also at work in the development of the other.

Speaking of one of the founders of modern psychiatry, Philippe Pinel (1745–1826), and of his *Traité médico-philosophique sur l'aliénation mentale ou la manie* (1801), Gladys Swain wrote the following:

Cést une *dimension réflechie*, pourrait-on dire, que Pinel introduit dans la folie: pas de pleine coïncidence de l'aliéné avec lui-même au sein de l'aliénation, mais un rapport de soi à soi maintenu en dépit de la menace de son annulation présente comme horizon de l'aliénation. Et les implications d'un tel déplacement de la problématique doivent être soulignées. Ainsi sont rendus dès lors virtuellement pensables le *conflit* interne en jeu dans l'aliénation et l'aliénation elle-même comme manifestation d'un conflit. Qu'est-ce qui transparait en effet au travers de cette tension mettant l'être subjectif en question, sinon cette singulière capacité d'essence du sujet à se porter contre lui-même, seulement poussée à son paroxisme dans l'aliénation?

Autant que l'aliéné est concu comme enfermé totalement dans son état, rien de plus est discernable dans ses actes et ses propos que la pure extériorisation d'un dérèglement, échappant par définition à la sphère du sens. (85–86; emphasis in the original)

(Pinel introduced what we might call a *reflective dimension* in [the concept of] madness: the alienated [subject] does not fully coincide with himself within his alienation. A relationship is maintained from himself to himself in spite of a threat of collapse, which is made present as alienation's own horizon. And the implications of such a displacement in the approach to alienation ought to be emphasized. Because now it becomes possible to think of the internal conflict at stake in alienation, as well as to think of alienation itself as the manifestation of a conflict. What is it that actually transpires through this tension that questions the subjective being but this singular essential capacity of the subject to drive himself against himself, only pushed to its limits in alienation?

As long as the alienated is conceived as totally enclosed within his condition, nothing can be discerned in his acts and intentions but the pure exteriorization of a derangement, which by definition escapes the sphere of sense.)

Quite clearly, for this modern psychiatrist and historian, the fundamental change in the conception of madness that allowed for the possibility of a new and scientific conception of mental alienation occurred when madness was no longer seen as a monolithic entity:

C'est sur une idée quant à l'être de la folie . . . que s'est fondée la connaissance [moderne] de la folie; c'est autour de cette idée et à sa poursuite que s'est jouée son histoire. *Elle surgit dans l'ouvrage de Pinel avec la critique de l'idée d'une folie complète.* L'aliénation mentale n'est jamais totale: l'aliéné conserve toujours une distance à son aliénation. (22; my emphasis)

(It is on the basis of an idea about what madness is . . . that modern understanding of madness is built; the history of this understanding is tied to this idea and its development. *It appeared for the first time in the work of Pinel with the critique of the notion of total madness.* Mental alienation is never total: the alienated always keeps a distance from his alienation.)

She brings none other than Hegel's testimony in support of her discovery concerning Pinel's fundamental contribution. According to Hegel, Swain avers,

[Avoir] découvert ce reste de raison dans les aliénés et dans les maniaques, l'y avoir découvert comme contenant le principe de leur guérison . . . c'est là un titre qui appartient surtout à Pinel, dont l'écrit sur cette matière doit être consideré comme le meilleur qu'on possède. (39–40)

(The discovery of this remnant of reason in the insane and the maniacs, and to have discovered it as holding the principle of their cure . . . that is a title that belongs above all to Pinel, whose writing on this matter ought to be considered the best we have.)

The conceptual centrality and the historical relevance of this new critique of the old idea of "complete madness" can hardly be exaggerated. But Swain wants equally to emphasize its profound originality, its radically unprecedented character:

[Ce] qu'il importe . . . de souligner, c'est le lien intime du fait psychiatrique tel qu'il se met en place à la charnière des XVIIIe et XIXe siécles, et de ce qui constitue l'originalité profonde de la societé qui advient alors: sa capacité à se penser sans garant dans l'au-delà et à se justifier dans son organisation sans recours au sacré. Ce qui émerge à ce tournant comme conditions nouvelles d'abord de la folie émerge sous le coup d'une rupture sans précédent dans l'histoire humaine et au sein d'une société radicalement distincte de toutes celles qui l'ont précédée. (52)

(What must be emphasized is the intimate connection between the psychiatric event such as it occurs at the turn of the century from the 18th to the 19th, and that which constitutes the profound originality of the society that emerges at that time: its capacity to view itself without warranty from the world beyond, to justify itself within its own organization without recourse to the sacred. What emerges at that time as the new conditions of madness does so under the impulse of a break without precedent in human history and inside a society radically different from all those that preceded it.)

In other words, the crisis of the old idea of "complete madness" is intimately tied to a profound process of desacralization undergone by European society—tied, therefore, to the emergence of a type of society "without precedent in human history." Swain explains what she means by a "desacralized society" ("une société qui cesse de se mirer dans son Autre pour se voir"; a society where "l'univers sensible n'est plus censé être habité par une virtuelle et permanente manifestation de l'au-delà."), but she is not very precise about when and how such a totally unprecedented society could have come about. In spite of the historical proximity of Pinel's treatise to the French Revolution, she is careful not to put much emphasis on this order of events. The French Revolution serves only as "a convenient benchmark" ("un repère commode").

Nevertheless, we learn that when that "liminal experience of the Other within oneself," which, according to Swain, is madness ("cette expérience-limite de l'Autre en soi-même qu'est la folie") becomes separated, disengaged, from the experience of the sacred, as the absolute Other ("Dieu créateur et législateur suprême," "l'invisible," "l'ailleurs"), that is to say, when the other becomes human and only human, the door is open for the establishment of the therapeutic relationship between physician and patient, which will form the basis for the medical treatment of alienation. Even though, in order to be properly therapeutic, the relationship must go beyond the purely medical, because it is a relationship that, while demanding the traditional authority of the medical doctor, requires that he or she not act as one. "[La demande] naît dans la relation médicale; elle ne peut viser sa satisfaction que dans une relation qui soit le contraire de la relation medicale" (56). One would be tempted to say that what the alienated patient demands is the kind of human relationship that he or she finds very difficult to maintain. At any rate, it seems perfectly clear that the desacralization of madness not only revealed an internal conflict, a subject divided against itself, but also a fundamental crisis in the very structure of intersubjective, or interindividual, relationships, a subject in conflict with the human other. And, as we already saw in Grivois, the individual crisis cannot be separated from the interindividual one: the conflict with the other and with oneself are two aspects of the same phenomenon.

Swain's insistence on the radical novelty of this new conception of madness, and of the social context in which it happens, is truly amazing. This revolution in thinking is a break not only with what immediately preceded it, but with the way humanity had conceived itself from the beginning ("... brisant bien plus qu'avec ce qui précédait immédiatement: avec la façon dont l'humanité s'est pensée depuis ses origines ..."; 51). And she knows, of course, that, in this regard, her view is totally opposed to that of Michel Foucault in his *Histoire de la folie à l'âge classique*, whose interpretation—she admits—is "la plus forte, à la fois la plus nourrie et la plus subtile, la plus étayée et la plus réfléchie qui ait été donnée du destin social de la folie dans l'Occident moderne et du sort qui lui a réservée la pensée médicale" (29; the strongest, both the most fulfilling and the most subtle, the most expansive and the most reflexive that has ever been given of the social history of madness in the modern West, and of the role that medical thinking has assigned to it). It is opposed to Foucault, because, in Foucault's view, nothing fundamental happened with Pinel and his disciple Esquirol at the turn of the century from the eighteenth to the nineteenth. The scientific objectivity of the psychiatric domain was, in his view, a direct result of the social and epistemological expulsion of madness that occurred *à l'âge classique* more than a century before, as Swain recognizes ("pour Foucault ... le foyer du sens est en l'occurrence du côté de ce geste originel d'exclusion où s'est décidé pour toute une époque le destin de la folie"; 30; for Foucault ... what is really meaningful in this case has to do with that original gesture of exclusion that decided for a whole epoch the destiny of madness). Swain thinks Foucault is an excellent example of how difficult it is at times to perceive the novelty of a given historical development.

But there is much more to it than that. It is not simply that Foucault seems to be incapable of perceiving the radical novelty of the new critique of the old notion of total madness, what we must understand (and I am not sure that Swain herself does) is that Foucault's discovery of the historical expulsion of madness to the margins of society is itself inseparable from the old notion of total madness. The crisis of that old notion, and the crisis of the logic that drives the expulsion, are one and the same. The revolutionary novelty of which Swain speaks occurs precisely at the expense of the logic of expulsion. Therefore, if the old notion, in one way or another, had always been part of the way humanity had taken account of itself from its very beginning, then the expulsion was also there, in one way or another, from that same beginning. And my argument is, of course, that what is really at stake in the desacralization perceived by Swain is precisely the social and mental mechanism of expulsion. That is the mechanism that ceases to be anchored in the sacred and, as a result, loses its ultimate justification, thereby forcing the members of the new society to become aware of its ultimate arbitrariness. The vision of those alienated human beings, many of them chained to a wall, locked up for life, becomes increasingly intolerable.

Swain laments the fact that the famous story about Philippe Pinel liberating the insane from their chains at Bicêtre (which she proves never really happened) has taken precedence over his theoretical accomplishment, that is to say, the development of the idea that alienation is never total (47). However, there is a profound historical logic in the process that grants precedence to the liberating gesture over the theoretical or ideological accomplishment. Because the liberation, a direct manifestation of the desacralizing of the mechanism of expulsion, is indeed the basis for the development of the new idea of mental alienation, and not the other way around.

On his part, Foucault is well aware that the mechanism of expulsion that he discovers operates at the most basic level in the constitution of human society. The gesture that expels madness and the madman is one of those "obscure" gestures—he tells us—whereby a human culture constitutes itself by expelling something, which becomes, in the eyes of that culture, the "Outside":

> On pourrait faire une histoire des *limites*—de ces gestes obscurs, nécessairement oubliés dès qu'accomplis, par lesquels une culture rejette quelque chose qui sera pour elle l'Exterieur; et tout au long de son histoire, ce vide creusé, cet espace blanc par lequel elle s'isole, la désigne tout autant que ses valeurs. Car ses valeurs, elle les reçoit, et les maintient dans la continuité de l'histoire; mais en cette région dont nous voulons parler, elle exerce ses choix essentiels, elle fait le partage qui lui donne le visage de sa positivité; là se trouve l'épaisseur originaire où elle se forme. Interroger une culture sur ses expériences-limites, c'est la questionner aux confins de l'histoire, sur un déchirement qui est comme la naissance même de son histoire. (iv)

(It would be possible to write a history of *limits or margins*, of those obscure gestures, necessarily forgotten as soon as they are made, whereby a culture rejects something that will become the Outside. All along its history, this void it has dug out, this blank space by which it isolates itself, identifies it as much as its [cultural] values. Because the culture receives its values and maintains them within the continuity of its history. But in this region of which we want to speak, the culture makes its essential choices, creates the separation that gives it the face of its identity; there lies the original density where it forms itself. To question a culture about its limit experiences is to question it at the margins of its history, about a tearing apart that is like the birth itself of its history.)

The problem is that, for Foucault, at that deep level where those culture-creating "obscure gestures" of expulsion operate, nothing fundamental ever happened, at least not in the history of the West. The expulsion of the madman that, in his view, characterizes the end of the Middle Ages simply substitutes the madman for the leper of the previous era. In other words, there have been changes in the way Western society has justified to itself its expulsion of madness, and these changes have produced certain cultural by-products, and even beneficial side effects. But no change at all has occurred in the fundamental operation of the mechanism of expulsion itself.

One of the purely modal changes, to which we will return in a moment, occurs *à l'âge classique*, that is, from the end of the sixteenth century through the seventeenth century. At that time, it looks "as if madness had been *desacralized*" ("la folie, aux XVIIe siècle, est comme desacralisée"; 76). What Foucault calls the "tragic" character of madness disappears, and the old madness becomes *déraison*, unreason. It is as such, as unreason, that the classical age, the Age of Reason, expels madness. But it does not quite expel it in the old way, by throwing it out of the city, where, half-hidden from view, it roams unchecked, and from where it continues to haunt the consciousness of the city. Instead, it builds a wall around it. This is the age of "the great confinement":

L'internement détache la déraison, l'isole des ces paysages dans lesquels elle était toujours présente et en même temps esquivée. . . . Par ce seul mouvement de l'internement, la déraison se trouve dégagée. . . . Et la voilà par conséquent, *localisée*; mais dégagée aussi de ses ambiguïtés dialectiques et dans cette mesure-là cernée dans sa *présence concrète*. Le recul nécessaire est pris maintenant pour qu'elle devienne objet de perception. (127)

(Confinement segregates unreason, isolates it from those landscapes where it was always present and at the same time avoided. . . . By this movement of confinement alone unreason finds itself detached. . . . And therefore there it is, *localized*; but detached also from its dialectical ambiguities, and to that same extent contemplated in its *concrete presence*. A necessary retreat is now taken so that unreason may become an object of perception.)

It is as such, desacralized, reduced to silence, as pure "object of perception," that madness, having now become "unreason," will develop, according to Foucault, into a scientific object. This means that psychiatric science has no right to proclaim itself the liberator of the old madman, as if it were innocent of any participation in the old expulsion, because it owes its very existence to the most recent manifestation of that expulsion, "the great confinement."

S'il est vrai que l'internement circonscrit l'aire d'une objectivité possible, c'est dans un domaine déjà affecté des valeurs négatives du bannissement. L'objectivité est devenue la patrie de la déraison, mais comme un châtiment. Quant à ceux qui proffesent que la folie n'est tombée sur le regard enfin sereinement scientifique du psychiatre, qu'une fois libérée des vieilles participations religieuses et éthiques dans lesquelles le Moyen Age l'avait prise, il n'est faut pas cesser de les ramener à ce moment décisif où la déraison a pris ses mésures d'objet, en partant pour cet exil où pendant des siècles elle est demeurée muette; il ne faut pas cesser de leur remettre sous les yeux cette faute originelle, et faire revivre pour eux l'obscure condamnation qui seule leur a permis de tenir sur la déraison, enfin reduite aux silence, des discours dont la neutralité est à la mesure de leur puissance d'oubli. (129)

(If it is true that confinement circumscribes the area of a possible objectivity, it is within a domain already touched by the negative values of the expulsion. Objectivity has become the fatherland of unreason, but as a punishment. With regard to those who believe that madness did not come within the purview finally serene and scientific of the psychiatrist, until it was liberated from the old religious and ethical attachments in which the Middle Ages had placed it, one must continue to bring them to that decisive moment when unreason took on its objective measures, by departing for that exile where it has remained mute for centuries; one must continue to place before their eyes that original fault, and revive for them the dark condemnation that alone made it possible for them to have with regard to unreason, finally reduced to silence, a discourse the neutrality of which was a measure of their capacity to forget.)

Fundamentally, therefore, nothing has changed. The new scientific detachment is still the direct heir of the entire history of expulsion:

Elle s'instaure dans un mouvement de proscription qui rappelle, qui réitère même celui par lequel les lépreux furent chassés de la communauté médiévale. (129)

(It installs itself within a movement of proscription which recalls, which even reiterates, the one by which the lepers were chased from the medieval community.)

To be sure, if the new science were nothing but that, pure detachment, cold objectivity, Foucault would be right. But is it, really? Historically speaking, it is impossible to separate the development of the new scientific way of looking at madness from the long sustained efforts to liberate the madman, to soften his isolation, to recover and strengthen his basic humanity. In other words, it is impossible to separate the birth of the new science from the modern accelerated erosion of the expulsion mechanism.

Gladys Swain is much more sensitive than Foucault to the connection between the new science and the liberating movement, which she explicitly links to the desacralization of the new society, as we have just seen. But she does not go far enough in her critique of Foucault's blindness. In the end, the desacralizing change that she sees at work in the development of the new science is still essentially ideological: society, somehow, changes its idea of the Other, of that which is other to it; somehow it stops believing in the sacred character of otherness and, as a result, it can see the existential otherness in the experience of madness as a purely human phenomenon. To which Foucault could rightly respond that such an ideological change in the perception of otherness is in no way an argument against the existence or the effectiveness of the social expulsion of madness. Isn't the expulsion itself a mechanism for the creation of otherness? Why does Swain assume that desacralization of the Other would change anything fundamental, and, in particular, why would it stop or interfere with the logic of the expulsion? I think that Swain's text provides an inadequate answer to these questions because she never demonstrates any fundamental connection between the sacred and the expulsion.

In other words, nothing of a purely theoretical or ideological character would touch the core of the social and cultural expulsion of which Foucault speaks. I think he could always maintain the historical priority of the expulsion over theory or ideology. He might even claim priority for the expulsion over the sacred itself, although in that case he would have to explain the connection between the two, just as he does in the case of theory and ideology.

But for that he would need a theory of the sacred, which he does not have.

But, in a sense, all this is beside the point. It is certainly not my intention to engage in a full-fledged critique of Foucault's view of history. The fact is that while it is true that "[o]ne could make a history of limits, of those obscure gestures, by which a culture expels something, which becomes the Outside," one can also write a history of the eventual erosion of all such "limits." As Foucault knows better than most, the history of those expelling gestures is a history of fear. But it is also possible to write a history of hope.

Take, for example, the expulsion of madness in the form of the "great [classical] confinement," which Foucault considers the historical and epistemological ground on which modern psychiatry rests. Let us assume that he is right, that there would have been no scientific objectivity in regard to madness, or "alienation," without this expulsion. Still, not even Foucault can hide the fact that the new science of the troubled mind has contributed in a very significant way to undermine the inhumanity of the expulsion, and therefore to liberate both society and its alienated members from all kinds of fearful taboos. For the new scientist not only sees the object of his study, human alienation, much more clearly, he also sees the suffering of the alienated human being with the same degree of additional clarity. So, even if he is right, we must ask, what has prevailed in the end, the logic of the expulsion—rooted in fear—or its opposite? From the point of view of the "confined" madman, the answer is not in doubt. Therefore, if Foucault is right, if it was the "great confinement" that made the new science possible, that means that even the expulsion can be made to work against itself, that even its victories can be ultimately placed in the service of its enemy. For the real enemy of the expulsion of madness, the one who bears witness against it, is not Nietzsche or Artaud, but the spirit of hope.

Even though he is right when he detects in Cervantes a "cosmic" sense of madness, Foucault does not understand the hopeful intention that drives Cervantes's novel. Even though Cervantes is in full agreement with his age that the roots of madness lie in a defect of the will rather than of the rational faculty ("[Àl'âge classique] c'est dans la qualité de la volonté, et non dans l'intégrité de la raison, que réside finalement le secret de la folie"; Foucault, 168), he is no witness to the spirit of expulsion that, according to Foucault, leads to the classical modality of the "great confinement." Nor is this defect of the will necessarily associated with "evil intention" or "wickedness" in

Cervantes's view, even though Foucault is still largely right in his appreciation of the difference between the medieval conception of madness, in which it is linked to mythical or imaginary forms of evil, and that of the age of Cervantes and Shakespeare, in which madness still "communicates with [Evil] through the more secret channels of individual choice and evil intention" (168; communique avec [le Mal] par les voies plus secrètes du choix individuel et de l'intention mauvaise).

One of the things Cervantes insists on throughout the *Quixote* is that the knight, even though a fool, never means ill to anybody. He meant well both as Alonso Quijano, *el bueno*, and as Don Quixote de la Mancha. As we said in the Introduction, Foucault's observation applies much better to Avellaneda's conception of Don Quixote's madness. And this means that he misses the character and meaning of Cervantes's geniality, his intelligent and clear-sighted compassion. And, in a more general sense, he misses what is of paramount importance in Cervantes: the study of interpersonal relations, which in Cervantes is inseparable from an understanding of the roots of madness. For, as Cardenio tells us, at the root of his madness lies the fact that "holy friendship" has gone to heaven, leaving a deceitful appearance below. It is always "holy friendship" that vanishes from the scene as soon as madness appears, and whatever takes its place is, by definition, not to be trusted. In other words, a lot more than a change in the victimizing of the fool, from expulsion from the city to confinement, was taking place in Christian Europe at the time.

Foucault's Misreading of Cervantes and Shakespeare

This is why I think Foucault is ultimately wrong regarding the conception of madness that can be found in Cervantes and Shakespeare:

> In Shakespeare or Cervantes, madness still occupies an extreme place, in that it is beyond appeal. Nothing ever restores it either to truth or to reason. It leads only to laceration and thence to death. Madness, in its vain words, is not vanity; the void that fills it is a "disease beyond my practice," as the doctor says about Lady Macbeth; it is already the plenitude of death; a madness that has no need of a physician, but only of divine mercy ["More needs she the divine than the physician. God, God forgive us all!"].) (31)[3]

3. A shorter version of Foucault's *Folie et déraison* appeared in English with the title *Madness and Civilization*, translated by Richard Howard (New York, 1965). The quote is from this translation. Previous passages from *Folie et déraison* did not appear in the English version.

What makes Foucault think that Lady Macbeth's madness is, in Shakespeare's eyes, "beyond appeal . . . already the plenitude of death"? When the doctor says that "[t]his disease is beyond my practice" or that "she needs the divine more than the physician," he is not saying that she is completely beyond hope. As a matter of fact, he refers to such a hope, following the words just quoted:

> This disease is beyond my practice. Yet I have known those which have walked in their sleep who have died holily in their beds. (5.1.54–56)

Of course, the reader should remember that Lady Macbeth appears to be walking in her sleep, for though "her eyes are open . . . their senses are shut." And the doctor knows he is not just witnessing a simple case of sleep-walking. Otherwise, why would he add that "she needs the divine more than the physician," why would he ask God "to forgive us all"? He knows that

> Foul whisp'rings are abroad. Unnatural deeds
> do breed unnatural troubles. Infected minds
> to their deaf pillows will discharge their secrets.
> (5.1.66–68)

He knows that Lady Macbeth's disease is of the soul and not of the body. There is nothing that he, a "Doctor of Physic," can do about it. But that does not mean that nobody can. People with that kind of disease "have died holily in their beds." But they have to repent, since it is guilt that is driving them mad. And that is something nobody can do for them; the patient alone must do it for himself, as the same doctor will tell Macbeth:

> Macbeth.
> How does your patient, doctor?
> Doctor.
> Not so sick, my lord,
> as she is troubled with thick-coming fancies
> that keep her from her rest.
> Macbeth.
> Cure her of that!
> Canst thou not minister to a mind diseased,
> pluck from her memory a rooted sorrow,
> raze out the written troubles of the brain,
> and with some sweet oblivious antidote

cleanse the stuffed bosom of that perilous stuff
which weighs upon her heart?
Doctor.
Therein the patient
must minister to himself.

(5.3.37–46)

If there is a text in Shakespeare where it is particularly inappropriate to see madness as something "beyond appeal" or "already the plenitude of death," it is probably *Macbeth*. Because there the cause of madness is perfectly explicit: a haunting and unshakeable sense of guilt deriving from what is described as a most "unnatural" and hideous crime: the murder of a just and generous king by his most trusted vassal, and all the subsequent murders commited to cover up the first one. The cure for such a madness was always ready at hand: a remorseful and public admission of guilt and a readiness to accept all its consequences. In fact, the suggestion was already there in the exemplary death of the Thane of Cawdor, "a gentleman—says the king—on whom I built an absolute trust," who betrayed his country and his king, which is what Macbeth (appearing before the king as he finishes pronouncing those words) will do. If we had any doubts about this suggestion, we should remember that the first thing the king does when he hears of Cawdor's treason is to transfer the title "Thane of Cawdor" to Macbeth. The contrast between the old and repentant Cawdor, asking for forgiveness and facing his own death "as 'twere a careless trifle," and the new Cawdor, the unrepentant Macbeth, haunted till the end by a maddening sense of guilt, is undeniable and striking.

What is typically Shakespearian is the idea that this maddening sense of guilt is something new. It did not happen "i' th' olden time," that is to say, among "gentiles." This is how Macbeth puts it:

Blood hath been shed ere now, i' th' olden time,
Ere humane statute purged the gentle weal;
Ay, and since too, murders have been performed
Too terrible for the ear. The time has been
That, when the brains were out, the man would die.
And there an end. But now they rise again,
With twenty mortal murders on their crowns,
And push us from our stools. This is more strange
Than such a murder is.

(3.4.75–83)

He is hallucinating. He sees the ghost of his latest victim, Banquo, rise up before him and take his place at the banquet. Nobody else sees the ghost, of course. It is a purely inward experience, prompted by Macbeth's inner sense of guilt. That is what pursues him. In the old days, if you murdered somebody, somebody else might come after you, the next of kin, for example, or the gods who favored the murdered one, or the Harpies from hell. But this is different. It is the very image of your crime that pursues you: the murdered one rises up and comes after you. That is the strange thing, not the murder itself, but the fact that you cannot get rid of it.

And that means that the old system, in which the murder and its aftermath remained external to you, where it was assimilated and explained by the system itself, is not working any more. In the old system you had to be on guard, of course, against the consequences of your crime. But you did not go mad from guilt. What is new is not what Macbeth did, but Macbeth's madness because of what he did. And this madness, in Shakespeare's eyes, has extraordinary historical significance because it is inseparable from the fact that the old system has collapsed, which is to say that Macbeth is no longer an old figure, but one who has already been "gospelled," to use his own words. He belongs to a new time in which human violence against humans finds no transcendant justification and is therefore turned back upon its human agent. Murder becomes a mirror for the murderer. Macbeth can no longer see himself without seeing his crime. He is terrified of what he did, and so he keeps on killing, not so much in order to defend himself from others, but to defend himself from himself—that is to say, in order to hide his murderous violence from his own sight, which only compounds his problem endlessly.

The reason for Macbeth's madness after he has killed the king is the same that makes Hamlet hesitate constantly in the face of his supposedly "sacred" duty to kill King Claudius in order to avenge the death of his father. Macbeth's real madness is what truly lies beyond Hamlet's fake madness. His antics, his paralysis of the will, his obsessive desire to put on a show, in every sense of the word, in the hopeless hope that if he pretends strongly enough the show itself will become reality, do nothing but testify to the fact that such a "sacred" duty is no longer sacred. Revenge, even of the most "sacred" kind, the one demanded by a murdered father, has lost its ultimate justification. His revenge has been hopelessly "dulled" (see Girard, *A Theater of Envy*, 271). He has also been "gospelled."

Madness in Shakespeare is not something of unknown or mysterious origin that for unknown and mysterious reasons strikes a human being without warning, and "without appeal," like an irrevocable death sentence, "the plenitude of death." And it is precisely because it is *not that*, because it is not entirely without hope, that a recourse to "divine mercy" is possible. This recourse to divine mercy is not at all what Foucault imagines. It is not a gesture of despair, not a way of saying "this is hopeless, there is nothing we can do, it's entirely in God's hands." Quite the contrary: it is a sign of hope. It is a way of saying that something can still be done, that we can petition God for help in order to do something that *we* still can do. Maybe "the patient" cannot do everything by himself, but he can certainly ask for God's help. For that is precisely the way "the patient must minister to himself." In Shakespeare a madness without hope is simply hell, or an existential anticipation of it. Which means that "the patient," perhaps like Macbeth, who tries to fight the problem without God's help—that is, without repentance—may in fact keep accelerating the maddening vicious circle in which he has trapped himself beyond all hope. At this juncture the only pertinent question would be whether "the patient" has now reached the point when divine mercy becomes to him a diving board from which he takes the final dive headlong into hell, into eternal hopelessness. I do not know if Shakespeare asked himself that question or not. But there is no doubt that he believed in the possibility of a Christian resolution for madness. We see a clear example of that possibility in the case of mad Leontes in *The Winter's Tale.*

The Cure of Madness and the Death of Don Quixote

Of Don Quixote, too, it can be said that "he needs more the divine than the physician." For it is by the mercy of God that he is saved at the last moment:

> He woke up and cried out loudly: "Blessed be Almighty God, who has vouchsafed me this great blessing! Indeed his mercies are boundless, nor can the sins of men limit or hinder them."
>
> His niece . . . asked him: . . . "What mercies are these, or what sins of men?"
>
> "The mercies, niece," answered Don Quixote, "are those which God has shown me at this moment, mercies to which, as I have said, my sins are no impediment. My judgment is now clear and free from the gloomy shadows of ignorance with which

my ill-starred and continuous reading of those detestable books of chivalry had obscured it.

. . .

Now I am the enemy of Amadís of Gaul and of all the infinite brood of his progeny. Now all profane histories of knight errantry are odious to me. I know my folly now, and the peril I have incurred from the reading of them. Now, by God's mercy, I have learnt from my own bitter experience and I abominate them."

God saves him, by clearing his judgment, by freeing him from his ignorance, but not because God perhaps thought that it was a pity for such a nice guy to have an unsound mind. God's help simply means that mad Don Quixote was on his way to hell. Madness took him away from God. He was moving toward Amadís instead of moving toward God, placing Amadís in God's place, turning Amadís into a god. The newly restored Alonso Quijano's acknowledgment of God's mercy is also an act of repentance. He now detests books of chivalry, which he declares to be "abominable," as he detests his own sins. Madness is not morally neutral in Cervantes's eyes any more than it was in Shakespeare's eyes. It may not be driven by deliberate malice, but it is definitely a form of evil, and its roots are within the human heart. It is precisely because of its moral character, that is to say, because it does not imply a complete loss of inner freedom, an inevitable and predetermined process ("Sans recours. Rien ne la ramène jamais à la verité ni à la raison," writes Foucault), that Don Quixote's madness may be remedied; and in the search for such a remedy, the will and the acts of the individual play a fundamental role, even if Cervantes is also convinced—as I think he was—that the individual alone cannot extricate himself from the terrible labyrinth in which he has placed himself, even if Cervantes was convinced, therefore, that divine mercy was necessary.

What we have to understand is that such a hope, based on deep religious convictions, becomes, historically speaking, the necessary prelude for the development of a scientific attitude regarding mental alienation. That kind of science becomes possible only when one believes in the possibility of a cure on the basis of a human decision (including the decision to ask God for help, accompanied by the proper attitude), because the disease in question is also of human, not sacred, origin. To Cervantes and to Shakespeare, the possibility of finding a scientific cure for madness would have seemed the most natural and marvelous thing in the world. It would have never occurred to either of them that hope in science and hope in God were incompatible, as Foucault appears to believe.

Without denying at all the historical reality of the "great confinement"—a modern, attenuated manifestation of the old expelling mechanism—I do not think that is where we can find the ultimate key to the historical possibility of a science of the mind that would look for experimental methods to cure madness. I think that Foucault remains blind and insensitive to a very different kind of attitude regarding madness, an attitude that is almost contemporary to the dates of the "great confinement," and of which both Cervantes and Shakespeare offer a clear and striking testimony. Foucault neither sees nor understands what they saw and understood. On the other hand, he sees and understands perfectly what somebody like Avellaneda sees in madness. However, if we are to choose the "heralds of the new age," *buccinatores novi temporis*, I think we would do much better with Cervantes and Shakespeare than with Avellaneda.

To be sure, it is both tempting and quite possible to read Don Quixote's sudden and full recovery from his madness at the end of the novel as something miraculous, a direct intervention of God on behalf of a good man who had never meant to do an evil thing. But such an intervention simply consists in making Don Quixote see himself, understand himself, return to himself. In other words, the miracle would be that of Don Quixote's conversion. Because the cure for his madness is a reordering or restructuring of his understanding and his will in the direction of clarity and hope, an overcoming of anguish, a peaceful reencounter with himself. What more could the most advanced psychiatric intervention hope for or achieve?

Whether or not we call this conversion and cure a miracle is not very important. What is important is to understand that the possibility of this cure and conversion is something inherent to the way Cervantes conceives of Don Quixote's madness. Within Cervantes's conception it is practically impossible to imagine an ending such as Avellaneda's, with the madman locked up in an insane asylum. I think everybody would agree with that. And if this is so, which of these two ways of conceiving madness anticipates better the spirit of modern psychiatry? I do not think there can be any doubt about the answer.

CHAPTER V

De te fabula narratur

—My name, sir, is Bachelor Sampson Carrasco, and I come from the same village as Don Quixote de la Mancha, whose madness and folly have excited the pity of all who know him. I have been among those who have felt most concerned and, believing that his health depends on his resting at home on his own land, I devised a trick to make him stay there. . . .

—Oh, sir—said Don Antonio—may God pardon you the injury you have done the whole world in your attempt to restore the most amusing of all madmen to his senses. Don't you see, sir, that no benefit to be derived from Don Quixote's recovery could outweigh the pleasure afforded by his extravagances? However, I fancy that all the worthy Bachelor's arts will not be sufficient to restore so completely crazy a man to sanity. And if it were not a sin against charity, I should say that I hope Don Quixote may never be cured, for with his recovery we not only should lose his pleasantries but his squire Sancho Panza's as well.

(2.65)

The Compassionate versus the Poetic View

That conversation took place in Barcelona, following the defeat of Don Quixote at the hands of the Knight of the White Moon, that is, Bachelor

Sampson Carrasco. On his way back from Barcelona, Sampson stops by the Duke's palace and explains to the court what had happened:

> [He] said that Don Quixote was already on his way back to fulfill his pledge like a good knight errant, and retire to his village for a year, during which time, said the Bachelor, he might possibly be cured of his madness. It was that in fact which had caused him to assume his disguise, for it was a pitiful thing that a gentleman of Don Quixote's intelligence should remain a lunatic. (2.70.916)

There are those who want to cure Don Quixote out of compassion, in the spirit of charity, because it is the decent thing to do, and those who don't, those, that is, who believe, as Don Antonio says, "that no benefit to be derived from Don Quixote's recovery could outweigh the pleasure afforded by his extravagances." Not only do they think that curing Don Quixote would actually be a loss to anybody who has ever been delighted with his madness, they do not even think that a cure is possible. How can you hope to cure "so completely crazy a man?"

One wonders what Don Antonio would have said if he ever found out about the complete recovery of Don Quixote before he died. Cervantes does not tell us, but I think we can guess: "Good for him! I hope he is now in heaven. But what difference does that make to the rest of us? The important thing is that we now have a permanent record of his crazy knight-errantries, thanks to the efforts of a wonderful author, who put everything in writing. What does it matter how Don Quixote died? The important thing is how he still lives in the memory of everybody!" There may be slight variations from one Don Antonio to another, but I think we have the gist of it. Such a reaction is quite in keeping with what Don Antonio did say to Sampson, and what his words clearly implied. Furthermore, if you listen carefully to Don Antonio's likely response, you may notice a certain undertone of admiration. He may still be laughing at Don Quixote, but he is clearly attracted by what he sees, especially because what he sees has now been cast in a literary mold by a real master of the genre. He is already taking Don Quixote's foolishness perhaps more seriously than he would like to admit. We could say of him what Cidi Hamete says of the Duke and Duchess: "that he considers the mockers were as mad as their victims" (2.70.916). Don Quixote's madness may become rather contagious in unsuspected ways. And the point is that, along the path of this contagion, the initial mockers may easily become the earnest defenders of Don Quixote's "originality." Don Antonio is not only a representative of all those who laugh at Don Quixote, he is also the precursor of later defenders of Don Quixote's heroic status.

I think it is fair to assume that most readers of the novel over the centuries would agree with Don Antonio. And, of course, they would believe that they have the very existence of the novel and its universal fame to prove their case. Compared with that kind of appeal, what possible interest could there be in a cured Don Quixote, or in a Don Quixote prior to his going crazy from reading novels, that is, in Alonso Quijano, a colorless, run-of-the-mill hidalgo like many others, "one of those who . . ."? They are right. Such a character, all by himself, has no literary interest.

And yet such a character is clearly not without interest to those who want to cure him. To the people in his village, to "all who know him," Alonso Quijano was not a colorless, run-of-the-mill individual with nothing of interest to offer. Quite the contrary: he was well liked, an honest man, "el bueno," and, as Sampson tells us, intelligent, and well informed ("bien entendido"). This is why all who know him feel that his best chance of recovery is among his own people, "at home on his own land." One thing is certain: the poor man does not have a chance among the Don Antonios of this world.

It is precisely because "all who know him" like him, see him as worthy of respect, that they refuse to think there is no cure for him, and that they refuse to see his madness as complete and hopeless, as Don Antonio sees it. This means that Don Antonio does not really know him. All he perceives in Don Quixote is the literary glitter, the interesting story. That is what dulls everything that is good, and decent, and worthy of respect in the human being Alonso Quijano. It is only when you look at this human being through the eyes of literary fiction that he immediately becomes colorless, run-of-the-mill, totally uninteresting.

So now we understand, perhaps, why Alonso Quijano went crazy reading literary fiction! The vision he had of himself changed. He must have started to see himself as colorless, run-of-the-mill, and totally uninteresting (as a worthy precursor of the provincial lady Emma Bovary). He must have started seeing himself in the same way the worst enemies of his sanity would see him. And of course he ran away from dullness, and colorlessness, and sheer boredom, to become glittery and interesting. But, alas! instead of becoming a hero in the eyes of those before whom he wanted to shine, the Don Antonios of the world, he became an antihero. In a way, the Don Antonios betrayed him. Nonetheless, he still shone in their eyes, and eventually, through the centuries, his glow managed to convince them that the antihero was in reality a hero. But one way or the other, whether antihero or hero, the damage was done: everything that did not shine with literary glitter became dull and run-of-the-mill.

Fortunately, in the midst of all that glitter, Cervantes never forgot the hidden value, the basic goodness, the inner peace, the honest and clear judgment of Alonso Quijano. Fortunately, all of that was still there in Don Quixote, in spite of his literary-induced madness. We have it in the words of Sancho, who came to know his master quite well:

> There is nothing of the rogue in [my master]. His soul is as clean as a pitcher. He can do no harm to anyone, only good to everybody. There is no malice in him. A child might make him believe it's night at noonday. And for that simplicity I love him as dearly as my heart-strings, and can't take to the idea of leaving him for all his wild tricks. (2.13.547)

The "clean soul," the "lack of malice," the "child-like simplicity"—none of this was acquired through his readings of literary fiction. Those qualities belonged to what was left of Alonso Quijano in Don Quixote. But those qualities became largely inoperative, seriously impaired, when he became mad through his reading of fiction—which makes his madness all the more regrettable. Because we cannot help thinking that his child-like simplicity and trusting disposition made him a particularly easy target for literary glitter. Seduction is always bad, but the seduction of a child-like soul is particularly shameful. In other words, if the *Quixote*, the best novel ever written (British historian Thomas Macauley called it "the best novel in the world, beyond comparison"[1]), is also a deliberate denunciation of novelistic fiction, such a denunciation is more than a mere warning to the reader not to become a Don Quixote and make a fool of himself. The danger is not in what others may think, it is in what one does to oneself inwardly, the destruction or the impairment of that "clean soul" of which Sancho speaks.

The fact, unfortunate or happy, depending on how one looks at it, is that

1. Quoted in *Masterplots: Plot-Stories and Essay-Reviews from the World's Fine Literature*, ed. Frank N. Magill (New York: Salem Press, 1964), 4.966.

an Alonso Quijano with the soul of a child, trusting, at peace with himself and his neighbors, is not an appropriate subject matter for literary fiction. Every great novelist knows that. One may remember Alessandro Manzoni, for example, when, toward the end of his famous novel *I promessi sposi (The Betrothed)*, he remarks regarding his finally married protagonists: "From that point on, in fact, they led the most peaceful, happy and enviable lives; so much so that if I told you about it you would be bored to death."

The *genuine* child-like simplicity of DonQuixote (child-like simplicity can be faked, of course, like everything else, for selfish, duplicitous reasons) is as much beyond the pale of literary fictional interest as the horrible darkness and anguish at the core of madness, discovered at the end by Don Quixote, of which we spoke in the last chapter. And if we were dealing with a run-of-the-mill specimen of literary fiction, we would not see either one of those two things. But Cervantes's *Quixote* is not run-of-the-mill. In Cervantes's hands, literary fiction is made to become aware of that beginning and of that end. In other words, it is made to become aware of itself as a vehicle or instrument of the loss of innocence.

I realize, however, that there is a certain danger in speaking this way. For I do not think at all that Cervantes set out to demonize literary fiction, to simply hang the blame for Don Quixote's madness on the stuff he was reading, as if it carried within itself some sort of poison. Obviously that is not what *Don Quixote* is really about. Nothing would be gained by turning an exalted view of literary fiction into its opposite, the blessing into a curse. Because one of the things we are already finding out about Cervantes's novel is how very difficult it is to isolate the blame, to hang it anywhere. Don Quixote's madness is not directly about literary fiction: it is about human desire. Don Quixote is out of himself, has become alienated from himself, on the wings of desire, so to speak; he is in pursuit of a desire that was not only alien to him, coming to him from the outside, but that made the outside itself attractive and alienation desirable. It could have happened without the aid of literary fiction because all it takes is the existence of another desire within sight—in other words, the existence of other human beings. This means that the seeds or roots of the problem are in the very nature of human desire and the fact that human beings live together in groups. Specifically, human desire is not self-generated in isolation, it is fundamentally mimetic, as René Girard has demonstrated.

But, even though it is not the ultimate root of the problem, novelistic fiction tends to aggravate it, as it prolongs and intensifies the inherent mimetism of desire. Literary fiction intensifies desire because it is itself a form of intensified desire. It is the great presenter and announcer of desire, making it desirable by the very act of presenting it, without regard for the reality of its object, making the desire for the object more attractive than the object itself. Literary fiction feeds on the contagious character of desire. It is the only aspect of desire without which it cannot live. It can live without an object; in fact, it invents its own objects. But it cannot live without desire.

Contagious Singularity and the Power of Self-Deception

Don Quixote's literary madness, which is what gives him his novelistic singularity, is made up of literary desire. It is something like the crystallization of mimetic contagion. Such an attractive singularity has no other reality or substance than that given to it by desire, a desire already mediated by desire, brought to life by contagion. What gives literary singularity, attractive power, magnetism, as it were, to Don Quixote's madness is nothing in particular, nothing real—it is simply the intensity of its desire. That is what makes it contagious. And the power of its attraction is in direct proportion to the extent of the contagion. As more and more people desire it, the more desirable it becomes. In other words, the desire attracted by such an exhibition of desire is, in its very essence (or lack of essence), a multitudinous desire, the desire of the crowd.

It will help us to understand what we are dealing with if we see how some of Don Antonio's most distinguished descendants have been misled by Don Quixote's poetic singularity. I have chosen two names that most *cervantistas* will probably be surprised to see together: Don Miguel de Unamuno and Don Américo Castro. Two of the most distinguished critical readers of *Don Quixote* in the twentieth century, they seldom agreed with each other. Castro, for example, never understood Unamuno's Olympian disregard, even scorn, for Cervantes, whom he dismissed as the "mediocre" inventor of sublime and immortal Don Quixote.

Since the case of Unamuno is, by far, the more complex of the two, perhaps we should begin with Américo Castro.

Américo Castro's View of Don Quixote's Singularity.

Here is what I consider to be one of Castro's most characteristic passages:

El núcleo radical del *Quijote* yace en el hecho de que sus mayores personajes—meras figuras sin correlación con nada existente—parezcan seres vivos, "de carne y hueso," según es uso decir. . . . Desde la firme base de lo singularmente voluntarioso, se proyectan las existencias quijotescas en todas direcciones: fantasía, ilusión, ironía, discreción, violencia. Mas en cualquier momento pueden retrotraerse esas actividades a su punto de arranque, a lo singular humano, a lo que no es divisible con nada que exista fuera de él—simbólico, religioso, social o lo que fuere. Tras don Quijote y Sancho actúa la voluntad de ser lo que son, y no consienten que nadie les arranque esa su última e irreductible naturaleza, que agota su significación dentro de ellos mismos. Don Quijote es un hidalgo que tiene la extraña ocurrencia de marcharse a realizar unos actos inusuales; Sancho va con él porque quiere ir, y, cuando le enoja el oficio, amenaza con tornar a su casa a seguir siendo Sancho, vértice postrero, un último absoluto. . . . Bajo don Quijote yace una entidad última independiente; no necesita de nadie ni de nada para dejar de ser caballero andante. Todo ello se nos hace sentir dentro de la obra, y no es una deducción nuestra. (*Hacia Cervantes*, 274–75)

(The radical nucleus of *Don Quixote* lies in the fact that its main characters—mere figures of fiction without correlation with anything existing—look like living beings, "flesh and blood," as the saying goes. . . . From the firm base of the singularly willful, these quixotic lives project themselves in every direction: fantasy, illusion, irony, prudence, violence. But all those activities can be brought back at any moment to that which is humanly singular, that which is distinct from anything existing outside of it—symbolic, religious, social, or whatever. Behind Don Quixote and Sancho there is the will to be what they are, and they will not let anybody take away from them that ultimate and irreducible nature, which does not extend its meaning beyond themselves. Don Quixote is an hidalgo who conceived the strange thought of going out to perform some unusual things. Sancho goes with him because he wants to, and, whenever he feels uncomfortable with the job, he threatens to go back home to continue being Sancho, his end point, his absolutely irreducible end point. . . . Under Don Quixote lies an ultimate and independent entity. He does not need anybody or anything to stop being a knight-errant. All of that we are made to feel within the novel itself, it is not a deduction of ours.)

I think Castro's intuition touches on something of great importance. One senses that ultimate core of vital individuality in Don Quixote and Sancho.

No matter how foolish, gullible, or insane they may be, one has the feeling, indeed, that it would be possible for them to do otherwise. I could not agree more. That is the fundamental difference between Cervantes's *Don Quixote* and that of Avellaneda, as we already saw. But this is much more than just a feeling, and it extends beyond Cervantes's masterpiece. This "feeling" is also essential to most of the *Novelas ejemplares*. It is essential, for example, in *La gitanilla (The Little Gypsy Girl)*, or *Rinconete and Cortadillo*, or *La ilustre fregona (The Illustrious Kitchenmaid)*, to name some of the more obvious cases. It is a constant theme in Cervantes that nothing external can destroy the fundamental inner freedom of the individual without the individual's own consent. The idea, of course, was by no means peculiar to Cervantes. It is a perfectly orthodox belief, and it shows up everywhere during the dreaded Counter-Reformation. And yet Castro is still right when he senses that in this regard *Don Quixote* may be something special because in *Don Quixote* that ultimate and vital core of individual freedom is much more than an orthodox belief or theme. In *Don Quixote* we see that ultimate nucleus of freedom as something particularly precious because that is precisely what is at stake in the novel; we see it confronted with its own catastrophe, shining as a ray of hope, a lifesaver of last resort. It is a lifesaver not only for Don Quixote, the character, but for the novel as well. We see that the novel would not be what it is without it.

In other words, we can agree with Américo Castro, we can sense that "flesh and blood" quality in Don Quixote and Sancho, that ultimate core of individuality that looks so real, and then ask the question that "all who know" and like Don Quixote and care for him must ask: Is it not a pity that such a fine gentleman, with such a warm, attractive personality, should go out of his mind, should go crazy? Because he did go crazy, although this elementary observation is completely ignored by Castro. What does it mean to say that Don Quixote "is in no need of anybody or anything to stop being a knight-errant"? Does it mean that he can stop being mad anytime he wants? What kind of a madness is that? Castro remains blind to Don Quixote's insanity. The fact that he is mad does not really mean anything to the critic. How could it? He mistakes a last hope for a guarantee, the most precious and fragile core of individuality and freedom for a proclamation of unbounded confidence. Castro turns Don Quixote's individuality into something totally unreal, a myth, some sort of ontological absolute, "*un último absoluto*." In the face of that absolute, the reality, the credibility, of Don Quixote's madness evaporates. Castro does not believe in the reality of Don Quixote's madness any more than Don Quixote himself does. And we know why Don Quixote cannot see the reality of his madness. It has to do with the fact that he sees reality only through the medium of literary fiction. Has Castro's vision of Don Quixote become contaminated by Don Quixote's madness?

The fundamental problem with Castro's interpretation is that he only conceives his ultimate and irreducible individuality in opposition to external interference or danger, be it "symbolic, religious, social, or whatever," especially if the danger comes with a Counter-Reformation label. And he would indeed be right if the dangers conceived by Cervantes were of that nature. But madness cannot easily be blamed on external cultural or ideological impositions. Madness threatens from within. It touches the individual precisely at that deep nucleus where the very possibility of individuality is at stake. So it tends to be diluted or simply to disappear from Castro's critical horizon. Willful individuality ("lo singularmente voluntarioso") is such a solid foundation ("firme base") that nothing can change it or make it doubtful. Human will sets its own goals, the objects of its own desires, in whatever direction it chooses, and it moves toward them unimpeded. And at any moment, if it so chooses, it returns home to its essence, its self, its undivided and whole self, the only source of its desires and goals. How could such an individual ever go mad, be out of himself, be divided against himself? He could not, of course. For Castro, Don Quixote's madness is not madness at all. It is simply an expression of his indestructible individuality, a spontaneous manifestation of his willfulness.

Or is it really? Fortunately for us, Castro's capacity for accurate textual observation is much better than his theoretical consistency. And he has observed a most interesting phenomenon about Cervantes's characters. The importance of Castro's observation (he calls it "*La estructura del Quijote*") deserves to be quoted at length:

La vida de los personajes mayores creados por Cervantes sería como el foco en donde coinciden una incitación venida de fuera y las acciones emergentes provocadas por aquella incitación.

El personaje comienza ofreciéndose a primera vista como un caso típico, encuadrado en un marco genérico y sin una peculiaridad que lo saque de su molde: un hidalgo lugareño, un tosco labriego, una linda aldeana de familia acomodada . . . etc. Tales figuras son en sí mismas inertes, y carecen de la posibilidad de avivar nuestro interés, pues ninguna de ellas, por sí sola, se crea un nuevo y propio rumbo partiendo de *la forma interior de su figura*. . . . El paso de la manera de vida borrosa y estática al existir dinámico y encendido (personalizado) se origina con motivo de una incitación venida del exterior, y que súbitamente transmuta la figura típica en una persona animada por los más inesperados propósitos y dificultades. Sobre la "materia" genérica se proyecta una "forma" animante, que la crea y la recrea, infundiéndole un nuevo sentido. . . .

La figura ahí a la vista fue concebida por Cervantes como un diálogo entre un "logos" vivificante, formativo, y una figura humana dispuesta a recibirlo para así salir de la quietud y encerramiento en donde existe. . . .

Tema capital del *Quijote* es la interdependencia, la "inter-realidad," del mundo extrapersonal y del proceso de incorporárselo a la vida de una persona. Los fantásticos libros de caballería se vuelven contenido integrante de la existencia de don Quijote; las etéreas narraciones pastoriles incitan a la linda Marcela a correr vagarosa por la real-irrealidad de unos bosques. . . . (304–7)

(The life of the main characters created by Cervantes would be like a focus where two things coincide, an incitement coming from outside, and the emerging actions prompted by such incitement.

The character begins by appearing at first sight as a typical case, inserted within the frame of its genre, without any peculiarity that would make it distinct from its own mold: a countryside hidalgo, a rustic peasant, a pretty village girl from a well-to-do family . . . and so on. Such figures are in themselves inert, they do not have the capacity to spark our interest, since none of them creates, all by itself, its own new goal out of *the inner form of its character*. . . . The transition from a blurry and static mode of life to a dynamic and inflamed (personalized) existence finds its origin in the promptings of an incitement coming from the outside, which suddenly transforms [what was nothing but] a typical figure into a person animated by the most unexpected purposes and difficulties. Upon a generic "matter" an animating "form" is projected, which creates and recreates it, instilling a new meaning into it. . . .

The [literary] figure before our eyes was conceived by Cervantes as a dialogue between a vivifying, formative "logos," and a human figure ready to receive it in order to come out of its quiet and enclosed existence. . . .

A capital theme in *Don Quixote* is that of the interdependence, the "interreality," of an extrapersonal world, on the one hand, and the process of incorporating it into the life of a person, on the other. The fantastic books of chivalry become an integral content of Don Quixote's existence; the ethereal pastoral narratives incite pretty Marcela to roam ethereally over the real unreality of some forest. . . .)

I could not agree more. But, then, the "ultimate absolute" of individual "willful singularity" is not so ultimate or absolute. For it needs "an incitement coming from the outside" to manifest itself. Without such an external incitement the novelistic "figures are in themselves inert, they do not have the capacity to spark our interest," because they are by themselves incapable of creating their own goals "out of *the inner form of* [*their*] *character.*" In other words, without the external incitement those figures do not have any significant individuality. At best they are some kind of inert matter waiting for the "vivifying and formative" action of some kind of "logos" to descend upon them. But once they are excited by the vivifying incitement, they come alive before our eyes; these figures of fiction, "who do not correspond to anything real," all of a sudden look to us as very real, "made of flesh and blood, as the saying goes," they look "autonomous." That is to say, once they are incited, they become, in turn, our external incitement, and we, inert stereotypes, routine-bound, uninteresting couch potatoes that perhaps we are, reading about the comings and goings of these fictional, but lifelike, figures, become energized, passing "from a blurry and static mode of life to a dynamic and inflamed (personalized) existence." For the first time, each one of us, under the spell of such a fascinating autonomy and individuality, feels what it is to be a real individual; we feel different, we feel we can do things, we feel we can be somebody, and so on.

Does that sound familiar? Where have we read that story before? The story, that is, of somebody "coming alive" by reading day and night, voraciously, about fictional characters that looked so real he could practically see them, feel their presence, almost touch them . . . :

> "Well, with your permission," replied the priest, "I will reveal my scruple. It is this. I cannot by any means persuade myself, Don Quixote, that all this crowd of knights errant . . . have really and truly been people of flesh and blood living in this world. . . ."
>
> "That is another mistake," replied Don Quixote, "into which the many have fallen. . . . I have tried to expose this almost universal error to the light of truth. On some occasions I have not succeeded in my purpose; on others I have, by supporting my argument with *evidence so infallible that I might say I have seen Amadís of Gaul with my own eyes. . . .* [*And*] *in the same way I have drawn Amadís, I could, I think, depict and describe all the knights errant in all the histories in the world.*" (2.1.478–79)

Clearly Don Quixote's excitement can be truly contagious. And, apparently, that of Sancho can be contagious too. For he could also see the characters in his story as if they were for real, like the shepherdess Torralba in the story he tells that frightful night of the fulling mills,

> "[She] . . . was a plump high-spirited girl, and rather mannish, for she had a slight moustache—I can almost see her now."
>
> "Really, did you know her, then?" asked Don Quixote.
>
> "I didn't know her," replied Sancho, "but the man who told me this story said that it was so true and authentic that when I told it to anyone else I could swear on my oath that I had seen it all." (1.20)

If there was ever a time when it was literally true to say *de te fabula narratur*, this must be it. But this is not a joke. There is something very important to be learned here. Castro has unwittingly discovered the solution to the problem that his view of the *Quixote* poses. The problem is this: What is the nature of the "external incitement" needed to bring the fictional character to life? In principle, the "external incitement" could be anything at all, with one condition: it cannot look inert, topical, routine in the eyes of the inert, topical character waiting to receive its vivifying influence. By definition, an inert, routine-bound character is not going to be brought to life by what looks in its own eyes inert and routine-bound. Routine only generates routine. Therefore, by definition, the "external incitement" must be . . . , well, inciting, exciting. Only excitement generates excitement. Only desire generates desire. By definition, Don Quixote must see in what incites him the same thing that Castro sees in Don Quixote, the same coming to life, the same vivifying experience. The difference is not in kind but in degree. That is to say, Castro is not quite as "vivified" by what he reads as Don Quixote was.

To repeat, only desire generates desire—at least the kind of desire that keeps literary fiction alive, looking and feeling real. It is caught only by contagion. We become contaminated by Don Quixote's desire, just as he was contaminated with the desire that had previously contaminated and found expression in books of chivalry. For the desire that animates books of chivalry does not originate there either. It is no different from the desire of all the quixotic readers, who could have written them just as they read them. Remember that Don Quixote was very tempted to write a romance of chivalry, and would have carried out his project if he had not had other more important projects to take on. This literary desire has no place of origin. It is never original. It only exists as a form of contagion among individuals. To be more precise, it is a form of contagion among individuals chasing after, to use Castro's phrase, "the illusion of autonomy." These individuals always see that "autonomy" in somebody else, never in themselves, or see it in themselves only on the rebound, as they catch it from the other, which is, of course, an inescapable contradiction.

Individuality, autonomy, by contagion? What else could that be but an illusion, a way of blinding oneself to the truth? Such individuality, no matter how intensily felt, how existential, is only a measure of the subject's blindness toward himself. And the force driving such blindness, the blindfold over those eyes, is desire, the force of desire. In reality, the only thing that the subject feels under the appearance of individuality is his own desire, and precisely the desire that makes him dependent on the other, on somebody else's desire, which is, in turn, totally unoriginal—dependent, therefore, on a desire that only mirrors the subject's own, and so on and so forth. The subject is caught in a situation in which nobody has any faith in his own willful individuality (he remains "inert") unless he sees it in somebody else; and the more the same thing bounces from one to another, the more "alive" and excited they all become.

Castro speaks of "interdependence" or "interreality" as a "central theme of the *Quixote*," but he never speaks of contagion. He sees, for example, how "the ethereal pastoral narratives incite lovely Marcela to roam ethereally over the real unreality of some forest." But he does not notice one of the most striking features of the story about Marcela: as soon as lovely Marcela, to the surprise of everybody, decides to don shepherdess's attire and live out in the fields, her adventurous gesture is immediately imitated by a host of other girls in the village:

> But, lo and behold, when we least expected it, the modest Marcela suddenly appeared dressed like a shepherdess and, in spite of her uncle and everyone in the village who tried to dissuade her, off she went into the fields with the other girls in the village [*con las demás zagalas del lugar*] and started to tend her own flock. (1.12.94)

Needless to say, the same thing happens among the young men of the region as soon as Chrysostom, Marcela's devoted worshipper ("he no longer loved her, he adored her"), follows her in dutiful imitation, dressed as a shepherd. First his close friend, Ambrosio, and then many others take to the fields:

I couldn't truthfully tell you how many rich youths, gentlemen, and farmers put on the same dress as Chrysostom, and wandered about these fields, courting her. . . .

If you were to stay here a while, sir, one day you would hear the hills and valleys echo with the lament of her rejected suitors. . . . Here one shepherd sighs; there another moans; from the distance you can hear songs of love; from near at hand dirges of despair . . . ; and over every one of them the beautiful Marcela triumphs, free and unconcerned. (1.12.94)

There are moments when the pastoral scene the goatherd is describing clearly reaches grotesque levels:

There will be one spending all the hours of the night seated at the foot of an oak or of a crag, never closing his tear-dimmed eyes till the sun finds him there next morning, sunken and lost in his thoughts; and there will be another giving no rest or truce to his eyes, but lying stretched on the burning sand in the most sultry heat of a summer afternoon. . . .

Cervantes is deliberately pushing the effects of the contagion into ridiculous caricature to emphasize the absurdity of it all. But let us not forget that these exagerated effects of the contagion, quite capable of triggering laughter in the reader, are simply a collective expansion of that "adoration," well beyond the normal expression of love, that leads Chrysostom to commit suicide, an event that is not meant to be laughable. No wonder the narrator compares the turbulence and damage done to the village by this unbelievable situation to the plague ("[Marcela] does more damage in these parts than if the plague had got in").

They all blame Marcela for it. But her role is simply that of a triggering mechanism. Once the contagion spreads, it is quite capable of sustaining itself through the reciprocal imitation of one another's desire. They do not really need the presence of Marcela to keep it going. Contagion feeds on contagion. This is precisely what happens in that other "pastoral" story, also told by a goatherd, almost at the end of Part 1, the story of Anselmo, Eugenio, the narrator, and beautiful Leandra, whose fame as a beauty seemed to surpass even that of Marcela, for "it reached to distant cities, and even entered the royal palace and came to the ears of many sorts of people, who would come to see her from all parts, as if she were a rare sight or a wonder-working image" (1.51.446).

As will be remembered, this rare icon of a woman, so rich and famous, fell for the colorful tinsel, fake military decorations, tall tales, and pretty voice of a deceitful soldier, who, after they eloped, robbed her of everything down to her underwear and abandoned her in a cave. He was the "external incitement" of wondrous Leandra. But the point is that the typical Arcadian scene we have just witnessed in the story of Marcela is here repeated and expanded *after the object of everybody's desire and adoration has been taken out of the picture completely*. For Leandra was immediately taken away and shut up in a nunnery:

> In Leandra's absence our sorrow increased. . . . In the end [Anselmo] and I agreed to leave the village and come to this valley, where we spend our lives among the trees. . . . Here we give vent to our passion. . . . Many others of Leandra's suitors have followed our example, and come to these wild mountains to follow the same employment; so many that this place seems to have become the pastoral Arcadia, for it is so crammed with shepherds and sheepfolds that there is no corner in it where you will not hear the fair Leandra's name. One man curses her and calls her fickle . . . ; another denounces her as forward and light; yet another absolves and pardons her; one more tries her and condemns her; one celebrates her beauty; another execrates her character; in fact all disparage her and all adore her; and the madness extends so far that some complain of her disdain *without ever having spoken to her*, and some bewail their fate and suffer the maddening disease of jealousy, for which she never gave anyone any cause. For, as I have said, her fault was discovered before her infatuation was known. There is not a hollow rock, nor river bank, nor shade of a tree that is not occupied by some shepherd or other recounting his misfortunes to the wind; and echo repeats Leandra's name wherever it can sound; the hills ring with Leandra, the streams mumur Leandra, and Leandra keeps us all distracted and enchanted, hoping against hope, and fearing without knowing what we fear. (1.51.449–50)

The Leandra that this crowd of feigned Arcadian shepherds worships is no more real than Don Quixote's Dulcinea. That is to say, the "madness" that spreads far and wide among these people is of the same character as that of Don Quixote. It is the madness of a desire that fictionalizes its object, destroys its reality. It does not make any difference whether lovely Marcela or beautiful Leandra are really there or not. What these madmen see in these beautiful creatures is not real. They could all use Don Quixote's words about Dulcinea: "Así que, Sancho, por lo que yo quiero a Dulcinea del Toboso, tanto vale como la más alta princesa de la tierra" (1.25; So, Sancho, for what I want of Dulcinea del Toboso she is as good as the greatest princess in the land).

Of course, the beautiful creatures themselves take the lead in this process of fictionalization of reality. For what they see in their "external incitement," be it pastoral novels or the swindler soldier Vicente de la Roca, is also a fiction—an attractive literary fiction, we may add. Because even this pretentious liar of a soldier, "who kept us all open-mouthed hanging on the exploits he described to us," was also "something of a musician," and "his accomplishments did not stop here, for he had also a talent for poetry." In other words, there was something artistic and literary about the fellow, which must have contributed powerfully to his capacity for incitement.

Castro's description of the "incitement" process as that of an external "vivifying form" or "logos" descending upon a receptive "matter," whereby this "matter" is formed, molded, into a real, that is, lifelike, individuality that gives the "illusion of autonomy," just will not do when you see dozens and dozens of identical "individualities" springing up all around you. There are far too many of them to maintain the "illusion of autonomy" in the eyes of any observer who has not yet fallen prey to the same contagion.

But, once again, what is it that they all see in the "external excitement" that makes it look so attractive, so real? What is it, for example, that Marcela sees in pastoral Diana, or Leandra in Vicente de la Roca, or all the others in either Marcela or Leandra? The answer, once again, is very simple: they see autonomy, self-sufficiency, singularity, differentiation. The "external incitement" comes to reveal to the unformed individual-to-be, to the inert personality caught up in everyday routine, something of which he or she may not have been fully aware, but which always lurks darkly in the background as a dreaded suspicion, namely, that he or she is indeed, as he or she had always dreaded, a nobody, a totally uninspiring individual, an empty personality; nothing at all like the "external incitement," which in the same gesture reveals itself to be somebody, different, full of itself, and therefore irresistibly attractive.

This is important. It is not the case that the "external incitement" comes to reveal to the inert individual that he or she is not inert, showing him or her his or her own worth, value, dignity, of which perhaps he or she was not aware. It is not God who speaks with the voice of the "external incitement," because the voice of God is only heard internally. The "external incitement," therefore, only reveals to the individual his or her own degradation. He or she follows the "external incitement" to hide the shameful "truth," to escape the accusation. His or her movement has little to do with real enthusiasm, and a lot to do with despair. If we pierced the protective rhetorical surface of Don Quixote's madness, that is what we would find. In fact, that is what he does find in the end. But, as we have already indicated, there are plenty of indications of that despair in the immediate vicinity of Don Quixote.

In other words, the spectacle of those "figures . . . in themselves inert [that] do not have the capacity to spark our interest," as Castro defines them, is a spectacle, a vision, already mediated, configured, by the contagion of the "external incitement." This is how they look when seen through such an external lens. And, of course, that must also be the way the characters see themselves, once they fall under the spell of the "external incitement." That is precisely how they lose what we might call their "original innocence," that childlike, trusting, malice-free disposition that Cervantes is still capable of seeing in them even through their very own foolishness. The "external incitement" shames them out of it. That innocence is turned into a stumbling block on their path, *una piedra de escándalo*. As the "external incitement" "vivifies" them, they become scandalized. It is in connection with the innocence of children that Christ pronounces those terrible words against scandal: "Whoever scandalizes one of these little ones who believe in me, it would be better for him to be drowned with a millstone around his neck, in the depths of the sea" (Matthew 18.6).

CHAPTER VI

Unamuno's Enthusiastic *Quijotismo* and the Envy of Cain

The crowd is untruth. Therefore was Christ crucified, because he, even though he addressed himself to all, would not have to do with the crowd. . . . And therefore everyone who in truth will serve the truth, is eo ipso in some way or other a martyr.

(Kierkegaard, *The Point of View*, 109)[1]

As soon as the category "the single individual" goes out, Christianity is abolished. . . . If this happens, then the God-man is a phantom instead of an actual prototype.

(Kierkegaard, *Journals and Papers*, 2.282)

Let us now turn to Unamuno, who is a much more complex case than Castro. Our own reading of *Don Quixote* from now on will be guided in part by our analysis of Unamuno's *quijotismo*.

While Américo Castro appears to be totally impervious to the value of Don

1. Quoted in Bellinger, 81

Quixote's innocence, Unamuno was clearly quite sensitive to it. He spoke repeatedly of Don Quixote's goodness and profound lack of malice. But that only served to make Don Quixote's madness appear in his eyes even more heroic, because Don Quixote's innocence—Unamuno thought—made his madness heroic in the eyes of God. In other words, not only did he see in Don Quixote's madness no danger to his innocence, he actually saw his madness as an extension, a magnification, of his inborn goodness to a heroic degree.

But Unamuno was no fool. It is important to emphasize from the start that he understood perfectly well that was not the way Cervantes saw Don Quixote's madness or the way it related to his innocence. Thus he accused Cervantes of being narrow-minded, mediocre, incapable of understanding the true meaning and greatness of Don Quixote's heroism, or, to be more precise, the truly heroic character of Don Quixote's madness:

> [Caso] típico de un escritor enormemente inferior a su obra, a su Quijote. Si Cervantes no hubiera escrito el *Quijote* . . . apenas figuraría en nuestra historia literaria sino como ingenio de quinta, sexta o décimotercia fila. . . . Cada vez que el bueno de Cervantes se introduce en el relato . . . es para decir alguna impertinencia o juzgar malévola o maliciosamente a su héroe. (*Obras completas*, 3.577–78)

> ([Cervantes is a] typical [case] of a writer enormously inferior to his work. If Cervantes had not written the *Quijote* . . . he would barely figure in our literary history as a writer of fifth, sixth, or thirteenth rank. . . . Every time good old Cervanters intervenes in his novel . . . it is to say something impertinent, or to judge his hero in a malicious way.)

I have no doubt that Unamuno would accept Sancho's words about Don Quixote's childlike absence of malice as being Cervantes's own words. It was the heroic character of his Quixote that mediocre Cervantes could not understand, and he couldn't understand it precisely because of his mediocrity. Unamuno thought that while Cervantes could conceive of an Alonso Quijano, *el bueno*, he could not conceive of Alonso Quijano's goodness to a heroic degree. Such heroic goodness would only look like madness in the eyes of mediocrity.

I think, however, that Unamuno's visceral anti-Cervantism is far more revealing of what is really happening in the novel than most of what the majority of defenders of Cervantes say. I think that Unamuno felt quite accurately what Cervantes was trying to do in his novel, and fully understood that such an intention was at its very core anti-Unamunian. Clearly, he did not like that at all. It is as if Cervantes would have tried to take away from him, from Unamuno, his own Quixote. There are moments in Unamuno's anti-Cervantine diatribe when one cannot help thinking that he feels Cervantes's ironic antiquixotism as something like a personal attack. And, in a certain sense, he was right. In other words, I think that implicitly, indirectly, in spite of himself, Unamuno can be an excellent guide to some of the most fundamental insights in Cervantes's novel.

In order to fully understand Unamuno's *quijotismo* we must keep in mind that he attached great religious significance to the heroic figure of Don Quixote. He tells us that Don Quixote, like any other true hero, can only be a hero insofar as he hears the voice of God internally and, as a result, his knightly adventures reveal their deepest level of meaning only when viewed as an answer to the divine call. To Unamuno, Don Quixote is "un loco sublime," and—borrowing Kierkegaard's phrase—a "knight of faith." At some point, half-jokingly, in his 1923 essay "Saint Quixote of La Mancha," he proposes that Don Quixote be elevated to sainthood by the Catholic Church. And without joking, in his "Don Quixote's Beatitude," he talks rather movingly of Don Quixote's fraternal encounter with Christ after the knight's death at the end of the novel:

> What he saw was Jesus Christ, the Redeemer. Don Quixote saw Him dressed in a purple mantle, a crown of thorns, and a reed scepter, as when Pilate, the great mocker, exposed Him to the multitude and said: "Behold the Man!" Jesus Christ, the Supreme Judge, appeared to Don Quixote dressed as He had been when mocked by the mob. . . .
>
> And he saw Christ upon a hill, at the foot of an olive tree, bathed in the light of the dawn of a spring morning, and he heard—it was as if the heavens sang—these words: "Blessed are the mad, for they shall be surfeited with reason!" (*Our Lord Don Quixote*, 427–28)

In Unamuno's view of Don Quixote's madness, "la locura de la cruz" (*Vida*, 111), the madness of the cross, is never far behind as a background, even though a basic sense of Christian prudence always kept him from fully equating the two. Toward the end of his life, commenting on his long-standing quixotism, he said the following:

> En cuanto a Don Quijote, ¡he dicho ya tanto! . . . ¡me ha hecho decir tanto! . . . Un loco, sí, aunque no el más divino de todos. El más divino de los locos fue y sigue siendo Jesús, el Cristo. (*Cómo se hace una novela*, 117)

(With regard to Don Quixote, I have said so much already! . . . [H]e has made me say so much! . . . He was a madman, yes, although not the most divine. The most divine of all madmen was and continues to be Jesus, the Christ.)

But this basic prudence, which causes him to maintains a certain distance between Don Quixote and Christ, practically vanishes when it comes to comparing the Manchegan knight with his saintly "contemporaries," such as Ignatius of Loyola and Teresa of Avila. References to and comparisons with these two saints in particular are constant—indeed, too numerous to mention.[2] The fact that the two saints, as we know, were avid readers of books of chivalry before they became committed followers, "soldiers," of Christ was, needless to say, of crucial importance in Unamuno's deeply personal reading of *Don Quixote.*

In his *Vida de Don Quijote y Sancho* he urges us to go, nay, to march, to "the tomb of our lord Don Quixote" and rescue it "from the power of bachelors, priests, barbers, and canons," and all other "gentlemen of Reason" (13; "hidalgos de la Razón"), in whose hands the foolish knight has remained for too long. This march, this "holy crusade," will, of course, be fully quixotic. So the marchers will not listen to anybody who demands a rational or a reasonable explanation, or to the insidious voice of those who may ask, "Where is the knight's tomb? In what direction does it lie?" Just follow the star! Have faith! Above all, do not analyze! If you stop to make analyses, the whole enterprise will be ruined.

An unquenchable thirst for immortality—says Unamuno—drives the faith of the true quixotic marcher or crusader, a thirst that no amount of rational logic will ever be able to eliminate:

Y así vamos a la toma de una nueva afirmación sobre los escombros de la que nos desmoronó la lógica, y se van amontonando los escombros de todas ellas, y un día, vencedores, sobre la pingorota de este inmenso montón de afirmaciones desmoronadas, proclamarán los nietos de nuestros nietos la afirmación última y crearán así la inmortalidad del hombre. (*Vida*, 120)

(And thus we struggle on to a new affirmation over the rubble of the one that logic has broken down; the rubble keeps on mounting, but one day we will triumph, on the

2. In his introduction to Kerrigan's translation of *Vida*, Walter Starkie refers to Aubrey Bell's view that "*The Life of Don Quixote and Sancho* is . . . a kind of lay sermon engrafted on the text of *Don Quixote* with parallels from the life of Ignatius of Loyola" (xxx).

pinnacle of this immense mountain of crumbled affirmations, until the grandsons of our grandsons may proclaim the final affirmation and thus create the immortality of man. [*Our Lord Don Quixote*, 169])

Thus man "creates" his own immortality by the very strength of his faith, a faith whose "affirmations" constantly crumble under the blows of rational logic. But as one affirmation crumbles, faith creates a new one, and so on generation after generation. In the end faith stands victorious atop that immense pile of debris caused by the relentless attack of reason on the affirmations of faith. (Of course, we have to believe in such a final victory of faith strictly on faith, a faith that is not supported by anything except its own blind intensity.)

The very logic of Unamuno's argument makes Don Quixote's foolish faith, foolish affirmation of himself as a knight, all the more genuine and significant the more foolish it appears to be, that is to say, the more it clashes with empirical reality, with anything standing beyond the pale of pure individual self-affirmation. At no time is Don Quixote more himself, more of a unique individual, than when he appears to be most insane. And even more importantly for Unamuno, at no other time is he—the unique individual Don Quixote, precisely because of his uniqueness—closer to God. Because it is indeed before God, and only before God, that the uniqueness of the individual human being is revealed. It is before God that the individual, in "fear and trembling," is made responsible for every single thought he ever had and every movement of his will. Or, as Kierkegaard said in his *Christian Discourses*:

> From "the others" a person . . . finds out what the others are. . . . "The others" in turn do not know what they themselves are either but continually know only what "the others" are. There is only one who completely knows himself . . .—that is God. And he also knows what each human being is in himself, because he is that only by being before God. The person who is not before God is not himself either. . . . If one is oneself by being in the one who is in himself, one can be in others and before others, but one cannot be oneself merely by being before others. (40)

Unamuno was attracted to Kierkegaard's Christian existentialism. He even read the Danish thinker in his native language. Reading certain passages in Kierkegaard it is easy to see why Unamuno may have thought them relevant to his view of Don Quixote. *Fear and Trembling* is especially noteworthy in this regard. Take, for example, the following passage, in which Kierkegaard explains the difference between the hero's path and the higher calling of the knight of faith:

[The knight of faith] knows also that higher than this [i.e., the ethical, the universal] there winds a solitary path, narrow and steep; he knows that it is terrible to be born outside the universal, to walk without meeting a single traveller. . . . Humanly speaking, he is crazy and cannot make himself intelligible to anyone. And yet it is the mildest expression to say that he is crazy. If he is not supposed to be that, then he is a hypocrite, and the higher he climbs on this path, the more dreadful a hypocrite he is. (86)[3]

The following words by Unamuno were probably inspired by Kierkegaard's idea of the existential situation of the knight of faith:

Puede el héroe decir: "yo sé quién soy," y en esto estriba su fuerza y su desgracia a la vez. Su fuerza, porque como sabe quién es, no tiene por qué temer a nadie, sino a Dios, que le hizo ser quien es; y su desgracia, porque sólo él sabe, aquí en la tierra, quién es él, y como los demás no lo saben, cuanto él haga o diga se les aparecerá como hecho o dicho por quien no se conoce, por un loco.

Cosa tan grande como terrible la de tener una misión de que sólo es sabedor el que la tiene y no puede a los demás hacerles creer en ella; la de haber oído en las reconditeces del alma la voz silenciosa de Dios, que dice: "tienes que hacer esto," mientras no les dice a los demás: "este mi hijo que aquí veis, tiene esto que hacer." . . . Y como el héroe es el único que lo oye y lo sabe, y como la obediencia a ese mandato y la fe en él es lo que le hace, siendo por ello héroe, ser quien es, puede muy bien decir: "yo se quién soy, y mi Dios y yo sólo sabemos y no lo saben los demás." Entre mi Dios y yo—puede añadir—no hay ley alguna medianera; nos entendemos directa y personalmente, y por eso se quién soy. ¿No recordais al héroe de la fe, a Abraham, en el monte Moria. (*Vida*, 38)

(The hero can truly say, "I know who I am!," and herein lies his strength and at the same time his misfortune. His strength because, since he knows who he is, he need fear no one except God, who made him who he is; and his misfortune, for he alone on this earth knows who he is, and since other people do not, everything he says or

3. It should be pointed out that Kierkegaard never made the association between the "knight of faith" and Don Quixote: "Miguel de Unamuno and W. H. Auden were two of the best-known authors to characterize the Manchegan knight by this term ['knight of faith']. . . . However, it should not be forgotten or overlooked, as it sometimes seems to be, that nowhere in *Fear and Trembling* is Don Quixote mentioned by name and that nowhere in Kierkegaard's other writings . . . is Don Quixote called a 'knight of faith' or vice versa" (Ziolkowski, "Don Quixote and Kierkegaard," 131). See also, by the same author, *The Sanctification of Don Quixote*, passim.

does will appear to them the words or acts of a man who does not know himself, of a madman.

It is a terrible thing, as terrible as it is great, to have a mission known only to oneself and in which others cannot be made to believe; to have heard in the secret places of the heart the silent voice of God saying, "This you must do," when He does not at the same time tell others, "My child, whom you see, has this to do." . . . And since the hero is the only one to hear it and know it, and since his obedience to this mandate and his faith in it are what make him what he is, so that he is himself and [by being himself] a hero, he may very well say, "I know who I am, and only my God and I know, and the others do not." Between my God and I—he might add—there is no mediating law. We understand each other directly and personally. Don't you remember the hero of the faith, Abraham, on Mount Moriah? [*Our Lord Don Quixote*, 49–50])

But Unamuno's Christian existentialism is of a rather peculiar sort that certainly would be difficult to shape into any kind of system. Unamuno himself declared repeatedly that he hated systems and that he did not want to be systematic. So we should not attempt what may be a hopeless task. But there are here and there some points about which Unamuno appears to be quite consistent. One of those points is of special relevance to our study. It concerns his "quixotic" understanding of Kierkegaard's knight of faith.

The difference between Kierkegaard and Unamuno on this point is already apparent in the passages quoted above, and we should expand on it. But it must also be noticed here that there are passages in Kierkegaard of a quasi-prophetic character regarding the possibility of an assimilation of Christ to Don Quixote. He could clearly see that in a world only nominally Christian, from which the spirit of the Christian word has vanished, Christ himself would inevitably be perceived as some sort of quixotic figure. In other words, in such a purely nominal Christian world, Christ becomes a poetic phantom who looks precisely like Don Quixote. The following quote from Kierkegaard's *Journals* is a revealing anticipation of that kind of grotesque situation that Unamuno would desperately try throughout his life to take in all seriousness:

When secular sensibleness has permeated the whole world as it has now begun to do, then the only remaining conception of what it is to be Christian will be the portrayal of Christ, the disciples, and others as comic figures. They will be counterparts of Don Quixote, a man who had a firm notion that the world is evil, *that what the world honors is mediocrity or even worse*. But things have not yet sunk so deep. Men crucified Christ

> and called him an enthusiast, etc.—but to make a comic figure of him! Yet this is unquestionably the only logical possibility, the only one, which will satisfy the demands of the age once the secular mentality has conquered. Efforts are being made in this direction—for the world progresses! (1.132–33; my emphasis)

It is interesting to notice Kierkegaard's perception of mad Don Quixote as a man convinced that the world is bad, and that the only thing that interests the world, the only thing that the world holds in high regard, is mediocrity. Is that not precisely the reason why Unamuno identifies with Don Quixote and despises "mediocre" Cervantes?

But let us look more closely at the significant differences between Kierkegaard's knight of faith and Unamuno's heroic Don Quixote. To begin with, the Kierkegaardian knight of faith is most definitely not a traditional heroic figure. He does not stand out like Don Quixote. In fact, he could be practically anybody, "a tax collector," for example, or "an accountant." "[If] one did not know him, it would be impossible to distinguish him from the rest of the congregation. . . . [W]hen one meets him on the Beach Road one might suppose he was a shopkeeper taking his fling . . . for he is not a poet, and I have sought in vain to detect in him the poetic incommensurability" (*Fear and Trembling*, 50). The hero, on the other hand, whether tragic or epic, is recognized by everybody. His gesture is, by definition, a public one, because he moves in the realm of the ethical, which is the realm of the universal. He sacrifices himself to express the universal, which everybody understands. Who wouldn't cry with Agamemnon who, submitting to the will of the gods, sacrifices his own daughter, beautiful Iphigenia? Everybody, even Iphigenia herself, understands that this awful deed is done for the public good. The hero sacrifices the individual for the benefit of the universal, the ethical, the public good.

But who can understand Abraham's faith? That is Kierkegaard's fundamental question. God gave him a son, Isaac, when his wife, Sarah, was too old to become pregnant, and God promised him a long and plentiful progeny. Now God calls on him, and him alone, to sacrifice Isaac, "your only son, whom you love," and gives him no explanation whatsoever. How does that terrible request square with God's promise? It does not make sense, either logically or ethically. And what if Abraham was mistaken? What if it was a temptation of the devil? And who would believe Abraham if he told them, in view of the irrational and ethical absurdity of the request? Wouldn't they all try to shake his faith and convince him that it was absurd to believe that such a command could come from the same God who made the promise? How can he be sure? But Abraham believes. Not knowing how he knows, he does know it was God who spoke to him. In spite of God's horrible request, he does not hesitate for a moment. For if he hesitated and still sacrificed Isaac, he would be crushed under his own suspicion of murder. Against all logic, he never stops believing that God somehow will give him Isaac back and keep his promise. For, as Kierkegaard points out, it is not simply that he is ready to sacrifice to God anything dear to him. He expects that God will give him everything He promised. But Abraham does not question, does not weep, does not complain, and does not tell anybody because nobody could understand. He does not understand either, but he has faith in God. He has a faith that now God is putting to the test, as only God can, because only God can call a man, single him out, in the way Abraham, the father of the faith, was singled out and put to the test.

Unamuno's hero, on the other hand, is someone not only very different from Abraham, but in some fundamental sense the very opposite. According to Unamuno, "It is a terrible thing to have a mission known only to oneself and in which others cannot be made to believe; to have heard in the secret places of the heart the silent voice of God saying, 'This you must do,' when He does not at the same time tell others, 'My child, whom you see, has this to do.'"

What is so terrible about that? Clearly the terrible thing has nothing to do with the character of the mission entrusted by God to the hero, as in the case of Abraham. In Unamuno, whatever that mission may be is not important. God's command is no cause for anxiety in the hero, since God does not demand anything unreasonable. For Unamuno the terrible thing is simply that God says "Do this," whatever "this" may be, but does not tell the others. In other words, the hero's relationship to God appears to be totally unproblematic. There is complete agreement between the two of them: "We understand each other directly and personally," says the hero, "and that is why I know who I am."

Clearly God made the Unamunian hero and remains solidly on his side. It's . . . the others who are not on his side! So perhaps there is a test, after all, involved in Unamunian God's command. Maybe God's silence with regard to the others is His way of putting the hero's strength to the test. That is to say, God tells the hero, "This is who you are and this is what you have to do," and then He leaves the hero alone in the midst of all those others who do not recognize him for who he is. That must be the test. Otherwise what could be the meaning of God's silence, why would God not tell the others, or why would the others not understand and believe him if the hero told them? The test, therefore, must be, as follows: Will the hero keep his faith in God, and therefore in himself, before all those skeptical eyes who do not believe a word he says and think he is crazy? If he does not, if he succumbs before the hostility of the others, what happens to him? What does it mean to succumb to the others, to fail the test? Can he fail the hero's test and still be a hero? That would not make any sense. We must assume that if he fails to maintain his heroic status, if the others win over him, he will simply become one of them, a part of the crowd, and lose his own unique God-given individuality. Thus being oneself includes not being like the others, resisting the power, the pressure, of the others. The hero's choice is therefore clear: either God or the others.

However, this is not at all the way Unamuno puts it. In Unamuno's scheme of things the hero is not put to the test. Once a hero, always a hero. The difference between the hero and the skeptical and taunting crowd never disappears. At no point do the others truly threaten the heroism of the hero. Quite the contrary: they are there to confirm the hero as a hero by making him suffer through their incomprehension. The idea that the hero could be tempted to become one of them, that he could feel pressured to conform to the crowd, would sound like blasphemy in Unamunian ears. The hero is the victim, the crowd the victimizers. If you erase in any way the difference between the two, the entire sacrificial scenario collapses, and with it the possibility of making a hero. For it is not enough for the hero just to be himself in order to be a hero, he must also bear his cross and suffer at the hands of the crowd *in order to be confirmed as a hero.* In spite of Unamuno's words, his hero is most definitely a public hero. He is perfectly recognizable as such, as a hero, by the way he stands before the crowd, victimized yet undaunted, face held high, ready to die a most beautiful death if necessary.

This Unamunian scenario is indeed the old sacrificial one, but with a Christian twist: Unamuno's God is definitely not on the side of the crowd. Because Unamuno is a good Christian, Unamuno's God is clearly on the side of the victim. The crowd does the sacrificial job it has always been supposed to do, but it gets no thanks for it, no recognition. In the old days the crowd would have sacrificed (to) the hero in a most reverent and commendable fashion. Unamuno's crowd, on the other hand, has no redeeming qualities. The others are simply those to whom God did not deign to communicate the message that the hero is a hero. So God uses them, and their incomprehension and their hostility, to confirm the hero as hero, and then blames them for it. Unamuno's Christian God ends up sacrificing the sacrificers.

In other words, Unamuno's "Christian" version of the old sacrificial scenario does not change anything essential. The relative roles of victim and victimizers continue to be as rigidly defined, as irreducible to each other, as ever. As I just said, the idea that the hero, the victim, anointed by God, could be tempted by the others, the crowd, to become one of them, not simply out of cowardice in order to escape his fate, but seduced by the desire to be like them; or, what amounts to the same thing, the idea of a contagious crowd that would spread its contagion to infect the hero, is something utterly alien to Unamuno. Even Christ was tempted, but not Unamuno's hero.

And yet, in true Christian terms, each and every one of those others, each member of the crowd, by the mere fact of being human, must be considered unique in principle—a hero in Unamunian terms—who either has not heard the word of God yet "in the secret places of the heart," or has not been faithful to it, has fallen from his heroic status. In other words, in that crowd there must be plenty of former heroes who chose to be part of it, to be one of them; heroes who were seduced by the human other, who ignored the word of God, or who did not have the strength to keep it; or maybe even heroes who mistook something that may have sounded like the word of God for the real thing. In true Christian terms, following the human other, wanting to become like the other for its own sake, instead of following God, becoming like God, is the temptation par excellence. Either God or the other, that is the fundamental, the most radical, choice. Everything is at stake in that choice. And if this is the case, the examination of what it means to fall away from God, to put the other in the place of God, becomes as important as examining what it means to follow God. (In Unamuno's words: "Quien no se cuida de la enfermedad, descuida la salud" (*Del sentimiento*, 94; Whoever pays no heed to disease is heedless to his health.) Above all, one must endeavor to maintain the difference between the two alternatives as clear as possible.

But that is not what Unamuno does. On the contrary, he tells us he does not understand how anybody can want to be somebody else. He can understand that one may want to have what somebody else has, but to want to *be* somebody else does not make sense to him:

> Eso es lo que yo no acabo nunca de comprender, que uno quiera ser otro cualquiera. Querer ser otro, es querer dejar de ser uno el que es. Me explico que uno desee tener lo que el otro tiene, sus riquezas o sus conocimientos; pero ser otro, es cosa que no me la explico. . . .
>
> Cierto es que se da en ciertos individuos eso que se llama un cambio de personalidad; pero eso es un caso patológico, y como tal lo estudian los alienistas. (*Del sentimiento*, 64–65)

> (That is something I have never understood: that one should want to be someone else, anyone at all. To want to be someone else is to want to cease being what one is. I can understand one's wanting to have what someone else has, his wealth or his knowledge. But to be someone else: that's something I do not understand. . .
>
> It is true that in some individuals there occurs something called a change of personality, but that is something pathological, and it is studied as such by mental pathologists.)

Is Don Quixote's madness not "pathological"? How can anybody who has read *Don Quixote* as many times as Unamuno did say that? Would Alonso Quijano not give an arm and a leg, as the saying goes, to transform himself into a second version of Amadís, to be himself by being exactly like Amadís? Or, from the opposite side, had Unamuno not read Kierkegaard and learned how much despair and hatred and willing self-destruction can be involved in wanting spitefully, resentfully, to be oneself? Nothing can be easier than to want to be somebody else, or not to be oneself, or to despair and to hate oneself at not being able to achieve either goal. Even more perplexing perhaps is to hear those words from the author of such works as the play *El otro* and the novel *Abel Sánchez*, a modern version of the story of Cain.

In other words, it is at first sight surprising that an author with such an interest in the phenomenon of fratricidal rivalry and envy should confess his inability to understand how anybody would want to be somebody else. And yet, when we find such a thought expressed by the protagonist of *Abel Sánchez*, Joaquín Monegro, supposedly the very personification of envy, we begin to suspect that this is by no means accidental. The question deserves closer scrutiny.

Unamuno's Modern Cain

Chapter 28 of Unamuno's *Abel Sánchez* consists entirely of the following conversation between Joaquín Monegro and a grey and secondary character toward whom Joaquín feels some pity:

> "Ah, to be you, Don Joaquín," said the poor disinherited Aragonese father of five to Joaquín one day, after he had succeeded in extracting some money from his benefactor.
>
> "You want to be me! I don't understand."
>
> "Yes, I would give everything to be you Don Joaquín."
>
> "What is this 'everything' you would give, now?"
>
> "Everything I can give, everything I have."
>
> "And what is that?"
>
> "My life!"
>
> "Your life to be me!" To himself Joaquín added: "I would give my own to be someone else entirely!"
>
> "Yes, my life in order to be you."
>
> "This is something I can't very well understand, my friend. I can't understand anyone's being ready to give up their life to be someone else. To be someone else is to cease to be oneself, to be the person one is." . . .
>
> When Don Joaquín found himself alone later he said to himself: "Ah, to be me! That man actually envies me, he envies *me*! And I, who would I like to be?"[4]

The question is left unanswered, but the answer is obvious. If that poor man envies him and the clear proof of his envy is that he would give everything to be him, to be Joaquín Monegro, and the latter envies his closest friend Abel (as much as Cain envied his brother), who else would he want to be but Abel? He would give his life to be Abel, and not simply—as he says to himself while listening to the man—to be other than he is. For it is easy to confess a desire to be other than who one is, to be a different person in general. But Cain wants more than that, he wants to be just like Abel, who is God's favorite; indeed, he wants to become Abel.

But that is precisely what Joaquín Monegro, filled with envious hatred of Abel, would never openly acknowledge. He would die rather than confess it.

4. I use Anthony Kerrigan's translation in the Bollingen Series (Princeton, N.J.: Princeton University Press, 1976).

And that is to be expected within the logic of such a character. What is more problematic is that Unamuno himself, the author, the one who tells us that he has taken his characters from the social life around him and from inside himself, never acknowledges that desire either. In fact, one has the distinct impression that the dialogue just quoted (and the entire short chapter of which it is a part) is a deliberate attempt by Unamuno to suggest the obvious in order to deny it—an attempt, furthermore, to separate the infernal but glorious and tragic envy of Unamuno's protagonist from low-level, ordinary envy. For, as he said in the Prologue to the second edition of the novel,

> [La] envidia que yo traté de mostrar en el alma de mi Joaquín Monegro es una envidia trágica, una envidia que se defiende, una envidia que podría llamarse angélica. . . . Y ahora, al releer . . . mi *Abel Sánchez* . . . he sentido la grandeza de la pasión de mi Joaquín Monegro y cuán superior es, moralmente, a todos los Abeles. No es Caín lo malo; lo malo son los cainitas. Y los abelitas.
>
> (The envy I tried to show in the soul of my Joaquín Monegro is a tragic envy, an envy that defends itself, an envy that could be called angelic. . . . And now, upon rereading . . . my *Abel Sánchez* . . . I have felt the greatness of my Joaquín Monegro's passion, and how superior he is, morally, to all Abels. Cain is not evil; the little Cains are the evil ones, and the little Abels.)

One is not surprised when the narrator tells us that

> Joaquín thought of himself as an exceptional spirit and, as such, more tormented and prone to pain than anyone else, a spirit marked by God with the sign of those predestined to greatness. (31)

But things get muddy when we discover that Unamuno agrees with the opinion his character has of himself. So that when we are told that Joaquín Monegro was planning to write a book entitled *Memoirs of an Aging Doctor*—

> Which would be a mirror to life, but revealing the very entrails, the darkest corners of it; a descent into the abysses of human vileness; a book of high literature and bitter philosophy. Into the book he would pour his soul, without speaking of himself . . . in it he would take vengeance on the vile world in which he had been forced to exist. (31)

—we must wonder to what extent Unamuno is actually talking about his own novel, a thought that would probably please him very much, for he took pride in considering his characters part of himself (or the other way around). "A descent into the abysses of human vileness, a book of high literature": this sort of contradiction in terms, this literary rescue of something repulsive in itself describes quite accurately the intention that guides the development of *Abel Sánchez*.

Unamuno is fully aware of the fact that this shameless exhibition of one's own spiritual sickness is itself a form of sickness, of vanity:

> Vanity consumes us—says Joaquín Monegro. We make a spectacle of our most intimate and vile diseases. I can imagine the existence of a man who would want to have a pestiferous tumor such as no one has ever had before, solely in order to vaunt it about. This very *Confession*, for instance, isn't it something more than a mere unburdening of the soul?
>
> I have sometimes thought of tearing it up, so as to free myself from it. But would that free me? No! It is better to make a spectacle than to consume oneself. After all, life itself is no more than a spectacle. (12)

It is true that *totus mundus agit histrionem*, the world is "a great theater," as Calderón called it. But in Calderón's *gran teatro del mundo* the spectacle takes place before God. He is the maker of it and the judge of it. The individual is what he or she is as an assignment from God (or from the "World," as God's stage manager). The worst thing that can happen to the human actor, for example, to the king, is to believe that he is king in his own right, all by himself, that is to say, to believe that he is what he is independently from God.

Joaquín Monegro's "vanity," on the other hand, offers the spectacle of his "most intimate and vile sickness" not before God, but before the other. It is not a true "confession," at least not a Christian one, for there is no repentance. It is indeed only a spectacle, an exhibition. He knows, as he says, that he will not get rid of his sickness by exhibiting it. But he still thinks he can profit from it in some way, that it will gratify his spirit. That may be true psychologically, but it will do nothing to cure the sickness, because the exhibition itself is an integral part of the sickness. It is hatred and envy that want to exhibit themselves for their own benefit as hatred and envy. But hatred and envy are in themselves hopelessly incompatible with the truth, at war with the truth, by definition. What hatred hates is the truth, what envy envies is the truth. This means that they exhibit themselves with duplicity, not with sincerity, and not to reveal the truth about themselves, but to hide it. They want exhibition, not truth, a simulacrum, an appearance of truth, behind which they will hide. Hatred and envy offer at the altar of the other, the idol before whom they "confess," the same thing that the most primitive sacrificer has always offered on the old altar: not the truth of violence, but a substitute for it, a ritual simulacrum, in the hope that the idol will accept it as if it were the truth in lieu of the truth. When one does not want to see the truth, but cannot avoid it either, one turns it into a show; or, as Joaquín Monegro puts it, one turns the *asquerosa dolencia*, the *tumor pestífero*, the nauseating inner gangrene, into "a book of high literature."

Antonio Machado, one of the best Spanish poets of the early part of the twentieth century, who declared his admiration for Unamuno's work repeatedly, had a very interesting and deep reaction to *Abel Sánchez*. Here are some extracts from a letter he wrote to Unamuno in 1918 on receipt of the novel:

> Bien hace V. en sacar al sol las hondas raíces del erial humano, ellas son un índice de la vitalidad de la tierra y, además, es justo que se pudra al aire, si es que ha de darse la segunda labor, la del surco para la semilla.
>
> Caín, hijo del pecado de Adán, desterronó el páramo virgen. . . . La segunda vuelta de arado la dio Jesús, el sembrador. . . . Su *Abel Sánchez* es libro precristiano que V.—el hombre del Cristo en el pecho—tenía que escribir para invitarnos a expulsar de nuestras almas al hombre precristiano, al gorila genesíaco que todos llevamos dentro. . . .
>
> Ahora tiene V. que escribir su novela cristiana, que es la suya, para curarnos de esa acritud de que V. se ha curado al escribir su libro. . . . (198–99)[5]

> (You do well in exposing to sunlight the deep roots of the human soil. They are an indication of the vitality of the soil. Besides, it is only just that they rot out in the open air, in anticipation of the second labor, the one that makes the furrows for the seed.
>
> Cain, the son of Adam's sin, harrowed the virgin land. . . . The second labor, the ploughing, was done by Jesus, the sower. . . . Your *Abel Sánchez* is a pre-Christian book, which you—the man with the Christ on his chest—had to write to invite us to expel from our souls the pre-Christian man, the original gorilla, which we all carry inside. . . .
>
> Now you have to write your Christian novel, which is the one that really suits you, in order to cure us from that harshness from which you have cured yourself by writing your book.)

5. A. Machado, *Prosas completas*.

He then proceeds to explain his view of the Old Testament as a gradual development of the "feeling of fraternity, which culminates in Jesus." I think the sense of his comments is quite clear: airing out Cain's sickness, allowing it to rot in the open, makes sense if it is a preparation for the second tillage or cultivation, when the good seed will be planted. Without that seed the soil, leveled by Cain, will remain barren, useless. *Abel Sánchez* is a "pre-Christian book." Its purpose can only be that of "an invitation to expel from our souls" that hate-filled Cain, that "gorila genesíaco," which all of us carry inside. The inevitable conclusion can only be that "now you must write your Christan novel in order to cure us" of the disease you have uncovered.

One cannot be any more delicate with a friend, while telling him that such an exhibition of human degradation and bitterness for its own sake is pointless; that such an exhibition without repentance, without turning from the envious hatred of the other to the love of your brother for the sake of God ("fraternity is the love of your neighbor for love of the common father"; 200; la fraternidad es el amor del prójimo por amor del padre común), as preached by Christ, is definitely something unchristian, and as such unworthy of an author like Unamuno, "the man with the sign of Christ on his chest" ("el hombre del Cristo en el pecho").

I think Machado was rather charitable. First of all, Unamuno never wrote the Christian novel that Machado saw as a necessary sequel to *Abel Sánchez*. Furthermore, I do not think he ever had such a sequel in mind when he wrote his novel, which means that he was not cured of his "bitterness" by putting it in his novel. Quite the opposite: I believe he put it in a novel because he could not cure himself of it. And because he could not eradicate it from himself, he did, in the absence of repentance, the only thing he could do: he turned it into literary fiction and shouted at the top of his lungs that life itself is literary fiction, a theatrical stage, and that the difference between reality and fiction is an illusion.

I have no reason to doubt Unamuno's religious desire to believe, as he stated so many times, together with his anxious desire for personal immortality. But the stumbling block in his path to faith was not rational logic and rational analysis, as he kept shouting in the defense of his quixotism, but the other, *el otro*. That was the real *skandalon*, stumbling block. He cannot hear the silent word of God in the "secret places of the heart," that is to say, he cannot be himself before God, because he remains scandalized before the other, trapped in a hopeless struggle to be himself before the other, *against* the other. It was his envy, it seems to me, the envy we all carry inside, as Machado said, not his reason, that blocked his way to God.

And exactly for that very reason he also tried to erase the difference between being oneself before God and being oneself before the other. He tried to turn a hopeless, envious, and degrading struggle with the other into some sort of epic struggle, a struggle that would make him a hero, which is the closest thing he could pretend to be if he could not be a saint, which is perhaps what he really wanted to be. And then, again, he tried to convince himself desperately that there is no real difference between a hero and a saint; and he talked about such things as "envy of Christ," and more, "I do not know, but I would dare say . . . envy of God."[6]

The envy of "Luciferian" Joaquín Monegro is meant to be "grandiose and

6. W. H. Auden also considered Don Quixote a religious hero: "a representation, the greatest in literature, of the Religious Hero, whose faith is never shaken" (103). Auden defines the religious hero as "one who is committed to anything with absolute passion, i.e., to him it is the absolute truth, his god. The stress is so strongly on the absolute that though he may be passionately related to what, ethically, i.e., universally, is false, he is a religious hero. . . . Thus, the distinction between being absolutely committed to the real truth, and being absolutely committed to falsehood, is not between being a religious man and not being one, but between the sane and the mad . . ." (97); this distinction, of course, applies specifically to the case of Don Quixote. In other words, even though Auden considers Don Quixote a religious hero, he would never equate him with a saint. Furthermore, in a rather interesting and insightful twist of his argument, Auden appears to imply that, as a religious hero, Don Quixote's place is not really in a novel:

> The only point to consider here is why Cervantes makes him [Don Quixote] recover his sanity at the end. Does this mean that he ceases to be a religious hero, that he loses his faith? No. It is because Cervantes realizes instinctively that the Religious Hero cannot be accurately portrayed in art. Art is bound by its nature to make the hero interesting, i.e., to be recognisable as a hero by others. Both the aesthetic hero and the ethical hero are necessarily interesting and recognisable by their deeds and their knowledge, but it is accidental and irrelevant if the religious hero is so recognised or not. Unless Don Quixote recovers his senses, it would imply that the Religious Hero is always also an aesthetic hero (which is what his friends want him to be). On the other hand, once he does, he has to die, for he becomes uninteresting and therefore cannot live in a book. (97)

Needless to say, Cervantes's "instinct," like that of Auden's himself, which tells them that literary attraction poses a threat to the religious character of the hero, is a specifically Christian "instinct." Inevitably Auden's reasoning also implies that while the religious heroism of a sane Quixote offers no novelistic interest, his madness does. Therefore, the religious character of his madness (the basis of Unamuno's *quijotismo*) is as fictitious, as false, as is his absolute commitment to knight-errantry. Therefore his mad literary heroism is only a fictitious semblance of true religious heroism. There is a world of a difference between Unamuno's view and Auden's.

tragic." But what is important to us here is the relation between that "Luciferian" or Cain-like heroism and the heroism that Unamuno sees in Don Quixote. The fact that the writer to whom, according to Marañón, we owe "the most profound pages about the passion of resentment, insidious and lethal sickness of Spanish life,"[7] is also the greatest *quijotista* in the history of modern Spain, the greatest defender of Don Quixote's heroism, does not seem to me to be accidental. I think that Unamuno himself would tell us that in order to understand in depth the heroism of Don Quixote, one also has to understand the terrible sickness that tortures the mind of envious Cain; that in order to understand the sublime in Don Quixote, we have to understand first the inner degradation of Cain. And I think he would also tell us that this connection between the infernal and the sublime is what mediocre Cervantes could not understand.

If this is true, then we should try to look at Don Quixote from inside that inner degradation of Cain. The question is the following: In what way does Don Quixote appear as heroic in the eyes of Cain-like Joaquín Monegro? What are the ingredients of such a heroism? In brief, the answer could be as follows: a combination of Don Quixote's innocence, his innate goodness, and the fact that he is mocked and ridiculed by everybody, that he is a victim of the incomprehension of people incapable of conceiving a great project, mediocre people who cannot understand what it is to go mad for the sake of something great.

To begin with, Joaquín Monegro, as we just saw, feels superior, considers himself "un espíritu de excepción" (an exceptional spirit) surrounded by mediocrity: "Ésta fue mi desgracia, no haber nacido entre los míos. La baja mezquindad, la vil ramplonería de los que me rodeaban, me perdió" (183; That was my misfortune, I was not born among my equals. The shallow paltriness, the vulgarity of those surrounding me, led to my downfall). He has always felt marginalized, an outcast. Everybody has ignored him. The favorite was always Abel, who was always successful. And this new Cain cries out against such an injustice. He is not the evil one; the true bad guy is Abel, he is the envious one. Was it not Abel who always took away from him what really belonged to him? He, the new Cain, knows what lies underneath that innocent-looking face. Abel may be able to fool everybody else, but not him,

7. Marañón's opinion is recorded by Unamuno himself; see *Obras completas*, 5.175.

not Cain. He knows that Abel is the one to blame for Cain's hatred, the hatred that consumes Cain from the inside.

But Cain's problem is even more complicated. Because, while he feels deeply that he is marginalized and scorned by the others, none of those others believes that is the case, least of all Abel. And that is too much: not only do they scorn him, and marginalize him, but they even refuse to believe that they are doing these things to him. They victimize him, and in addition they want to take away from him the only thing he's got left: the mark of the victim, the right to be recognized for what he really is, a victim and an outcast.

It is during those black moments, while consumed by resentment, when Unamunian Cain lifts his eyes and looks at Don Quixote. Don Quixote appears to him wearing all the marks of the victim, and not just any victim: he appears like the sublime Christian victim, anointed by God, the one mocked by everybody. Don Quixote does not have to convince anybody that he is a victim. He does not even try! He does not have to hate anybody. This makes it possible for his innocence, his innate goodness, to shine forth. He has the same innocence and goodness that Abel has taken away from him, and that is also denied to him by all the others in their refusal to believe that he is really a victim. "Y lo más grande de [don Quijote] fue haber sido burlado y vencido, porque siendo vencido es como vencía: dominaba el mundo dándole que reir de él" (*Del sentimiento*, 351–52; And his greatest attribute was that he was mocked and conquered: for being conquered is how he conquered; he mastered the world by giving the world cause to laugh at him). I have no doubt that Joaquín Monegro would make these words his own without hesitation.

Would all the Joaquín Monegros of this world not love such quixotic sublimity? Wouldn't they all look up to him as their savior? To the envious eye the difference between reality and fiction, between following Christ and following Amadís, is irrelevant. What is important is not what Don Quixote does, or what model he follows, but the fact that he stands tall, as a victim, before the other. What matters is his heroic stance, which, of course, has nothing to do with Christ's humble submission to the will of the Father. Unamuno's heroic Don Quixote is exactly what his envious Cain would like to be before the other, because that is the only kind of being in which the envious one, as such, has any interest.

When he sees Don Quixote, he sees not only the one he would like to be, he sees in the knight a revelation of his own true self, the one he really is, a mirror of his deepest and truest reality, precisely the reality that the other obstinately persists in not seeing—nay, the reality that the other takes away from him in a most despicable and unfair manner. If it were not because of the other, his true quixotic self, and quixotic innocence, would shine forth in splendor.

The envious one fools himself, of course, because he sees everything through the distorting lens of his envious desire. But his foolishness is far from haphazard or arbitrary. For he fools himself with the truth by understanding it in reverse. What he takes to be an image—a Don Quixote–like image—of his liberation from the other, and therefore from the anguish of his own self-consuming envy, is in fact the trap that his envy lays out for him, the disguise or veil of his envy.

But if this is so, we ought to pay attention to the envious one when he tells us that Don Quixote is the perfect image of his "true" self. We must pay attention not because we can take his word at face value, but because there is only one thing we can trust about the voice of envy: its denial that it is really envy, its obsessive need to hide itself from the other, to hide its hate-filled fascination with the other. So when he tells us that Don Quixote reveals his true nonenvious self, he is in fact telling us that the quixotic attire is the perfect cover for his envy. For he definitely ought to know what envious desire considers good for itself, that is to say, good for its own preservation, for continuing to be itself without appearing to be so.

We should, therefore, consider Unamuno to be the first (and to my knowledge, the only one till now) to have felt intuitively, without seeing it clearly, the relationship between the quixotic figure and the figure of Cain, between quixotic madness and envy. The question is whether Cervantes was fully aware of these relationships. And I think there can be no doubt about it. Furthermore, if we can find the evidence for it, we will have discovered not only the secret of Unamuno's fascination with Don Quixote, but also the secret of his persistent animosity toward Cervantes, for they are the two intimately connected sides of the same attitude. The reason is quite simple: while Unamuno used literary fiction, the spectacle, the exhibition, to ennoble the ignoble face of envy, Cervantes discovered that under the pleasing veil of literature lies the ugly face of envious desire. Cervantes discovered what Unamuno tried his best to cover. This is why, in spite of himself, Unamuno is probably the best guide we can have to some of the most profound insights into Cervantes's novel.

But where would we look for the textual evidence? Logically we should look in Cervantes's novel for anything that Unamuno consistently declares to be irrelevant or impertinent. And I think there is nothing so consistently avoided by Unamuno as the interpolated stories. In his *Vida de Don Quijote y Sancho* he bypasses every single one of them, at times with a derisive comment, as in the case of *El curioso impertinente*: "A story altogether impertinent and alien to the action of our history." In one of his essays he explicitly declares that "[i]f Cervantes had not written the *Quixote* . . . the very novelas and digressions that appear in the *Quixote*, like that most impertinent one about *El curioso impertinente*, would not deserve people's attention" (*Obras completas*, 3.577).

This quasi-instinctive avoidance of the interpolated stories in Cervantes's novel is all the more revealing because at the core of the story of Unamuno's own *Abel Sánchez*, and therefore at the core of Joaquín's hate-filled envious relationship with Abel, we find a situation structurally similar to the one we find in most of Cervantes's interpolated narratives: a frustrated love story. In fact, the similarity goes much further when we compare it with the two most prominent stories in Cervantes, the story of Cardenio, Luscinda, and Don Fernando, and the story of Anselmo, Lotario, and Camila. The two stories both involve two close male friends, one of whom intends to marry (or is already married to) a woman who will eventually be taken away by the other, to the logical dismay and despair of the aggrieved friend, who, in both cases, was quite instrumental in establishing the contact between the woman and the friend, which is exactly what happens also in *Abel Sánchez*. It does not take much to see in Joaquín Monegro an Unamunian version of Cardenio or Anselmo. Why would Unamuno consider such a type of love story so utterly irrelevant to the story of Don Quixote? Or perhaps we should rephrase the question: What is it that Cervantes says in those stories that triggers Unamuno's derisive hostility? What does Cervantes say that Unamuno does not want to hear?

We will explore this question at length in a later chapter. But before we do that, we should reflect further on what lies at the root of Unamuno's basic misunderstanding of the *Quixote*, and of his animosity against Cervantes: his deliberate and insistent blurring of the difference between the saint and the hero, between the follower of Christ and the follower of Amadís.

CHAPTER VII

From Don Quixote's Penitence to the Episode of the Lion

What is more I say that when any painter wishes to win fame in his art, he endeavours to imitate the pictures of the most excellent painters he knows. . . . In the same way, Amadís was the pole star, the morning star, the sun of all valiant knights and lovers, and all of us who ride beneath the banner of love and chivalry should imitate him. . . .

Have I not told you—replied Don Quixote—that I intend to imitate Amadís, and to act here the desperate, raving, furious lover, in order to imitate at the same time the valiant Sir Roland . . . ?

It seems to me—said Sancho—that the knights who did things like that were provoked and had a reason for their follies and penances. But what reason has your worship for going mad? . . .

That is the point—replied Don Quixote—and in that lies the beauty of my plan. A knight errant who turns mad for a reason deserves neither merit nor thanks. The thing is to do it without cause. . . . So, friend Sancho, do not waste any time advising me to give up so rare, so happy, and so unprecedented an imitation. I am mad and mad I must be till you come back with the reply to a letter which I intend to send by you to my lady Dulcinea. . . .

> *[And] I would have you know that all these things which I am doing are not in jest, but very much in earnest. Otherwise I should be infringing the laws of chivalry, which bid us tell no lie. . . . Therefore the blows on my head must be real, hard, and true, without any sophistry or deception.*
>
> *So, Sancho, for what I want of Dulcinea del Toboso, she is as good as the greatest princess in the land. For not all those poets who praise ladies under names which they choose so freely, really have such mistresses.*
>
> (1.25.202–10)

Don Quixote's model is radiant Amadís, "the pole star, the morning star, the sun of all valiant knights and lovers." However, his explanation should not fool anybody, nor should we make light of it and charge it all to Cervantine irony without further ado. Don Quixote's imitation of Amadís clearly goes far beyond the limits of a master-apprentice relationship. In a genuine healthy relationship between master and apprentice there is a third element, the object of the imitation (the painting, in Don Quixote's own example), with a reality of its own, independent from both master and apprentice. The latter imitates the former only in reference to that particular object, the reality of which sets limits to the imitation itself. But this is not the case in Don Quixote's fascinated imitation. There is no independent reality between model and imitator. To be a good knight errant is not *to do something* as well as Amadís would do it. To be a good knight errant is *to be like* Amadís. This model does not tell his imitator "Watch me do this or that," but rather "Watch me," "Be like me." That which is to be imitated is anything at all that the model does, feels, or even thinks. To be the best knight errant is to do, feel, think exactly like Amadís. "Amadís lives in me as I live in Amadís," the faithful chivalric disciple could very well say.

So what if Dulcinea del Toboso is not real? Why should that change anything? Don Quixote is perfectly willing to grant that Dulcinea's existence may be purely poetic. That does not change the absolute necessity in which he believes he is of having her as the object of his chivalric love because that absolute necessity of his is dictated by Amadís, not by empirical reality in any shape or form. Dulcinea is just as real as she has to be for the imitation of Amadís to be genuine. For that is the only thing that has to be genuine and true, the only thing with which Don Quixote cannot compromise. In the final analysis, the only thing that has to be real for Don Quixote to be Don Quixote, for Don Quixote, that is, to be sure of himself, is Amadís. Everything is real not in itself, but in reference to Amadís, whose reality, in turn, is not subject to empirical confirmation, for it is he, Amadís, who gives meaning to reality, who makes reality real, and not the other way around. In other words, in Don Quixote's mind at this point, for all intents and purposes, Amadís is God. He functions in the don's mind as God.

At no time is mad Don Quixote madder than when he deliberately decides to become mad in imitation of the chivalric model. But also at no time is he closer to revealing the true cause of his madness because he has indeed become truly mad by imitating the chivalric model. Of course, you have to be mad to want to do the kind of imitation that Don Quixote intends to do in Sierra Morena. But we miss the point if we think that he has turned radiant Amadís into a God-like model because he is already mad; rather, he is mad because his desire has already turned radiant Amadís into a god. His mad imitation of Amadís in Sierra Morena reveals the formidable power that the chivalric model has over him, the complete dependence in which he has placed himself at the feet of Amadís. In this moment of supreme irony, Don Quixote's madness doubles, as it were, on itself, looks at itself in a mirror without recognizing itself. But Don Quixote's blindness before the mirror becomes Cervantes's ironic revelation. It was indeed the blinding light of the model, God-like Amadís, "the sun of knight errantry," that turned Don Quixote mad in the first place.

The problem is, of course, that God-like Amadís is not God. God transcends empirical reality but does not ignore it or make it irrelevant. On the contrary, He transcends it in the very act of confirming it and declaring it to be true. External reality is true because it is God's work. And because it is God's work, every concrete detail, including concreteness itself, the palpable density of the real, becomes meaningful. Whether something is empirically real or a poetic fiction is of crucial importance in reference to God's transcendent reality. He demands an absolute act of faith beyond empirical reality, but such an act of faith does not obliterate the inherent rationality of the world "out there." The act of faith is essential only to prevent empirical reality from becoming a god unto itself, an idol. For empirical reality is true but it is not the ultimate truth. This situation of empirical reality's dependence on a higher authority is formally maintained when Amadís substitutes for God. The difference is that when empirical reality depends on Amadís, who did not create it, it loses its moorings, as it were, it becomes fictionalized, it becomes a pure appearance to be changed at will.

Unamuno was not alone in seeing profound religious meaning in Don Quixote's madness. Cervantes himself saw religious meaning in this madness, but meaning of a different kind. The quixotic imitation of Amadís is not compatible with the imitation of Christ. For the question is not whether one can be a good knight errant and a good Christian at the same time. The answer to such a question could only be that it all depends on what it takes to be a good knight errant. The incompatibility arises when it becomes clear that in order to become a good knight errant one has to do, feel, and think as much as possible like Amadís (or any other chivalric hero)—that is, when it becomes clear that the ultimate model of our behavior, whatever that behavior may be, is not Christ. Don Quixote is mad because he has lost that ultimate point of reference and control, because there is no limit to his imitation of Amadís, and therefore no limit to the power that Amadís (i.e., fiction) has over him. In any case, it would be absurd to think that Don Quixote can make his imitation of Amadís compatible with the imitation of Christ. The imitation of Christ would never produce a Don Quixote, nor can it support the novel that Cervantes wrote; and, of course, Cervantes knows that. Any attempt to write a Don Quixote *a lo divino* would be a complete fiasco.

In addition to its function as an ultimate point of reference, the choice of model affects the quality of the relationship between the model and the imitator. One does not follow Christ in the same manner in which one follows Amadís. One is supposed to follow Christ in the same manner in which Christ obeys the Father, that is to say, to love and honor Him, to be ready and willing to lose one's life for Him, just as He was willing to give His life for each and every human being. Following Christ does not involve competing with Christ. Quite the contrary, the imitation of Christ is offered as the safest antidote against the all-too-human drive of competition and rivalry.

But that is certainly not the way Don Quixote follows Amadís. What fascinates Don Quixote about the chivalric hero is that the hero is number one. To be Amadís is to be the one and only, that is to say, to be above all the others—and that is precisely what Don Quixote wants to be:

> Sancho, my friend . . . it is for me that are reserved perils, mighty feats, and valorous exploits. It is I, I say once more, who must . . . consign to oblivion the Platirs, Tablantes, Olivantes and Tirantes . . . and all that herd of famous knights errant of

olden times, by performing in this age in which I live such prodigies, such wonders, and such feats of arms as to eclipse the most famous deeds they ever performed. (1.20.149)

To imitate Amadís is to compete with Amadís, to challenge or be challenged by Amadís at every turn. Amadís is the fascinating goal, but he is also the ultimate obstacle and rival. One cannot truly be Amadís without first defeating Amadís, for, unlike Christ, Amadís cannot give his follower what he wants without ceasing to be Amadís. The problem is that as soon as one defeats Amadís, the ultimate goal becomes meaningless, since Amadís loses his meaning, his godlike attraction, as soon as he is no longer number one. A defeated Amadís is a terrible disappointment in the eyes of his worshipper, for it reveals to the latter that his supposed god was no god at all, for which he may hate him now as much as he adored him before. The worshipper has to look immediately for another Amadís, another fascinating obstacle, another challenge. The search is clearly endless, and endlessly self-defeating, since every triumph turns out to be hollow.

Don Quixote's fascination with the chivalric model is, therefore, a very ambivalent affair, a mixture of admiration and hatred—in other words, something incredibly close to envy. He was lucky never to meet Amadís face to face along the paths of La Mancha. Had this fateful event happened, sooner or later I am sure Cervantes would have shown us the other side of Don Quixote's admiration.[1] Other Cervantine characters in the novel were not so lucky with their respective objects of intense and adoring desire.

As an immediate consequence of pursuing his inherently endless chi-

1. Talking about what he calls the "Religious Hero," W. H. Auden, to whom we have already referred (see Chapter VI, note 6), explains the two dangers that threaten such a hero, of which "the greatest [representation] in literature is Don Quixote," as follows: "firstly, that he may lose his faith, and so cease to be absolutely committed, and secondly and much more seriously, that while continuing to recognise the absolute commitment he should transmute its nature from positive to negative, so that he is committed to the truth [as he sees it] in an absolute passion of aversion and hatred. In the first case, he simply ceases to be a religious hero; in the second, he becomes the negative religious hero, i.e., the devil, the absolute villain, Iago or Claggart" (98). Or, we may add, Cain. Unfortunately, Auden does not explain how "the greatest literary religious hero," Don Quixote, would have transmuted his absolute commitment to Amadís from positive to negative. But having learned through Unamuno how close Cain-like Joaquín Monegro felt to the spirit of Don Quixote, we can be sure that such a transmutation would have involved a lot of hate-filled envy.

valric goal, Don Quixote plunges into a mental world of numberless challenges and countless enemies forever waiting in ambush to destroy him or throw obstacles in his path to glory. The ever present enchanters, to whom Don Quixote refers so frequently (e.g., "there is a crew of enchanters always amongst us who change and alter all our things"; 1:25.204), are not only a parodic device they are also an accurate representation of Don Quixote's psychological pathology. In the mental world in which he lives, he must indeed feel that anything can happen at any time. Why? Because everything hangs from an ultimate point of reference, radiant Amadís, who cannot be trusted to always show the same face to his worshippers: he can appear fascinating one moment and hateful the next.

The follower of Christ, the supreme realist, does not perceive danger and death as a challenge, as a way to prove himself or herself, by overcoming the obstacles thrown on his or her path, that is to say, by proving himself or herself to be greater and more powerful than the obstacle. Quite the opposite: this supreme realist is supposed to look danger and death straight in the eye, as it were, and recognize it exactly for what it is, namely, something against which he or she, standing alone, is utterly powerless, something before which, in anguish, he or she will be sweating blood, and yet he or she will not retreat, will remain confident, not in themselves, not in their own strength, but in the model they follow, Christ, who will show them the way.

Perhaps at no other time in Cervantes's novel is the contrast more deliberately explicit between Christian realism and the "heroic" imitation of a false idol than in the episode of the lions, "the most original in the *Quixote*," as Antonio Machado called it (*Mairena*, 2.103).

The Adventure of the Lions

At this moment the cart with the flags arrived, and with it was nobody but the carter on one of the mules, and a man seated in front. Don Quixote, however, took up his stand before it and called out: "Where are you going, brothers? What cart is this? What have you in it? And what flags are these?"

To which the carter replied: "The cart's mine. In it are two fierce lions in a cage, which the General is sending from Orán to the capital as a present for his Majesty. The flags are the King's our Master's, for a sign that there's something of his in my cart."

"And are the lions big?" asked Don Quixote.

"Very big," replied the man at the door of the cart. "There have never been any so large that have ever crossed from Africa to Spain. . . ."

To which Don Quixote replied with a slight smile: "Lion cubs to me? To me lion cubs, and at this time of day? [¿Leoncitos a mí? ¿A mí leoncitos, y a tales horas?] Then I swear to God the gentlemen who have sent them here shall see if I am a man to be frightened by lions. Get down, my good fellow, and . . . open these cages and turn out these beasts for me. For in the middle of this field I will teach them who Don Quixote de la Mancha is, in despite and defiance of the enchanters who have sent them to me."

. . . .

At this point Sancho came up to [the gentleman in green] and cried: "Sir, for God's sake do something to stop my master fighting with these lions. . . ."

"I will see that he does not," promised the gentleman. And going up to Don Quixote, who was pressing the keeper to open the cages, he said: "Sir Knight, knights errant should engage in adventures which offer a prospect of success, and not in such as are altogether desperate. . . . What is more, these lions have not come against you, nor do they dream of doing so. They are going to be presented to his Majesty. . . ."

"Pray go away, my dear sir, and see to your quiet pointer and your good ferret," replied Don Quixote, "and leave every man to do his duty. This is mine, and I know whether they are coming against me or not, these noble lions."

(2.17.572–73)

To believers in Don Quixote's fundamentally heroic character and meaning, this episode, Don Quixote's encounter with the lions, tends to be seen as the pinnacle of his heroism. Even to those readers who pay attention to Cervantes's ironic treatment of his protagonist and to the parodic intention of the novel, Don Quixote's gallant attitude in the face of such danger inevitably looks heroic, in particular because it contrasts with the behavior of the exemplary but circumspect gentleman in green, who tries his best to dissuade our hero and even thinks of restraining him by force ("but not being as well armed, he thought it unwise to fight with a madman"), but finally decides to leave the field for his own safety in the company of the hurrying Sancho and the carter with his mules.

We should concede at once that the literary attraction of this exemplary gentleman cannot possibly compete with that of Don Quixote. Can anybody imagine a novel being written around such a circumspect and prudent character? It would probably be the most boring thing in the world. Of course, we could say exactly the same thing about these particular lions. For, as we will see in a moment, their behavior is most definitely of a nonliterary variety. So much so in fact that one would be inclined to suspect that they were perhaps in connivance with the exemplary gentleman. . . .

Cervantes knows all of that better than anybody. Everything about the gentleman is meant to serve as a contrast to Don Quixote's quintessentially literary character. The question is, Why did Cervantes create this contrast, and why did he do it at this particular time, that is to say, in the context of the "heroic" attitude of Don Quixote before the lions? For it is not enough to say, as countless critics have already said, that Don Quixote and Don Diego stand in sharp contrast to each other. What does Don Diego's deliberately contrasting personality tell us about Don Quixote's behavior in this particular instance? For we want to know about Don Quixote, not about Don Diego. Don Diego is there to throw light on Don Quixote, not the other way around. Ultimately the question can only be, Do we understand Don Quixote any better, in greater depth perhaps, after his encounter with the lions in the presence of Don Diego? Which is, of course, the wrong question for believers in Don Quixote's heroism to ask. They all think the question is about Don Diego, not about Don Quixote, because they all think they already know everything about Don Quixote. But, as an individual, Don Diego is presented to us in a rather one-sided way. We only know about him those things that are relevant for Cervantes to create a contrast with Don Quixote in those circumstances. His exemplary character is strictly ad hoc, consisting of no more than is demanded by the episode. In those circumstances Don Quixote should have followed the model of behavior and reason offered at that moment by Don Diego. Cervantes is not suggesting at all that Don Quixote substitute Don Diego for Amadís as an ultimate model or point of reference. That would be precisely as simplistic and even ridiculous as Sancho's reaction to the "account of the gentleman's life and occupations; for it seemed to him that this was a good and holy life, and that the man who led it must be able to work miracles. So, flinging himself off Dapple and hastily seizing his right stirrup, with devout heart and almost in tears he kissed the gentleman's foot again and again" (2.16.567). Don Diego is not there to become a Christian substitute for Amadís, but rather to illustrate something of fundamental importance about Don Quixote's foolish heroism.

The fact is that Don Quixote's heroism would look far more convincing if he really knew what he was up against. But does he? In other words, does he see reality here any more clearly than he does, for example, in the case of the windmills? For, courage for courage, I do not see why facing a huge and hungry lion should be any more dangerous than facing "more than thirty monstrous giants." The point is that, in spite of appearances, *the lion that Don Quixote perceives* is no more real than were the giants in the earlier episode. The lion that Don Quixote sees is definitely not the real lion that the general of Orán is sending as a present to the king, one of those lions which, as the gentleman in green, Don Diego de Miranda, tells him, "have not come against you, nor do they dream of doing so." The view that Don Quixote has of the lion in front of him is as mediated by literary fiction as the earlier giants had been. He is simply incapable of seeing the reality of the lion, a reality that has absolutely nothing to do with the fact that he, Don Quixote, happens to be there at that particular time. And that is exactly the lesson that the fierce and hungry lion, with a most deliberately unrealistic behavior, teaches our would-be hero, a lesson that will, of course, be wasted on him, as it has been wasted on so many generations of romantic readers of the novel:

> When the keeper saw Don Quixote firm in his position . . . he flung open the door of the first cage, in which, as we have said, was the beast, which seemed to be of extraordinary size and of a fearful and hideous aspect. The lion's first action, however, was to turn round in his cage, extend his claws, and stretch his full length. Then he opened his mouth and yawned very leisurely, and sticking out almost two foot of tongue, licked the dust out of his eyes and washed his face. This done, he put his head out of his cage and looked in all directions with eyes blazing like live coals, a sight to strike terror into the bravest heart. Alone Don Quixote watched him attentively, hoping that he would now jump out of the cart and come within reach of his hands, for he intended to tear him to pieces. To such a height of extravagance was he transported by his incredible madness. But the noble lion, more courteous than arrogant, took no notice of this childish bravado, and after looking in all directions, as we have said, turned his back and showed Don Quixote his hind-quarters. Then he lay down again in his cage with great calmness and composure.

Obviously Cervantes could not be very realistic about this encounter with the lion if he wanted to keep his hero alive and well enough to continue on his knightly journey. But he could have solved the problem in any number of ways (e.g., by using the sheep, which the shepherds were milking nearby, as a decoy in extremis—those same sheep that apparently the hungry lion did not even notice, or that Cervantes had completely forgotten). Paradoxically, however, this lack of artistic verisimilitude is motivated by a clear desire to give special emphasis to the fact that the lion was meant to be a real lion. Precisely because it was meant to be real, it could have nothing to do with Don Quixote's literary game. They indeed "have not come against [him], nor do they dream of doing so," as Don Diego tells him. And there was only one way to show this unmistakably: to ignore Don Quixote's poetically inspired challenge as completely as if he were not there at all, as if he were nonexistent. The real lion is as ignoring of Don Quixote's literary posture as Don Quixote is of the lion's reality. It is as if the two had never met.

Unamuno probably knew quite well what Cervantes meant by such feline behavior. But, of course, he did not like it:

> Ah, damnable Cidi Hamete Benengeli, or whoever it was who wrote up this feat, how vilely and pettily you understood it! One would think that envious graduate Samson Carrasco was whispering in your ear as you wrote it down. No, it did not happen in this wise; what really happened was that the lion was frightened away or was shamed to see the ferocity of our Knight, for God permits beasts to feel more vividly than men the invincible power of faith. . . .
>
> No, the lion could not or should not mock Don Quixote, for he was not a man but a lion, and wild beasts, since their wills are not depraved by any original sin, never make mock. Animals are entirely serious and entirely sincere, and neither slyness or malice has any place in them. Animals are not graduates, from Salamanca or anywhere else, for what they are given by nature suffices them. (*Our Lord Don Quixote*, 187–88)

This idea about the lack of malice in animals or, in general, in nature is repeated elsewhere by Unamuno: "What raises Nature to a higher level of greatness is the fact that it harbors no intention" (Lo que hace más grande a la Naturaleza es el ser desintencionada; *Obras completas*, 3.241).

He wants to turn the tables on Cervantes, for he accuses him of exactly what Cervantes accuses Don Quixote. In Cervantes's text it is clearly Don Quixote who does not see the lack of malice in the lion, the innocence of nature. In his madness Don Quixote is incapable of accepting or living with the fact that there is a world out there, the reality of which is totally independent of his own reality, of who he is, of what his desires are, or of why he happens to be there—a world that does not either beckon him or threaten him in any way by its simply being there. In his madness the distance between him and the world disappears. Nothing is indifferent to him or toward him. Everything is ultimately either a friend or an enemy. And, since he does not know friend or enemy in advance, he must be prepared at all times:

> Forewarned is forearmed. Nothing is lost by taking precautions. For I know by experience that I have enemies visible and invisible, and I do not know when or where, nor at what time or in what shape they will attack me.

Unamuno knows, of course, who those "enemies visible and invisible" are. They all look like the envious graduate Sampson Carrasco, or maybe the priest, or the barber. In other words, they all look like "petty" Cervantes, who never really understood the sublimity of his hero. And I must emphasize that, within Unamuno's own logic, they must all be motivated by envy. For why would they otherwise twist things around to make Don Quixote look ridiculous? At this point Unamuno should have quoted Don Quixote himself, who, after the disastrous encounter with the windmills, told Sancho that "the same sage Friston who robbed me of my room and my books has turned those giants into windmills, to cheat me of the glory of conquering them. Such is the enmity he bears me." For, in his own way, Don Quixote was right. Those windmills were not just there as Don Quixote just happened to pass by. Their similarity with real windmills was purely fictional. The Cervantine windmills were not there to serve their grinding purpose. They were placed there deliberately, in Don Quixote's path, for the purpose of confusing him and making him look crazy and ridiculous. The same thing is happening now with the peculiar behavior of this lion who just happens to come by at this particular time, just as Don Diego de Miranda also happens to pass by. . . .

But why should either Don Quixote or Unamuno complain about it? That is how things are supposed to happen in the world of fiction. In fact, Don Quixote knows that much better than Unamuno. He knows that nothing "just happens" in books of chivalry. Everything is supposed to be there *de industria* (as the priest tells the barber during their scrutiny of Don Quixote's library), deliberately. What one does not find in books of fiction is lions who behave simply according to their malice-free nature, or totally unintentional natural events. There is nothing naturally innocent in the world of fiction, and to pretend otherwise is to deceive oneself or to lie. Cervantes is not changing the rules of the game. He is simply using them masterfully to his advantage.

This is why Unamuno is badly mistaken when he tells us that what Don Quixote really saw in the lion was the will of God:

> We might also stop to consider how this affair of the lion was an adventure, as far as Don Quixote was concerned, of complete obedience and perfect faith. The Knight encountered the lion by the chance of the road because, without any doubt whatever, God sent the beast to him, and the Knight's strong faith made him declare that he knew whether or not Master Lions were sent against him. . . . And God wished, doubtless, to try the faith and obedience of Don Quixote, as He had tried the faith of Abraham. . . . (*Our Lord Don Quixote*, 187–90)

There is where Unamuno went astray. "As far as Don Quixote was concerned," it was not God who sent the lion, but his enemies "visible and invisible"—his envious enemies, he might add. And he knew it, because he also "knew" that he was writing a novel of chivalry with his own life, that he was living a novel, and even though he was mad, he was still aware that God does not write novels of chivalry.

The problem with Don Quixote's transformation of his life into a novel is that he is deceiving himself by thinking that he will live the novel of his own desire, that he will be in control of things. But this is no more true in a novel than it would be in real life without such a transformation. In both cases he has to deal with a high degree of uncertainty. The difference is that real uncertainty is in the hands of God, who is not out to get you, while fictional uncertainty is in the hands of a human other who may not like you very much. So when you live in a world of fiction you have to be on your toes all the time.

Historical Background

In Cervantes's penetrating insight the world of fiction is the representation of a world dominated by the ubiquitous and ambivalent presence of the other, a world in which everything is caught in, and becomes a reflection of, the relationship between the I and the other. And it does not take much to realize that, in this regard, what Cervantes sees is only the tip of an enormous human iceberg. The fact of the matter is that most humans throughout most of their history would have found it much easier to agree with Don Quixote than with Don Diego de Miranda. They, in complicity with Don Quixote, would have nodded their assent at his words: "I know whether they are coming against me or not, these noble lions." And the further back we go in the development of human society, the more this is so. There are societies in which the very notion of randomness does not exist, where nothing ever happens by mere accident, where everything is the result of either the evil eye or some other form of deliberate intention. "The most envy-ridden tribal cultures—such as the Dobuan and the Navaho—do not in fact possess the concept of luck at all, nor indeed the concept of chance. In such cultures no one is ever struck by lightning, for instance, without a malignant neighbor having willed it out of envy" (Schoeck, 6).

The further back we go, the deeper we sink into a world of magic and violent divinities as prone to envy and jealousy as your nextdoor neighbor—a world of magic ultimately dominated by the terror of the sacred, the persecuting sacred that follows you at every turn. As María Zambrano has profoundly intuited,

> En lo más hondo de la relación del hombre con los dioses anida la persecución: se está perseguido sin tregua por ellos y quien no sienta esta persecución implacable sobre y alrededor de sí, enredada en sus pasos, mezclada en los más sencillos acontecimientos, decidiendo y aun dictando los sucesos que cambian su vida, torciendo sus caminos, latiendo enigmáticamente en el fondo secreto de su vida y de la realidad toda, ha dejado en verdad de creer en ellos. (*El hombre y lo divino*, 27)

> (At the bottom of the relationship between man and the gods lies persecution: one is being constantly chased by them, and whoever does not feel this implacable persecution on and around himself, tangled around his steps, mixed up in the simplest events, deciding and even dictating events that change his life, twisting his path, palpitating enigmatically in the secret depths of his life and of all reality, has, in truth, ceased believing in them.)

To which I would only add that when society has ceased to believe in those persecuting gods, such gods or their domesticated descendants still find refuge and a new lease on life in literary fiction. For in our society, the modern society that was still emerging at the time of Cervantes, in principle, things are only supposed to happen that way in fiction—not necessarily in the sense that fictional forms may portray explicitly a world full of magical forces and hidden intentions governing everything that happens (as Don Quixote believes), but in the sense that, if the author knows his or her art, knows what he or she is doing, nothing will happen within the fictional domain that is not meant to be there for a purpose, *de industria*. It is in this sense that the modern poet is the direct heir of those magical forces when they are no longer credible. And this is also why any blurring of the difference between reality and fiction automatically implies a historical regression.

To be able to talk about things, things out there, independently of interindividual relationships, was an extraordinary step in the evolution of human society. As Gregory Bateson has said, "What was extraordinary—the great new thing—in the evolution of human language was not the discovery of abstraction or generalization, but the discovery of how to be specific about something other than relationship" (*Steps to an Ecology of the Mind*, 367). But this extraordinary discovery, when *the thing*, the specific thing as such, appears independently of who I am or who you are, or what our relationship may be, is something as formidable as it is precarious and fragile. Any disturbance in the realm of interpersonal relationships may affect the perception of the independent status of the thing out there. It does not take much to feel the invisible presence of the human other where the thing is. To put it in the ecological terms used by Bateson, "our mammalian ancestry is very near the surface." In order to keep the reality of the thing out there in view, a certain peaceful consensus must be maintained. For "[the] very origin of the conception of reality shows that this conception essentially involves the notion of a *community*," as Charles Peirce observed (*Selected Writings*, 69). And this idea suggests that the clarity of our perception of external reality is an excellent indicator of the peace we keep with our neighbors.

Any form of alienation before the other, of fascinated servitude, of envy, will distort our perception of the real world out there. The threat to our view of reality always comes from the other, or, rather, from the way we deal with its or their unavoidable presence. To the extent that one can remain oneself, not against the other, which is the typical form of alienation, but by achieving a higher form of self-identity in communion with God, for example, to that precise extent one truly sees. As María Zambrano said, in the final instance, perhaps it is true that "Ver, de verdad, deben poder sólo los angeles" (Seeing, in truth, perhaps is possible only to angels; *El hombre y lo divino*, 295).

Unamuno himself had expressed similar ideas before. It can only be regretted that he did not think them relevant when he commented on Don Quixote's attitude in the episode of the lions. In my opinion, his ideas in this regard are very relevant:

A lo contrario de la verdad lógica se llama error, y a lo contrario de la verdad moral se llama mentira. Y es claro que uno puede ser veraz, decir lo que piensa, estando en error, y puede decir algo que sea verdad lógica mintiendo.

Y ahora digo que el error nace de la mentira. . . .

El hombre miente y aprende de otros hombres la mentira. En el trato social hemos aprendido la mentira, y como el hombre lo ve todo con ojos humanos, todo lo humaniza. Humaniza el hombre a la Naturaleza, atribuyéndole cualidades e intenciones humanas; y como el hombre dice una cosa y piensa o siente otra, suponemos que también la Naturaleza suele pensar o sentir de un modo y presentársenos de otro; suponemos que la Naturaleza nos miente. Y de aquí nuestros errores, errores que proceden de suponer a la Naturaleza, a la realidad, una intención oculta de que carece. . . .

Estoy persuadido de que si la absoluta veracidad se hiciese dueña de los hombres y rigiese sus relaciones todas, si acabase la mentira, los errores desaparecerían y la verdad se nos iría revelando poco a poco.

El único culto perfecto que puede rendirse a Dios es el culto de la verdad. Ese reino de Dios, cuyo advenimiento piden a diario maquinalmente millones de lenguas manchadas en mentira, no es otro que el reino de la verdad. (*Obras completas*, 3.692–93)

(The opposite of logical truth is called error. The opposite of moral truth is called a lie. And it is clear that one can be truthful, saying what one thinks, and be in error, and one can say something that is true logically, and still lie.

And now I say that error is born out of lying. . . .

Man lies and learns to lie from other men. We have learned to lie through our social dealings, and since man sees everything with human eyes, he humanizes everything. Man humanizes Nature, attributing to it human qualities and intentions; and since man says one thing and thinks or feels something else, we assume that Nature will think or feel one way and offer a different appearance. We assume that Nature lies to us. Hence our errors, which proceed from assuming a nonexistent hidden intention in Nature or reality. . . .

I am convinced that, if absolute veracity would reign among men, and would govern all of their relations; if lying disappeared, errors would disappear, and the truth would reveal itself to us little by little.

The only perfect worship that can be offered to God is the worship of truth. That kingdom of God, whose coming is implored daily, in a routine manner, by millions of tongues stained with lies, is none other but the kingdom of truth.)

And a little later in the same text, he writes:

Eso que llamamos realidad, verdad objetiva o lógica, no es sino el premio concedido a la sinceridad, a la veracidad. Para quien fuese absolutamente y siempre veraz y sincero, la Naturaleza no tendría secreto alguno. ¡Bienaventurados los limpios de corazón, porque ellos verán a Dios! Y la limpieza de corazón es la veracidad, y la verdad es Dios. (700)

(What we call reality, objective or logical truth, is only the prize given to sincerity, to veracity. To him who were always and absolutely truthful and sincere, Nature would have no secrets. Blessed be the clean of heart, because they will see God! And cleanness of heart is truthfulness, and truth is God.)

This is a bold and far-reaching statement. But how could this conclusion be compatible with the blurring or the inversion of the difference between reality and fiction that allowed Unamuno to proclaim that Don Quixote is more historically real than either Cervantes or himself?[2] Is Amadís as real as Don Quixote? Don Quixote certainly thinks so. How does that reflect on Don Quixote's sincerity and "cleanness of heart"? Don Quixote is not a liar, of course, but he has been seduced by a lie, and he is trying to live by it. If the real world of nature, where real human beings live, is revealed in its true reality, its God-given reality, to those who are "clean of heart" and "always truthful and sincere," how does that reflect on Unamuno's proclamation about the historical reality of Don Quixote? For, on Unamuno's own terms, cleanliness of heart and truthfulness are the characteristics of a person who trusts in the existence of a reality and rationality out there ultimately grounded on God's own truthfulness, the God who, as Descartes said, does not play tricks on humans, the God who is the author of a reality beyond our own deceptive perceptions and desires.

The point is that there is a profound connection between the status of our interpersonal relations and our ability to perceive the independent reality of the thing out there, to see and accept the fact that the perceived thing is itself quite independent of the way it affects us, whether positively or negatively. And this way of thinking is by no means confined to the Christian worldview. It can be found throughout the classical Greco-Roman world, particularly

2. "Los que conocen nuestra filosofía de la historia . . . expuesta en nuestra *Vida de Don Quijote y Sancho* . . . saben que creemos que Don Quijote y Sancho tienen más realidad histórica que Miguel de Cervantes Saavedra—y más que la del que esto escribe—y que lejos de ser éste, Cervantes, el que creó a aquellos, son ellos los que crearon a Cervantes" (*Obras completas*, 5.638).

among the Epicureans, the philosophers of the garden, who secluded themselves from the public agitations of the agora, avoided the crowds, and lived in small communities of friends. Although I must also point out that there is a fundamental difference between the way the pagan world in general, and the Epicureans in particular, understood the connection between interpersonal relations and the perception of external reality, and the Christian understanding of it.

Epicurus plunges into the study of the rational causes of all physical phenomena and things in order to escape from the troubles of the mind. For, as he tells his disciple Pythocles, "In the first place, remember that, like everything else, knowledge of celestial phenomena, whether taken along with other things or in isolation, has no other end in view than peace of mind and firm conviction" (Diogenes Laertius, *Lives*, 10.85.615). On the other hand, the Christian is enjoined to achieve peace and purity of mind first in order to be able to see things the way they really are.

Don Diego de Miranda, the Gentleman in Green

It is at this point that we must remember that the adventure of the lions occurs within the context of Don Quixote's encounter with Don Diego de Miranda, "a sensible gentleman of La Mancha," *el Caballero del Verde Gabán*, the gentleman in green, whose attire and demeanor are described by Cervantes in minute detail. There is no other character in the entire novel quite like him. Everything about him is peaceful, reasonable, dignified, and pleasantly admirable. His words are few, timely, and polite. He is courteously deferential, answering fully when asked, but does not volunteer unrequested opinions. He does not rush to conclusions and always gives the other the benefit of the doubt. In fact, no other character in the novel treats Don Quixote with such genuine respect, even after he has come to the unavoidable conclusion that the man is crazy. In sum, he is exemplary in a deliberately subdued, nonheroic manner. In other words, one could not have imagined a sharper contrast with Don Quixote. The contrast becomes evident from the very first moment, in the manner they meet on the road. The passage is sufficiently important for me to quote it at some length:

While they [i.e., Don Quixote and Sancho] were engaged in this conversation they were overtaken by a man who was riding on their road behind them, mounted on a very handsome grey mare, and dressed in a fine green cloth overcoat slashed with tawny velvet, and wearing a hunting cap of the same material. . . . Now when the traveller caught them up, he greeted them politely and, pricking his mare, was going to pass on ahead, had not Don Quixote adressed him, saying:

"Gallant sir, if your worship is taking the same road as we are, and haste is not important to you, I should esteem it a favour if we could ride together."

"Really," replied the man on the mare, "I should not have pressed on ahead of you if I had not been afraid that your horse would be disturbed by my mare's company."

"Sir," broke in Sancho, "you can safely, very safely, rein in your mare, for our horse is the chastest and best-behaved in the world. . . ."

The traveller drew in his rein, gazing in astonishment at the figure and the face of Don Quixote. . . . And the more the man in green stared at Don Quixote, the more did Don Quixote stare at the man in green, who seemed to him a man of substance. His age appeared to be about fifty; his grey hairs few; his face aquiline; his expression between cheerful and grave—in short, from his face and appearance he gave the impression of a man of good parts. But what the man in green thought of Don Quixote was that he had never seen anyone of that kind or anyone looking like him before. He was amazed at the length of his neck, the tallness of his body, the thinness and sallowness of his face, his armour, his gestures and his carriage—for his was a shape and figure not seen for many a long year in that country. Don Quixote observed the attention with which the traveller gazed at him and from his amazement assumed his desire. So, being so courteous and anxious to please everybody, before the other could ask him a question he took the initiative by saying:

"I should not wonder if your worship were surprised at this appearance of mine, for it is both novel and out of the common. But you will cease to be so when I tell you, as I now do, that I am a knight [errant]. . . ."

After this speech Don Quixote fell silent, and the man in green took a long time to reply, for he seemed unable to find words. But after a while he said: "You guessed my thoughts, Sir Knight, when you observed my surprise; but you have not succeeded in dispelling my amazement. . . . On the contrary now that I know, I am the more astounded. What! Is it possible that there are knights errant in the world today, and histories printed about real knight errantries? . . . Heaven be praised, for that history of your noble and authentic chivalries, which your worship says is printed, will consign all the innumerable stories of imaginary knights errant . . . to oblivion, such harm they do to good manners, and such damage and discredit to genuine history."

"There is much to be said," replied Don Quixote, "on this question of whether the histories of knights errant are fictions or not."

"But is there anyone," asked the man in green, "who doubts their falsehood?"

"I doubt it," answered Don Quixote. . . . "[And] I trust to God I shall convince your worship that you have done wrong in going with the stream of those who affirm that they are not true."

From this last speech of Don Quixote's the traveller suspected that he must be an idiot, and waited for some further remarks to confirm his suspicions. But before they could turn to any other subject, Don Quixote begged his fellow-traveller to tell him who he was, since he had already told him something of his own condition and way of life. (2.16.563–66)

So far we do not know who this gentleman is, how he lives, or what his philosophy of life may be. And yet we have seen enough already to realize how sharply different he must be from Don Quixote, quite apart from his opinion about books of chivalry. Can anybody imagine Don Quixote passing by such a "gallant" gentleman (or anybody, for that matter, gallant or not) on the roads of La Mancha with just a "hello" or a "good day, sir"? Impossible. It would be totally out of character. It would be as impossible as it was for him to keep his promise of silence when Cardenio mentioned the name of Amadís de Gaula during the narration of his story. For, as he said then, "I can no more prevent myself from talking of [chivalry matters] than the sun's rays can help giving heat" (1.24.197).

The gentleman in green must have been amazed at the strange-looking pair as he approaches them from behind, in particular the tall thin figure of Don Quixote, "for he had never seen anyone of that kind or anyone looking like him before . . . for [Don Quixote's] was a shape and figure not seen for many a long year in that country." But he is in complete control of his amazement. He greets the strange pair politely and moves on. "He is strange," he must have thought looking at Don Quixote, "but that is none of my business." He shows respect, but expresses no curiosity. He is definitely not intrusive or inquisitive. He does not intervene where he is not called.

All of which makes us realize that this man is precisely the right person to tell Don Quixote a few moments later: Sir Knight, listen, these lions have nothing to do with you, they are really not your business ("these lions have not come against you, nor do they dream of doing so"). Everything we have known about him from the very first moment we met him is a preamble to that statement. The statement flows easily and logically from everything that describes or defines this man's behavior. It is not just something this man says, it is precisely what you would expect this particular man to say in those circumstances.

But there is more. The statement is not only typical of this man, that is to say, not only reveals or confirms the kind of person he is, it also anticipates fully and accurately what is going to be the most peculiar and totally unexpected behavior of the lion. For the beast will react to Don Quixote's challenge in a manner fully consistent with the fact that he indeed has not come against the knight nor does he even dream of doing so. There is a direct and undeniable link between the lion's behavior and that of the gentleman in green, Don Diego de Miranda. This proves conclusively that in Cervantes's mind such a strange beastly behavior emerges from, and in accord with, his reflection on the kind of person he is describing in Don Diego. In other words, the entire episode of the lions does not just happen in the presence of Don Diego as if by accident. Quite the contrary, the episode and Don Quixote's behavior in it are meant to acquire their proper meaning in reference to the gentleman's specific kind of exemplary personality: one who is not inquisitive or intrusive, who is not curious about other people's affairs, and who tries his best to maintain a healthy and peaceful relationship with others; precisely the kind of person least likely to see hidden intentions or magical forces of any kind around him; the kind of person, therefore, whose eyes are best equipped to see reality and truth.

We can go even further. Beyond the obvious contrast between Don Quixote's "heroic" behavior and that of Don Diego, there is something about the "gentleman in green" that brings to mind the underlying childlike innocence of Don Quixote, of which we spoke in a previous chapter; that absence of malice, that fundamental openness and trust in the presence of the human other, which Sancho has detected in his master, prompting him to say that "his soul is as clean as a pitcher. He can do no harm to anyone, only good to everybody. There's no malice in him. A child might make him believe it's night at noonday." How else can we interpret Don Diego's initial, spontaneous reaction of genuine surprise, and genuine belief, when Don Quixote informs him that he is a knight errant? Don Diego is clearly an intelligent man. He had never imagined there could be such a thing in the flesh. And yet, amazingly, he accepts, at that moment, the idea that he is truly in the presence of a real knight errant simply because this man, whom he has no reason to mistrust, tells him so. In other words, I think we have here another indication of Cervantes's increasing emphasis on the fundamental human value of his madman, which is the reason why it becomes increasingly imperative to cure him of his madness, the madness that wastes that value, that turns it into a fiction. Don Diego is what Don Quixote could be if he had not become a fascinated follower of Amadís. And we can know all that even before the gentleman begins to tell us about himself, because it is all in the way he relates to Don Quixote. But let us see what he has to say about himself.

> I, Sir Knight of the Sad Countenance, am a gentleman and native of a village where, please God, we shall dine today. I am more than moderately rich, and my name is Don Diego de Miranda. I spend my life with my wife, my children and my friends. . . . I have about six dozen books . . . some historical and some devotional, but books of chivalry have never so much as crossed the threshold of my door. . . . Sometimes I dine with my neighbours and friends, and very often I entertain them. . . . I do not enjoy gossiping, and do not allow any in my presence. I do not pry into my neighbours' lives, nor do I spy on other men's actions . . . I try to make peace between those I know to be at odds. I am devoted to Our Lady, and always trust in the infinite mercy of our Lord God.

It is not enough to say that Cervantes is presenting here an exemplary Christian person. He is doing that, of course, but what is particularly relevant at this point is the specific human features of the exemplum, features that might not be equally relevant or even appropriate in a different context. Suppose the author wanted to offer a model for Christian missionary work; clearly the image that Don Diego offers of himself would not be appropriate. What is appropriate here, given Don Quixote's primitive and paranoid distortion of the empirical reality of the lions, is a Christian version of the old Epicurean ideal of living a life conducive to inner peace and a proper view of the reality of the world out there. Apart from its profound expression of Christian faith, the key element in this description of Don Diego's lifestyle is its emphasis on the quality of human relationships, which are few (wife, children, friends, and neighbors), and completely free from any sense of rivalry or envious curiosity: "I do not gossip . . . I do not pry . . . nor do I spy. . . . I try to make peace."

What modern critics, it seems, have never understood is that this type of lifestyle is not only that of a man at peace with himself and genuinely respectful of, and concerned with, those around him, but, as a consequence of this, also of a man whose view of reality is not distorted, who does not look for hidden intentions or conspiratorial manipulations, a man, therefore, in whose world there are no evil enchanters, where lions are real lions and windmills are real windmills.

Needless to say, to critics for whom Don Quixote's madness is not real but only a very personal way, a heroic way, of being himself, Don Diego de Miranda is not only utterly unexemplary but has actually been placed there by Cervantes, next to heroic Don Quixote, with the perverse hidden intention ("con genial perversidad") of ridiculing such an unheroic lifestyle. This is, once again, the case of Américo Castro and, to a greater or lesser degree, that of his followers.

It is not my intention to engage in a detailed analysis of Americo Castro's view of the subject. But there is an aspect of it that is very relevant to what I am trying to emphasize here: the importance of human relationships in Cervantes's novel, the way the self relates to the other, for a proper understanding of Don Quixote's madness. In Castro's view, Don Diego de Miranda's admirable way of behaving with Don Quixote, so full of respect, and so unique in the entire novel, is not only totally ignored, it is in fact equated with the behavior toward Don Quixote of another character who appears to be a clear antithesis to Don Diego, namely, the irascible ecclesiastic who sits at table with the Duke, the Duchess, and Don Quixote, when the latter first arrived at the ducal castle. These are the two "prime examples [who] are attacked ad hominem by Don Quixote, thus showing how fragile or exceptional their position is," in the words of Castro (*Hacia Cervantes*, 317).

But the text of the novel tells in a most explicit manner a very different story. In sharp contrast with the way Cervantes introduces the reader to the gentleman in green, who from the beginning "gave the impression of being a man of good parts," this is how the ecclesiastic is described: "[One] of those grave ecclesiastics who rule the houses of princes; of those who, not being born princes themselves, do not succeed in teaching those who are how to behave as such; who would have the greatness of the great measured by the narrowness of their own souls; who, wanting to show those they rule how to be frugal, make them miserly" (2.31.675). And the reason why Castro equates this ecclesiastic with Don Diego is what he says at table, reproving both the duke and Don Quixote:

He turned to the Duke in great anger:

"Your Excellency, sir, will have to account to our Lord for this good man's doings. This Don Quixote, or Don Fool, or whatever you call him. . . ."

Then, turning to address Don Quixote, he said: "And you, simpleton, who has driven it into your brain that you are a knight errant and conquer giants and capture malefactors? Get along with you, and take my advice: go back to your home, and bring up your children, if you have any. Look after your estate, and stop wandering about the world, swallowing wind and making yourself a laughing-stock. . . . (2.31.675)

All we can say in response to Castro is this: if there is one person in the entire novel who would never, ever, speak to Don Quixote that way, it must be without a doubt Don Diego de Miranda. As I just said, it is hard to imagine a greater contrast between two people. This obtuse ecclesiastic seems to be everything that Don Diego is not. But this contrast is meaningless to Américo Castro and his followers, because, in the end, the ecclesiastic advises Don Quixote to lead a kind of nonheroic, nonliterary life, looking after his children and his estate, which has, in its nonheroic aspect, an obvious similarity with the kind of quiet existence led by Don Diego, but which Don Diego never tries to impose on or even recommend to Don Quixote. Castro finds it impossible to see any meaningful individuality, anything profoundly personal and irreplaceable, in this quiet existence; for him, Don Diego's quiet existence can be nothing but monotonous mediocrity, for it lacks any "external incitement." It goes without saying that Castro shows no interest in the underlying innocence of Don Quixote, the innocence that links him to Don Diego beyond the madness.

At the very least Castro ignores the kind of elemental wisdom that says that actions speak louder than words. *Operibus credite, non verbis*, shrewd Maese Pedro advises us, or, in the words of one of Molière's characters, "all men are similar by their words, it is only their actions that prove them different" (*L'avare*, 1.1). And the insulting action of the ecclesiastic proves him to be the exact opposite of a man whose actions as well as his words proclaim the wisdom of not meddling in other people's affairs, never doing anything to destroy a person's reputation, and not offering advice where it is not asked for.

On the other hand, given Castro's pronounced tendency to see deliberately hidden Cervantine intentions all over the text, always secretly directed against something or somebody, we should not be surprised at his intense dislike of a character who has been placed there to warn Don Quixote against seeing secret intentions and evil manipulations where there really are none. It would indeed be "perverse" (not "genially perverse," just perverse) of Cervantes to create a character who treats Don Quixote with more respect than anybody else in the novel; who invites him to his home and introduces him to his family; who, even after realizing that the man is insane, wonders in admiration at his ability to converse in a most rational and sensible way about all kinds of subjects; who never for a moment thinks of playing games or tricks on him, as almost everybody else does; and all of this in order to show that such exemplary behavior is not all it is made up to be, that it is really very "fragile," very pedestrian and uninspiring, compared with Don Quixote's heroic way.

As unlikely and anticervantine as such an interpretation really is, it might convince those who are already convinced of Don Quixote's unimpeachable heroism, except for one central detail: the behavior of the lion. For the lion, as we have already observed, is decidedly and unambiguously on the side of Don Diego de Miranda. The lion is there in order to prove how foolish and dubious Don Quixote's heroism is, and how clear and without duplicity Don Diego's perception of reality is.

Behind Castro's critical blindness in this case lies a fairly widespread critical weakness, a lack of appreciation or understanding of what, in my opinion, is the key to all of Cervantes's characterizations: the structure and the quality of interpersonal, interindividual relations. Individual characters are always ultimately defined through their relations with others. Opinions and ideas may be important in themselves, but they are never enough to give us an accurate profile of any character. Even the objective truth or falsity of what is said is not as important as the effects or consequences that such saying may have on other people. A character may tell the truth about somebody and still be, in Cervantes's eyes, a negative counterexample if the telling of it does not bring any rightful benefit to anybody and may hurt or show disrespect to the person concerned.[3] The best-known case is that of Clodio, the *maldiciente*, the evil-tongue, in *Los trabajos de Persiles y Segismunda*, who suspects and tells the truth that for valid reasons the two exemplary protagonists are

3. This is one of the leading ideas in one of Cervantes's exemplary stories, *The Dogs' Colloquy*, best discussed by Forcione (1984).

hiding, the truth of their real identities. In the end Clodio is killed, quite appropriately, with an arrow through his mouth. There are no isolated destinies in Cervantes. The individual is always defined in relation to the other, the neighbour, the *proximus*. It must be insisted upon: what holds Cervantes's novelistic attention and drives his reflection is not the individual psychology of the character in isolation but his or her sociability, so to speak.

Critics have spoken often of Cervantes's *perspectivismo*, his interest in and tolerance of different points of view on any given subject (and have almost as often overloaded this observation with heavy ideological attachments). It is true, but I would also like to point out that this *perspectivismo*, as manifested in the novel, is inseparable from, is an aspect of, his novelistic interest in interpersonal *relations*. There is hardly anything that happens in the novel, both in terms of action and of characterization, that is not also, in the best sense of the word, *relative*, or perhaps I should say *relational*, that is, deriving its novelistic significance from the network of human relations within which it happens.

How could it be otherwise in a novel that gives such a paradigmatic importance, such a centrality, to the profoundly human, rich, and complex relationship between the knight and his squire? Harold Bloom is undoubtedly right when he tells us that "[t]he loving, frequently irascible relationship between Quixote and Sancho is the greatness of the book, more even than the gusto of its representations of natural and social realities. . . . I cannot think of a fully comparable friendship anywhere else in Western literature" (131). Nothing in the novel stands more clearly beyond or outside the heroic-antiheroic traditional parameters than the relationship between Don Quixote and Sancho. When we speak of their basic decency and goodness, we speak of the quality of their relationship. Their friendship endures and thus sustains the novel beyond Don Quixote's madness, as it is also their friendship that becomes strained and placed at stake by his madness.

By placing the exemplary Don Diego next to the obviously foolish heroism of Don Quixote, inspired by his perception of the world as ruled by the secret manipulations of enchanters, Cervantes's profound intuition is also telling us that there is something wrong with this basic interindividual, relational structure of the human personality in the case of Don Quixote's foolishness. The secret manipulations of the world, the distorted and paranoid perceptions of reality, are now revealed as the logical offspring of Don Quixote's maddening relationship with the other, the idolized other, radiant Amadís, model and obstacle.

This intimate association of madness with the deterioration of the self-other relationship has a clear traditional theological foundation in Cervantes's mind, but it is also no less modern because of that. "The place where madness is born . . . is also the place where we all live together," says a modern psychiatrist (Grivois, "Adolescence," 117) we have already quoted in a previous chapter. In fact, he also told us that all his patients recognize "the interpersonal origin of their travail. It is even the single point they never question" (107).

Amadís is a fictional representation of the human other. When Don Quixote sets this fictional hero up on his idolatrous pedestal, he is setting up the human other as an idol. But in Cervantes even the fact that it is a fictional representation is in itself significant. Because to idolize the human other and to fictionalize it are one and the same thing. The problem is that as soon as Don Quixote does that, his relationship with the other, now turned into a fiction, a false god, becomes itself fictionalized, uprooted from reality, unstable, both itself and its opposite in endless self-contradiction, hopelessly ambivalent. At that point Don Quixote's fascination with radiant Amadís is only one of the two sides of envy; the other side, covered by the fascination, is hatred.

How could Unamuno, of all people, have missed the implication that behind Don Quixote's mimetic fascination with heroic Amadís, lies something hidden and unspeakable, something that should have interested him very much, the prototypical story of a diseased human relationship with the other, that is to say, the universal story of Cain's relationship with his brother Abel?

CHAPTER VIII

Unamuno's Story of Cain and Abel and the *Curioso impertinente*

As we were saying before, as far as Unamuno, creator of *Abel Sánchez*, is concerned, the heroic sublimity of mad Don Quixote would shine with particular intensity in the eyes of his tragic Cain-like character Joaquín Monegro. Don Quixote is a hero not in the eyes of Abel (who, in Cervantes-like fashion, might even pretend to be sorry that Don Quixote is mad, without understanding a thing about the sublimity of his madness), but in the eyes of Cain. There is little doubt that Unamuno would be more than willing to accept an underlying similarity, a subterranean link, between his sublime Don Quixote and his tormented, tragic, and resentful Cain. This leads us to believe that Unamunian Cain must have seen in Don Quixote the embodiment of his own deepest desire.

But what could Cain's deepest desire be except to rid himself of Abel? To rid himself of Abel not just physically, but—far more important and far more difficult—to free his own mind and soul of the haunting, maddening presence and influence of Abel, that hateful and fascinating other, that other on whom God seems to be smiling all the time, the one who can fool everybody (even God, it seems), but not him, not Cain. That's what Don Quixote's madness is all about, says Cain. Don Quixote appears to be mad because he is all alone. He is the one who finally triumphs over the haunting other, he is the one who is alone with himself, which is the reason why he can hear the voice of God and know that God is on his side. This is also why Don Quixote can be such a hopeful sign for the troubled soul of envious Cain. But to all those secretly envious Abels, *abelitos*, little Abels, how could such a lonely hero appear to be anything except raving mad? An envious Don Quixote? Perhaps, but certainly not envious of any little Abel. If Don Quixote is envious, his envy is of a different sort, of a higher caliber—envy of Christ perhaps, or even of God, that is, a Luciferian but definitely ennobling kind of envy. Don Quixote is the redeemer of envious Cain because he understands Cain's tragedy; he knows that he, Cain, is the real victim, and he is on his side.

However, it is difficult to reconfigure the biblical story in such a radical fashion if one keeps close to the biblical text. For the biblical text is unambiguous about Cain: he is a murderer, he killed his brother Abel with premeditation and treachery, and the blood of Abel cries out to God from the soil. It is not easy to turn the biblical Cain into a modern tragic hero. And so, indeed, in Unamuno's modern rendering of the story, Cain, that is to say, Joaquín Monegro, does not quite soil his hands with the blood of Abel. He thinks about killing him, but there is something in Joaquín, some kind of inner nobility, that prevents him from descending to such a low level. In the end the murder turns out to be purely symbolic. Joaquín, livid with rage, grabs Abel by the throat, but immediately lets go. Nevertheless, the attack is too much for Abel Sánchez, who has a weak heart: he grips his chest and dies. Joaquín, who is a medical doctor, accurately diagnoses the situation, saying to himself: "An angina attack . . . , there is nothing to be done. It's the end!" (37.373).[1] So all the talk later on about he, the new Cain, having killed Abel, is not really true. Likewise, on a previous occasion, when Helena, the woman he loves who ended up marrying Abel, is about to give birth to their first child, Joaquín says, "[M]y own evil spirit suggested a ferocious

1. From *Novela/Nivola*, trans. Anthony Kerrigan (Princeton, N.J.: Princeton University Press, 1976). Occasionally I change Kerrigan's translation slightly to bring it closer to the original text.

temptation: attend her [as a doctor] and smother the child surreptitiously. I was able to . . . suppress this revolting thought [vencí a la asquerosa idea]" (10.285). Clearly, Joaquín Monegro is a rather dignified sort of Cain, as befits a tragic hero. In other words, Unamuno's Cain is far from being the bloody murderer of the biblical story. He can feel an enormous turbulence inside, the icy cold grip of profound hatred, and so on. But that only adds to the magnificence of his tragic stature. You would never see Unamuno's Cain, for example, crouching in the dark, knife in hand, waiting for unsuspecting Abel in order to jump out and kill him from behind; you would never see him strangle an infant in his crib when nobody is looking. What kind of a hero would that be? And yet a real Cain could do those things—that is to say, a Cain who really felt the kind of unbounded envious hatred that Unamuno's Cain says he feels, could do those things. So perhaps Unamuno's Cain was just putting on a show for the benefit of the expectant literary audience, an audience whose literary sensitivity would hardly tolerate the unsightly degradation of a real Cain. In other words, I suspect that mostly Unamuno was just making literature, which is the reason why the loneliness that he perceives and admires in the heroic figure, whether quixotic or Cain-like, the loneliness that supposedly places him closer to God, humbly or as a rebel, is not very convincing.

But in his own negative way Unamuno can be an accurate guide, as I have been saying all along. If we want to know what really lies behind the literary façade of Unamunian Cain, all we have to do on the one hand is look at that to which Unamunian Cain points in order to tell us that he would not do such a thing because he is not that kind of low and degraded creature, or in order to tell us that the very enormity of the envious hatred he feels, its greatness, prevents him from doing it, from doing the sort of thing that a disgusting, undignified, mediocre Cain would surely do; and, on the other hand, look at everything that this admirer of Don Quixote's heroism attributes to the mediocrity of a Cervantes incapable of understanding the greatness of his hero.

We have already seen how surprisingly similar the basic story line in Unamuno's *Abel Sánchez* is to the most prominent interpolated stories in Cervantes's novel. They are surprisingly similar and yet different in a crucial sense because they are driven by opposite intentions. We should be in a position now to see more clearly why, in spite of such obvious similarity, Unamuno considers those Cervantine stories so utterly uninteresting and so irrelevant to a proper understanding of the main story of Don Quixote—why, in Unamuno's eyes, they are clear proof that Cervantes was a mediocre author who did not know what he was doing. He seemed to be particularly hostile to and derisive of that "most impertinent story of *El curioso impertinente*." And, needless to say, Don Quixote himself is squarely on Unamuno's side: "Now I believe that the author of my story is no sage but an ignorant chatterer. . . . I do not know what induced [him] to make use of novels and irrelevant stories, when he had so much of mine to write about" (2.3.489–90).

One can easily understand Don Quixote's displeasure. But why would such a story appear to be so "impertinent" to the man who wrote *Abel Sánchez?*

Let us begin by reviewing the main events in the development of Unamuno's novel, the events that provide Joaquín Monegro with the clearest motivation (or excuse) to hate his closest friend Abel. The novel is, as I already reminded the reader, a love story, or to be more precise, the story of a love triangle.

Joaquín is in love with his cousin, Helena. Perhaps "love" is not the word. He was trying to overpower, to conquer the heart of Helena: "Joaquín was, in fact, laying seige to his cousin Helena and was burning with the fire of his intense and jealous nature" (1.253). Naturally he talks a lot about it with Abel: "he unburdened himself—the inevitable and healthy unburdening of the embattled lover—to his friend Abel" (1.253). Helena is making him suffer terribly because she keeps him at bay in a rather ambivalent fashion. He is convinced that she is in love with another, even though that other may not be aware of it yet: "She must be in love with someone else, even though the other person doesn't know it. I'm certain she is in love with someone else" (1.253). Here is part of this conversation between Joaquín and Abel, who is a painter:

> "It's just that this woman is toying with me. And it is not honorable to play this way with a man who is loyal, open, above board. . . . If you could only see how beautiful she is! And the colder and more disdainful she grows, the more beautiful she becomes! There are times when I don't know if I love her more or hate her more. . . . Would you like me to introduce you to her?"
>
> "Well, if you. . . ."
>
> "Good, I'll introduce you."
>
> "And if she likes, if she wants it. . . ."

"What?"

"I'll paint her a portrait."

"That's wonderful!"

But that night Joaquín slept badly, envisioning the portrait and haunted by the idea that Abel Sánchez, the guileless natural-born charmer, the one everybody favored, was going to paint Helena's portrait. . . . He thought of calling off the proposed introduction, but, since he had already promised. . . . (1.254–55)

The modeling sessions begin. "Within a couple of days Abel and Helena were addressing each other using the familiar *tú*. Joaquín wanted it that way. On the third day, Joaquín missed the painting session" (2.257). At the end of that third session from which Joaquín had absented himself, Abel and Helena became *novios*, lovers. After all, if Joaquín insisted that she must be secretly in love with someone else, as Helena said, "he'll succeed in having me fall in love with someone else. . . " (2.259). Joaquín will have terrible nightmares about that. "I began to hate Abel with all my soul, and, at the same time, to plan the concealment of this hatred, which I would cultivate and tend deep down in my soul's entrails. Hatred? I did not yet want to give it that name. Nor did I want yet to recognize that I had been born predestined to carry the substance and the seed of hatred within me. That night I was born into my life's hell" (3.264). He recognizes that he has no right to complain. He was never engaged to her, he cannot and should not try to force her affection, and so on.

And still, confusedly I felt that it had been I who had brought them, not only together, but to the point of love; that they had come together because they both wished to spurn me; that Helena's decision was largely determined by an urge to see me suffer and rage, to set my teeth on edge, to humiliate me before Abel; on his part I sensed a supreme egotism which never allowed him to take notice of the suffering of others. Ingenuously, he simply did not pay attention to the existence of others. . . . He did not even hate, so full of himself was he. (5.268)

"I felt confusedly . . ." . There was no confusion about the facts. It was his idea that Abel should meet Helena. He applauded the idea of having her pose as a model for him. He insisted that they drop the formal form of address with each other, and use the familiar "tú." And then he left them alone. And he did all this in spite of the fact that he had misgivings about the whole situation from the very beginning, misgivings that kept him awake at night. In fact, it was as if he had anticipated everything, since he told Abel he was convinced she must be in love with someone else. Was he a masochist? I do not think masochism is the most appropriate interpretation in this case. It does not explain adequately the overpowering hatred of Abel that Joaquín Monegro nurtures secretly in his heart.

This modern Cain was clearly the Galeotto, the procurer, between the object of his own desire and his rival. This means that he places his rival between himself and the object of his desire; he desires through the rival. And he "confusedly" knows this to be true. But he does not seem to feel any responsibility for the pain and mental disturbance that his own actions have brought upon himself. Quite the contrary: he, the go-between, feels victimized because the two lovers took advantage of him when he was right in the middle of them to hit him from both sides. For "it was out of contempt for me that they started seeing each other." They were really looking for an opportunity to show him how little they thought of him, how insignificant he was in their eyes, and he innocently provided them with such an opportunity. Of course, knowing them as well as he did, he had some premonitions, but who could have thought that they would reach such a disgusting level of depravity and do to him what they did!

All of this is quite in character for any Cain worth his salt. The problem is that none of this hate-filled distortion of the truth seems to affect in any way the tragic grandeur of the character in Unamuno's eyes. He never casts any doubts, ironic or otherwise, on Joaquín Monegro's view of the events that led to the "treacherous" behavior of his girlfriend and his best friend. And yet Unamuno's presentation of those events is clear-sighted enough to suggest quite a different view, a view that would radically undercut the tragic pose, the claim to innocence, of his protagonist. It is as if Unamuno deliberately intimated such an unflattering view in order to avoid it. He probably considered this view too mean-spirited, too degrading, too unworthy of the turbulent grandeur of his modern Cain. The fact of the matter is that Unamuno never interrupts his character's poetically sanctioned story in the way Cervantes does with the stories of his own characters.

According to Joaquín Monegro, he became interested in Helena quite independently of his Cain-like relationship with Abel. And once that happened, what could be more natural than talking with his closest friend about it, and wanting his friend to meet and befriend her? Therefore, the only possible explanation for the betrayal of Helena and Abel is that they thought nothing of him, that they cared nothing about his feelings, in fact that they probably enjoyed hurting him. Joaquín Monegro would probably admit that he was a little imprudent, but, once again, who would have thought!

But this is not a very credible version of the story. If envious Cain could fall in love with a woman, without thinking about Abel, that is to say, quite independently of what Abel may or may not think about it, then indeed he does not have a problem, least of all with Abel. But he does have a problem with Abel: that is precisely what defines him as envious Cain. He cannot get Abel off his mind. Nothing that he does or feels is immune to what he both hopes and fears that Abel may or may not do or think about it.

In fact, Cain's problem is even deeper and more absorbing than that. The real question is, Could Cain, consumed as he is with envy of his brother Abel, ever be able to desire anything in which his brother Abel would show no interest? It does not seem possible, because, once again, if it were possible, it would mean that Cain would have found a way to overcome his envy. As long as Cain is in the grip of his fratricidal envy he can have no desire that he can truly call his own, that is to say, a desire independent of Abel.

Nevertheless, let us assume for a moment that Cain's envy is not so overpowering as to completely obliterate natural urges or needs. Let us assume that a past-puberty young Cain would feel naturally attracted to a young woman. Would he not think immediately of using the object of his attraction to excite Abel's envy? Would he not give an arm and a leg, so to speak, to get Abel to desire the woman, his woman? Of course he would. And he would feel dejected and frustrated if Abel showed no interest whatsoever in this woman. One can easily picture him complaining to Abel that he only thinks of himself, that he takes no notice of the things that he, Cain, really likes, and so on. And here is an even more interesting possibility: he may very well end up blaming the woman for it, that is to say, blaming her for being so . . . so . . . uninteresting. Because if Abel persists in his lack of interest, Cain's own interest will quickly dwindle. He may actually wake up one day and find himself wondering what he ever saw in that woman that attracted his interest, because now that his passion has abated he can see clearly that she is not such a great thing at all.

Perhaps Joaquín Monegro was lucky, after all, that Helena married Abel Sánchez, not him. Because if she had married him, and Abel Sánchez, in spite of Joaquín's efforts, remained indifferent to her, heaven knows what envious Joaquín would have been capable of thinking. He could have thought of truly shameful things involving Abel and Helena in order to make her attractive again. To be sure, Unamuno would have considered such things to be incompatible with the dignity of his tragic hero. We have to go to Cervantes's story to find out about those things.

El curioso impertinente, or *The Tale of Foolish Curiosity*

The Tale of Foolish Curiosity is the story of two very close friends, Anselmo and Lothario, and a woman, Camilla. In sharp contrast with Unamuno's story, here at the beginning nothing appears to foretell the tragedy to come. The relationship between the two best friends could not be better. They are known in their native Florence for their exemplary friendship—indeed, people call them "the friends." This kind of ideal initial situation appears frequently in Cervantes. It appears, for example, in the other two important interpolated stories, the Marcela-Grisóstomo story and the one about Cardenio and Luscinda. It is no accident. Cervantes does not like to begin with characters already marked for destruction, predestined to evil. You will never hear a Cervantine character say something like what Joaquín Monegro says: "[N]ací, predestinado, con su masa [la del odio] y con su semilla" (I was predestined. I was born with the substance and the seed of hatred). In Cervantes's world bad things, tragic things, do not just happen to the bad people. They can happen to the best people. In Cervantes's world nobody can say "That would never happen to me." That also means that in Cervantes's world evil never becomes a tragic mark, a mark of distinction.

Anselmo and Lothario were excellent friends. "Their minds, in fact, worked in such unison that no clock could keep better time." Then,

> Anselmo fell deeply in love with a noble and beautiful damsel of that city. So good was her family and so good was she that he decided, *with the approval of his friend Lothario, without which he did nothing*, to ask her parents for her hand. And this he did. *Lothario himself was the messenger; and it was he who concluded the business* so much to his friend's satisfaction that in a short time Anselmo gained the object of his desires. Camilla too was so pleased to have got Anselmo for a husband that she never ceased to thank heaven and Lothario, the joint agents of her good fortune. (1.23.282–83; emphasis added)

For a while after the wedding Lothario continued to come to his friend's house as he had done before. "But once the wedding celebrations were over . . . he began deliberately to visit Anselmo's less often. . . . For though good and true friends should not be in any way suspicious, yet a married man's honor is so delicate that it can be injured even by his own brother. How much more so by his friend." Anselmo complains loudly. He even tells his friend that "he would never have married if he had known that his marriage was going to deprive him of his friend's company. He begged him . . . he implored him . . . to treat his house as his own again. . . . He assured him that his wife Camilla . . . was troubled to see Lothario turned so shy, knowing as she did the warmth of their friendship." Lothario replied so judiciously that Anselmo was forced to accept a certain limitation to the visits: "twice a week and on feast-days." Nevertheless, Lothario, still thinking of his friend's honor, "tried to reduce, shorten, and diminish the agreed times for his visits to the house. . . . Therefore he spent most of the days agreed upon in other business and amusements. . . . . So it was that a great part of the hours they spent together passed in complaints on one side and excuses on the other."

And so it went for a while. It was then that Anselmo developed, in his words, "a desire so strange and peculiar that I am astonished at myself," and he decides to tell his friend: "I will tell you, friend Lothario, what distresses me. It is the question whether my wife Camilla is as good and perfect as I think." As a consequence of this unexpected doubt, he is seized by an obsessive desire to test the goodness, the virtue, the value of his wife. He is obsessed and anguished with the thought that such value may be only apparent. How can he be sure that she really is as good as she appears? There is only one way to find out: she must be tempted. And the tempter should be none other than Lothario himself. That is to say, let her be desired by Lothario. For as long as she resists Lothario's desire, as long as she, having attracted Lothario's desire, rejects it, remains beyond Lothario's reach, Anselmo will be sure that his wife is as good as she appears to be.

Obviously Anselmo does not quite put it this way to his friend. He rationalizes his "strange and peculiar" desire, an obsessive desire for which "I blame and scold myself when I am alone, and try to stifle it and conceal it from my own thoughts," in a more general and philosophical way: "For it is my opinion, my friend, that a woman is good only in proportion to her temptations, and that the only constant woman is one who does not yield to promises, gifts, tears, or the continuous importunities of persistent lovers. What reason has one to thank a woman for being good . . . if no one has tempted her to be bad?" However, one must wonder, if such a rational "opinion" is the reason for what Anselmo is about to ask his friend, why does he feel so distressed with himself, so ashamed?

It is amazing to see how many critics have taken this general and moralizing rationalization of the "test" at face value. Of course, they all realize that such a test is very unwise, but they do not question its internal logic. They seem to accept the fact that what Anselmo really wants, no matter how unwisely, is to have an objective, rational proof of his wife's virtue. Many, though by no means all, read the text in this fashion. But Francisco Ayala, for example, discovers a subconscious or latent homosexual (though Ayala never uses this word) desire in Anselmo, which remains "impenetrable para su propia mente" (175). Ayala views the "test" as a cover-up for a "proceso enfermizo . . . durante el cual pretenderá conseguir el nuevo esposo satisfacción vicaria a través de su mujer . . . para los turbios deseos que hasta entonces había mantenido larvados o, mejor dicho, sublimados en las formas nobles de la camaradería" (175; a sick progress . . . during which the new husband will try to get vicarious satisfaction through his wife . . . for the dark desires that he had kept latent, or rather sublimated, in the noble forms of caomaraderie).

There is nothing in the text that would clearly prevent us from assuming some sort of latent homosexual desire in Anselmo, but neither is there any unmistakable indication that Cervantes intended to suggest such desire, as Ayala himself recognizes. The critic seems to feel uncomfortable with his own assumption, but he has no other explanation for what he has discovered, which is, in my opinion, unquestionable: what is of primary importance in Cervantes's story is not the relationship between Anselmo and his wife, but the relationship between Anselmo and Lothario. The former relationship is only a function of the latter. And Ayala is also right in noticing how "dependent" ("supeditado") "weak and sensual Anselmo" is on Lothario.

The problem with the assumption of subconscious homosexuality is that it bypasses almost completely the idea of the "test." Within this view of the story the test itself is not significant. Any other strategic maneuvering would have functioned just as well as long as it brought Lothario and Camila together for the subconscious "vicarious" erotic satisfaction of Anselmo.

But I think the idea of the test is in itself significant. It is by no means arbitrary that such an idea suddenly comes to Anselmo's mind. Because what he actually feels is that the object of his desire, that is, beautiful, sensitive, intelligent, noble Camilla, all of a sudden has ceased to attract him, or is no longer as attractive as she used to be. Psychologically, he experiences doubts about her, about how real her worth, her value, is. It is therefore no accident that the idea of the test suggests itself to him insistently. Of course, inseparable from such doubts is the acute psychological experience of the friend's absence, the unbearable thought that the friend, the mediator of his desire, has lost interest in what he, Anselmo, has; that Camilla—it appears—is no longer, in the friend's eyes, as desirable as he was convinced that she was. The two things go together—the perception of a lack of reality or authenticity in Camila's value, and the feeling of a lack of interest in her on the part of his friend—even though these two things remain disconnected at the conscious level. Hence the idea of the test and the manner of the test. There is a profound logic in this "underground process," to use Dostoyevsky's terminology. After all, who is the only person who can "test" the value of Camilla in a way that would convince Anselmo? Obviously, the very person who gives meaning, and reality, and authenticity to the value of Camilla. And how would he confer such authenticity? Clearly not by some pronouncement ex cathedra, but by becoming interested in her, by desiring her.

In psychological terms, Lothario has become a god to Anselmo. But Lothario is not a giving and generous god, but a jealous one. For this kind of god only grants meaning and reality to what the worshipper has by desiring it himself, in other words, by becoming his rival. This "divine" attitude is mimetically reproduced by the worshipper, who is condemned forever to desire only what the jealous god desires. Anselmo could very well discover in himself the same feelings that Cardenio had: "vague apprehensions which made me fear that my desires would never be realized." (This is the same kind of logic that led to Joaquín Monegro's "certainty" that Helena had to be in love with someone else.) Comparing El *curioso impertinente* and Dostoyevsky's *The Eternal Husband*, René Girard has said the following:

> It is clear that their [Anselmo and Lothario's] ardent friendship is accompanied by a sharp feeling of rivalry. But this rivalry remains in the shadows. In *The Eternal Husband* the other side of the "triangular" feeling remains hidden. The hatred of the be-

trayed husband is obvious; we gradually guess at the admiration which this hatred hides. . . . (*Deceit*, 50)

If we substitute Unamuno's *Abel Sánchez* for Dostoyevsky's *The Eternal Husband*, we can still say the same thing. When we compare Unamuno's novel and Cervantes's story, what we see is the two opposite sides of the same envy. Anselmo's behavior reveals what Joaquín Monegro (or Unamuno, as opposed to Dostoyevsky) would never openly admit about his relationship with Abel: the fact that he "worships" him, that he has no desires of his own, that everything he has only has value in reference to the other, "el otro," the hated friend. And, conversely, the hate-filled envy that we see in Joaquín Monegro should be a clear indication of the nature of that obsessive and unspeakable feeling that Anselmo openly admits that he wants to hide from his very own thoughts (an open admission, by the way, that speaks highly of Anselmo's fundamental honesty). For Anselmo truly believed that he loved and honored his friend just as his friend loved and honored him. But now he is terrified by his own feelings toward his friend and his wife. He is profoundly distressed because he is truly sensitive to his own dishonor. To judge by the way Cervantes introduces the story of the two friends, what is happening to Anselmo appears to have caught him by surprise. Nobody anticipated that such a shameful and dishonoring relationship could be generated out of what everybody—including the two friends themselves—thought was clear and exemplary. And of course Anselmo tries to dress it up as best he can, to lie to himself, in order to be able to live with it, because the one thing he tells us he cannot do is shake it off his mind. But, thanks to Cervantes, we are able to see what he is doing. Cervantes goes to great lengths to tell us that Anselmo is trying desperately to deceive himself.

That is the enormous difference between Cervantes and Unamuno. Cervantes tells the truth about his character, he sees the two sides of the relationship. Unamuno does not. He is as interested as his character is in hiding the truth, which he does (or thinks he does), as we have seen, by turning something unspeakable and shameful into an unchanging predetermined heroic essence, a tragic human destiny in accordance with the requirements of a piece of high literature. It was while reading Lord Byron's *Cain* that Joaquín discovered that his hatred had to be immortal, that his soul was his hatred: "A corruptible organism could not hate as I did. Lucifer had aspired to be

God, and I, ever since I was very young, had I not aspired to reduce everyone else to nothing? But how could I have been so unfortunate, unless I was made that way by the creator of all misfortune?" (12.292).

Joaquín Monegro and his envious hatred of Abel belong together, they are of one piece, there is nothing left beyond such union of the two. Cervantine Anselmo, on the other hand, is not of one piece with his own dishonor and shameful behavior. This is why he has such a problem living with it. He finds himself in contradiction with himself. And that awareness allows him in the end to recognize that he was his own worst enemy, that he brought his own dishonor and destruction upon himself. We can say of his dishonor what we said of Don Quixote's madness: he is mad but not totally and irremediably mad, his self does not fully coincide with his madness. This is why there is something about Don Quixote, as there is about most of Cervantes's characters, that transcends the limits of literary fiction. They are never exhausted by what they do or think at any given moment in accordance with what the literary form demands of them.

That does not mean that Cervantes is incapable of contemplating a complete breakdown of the individual self, a mind so overwhelmed by its internal conflict that it just gives up. Quite the contrary: precisely because Cervantes envisages an internal conflict that is truly a conflict, the possibility always exists for the conflict to intensify and to end with a total collapse of the self. That is the possibility that Cervantes contemplates in the madness of Cardenio, the suicide of Chrysostom, or the fate of Anselmo in the *Curioso* when, confronted with the disastrous news of his friend's betrayal and his wife's infidelity, "Anselmo was not merely on the point of going out of his mind, but on the verge of putting an end to his life." In the end, "he was so overwhelmed by the thought of his disaster [la imaginación de su desventura]" that he seems to lose the will to live and lets himself die. Unamuno never contemplates that final collapse seriously, because even if he tells us that his Cain lives constantly under incredible inner pressure, this pressure turns out to be the very stuff he thrives on, the stuff that makes him immortal, perhaps like the damned in hell are immortal, except that Unamuno's hell is only the stuff of "high literature," not the real thing. In Cervantes's hell, on the other hand, there are great sufferings, but no heroes.

Can anybody imagine how Unamuno would react if we told him that in the story of Anselmo Cervantes performed a much more truthful analysis of envious desire than he did in the story of Joaquín Monegro? I suppose he might laugh in our face or become outraged. Because, from his perspective, the character Anselmo is the very proof of how pedestrian and mediocre Cervantes was. And in a certain literary sense he would be right, because the truth of that final collapse of the self that Cervantes contemplates is not at all the way "high literature" would make it out to be. Pedestrian Cervantes is the great revealer of Unamuno's literary cover-ups.

But, to repeat, while in Cervantes the inner conflict does threaten the individual with the possibility of total collapse, such a collapse is no more than a realistic possibility. There is no predestined necessity between the Cervantine individual and the problem he or she faces. The individual is one thing, the problem is another. In the literary world of Cervantes there are all kinds of individual characters with different personal predispositions or natural inclinations (Anselmo, for example, "was more inclined to affairs of the heart than was Lothario, who preferred hunting"), but no such inclinations or personal characteristics are ever sufficient to explain the nature of the problem itself.

This separation between individual character and circumstances, on the one hand, and the fundamental nature of the problem, on the other, not only confers on the individual his or her characteristically Cervantine freedom, but allows simultaneously for a clearer (one might even say scientific) understanding of the problem itself—much clearer than would be the case if Cervantes were primarily interested in the psychological analysis of different individual cases. Cervantes's extraordinary inventiveness is not aimed at the creation of multiple psychological cases, each one different from the others. He is rather an extraordinary inventor of all kinds of specific individual circumstances, all of which, however, are susceptible to becoming a breeding ground for the development of the fundamental problem. In the literary world of Cervantes nobody can say "That would never happen to me," "My circumstances are different," or "I am not that kind of a person." This is so because ultimately the problem that Cervantes illustrates time and time again is an ever-present danger in all human relationships: envious desire, or as Girard has called it, "internal mediation" (it might be better to call it "mediation denied" because envious desire denies being mediated by the model it envies), the loss of transcendance in the relationship between the I and the other, the ever present possibility of a relationship without any point of reference beyond the relationship itself. It is within this immanent reciprocity that envy thrives and the object of envy may easily become a profoundly ambivalent idol both fascinating and hateful, a model and a rival, a stumbling block, *piedra de escándalo*, a scandal.

Existentially this loss of transcendance, the point at which a healthy relationship becomes an invidious one, can be extremely difficult to detect, for at the beginning of the change both things may look exactly the same. That which deserves healthy respect and admiration is in itself no different from the object of envy. The same thing that triggers the one may also trigger the other. We find the idea repeatedly in Cervantes. We find it, for example, in Cardenio's story, when he tells us that although he found Don Ferdinand's praise of Luscinda's virtues justified, "This awoke a vague jealousy in me; not that I had any reason to fear a change in Luscinda's faith and virtue, yet, for all that, my fate made me dread the very danger against which she seemed to secure me [me hacía temer mi suerte lo mesmo que ella me aseguraba]." And we also find it in the *Curioso*: "Camilla's modest behaviour and gravity of expression . . . were sufficient to curb Lothario's tongue. But whatever advantage they gained from Camilla's virtues silencing Lothario's tongue led to even greater harm for both of them [redundó más en daño de los dos]. For if his tongue was silent, his thoughts ran on; and he had time to contemplate, one by one, all of Camilla's perfections of mind and body. . . ." In other words, the same attitude in Camilla that commanded respect and admiration, holding Lothario's verbal advances in check, also contributed to making her even more invidiously desirable in the eyes of Lothario; the same thing that gave Cardenio confidence in his relationship with Luscinda made him fear that he might lose her.

In principle, therefore, it is not the case that the healthy and the envious ways of looking see different things or different qualities in the object. They both see something that is good in itself, worthy of admiration and respect. The envious one desires the same object as the nonenvious one. It is indeed this convergence toward, or coincidence in, the object that establishes an uneasy proximity between radically different ways of seeing, a constant danger that the good may become evil, or, as we read in the *Persiles*: "Parece que el bien y el mal distan tan poco el uno del otro, que son como dos líneas concurrentes, que, aunque parten de apartados y diferentes principios, acaban en un punto" (4.12; It seems that good and evil are so close to each other, that they ressemble two converging lines, starting at separate and different beginnings, and ending in one point).

Since there is desire involved in both ways of looking at the attractive object, we could simply say that in one case desire is ruled by reason, does not overstep its rational boundaries, while in the other case we have a desire that recognizes no rule outside itself, an obssesive, selfish form of desire. And that, I think, would be a sufficient explanation of the difference between the two desires, the two ways of looking at the attractive object. But that may not explain with sufficient clarity one of the inmediate consequences of lapsing into the invidious, selfish way of looking that we see time and again in Cervantes. For as soon as the Cervantine character falls prey to selfish desire, he or she loses self-confidence, becomes radically insecure and prone to jealousy. For example, as soon as the respect and admiration that Lothario and Camilla feel for each other turn into selfish desire "without thought for anything but [its] own gratification" (33.299), they both become very vulnerable to feelings of jealousy. In fact, the course of their adulterous relationship is a series of episodes of jealousy and their immediate consequences for both of them. That is by no means accidental. The only accidental thing about those bouts of jealousy are the specific circumstances in which they occur. But any attentive reader of Cervantes, or indeed of sixteenth- and seventeenth-century literature in general, knows that they will occur. Jealousy is the ever present danger to any healthy human relationship. No such relationship is inmune to it. In other words, it happens not only to the bad people but to the very good ones too—for example, to the marvelous and exemplary Auristela of the *Persiles* (1.23).

This feeling of insecurity that overtakes a character as soon as the object of respect and admiration becomes an object of invidious desire suggests that the very distance that genuine respect and admiration establishes between subject and object, admiring and admired, all of a sudden is experienced by the subject as an obstacle, a barrier, a denial, a form of exclusion that places the admired and respected object beyond the reach of the subject. At that moment, in the experience of the subject, the distance is no longer there only to highlight and to make visible the value of the object, but *also*, simultaneously, to exclude the subject, to show him or her as lacking in value in the light of the admired and respected object. At that moment objective rationality disappears because nothing of real value is just there in itself, independently of the subject. Valuable things are there *ad hominem*, pointing a finger toward the valueless, excluded subject. They are valuable *against* him or her. They exist either as a testimony against the invidious subject and/or as a challenge.

Within the internal dynamics of this situation, the experience of being excluded, which occurs simultaneously and inseparably from the perception of the value of the desired object, ends up becoming the *proof* of such a value. Any object which, for any reason, is denied to the subject will tend to become immediately an object of his or her desire. The more insecure and excluded the envious subject feels, the more convinced he or she will be of the intrinsic value of that which is denied to him or her; and the greater this perception of value, the more deeply and intolerably will he or she feel his or her own inadequacy, his or her own exlusion, and so on, in an endless vicious circle.

There is an immediate and direct relation between the denial, the obstacle, and the intensity of the desire. We see this constantly in Cervantes. Chrysostom, for example, initially loved Marcela, it seems, in a perfectly healthy way. But as soon as she decided to become a Diana-like virginal shepherdess for the rest of her life, thereby placing herself beyond his reach, we are told that he "no longer loved her, but adored her." We find the same development in Cardenio regarding his feelings for Luscinda. As soon as Luscinda's father bars him from coming to the house as he used to, "[the] denial added flame to flame and desire to desire." In fact, in the case of Cardenio we see how this intensification of desire is immediately followed explicitly by a certain paralysis of the will. Cardenio, as we will see, is the very epitome of indecision and insecurity. And in this too Cervantes teaches us a very anti-Unamunian lesson: intensity of desire is by no means an indication of self-confidence and hope, and may well be just the opposite.

That is probably the reason for Cervantes's profound sense of balance and moderation (which Unamuno would wrongfully interpret as weakness and mediocrity). After all, mad Don Quixote is the prototypical example of intense desire, a desire that, as we have seen, idolizes its object, transforms it into a false god. In this particular regard, what the story of the *Curioso* reveals is that even the best feelings of friendship can actually be carried too far and thus turned into their very opposite. For this seems to be what happened to Anselmo. Not only could he not live without his friend Lothario, he could not even desire anything important to him that Lothario would not also desire.

At which point, of course, the very logic of the situation inevitably turned the two friends into virtual rivals competing for the same desirable object. The story of the *Curioso* could also be called the story of the two friends turned into rivals. The literature of the period is full of such stories both in narrative and dramatic forms. It could also be called the story of how envy or jealousy destroyed their friendship. Anselmo's sickly desire is an envious, jealous desire. In fact, it was Cervantes himself, long before the *Quixote*, who defined jealousy as "impertinent curiosity" ("no son los celos señales de mucho amor, sino de *mucha curiosidad impertinente*"; *La Galatea*, 1.230; my emphasis).

Indeed, *La Galatea* offers another Cervantine version of the traditional story of "the two friends" that is an interesting antecedent and point of reference for the later story in the *Curioso*.[2] It is the story of Timbrio and Silerio, two gentlemen from Jerez. Their friendship was such that, in the words of Silerio himself, the narrator, "those who knew us almost forgot our names, Timbrio and Silerio, and only called us *the two friends*" (128). It was, in fact, Silerio who made every possible effort to become a friend of Timbrio: "Let it suffice to say that whether it was because of Timbrio's abundant goodness or by the influence of the stars, which inclined me to it, I tried in every way I could to become his special friend, and heaven was in this regard so favorable that those who knew us . . . only called us *the two friends*." Timbrio has to leave Jerez and eventually ends up in Rome, where he falls in love with beautiful Nísida. Silerio follows him there, meets Nísida, and immediately falls in love with her too.

But the Cervantes of *La Galatea* (1585) is not yet the Cervantes of the *Quixote*. The friend falls in love with the same woman, because, we are told, he would not be in his right mind if he did not fall in love with such beauty. And since the story is meant to depict exemplary friendship, loyalty to his friend will prevail, and Silerio will sacrifice his love for Nísida and leave Rome. In other words, there is no suggestion that the desire of one *for this particular lady* may have actually influenced or even triggered the desire of the other for the same lady. But how credible is it that a man like Silerio, who has tried "in every possible way" to become a special friend of Timbrio; who could not bear the thought of staying behind when Timbrio had to leave; who then

2. See Avalle Arce, *Deslindes*, 197–207, for an interesting comparison between the two stories.

followed him by land and sea; who risked his life for him; and who as soon as he learned of Timbrio's love immediately offered himself to become his go-between, the mediator between Timbrio and Nísida—how credible is it that his desire for Nísida had nothing to do with Timbrio's desire for Nísida? Of one thing we can be sure: the Cervantes of *Don Quixote* did not think that to be very credible. At the very least, Silerio could have expressed the same doubts as Proteus, one of the two main characters in *The Two Gentlemen of Verona*, when, recently arrived in Milan to join his best friend, Valentine, he found himself in a similar situation of falling in love with Silvia, the woman his best friend is already in love with, and has been praising to the sky:

> Is it mine eye, or Valentine's praise,
> Her true perfection, or my false transgression
> That makes me, reasonless, to reason thus?
>
> (2.4.194–96)

This is one more reason, perhaps, why Cervantes thought that his *Galatea*, in the words of the priest at the scrutiny of Don Quixote's library, "proposes something, but does not conclude anything." If one looks for a clear precedent to Cervantes's treatment of human desire in the *Quixote*, the place to look is not *La Galatea* but the two *Dianas*, in particular the first one, by Montemayor, the originator of the genre (apart from Sannazaro's *Arcadia*, which may not yet be fully a novel). From a historical point of view, no study of Cervantes's penetrating analysis of desire can be complete without seeing what Montemayor had done with it a generation before. It may be worth mentioning as well that, in the opinion of many,[3] Montemayor's *Diana* is also a clear precedent for, and a source of, Shakespeare's *A Midsummer Night's Dream*. We should now have a look at some of the things that went on in these pastoral precedents.

3. See "*Diana* in England," in Judith M. Kennedy, ed., *A Critical Edition of Yong's Translation of George of Montemayor's* Diana *and Gil Polo's* Enamoured Diana (Oxford, U.K.: Clarendon Press, 1968).

CHAPTER IX

The Pastoral Precedent

[In] ogni libro, in ogni foglio, misero amante, infelice amante e si legge e si scrive. Senza fallo esso Amore niuno è che piacevole il chiami, niun dolce, niuno umano il nomò giamai: di crudele, d'acerbo, di fiero tutte le carte son piene. Leggete d'Amore quanto da mille se ne scrive: poco o niente altro in ciascun troverete che dolore.[1]

(P. Bembo, 334)

Lysander.—Ay me! For aught that ever I could read,
Could ever hear by tale or history,
The course of true love never did run smooth.

(*A Midsummer Night's Dream*, 1.1.142–44)

1. "In every book, on every page, what one writes and what one reads is [always] miserable lover, unhappy lover. Nobody has ever called that love pleasant, sweet, or humane; [on the contrary,] the pages are full of [words] like cruel, bitter, violent. Read what thousands have written about love: little or nothing you would find there other than pain."

Piénsese bien: el amor feliz no tiene historia literaria propia. Siempre que el amor ha sido eje argumental ha tenido un signo trágico, o bien se ha tratado de un amor contrariado.[2]

(Juan Bautista Avalle-Arce, "Estudio preliminar," in *La Diana*, ed. Juan Montero, 14)

In the Italian passage quoted above from Pietro Bembo's dialogues *Gli Asolani*, the character speaking, Perottino, is violently against love because he suffers grievously from it. Some other character will answer him by saying that what he feels is not love because love is rational and temperate. If he really loved, he would not suffer for things that have not happened, or desire and look for that which he cannot have. "Because . . . it is a most stupid thing and intemperate beyond measure to keep on looking for and desiring that which cannot be had as if it could be had."[3]

In the highly stylized world of the pastoral novel, everybody seems to be suffering from Perottino's problem. Everybody is looking for something they cannot have. And what is even worse, if they finally get what they want, their interest seems to dwindle rather quickly as they become attracted to something else beyond their reach. In the interminable web of love relationships that structures these novels, two lovers who love each other at the same time is indeed a rare and fleeting sight. What keeps these novels going is the rather simple fact that when A loves B, B does not love A, usually because he or she loves C, who, of course, does not reciprocate, because, in turn, he or she loves D, who does not reciprocate, because . . . , and so on, in principle, endlessly.

Given the fact that in literature "the course of true love never did run smooth," that is to say, given the fact that "happy love does not have a literary history of its own," obviously these characters are true to type. They all feel and act as if inspired by their reading of poetically painful love stories. They seem to embody the very spirit that keeps the poetic love story alive. For they are attracted to all those obstacles that keep the genre alive, which means those same obstacles that keep attracting us, we avid readers of poetic love

2. "Think carefully: happy love has no literary history of its own. Whenever love has been central to the plot, it has always ended tragically or it has encountered obstacles."

3. "Perottino, tu non ami. . . . Perciò che se tu amassi, temperato sarebbe il tuo amore, et essendo egli temperato, né di cosa che avenuta ne sia ti dorresti, né quello che per te avere non si può disidereresti tu e cercheresti giamai. Perció che . . . stoltissima cosa é e fuori d'ogni misura stemperata, quello che avere non si possa, pur come se egli aver si potesse, andare tuttavia desiderando e cercliando" (410).

stories. Their desires seem to be a reflection of our own desires as readers of love fiction, or the other way around.

When critics frequently speak of the highly stlylized, artificial, conventional "literariness" of these novels, they usually do not realize the extent to which they are indeed right. For the readily apparent conventional literariness of these novels is not only one formal characteristic of their narrative content but their very essence. The amorous desire of all these pastoral characters, the desire of which Perottino says that "senza fallo niuno è che piacevole il chiami, niun dolce, niuno umano il nomò giamai: di crudele, d'acerbo, di fiero tutte le carte son piene"—in other words, the desire based on frustrated love—is quintessentially literary. The other kind of love, the rational, temperate, nonfrustrating one, "has no literary history of its own"—in other words, it does not interest anybody.

The difference between this new pastoral version of the typical love story and most of its predecessors is that here the amorous desire itself takes center stage. The surrounding world, mythical Arcadia, is no more than the backdrop demanded by that desire; the outer world adapts itself submissively to such a desire. This means that the typical causes blamed for the typical frustration of the typical love relationship (e.g., parental opposition, unexpected absence, storms at sea) are reduced to a minimum or simply disappear, allowing the amorous frustration essential to the plot to be generated by the internal dynamics of the love relationship itself.

The characters themselves blame "Time" and the mutability of "Fortune" for their frustration. However, the frustration itself is perfectly predictable, and its inner structure is always the same. In fact, the best among these authors, Montemayor, is quite capable of playing ironic games with his own characters by bringing forth the obvious automaticity and predictability of what is going on, while his characters keep talking about haphazard events and silly coincidences. Of course, the willing self-deception of the character, who always finds his or her situation unique, tied to very specific circumstances, is of the essence to keep the game going.

Let us examine what this great master of the pastoral is capable of doing. The story we will examine is the leading one in the *Diana*, within the general frame story of the frustrated relationship between Diana and Sireno, a framing frustration that has already happened when the novel begins. Our story is that of Selvagia and her frustrated love of Alanio.

Selvagia first appears on the scene at the beginning of the novel, in the place where Sireno and Silvano, both in love with absent Diana, have been telling each other their love woes. She greets the shepherds:

—What are you doing, unloved shepherds, in this green and delightful prairie?

—You ask indeed the right question, beautiful Selvagia—said Silvano. For we do so little in respect of what we should do, that we can never conclude or bring to pass anything that love makes us desire.

—Don't be surprised—said Selvagia—for there are things that, before they can be finished, finish the one who desires them. (39)[4]

Quite a fitting prologue for what is coming, or indeed for the entire novel. Their words summarize in a convenient and emblematic nutshell the basic problem all these characters face. Here is Selvagia's story: one day she and some other shepherdesses, her friends, are attending a celebration in the temple of Minerva. A new group of mysterious shepherdesses enters the temple. They all have their faces covered with white veils, which immediately attracts the attention of Selvagia and the other girls. Selvagia continues:

I was looking at the one sitting next to me, and noticed that, while I was not looking, she wouldn't take her eyes off mine, and that, as soon as I looked at her, she would lower them, seemingly wanting to look at me without my noticing. I was burning to find out who she was . . . for she continued to keep her eyes on me, as soon as I diverted mine for a moment; so much so that a thousand times I was about to talk to her, as I was in love with those beautiful eyes, which were the only thing I could see. It was then, while I was paying her all possible attention, that she extended toward me the most beautiful and delicate hand that I have ever seen, and, taking mine, looked at it for a short while. I, who was feeling more in love with her than I could tell you, said to her:—"Beautiful and gracious shepherdess, it is not only this hand that is ready to serve you, but the heart and the thought as well to which the hand belongs." Ismenia, for that was her name . . . answered in a very low voice, that nobody could hear:—"Gracious shepherdess, I am so much yours that as such I dared to do what I did. I beg you not to be scandalized, for as I looked at your beautiful face I could not control myself." . . . After this we gave each other so many hugs, the love words we said to each other were so true, at least on my part, that we paid no attention to the songs of the shepherdesses, nor did we watch the dances of the nymphs and other rejoicings that were taking place in the temple. (45–46)

4. English translations from the two Dianas are mine.

What is this? Are we witnessing the beginning of a lesbian relationship? It certainly looks that way. Would Selvagia feel the same way if her new friend were a man? We will soon find out, because Montemayor has a surprise in store for the reader.

Selvagia keeps pressing the beautiful shepherdess to reveal her face and her name, against which the girl always found some excuse and kept changing the subject. But it was past midnight, and Selvagia's desire and insistence were becoming obsessive. She started crying and begging. Finally Ismenia, of the beautiful eyes, takes Selvagia apart and in great secrecy reveals to her that she is really a man, not a woman, that "he" has disguised himself as a girl in order to be able to stay inside the temple with all the other girls and the nymphs, because the rule of the place prohibits men from doing that. Selvagia is, of course, surprised. However, now she notices a certain masculinity in beautiful Ismenia's face. But she is already so much in love with her/him that she does not mind at all. She would have preferred that "he" would have put on "his" disguise for her sake, that is to say, in order to be able to stay in the temple with her (not just with "the girls" in general). But other than that, everything is all right, and Selvagia fully expects to see "the boy" in the days ahead.

We soon find out that Ismenia, who is not in fact a boy at all, is almost a perfect replica of her male cousin Alanio, with whom she is very much in love, although her love is not reciprocated with quite the same intensity. She tells Alanio, jokingly, what happened to her in the temple. Needless to say, Alanio's interest and curiosity are greatly aroused, and he looks for an opportunity to meet beautiful Selvagia. When he does meet her, she of course believes that she is meeting the "real" Ismenia, and is all happy about it, promising Alanio eternal love. It does not take long before Alanio is seduced by the game instigated by Ismenia, and falls in love with Selvagia. At this point Ismenia, who sees that her joke has backfired on her, for she is losing Alanio, begs Selvagia to have pity on her and give up her old boyfriend for her sake. Of course, Selvagia refuses, for she is now eternally devoted to Alanio. (Although in the end she will be cured magically of her attachment to Alanio and made to fall in love with Silvano, who has, in turn, been cured of his love for Diana, and made magically to fall in love with Selvagia.)

Let us pause for a moment to reflect on these events. How are we to understand that scene in the temple and Ismenia's "joke"? Was it really all a "joke" to her, and nothing else? Why would she do such a thing? In the way it is presented to us, the "joke" was entirely unpremeditated. She did not have it in mind when she entered the temple. This is indirectly acknowledged by Selvagia's complaint that she would have preferred for the "boy" in disguise to have come to the temple with her already in mind, as well as by the fact that none of the other veiled girls who came with Ismenia shows any indication of knowing anything about it. Nor will Ismenia acknowledge any premeditation when she "jokingly" tells Alanio. In other words, the "joke" must have been suggested to her by the very play of desire between the two girls as it occurred and intensified. There was an obvious crescendo as the desire of each of the girls fed on the desire of the other. First, it's hide-and-seek with the eyes, with each one baiting the other, showing and hiding. With every exchange desire increases. Then it's the hand game. They can hardly control themselves any longer. Then come the hugs and passionate expressions of love. Selvagia breaks down in tears. She must know who this fascinating creature is. For she has only seen her eyes, and knows absolutely nothing about her. According to Selvagia's account, it is precisely at that point, at the peak of this mutually fed desire, that Ismenia reveals herself to Selvagia by assuming the identity of her own boyfriend. In other words, *she presents, she offers, the image of her own boyfriend as a bait, an enticement, to the intensifying desire of Selvagia, automatically turning her, Selvagia, into her own rival.* Fascinated by Selvagia's desire for her, she has been feeding it to a frenzy, and as it reaches that peak she substitutes her own boyfriend for herself. At the peak of her own fascination with Selvagia's desire, she sees it, she perceives that desire, as a rival desire, as the desire of her rival. Selvagia becomes much more fascinating to her as a rival than as a friend.

Needless to say, in the character's discourse, the triangle Ismenia-Alanio-Selvagia created by Ismenia's "joke" was totally unintentional, the result of a series of actions each one of which was perfectly innocent. For example, since Alanio was always in Ismenia's heart, what could be more natural than for her to think of Alanio when her innocent "joke" forced her to come up with a boy's name? It was just the first thing that popped into her mind ("[Cuando] yo a ella le pregunté su mismo nombre . . . el primero que me supo nombrar fue Alanio, porque no hay cosa más cierta que en las cosas súpitas encontrarse la lengua con lo que está en el corazón"). Likewise, when she told Alanio everything that had happened in the temple (thereby completing the triangle), she did it just as innocently, so he could have some fun, because she always wanted to please him, "without thinking about it" ("sin mirar lo que hacía"). Clearly, Montemayor knew better than that. After all, what he observed beyond the speech of his characters was not so unique in the context of sixteenth-century literature, even though he was unsurpassed in the way he manipulated it for literary purposes.

As a point of comparison, we may bring to mind a similar attitude in one of Lope de Vega's shepherdesses, in his own pastoral *Arcadia* (1598), on which the author comments as follows: "Es muy de celosos agradar más al competidor que los mismos ojos que se aman" (4.1304). That is to say, it is typical of the jealous person to want to look more pleasing before the eyes of the rival than before those of the person he or she loves. This is another way of saying that, to the jealous person, the desire of the rival is preferable to, is more attractive than, the desire of the beloved.

Before Ismenia's boyfriend meets Selvagia, or even knows of her existence, Ismenia is already looking at her with jealous eyes. Her mounting fascination with Selvagia during the temple scene is already filled with jealousy. It is indeed this jealousy that Selvagia triggers in her, that seduces her and keeps her desire glued, as it were, on her rival. She will nurture this jealousy. She will do anything to arouse Selvagia's interest in, and desire for, her boyfriend Alanio, as well as her boyfriend Alanio's desire for Selvagia. One could not find a clearer precedent to *El curioso impertinente*.

And she succeeds, of course. And as soon as she succeeds, she hates it. Now she will do anything to spoil the relationship between Alanio, her "inconstant" and "unfaithful" boyfriend, and "cruel" Selvagia. She tries pleading first, but it does not work because Selvagia has by now transferred all her fascinated desire for the beautiful Ismenia over to the equally beautiful Alanio, as suggested by Ismenia herself. Then it dawns on Ismenia that jealousy is a much more powerful weapon of seduction than pleading. She ought to know, of course. Whereupon she, in order to make Alanio jealous, sets her eyes on Montano, a bitter rival of Alanio, who is in love with her. It works. Now poor Selvagia suffers: Alanio's interest for her cools down rather quickly, and he increasingly turns his attention back to Ismenia. But the situation gets even more complicated. For it turns out that the jealousy game Ismenia is playing with Montano catches up with her, and she ends up falling in love with him, as her old beloved reaches out to her in vain. Montano, Alanio's old rival, ought to consider himself the happiest man in the world because his triumph is now complete: he has gotten Ismenia's love and, on top of that, he sees his old rival, Alanio, not only defeated, but pleading for attention from Ismenia, who rejects him. What more could he hope for? Well, contrary to rational expectations, it seems that the triumph itself cools down his interest in Ismenia. Shortly after desired Ismenia stopped loving Alanio in order to love him, he starts finding her adoration a little too much ("los sobrados favores que Ismenia le hacía . . . en algunos hombres de bajo espíritu causan fastidio"; 53). Furthermore, from that moment on he begins to fall in love with Selvagia, who not only has no interest in him, but is totally in love with his rival of old, Alanio (who, of course, is no longer interested in Selvagia). It seems, therefore, that Montano only falls in love with women who are in love with his rival. He loved Ismenia when she was in love with Alanio, and lost interest in her when she lost interest in Alanio; now he falls in love with Selvagia, who is in love with Alanio. All this means that he is more interested in the triumph and prestige of his rival than in his own triumph. A pleading rival, which is now Alanio's case before disinterested Ismenia, does not attract him at all. Selvagia's unrequited love for Alanio, however, keeps the shining prestige of the rival on its pedestal. She basks in the glow of that prestige, and that is what makes her attractive. So there we are: Selvagia chases after Alanio, Alanio chases after Ismenia, Ismenia chases after Montano, and Montano chases after Selvagia in a perfect circle of frustrated desire:

Ved que estraño embuste de amor: si por ventura Ismenia iba al campo, Alanio tras ella; si Montano iba al ganado, Ismenia tras él; si yo andaba en el monte con mis ovejas, Montano tras mí; si yo sabía que Alanio estaba en el bosque . . . allá me iba tras él. Era la más nueva cosa del mundo oir cómo decía Alanio sospirando:—"¡Ay, Ismenia!"; y cómo Ismenia decía:—"¡Ay, Montano!"; y cómo Montano decía:—"¡Ay, Selvagia!"; y cómo la triste de Selvagia decía:—"¡Ay, mi Alanio!" (53–54)

(See what a strange tangle of love: if by chance Ismenia went to the fields, Alanio would follow her; if Montano went to his herd, Ismenia would follow; if I was in the hills with my sheep, Montano would follow after me; if I knew that Alanio was in the forest . . . I went after him. It was the most unheard of thing in the world to hear Alanio sighing, "Ay, Ismenia!," and Ismenia, "Ay, Montano!," and Montano, "Ay, Selvagia!," and sad Selvagia, "Ay, Alanio!")

One day the four of them run into each other in the forest:

Y cuando allí los cuatro discordantes amadores nos hallamos, no se puede decir lo que sentíamos, porque cada uno miraba a quien no quería que le mirase.

(And when the four of us disaccordant lovers found ourselves there, it cannot be imagined what we all felt, for each one looked at the one who did not want to be seen by those eyes.)

This scene in the forest is a clear precedent to the one in *A Midsummer Night's Dream* with its own four disaccordant lovers and all their mismatches, aggravated by the blundering and mischievous Puck, jester to Oberon, king of the fairies, and their magic potion, Shakespeare's way of playing ironic games with the mimetic desires of his characters. In Montemayor, also, the mismatches will be straightened out in the end with the magic potion of the sage Felicia, Montemayor's version of the queen of the fairies.

It is during this scene in the forest that one of the shepherds, Montano, the one who is now pining away for Selvagia, who is pining away for Montano's archrival, Alanio, sings an old popular ballad, which fits perfectly in their situation, and reads in part as follows:

Amor loco, ¡ay, amor loco!
Yo por vos y vos por otro
. . . .
Ya que viéndoos no me veis
Y morís porque no muero,
Comed ora a mí que os quiero
Con salsa del que quereis.
(58–59)

(Foolish love, ah foolish lover,
I for you, and you for another.
I see you, you don't see me,
And you die because I don't.
Then, eat me, who love you,
With the sauce of the one you love.)

In spite of the "strange agony" ("extraña agonía") they all felt, everybody laughed when they heard Montano, especially Selvagia on seeing that "Montano wanted me to deceive my taste of him with the sauce of his rival Alanio, as if I could entertain the thought of allowing myself to fall for an appearance instead of the real thing" ("que quería que engañase yo el gusto de miralle con salsa de su competidor Alanio, como si en mi pensamiento cupiera dejarse engañar con apariencias de otra cosa"). Montemayor's clear insight is the exact reverse of his characters' blindness. What Selvagia says she would not think of doing is precisely what she and everybody else *are* doing. Selvagia "eats" Alanio with the sauce of her rival Ismenia. For we must remember that, as an object of desire, Alanio is merely substituting for Ismenia in Selvagia's eyes. Alanio would become rather insipid to Selvagia's taste if rival Ismenia were not there to take Alanio's desire away from her. Likewise, Ismenia "eats" Montano with the sauce of her rival Selvagia, Alanio "eats" Ismenia with the sauce of his rival Montano, and Montano "eats" Selvagia with the sauce of his rival Alanio. So, says Montano, in fact, to Selvagia in his song: your love is as foolish as mine. If you love the one who does not love you with the sauce of the one he loves (your rival), why can't you love me with the sauce of the one you love, for he is already a substitute anyway.

The secret recipe to the love of all these characters is "rival sauce." Without the rival who takes away from them what they desire, they would not desire it. What is also interesting is that the rival does not take it away by desiring it himself, but *by not desiring it*, because in this pastoral world the one who triumphs is not the one who desires more, but the one who desires less. Indeed, the one most desired is the one who desires least. We are dealing, then, with a desire that is inherently self-contradictory: it grows all the more intense the less hope there is of satisfying it. It desires through its own frustration. It only desires the object that denies itself to it. That is to say, it only desires its object if there is an obstacle in its path, an explicit or implicit rival. What really attracts this pastoral lover is not the reciprocal love of the beloved, but the love of the beloved as it is drawn away toward a third party, who is thus confirmed as a successful rival, and being thus confirmed, in turn confirms the value, the desirability, of the love denied to the lover. Only that love is attractive whose value is confirmed, validated, by the successful rival, who is successful precisely because he or she does not desire it.

What all this means is that we are dealing with a desire that pays no attention whatsoever to particular circumstances or personal characteristics of any kind, including gender, for it does not matter whether the subject or the object of this desire is a man or woman. Girard has called it, quite appropriately, *metaphysical desire*. It does not love anything that could truly be called real. It is haunted by its own emptiness, by absence, not presence. This Arcadia is the kingdom of the Goddess Diana, the one who keeps herself beyond the reach of lovers.

I think it was a stroke of intuitive genius on the part of Montemayor to keep his character Diana, the one who "presides" over the whole book, the book that carries her name as a title, literally absent almost until the end of the book. She is the shepherds' absent object of desire. The literal reason given for her absence is a very traditional one: she, an obedient and dutiful daughter, has been married to an equally absent shepherd by her father. And, of course, as we know from the entire courtly love tradition, marriage and romantic, courtly, pastoral love are incompatible with each other. However, Sireno, her main lover, does not find this explanation very convincing. He thinks she is using marriage as an excuse for the fact that she has really forgotten him, that his love is no longer of any interest to her, which is the typical complaint of all these shepherds and shepherdesses. As we will see in a moment, the fact that Diana is married does not change anything in regard to the internal dynamics of the desire that moves all these characters, including Diana herself.

She is the absent desire-free lady as long as she reigns supreme over the desire of her worshipping lovers. But is she really such an unconcerned divinity? We will find out what happens to the little goddess as soon as her power over her lovers is broken by sage Felicia and her magic potion. For it is precisely at that moment, when her former lovers are returning home cured of their dependence on her, that, lo and behold! shepherdess Diana finally appears literally on the scene. This is hardly a coincidence, in my view. For it is now, when they no longer desire her, that we will be able to see whether the absent lady is any different from anybody else.

And, of course, she is not. As she learns from her previous lovers what has just happened at Felicia's palace, and how much they are enjoying their newly found freedom from her,

> Each one of those words was like a spear thrown against Diana, for God knows how much she would have liked hearing complaints [of love] rather than having to believe in their freedom.
>
> (Cada palabra destas para Diana era arrojalle una lanza, que Dios sabe si quisiera ella más ir oyendo quejas que creyendo libertades. [237])

In fact, Montemayor is even more precise than that. Diana is not equally hurt by the new freedom of her two former lovers, Sireno and Silvano. We should remember that she had been totally in love with Sireno at a time prior to the beginning of the novel, while she had always hated Silvano. One would think, therefore, that she would be particularly hurt by Sireno's new attitude, rather than by Silvano's, about whose attitude, one would think, she would not care at all. And yet what happens is precisely the opposite, because Sireno is now free from any romantic desires, while Silvano, thanks to Felicia, has now fallen for Selvagia (and Selvagia for him), and that hurts much more than Sireno not loving her any longer:

For even though she had loved Sireno more than her life, and had hated Silvano, it was Silvano's forgetting that hurt her most, because it was for another woman, the sight of which he was enjoying every day to the great contentment of their [mutual] love, while Sireno was not moved by any new desire.

(Puesto caso que ella hubiese querido a Sireno más que a su vida, y a Silvano le hubiese aborrecido, más le pesaba del olvido de Silvano, por ser a causa de otra, de cuya vista estaba cada día gozando con gran contentamiento de sus amores, que del olvido de Sireno, a quien no movía ningún pensamiento nuevo. [255–56])

The difference, once more, is the presence or absence of a rival. The words just quoted clearly imply that, if given the opportunity and the choice at that moment, Diana would have been more attracted by the thought of seducing Silvano, the hated one of old, than by her desire to recapture the love of her dear Sireno. It is the "rival sauce" that makes Silvano more attractive now, and, as a result, his forgetting her more painful.

What about her husband? Does he have a role to play or is he just a prop, part of the marriage device to keep her distant from the love games of her worshippers? We know his name is Delio, although we never see him in the book. Nevertheless, one would think he must be a very happy fellow, for he has gotten the object of everybody's desire. But he is not happy at all, to judge by what Diana tells us about him in her song. In fact, he must be the unhappiest person in the whole book. As it turns out, the poor devil cannot help seeing rivals all over the place. He is jealousy personified. Here is, in part, Diana's song, which she sings as she makes her entrance in the book:

Celos me hacen la guerra
sin ser en ellos culpada:

con celos voy al ganado,
con celos a la majada,
y con celos me levanto
contino a la madrugada;
con celos como a su mesa
y en su cama só acostada.
Si le pido de qué ha celos
no sabe responder nada.
Jamás tiene el rostro alegre,
siempre la cara inclinada,
los ojos por los rincones,
la habla triste y turbada.
¿Cómo vivirá la triste
que se ve tan mal casada?

(Jealousy makes war on me / and I am not at fault: / jealousy follows me in the fields / and comes with me to the sheepfold, / and with jealousy I get up constantly in early morn; / with jealousy I eat at his table / and lie down on his bed. / If I ask him what he's jealous of / he knows not what to answer. / His visage is never happy / his face is always down, / his eyes peering in the corners, / his talk sad and disturbed. / How will the sad one live, who finds herself in such a marriage?)

In Gil Polo's excellent continuation of Montemayor's *Diana*, the *Diana enamorada*, the author expands on this brief sketch of Diana's jealous husband. There he is clearly presented as some sort of ugly personification of everything antipastoral, antiromantic. In the end he will die of a lethal combination of frustrated love for a fleeing shepherdess and jealousy of his rival Sireno, thus making it conveniently possible for the latter to be reconciled with Diana in happy marriage, through the good offices and magic herbs, once again, of sage Felicia, thereby ending the whole Arcadian saga.

Diana's husband seems to be the ugly scapegoat of this idyllic Arcadia, on whom everything that this world wants to expel from itself accumulates. When he dies, everything that is dark and ugly in that world seems to die with him. But both Montemayor and Gil Polo know—and that is part of their greatness—that his self-consuming disease is in reality spread all over the place. This miserable creature, forever frustrated, consumed with jealousy, "peering in the corners" for hidden rivals, is indeed married, in more senses than one, to beautiful, godlike Diana. He is the other hidden side of the radiant absent goddess. Gil Polo appears to be more explicitly concerned with, and insistent on, this other hidden side of the ideal. After all, he is the one who understood perfectly that the way to continue what Montemayor had already done, the way already suggested by Montemayor's novel, was to turn the image of the absent and distant Diana around, to make her plead now for what she disdained before, to change the roles of pursued and pursuer.

This is how Gil Polo begins the last book of his *Diana*, right after sage Felicia has accorded all the disaccordant lovers, and arranged their proper marriages, including, of course, the central one between Diana and her former lover Sireno. He is talking to the reader directly:

> Tan contentos estaban estos amantes en el dichoso estado, viéndose cada cual con la deseada compañía, que los trabajos del tiempo pasado tenían olvidados. Mas los que desde aparte miramos las penas que les costó su contentamiento, los peligros en que se vieron y los desatinos que hicieron y dijeron antes de llegar a él, es razón que vamos advertidos de no meternos en semejantes penas, aunque más cierto fuese tras ellas el descanso; cuanto más siendo tan incierto y dudoso, que por uno que tuvo tal ventura, se hallan mil cuyos largos y fatigosos trabajos con desesperada muerte fueron galardonados. (265)

> (So happy were these lovers in their fortunate state, each one being with the desired companion, that they forgot all their former troubles. But we, who look from afar and see the pains that their contentment cost them, and the dangers in which they found themselves, and the insane things they did and said before they came to their happiness, must be well advised and take heed not to put ourselves in such pains, even if our rest were more certain than theirs; a rest which is in fact so uncertain and doubtful, that for one who is fortunate enough to get it, there are thousands whose long and anxious travails are only rewarded with a desperate death.)

Gil Polo is not exaggerating. The internal logic of the desire that moves these novels and their characters is a feedback mechanism that, left to itself, will only accelerate until it self-destructs. Existentially speaking, a desire that feeds and grows on its own negation, on the obstacle in its path, on the presence real or imagined of the rival, if left to itself, can only lead to a mental breakdown or death.

Critics have spoken at length about the difference between Montemayor and Gil Polo regarding their respective "concepts" of love.[5] But the only real

5. See A. Solé-Leris, "The Theory of Love in the Two *Dianas*: A Contrast," *Bulletin of Hispanic Studies* 34 (1959): 65–79; "Psychological Realism in the Pastoral Novel:

difference between the two is Gil Polo's greater alarm, on both moral and psychological grounds, at what is really going on in this pastoral world behind its bucolic facade. Montemayor appears to be more interested in, perhaps even fascinated by, the quasi-mathematical predictability of his characters's desire. For in this world of idyllic "freedom," nobody desires freely, that is to say, rationally. Their desires are not only prompted by somebody else's desire (which would not be a problem in itself), but they remain irrationally at the mercy of that alien desire, and always for the same reason. They may believe that they are in the hands of a blind destiny that they do not control. And, in a sense, they are right. For their desires, as I say, are not truly in their control. But, as Gil Polo's Felicia tells them (313), there is no such thing as a blind Cupid pulling the strings. What we find in the novel is the pure immanence of a web of interpersonal, intersubjective desires in which each one eagerly participates, and which nobody controls. However, the movement of each individual desire caught in the web, ruled by the web, is by no means anarchic; it has its own logic, which could be called the "logic of the obstacle." That is to say, it is the logic of a desire possessed by the obstacle, the stumbling block. It is a kind of petrified desire. Caught in the web, each individual desire is both a prompt and an obstacle to other desires.

Montemayor and Gil Polo created the pastoral novel and took it to its limit. How long could the conventional, the required, tranquility of bucolic Arcadia last when one could already see the seeds of its own destruction germinating at its very core, that is, within the traditional love relationship? What Montemayor and Gil Polo did was to prepare the ground for Cervantes, not so much the Cervantes of *La Galatea* as that of *Don Quixote*. Because, regarding the analysis of frustrated desire within the love relationship, I think Montemayor and Gil Polo went further, or deeper, than the Cervantes of *La Galatea*, but neither went as far as the Cervantes of *Don Quixote*.

In the next chapter we will study the main interpolated love stories of Part 1 of *Don Quixote*. But let us think here for a moment about those little Manchegan Arcadias which, all of a sudden, appear along Don Quixote's route, and to which we have already referred in Chapter V: the one formed around Marcela and the one whose object is Leandra. The reference to pastoral Arcadia

---

Gil Polo's *Diana enamorada*," *Bulletin of Hispanic Studies* 39 (1962): 43–47; and *The Spanish Pastoral Novel* (Boston: Twayne Publishers, 1980).

is perfectly explicit in both cases. Cervantes is clearly imitating the pastoral world we see in the two *Dianas*, among others. But that imitation is already an interpretation. Cervantes is reading that pastoral world in his own way. The most obvious difference is the following: instead of a countless number of "discordant" relationships or couples, everything is reduced to one relationship with one fixed point, the unreachable shepherdess, the one object of desire. It is this desire, this frustrated relationship, that spreads everywhere, like "pestilence," by contagion, through imitation. All the "shepherds" desire exactly the same thing, even though each one may complain in his own way. It is not a multitude of desires, but just one extremely contagious desire. Grisóstomo's frustrated desire, as well as that of shepherd Anselmo, are immediate best-sellers, so to speak.

But this contagious desire, glaringly mimetic, is already announced in the repetitive and circular development of the love relationship we have observed among the different couples in Montemayor's *Diana*: A loves B, who loves C, who loves D, who loves A. It would not make much sense to speak of different individual desires in this situation. There is just one desire traveling in a circle through each of the individuals involved. Each individual keeps the desire circulating by running away from it, by becoming an obstacle to the one running behind him or her. In other words, Montemayor's quasi-mathematical anlysis of the love relationship is the immediate precursor, the herald, of the amorous "pestilence," the contagion, of the quixotic Arcadias.

CHAPTER X

The Desire of the Obstacle

The Challenging Adventure

We return now to Don Quixote on the road. He is out in search of adventures. An adventure is a challenge, a challenging obstacle in his path. He is looking for challenges. Occasionally he may become impatient if he does not find one as quickly as he would like:

> Almost all that day he rode without encountering anything of note, which reduced him to despair, for he longed to meet straightway someone against whom he could try the strength of his strong arm. (1.2.37)

And we know, of course, that most of these challenges end in failure. It is equally worth noticing that in spite of so many failures, he remains undeterred. In Part 1 in particular Cervantes appears, in this regard, to be merciless with his fool. The failures and the beatings come one after another with cruel and hilarious predictability. Not even Avellaneda behaved like that with his spurious Quixote. If Cervantes is trying to teach his fool a hard lesson for our entertainment, what becomes obvious after a while is that the fool is not learning that lesson. If anything, with every failure and every beating, he appears to sink deeper into his madness, desperately trying to find a way to fit the failure and the beating into the context of the world of knight-errantry. For he cannot bear the thought of being excluded from that world.[1] He is clearly not like the madman from Córdoba, of whom Cervantes speaks in the prologue to Part 2, who really learned his lesson after being beaten by the angry hatter. He remembered the beating. Don Quixote, on the other hand, seems to have an extraordinary capacity to forget or completely ignore his failures and beatings. But then, of course, the madman from Córdoba, as best as we can tell, was not responding to challenges, he was not trying to be a hero. Apparently he could, in his own mad way, learn from experience.

But when you are trying as hard as you can to be a hero, when you must be a hero, because not being one is a possibility too humiliating and too devastating to contemplate, then failure is not an option. Failure will only make Don Quixote's need to prove himself even more urgent, insanely urgent. Because Don Quixote the knight is not seeing himself through the eyes of God, as Unamuno thought: instead, he is seeing himself through the eyes of the invincible knight Amadís. And at no time is the need to be like Amadís more anxious, more desperate, more urgent than when the poor knight is being beaten to a pulp. This is also why, when he triumphs, Don Quixote feels on top of the world. The importance of the triumph for him gives us the measure of how intolerable the failure is. This is his exaggerated reaction to his triumph over the badly protected and ill-advised Basque:

> But tell me, on your oath [Sancho], have you ever seen a more valorous knight on the whole face of the earth? Have you ever read in histories of one who has or had more

1. Luis Rosales, ignoring the connection between the failures and Don Quixote's madness, wanted to turn Don Quixote's repeated failures into some sort of Christian lesson: "Don Quijote fracasa en todas sus empresas, y el fracaso . . . es inherente al quijotismo. Vivir is fracasar. Todo lo humano se verifica en el fracaso. La historia de don Quijote nos enseña—golpes, violencias, burlas, humillaciones—que el fracaso es inherente al destino del hombre, pero que el heroísmo se demuestra en la manera de aceptar su lección. . . . Desde el punto de vista de la moral cristiana, sus continuas derrotas implican el perfeccionamiento de su virtud" (2.365). The critic seems to forget that it was Don Quixote himself who provoked those failures. I do not know what the Christian meaning could be of refusing to, or being incapable of, learning from one's own experience.

spirit in the attack, more wind in the holding, more art in the wounding, or more skill in the overthrowing? (1.10.80)

Logically, when he is defeated, Don Quixote must feel like the least deserving knight "on the whole face of the earth," the worst that has ever been read about in "histories"—in other words, as someone unworthy of being in the company of well-known heroes. Victory, no matter how insignificant when viewed objectively, holds off a danger far more terrible than the power of any given adversary: the danger of being excluded, of being denied the identity of a true knight-errant. It will indeed be a hopeful sign of mental recovery in Part 2 of the novel when Don Quixote becomes capable occasionally of accepting defeat or of declining to take up the challenge of an adventure, as we see in the episode of the cart with *The Parliament of Death* actors (Las cortes de la muerte) or the episode about the enchanted boat. Apart from those hopeful signs, however, he cannot resist a challenge and is always looking for one.

We also know by now that he does not think for a moment that he encounters these challenges by accident. Like the lions discussed in Chapter VIII, they are planted in his way, are meant for him. It would be shameful and cowardly to ignore the challenge, as Don Diego de Miranda wanted him to do. There is always a rival intention behind the challenge, a throwing down of the gauntlet that he unfailingly takes up, because that is the only way in which he can prove himself before, and compete with, God-like Amadís. To use the expression we learned in the last chapter, Don Quixote always "eats" his adventures with "rival sauce"; without such a "sauce" the adventure would lose its flavor entirely.

What all this means is that, regardless of the circumstantial defeat or triumph, Don Quixote is tied to a deeper and permanent kind of failure in comparison with which the occasional triumph will always be momentary and without lasting consequences. No success will ever be enough to prove to him, once and for all, that he is worthy of the company of Amadís. With each new challenge that worthiness will be as radically and anxiously in need of proof as it was the first time. Even the ultimate triumph over the ultimate and definitive rival, Amadís himself, could turn out to be a bitter disappointment. Because, as I have indicated already, a defeated Amadís would, ipso facto, deprive Don Quixote of the very ground for his knightly desire. A defeated

Amadís is of no interest at all to Don Quixote. He would have to look immediately for a new incarnation of invincible Amadís. In other words, Amadís, the knightly model, must remain undefeated to sustain and give meaning to Don Quixote's rivalry driven desire for knightly adventures. And that means that the price he has to pay to maintain his idol on his pedestal is the ultimate failure of the sum of all his adventures, regardless of the specific outcome of any one of them: the failure to settle the issue of whether he is equal to Amadís. As long as he remains trapped in his madness, Don Quixote's literary knightly desire will forever be frustrated. Indeed, in Cervantes's novel, Don Quixote's madness is but a literary expression of being trapped in a self-frustrating, self-defeating desire. Cervantes's Don Quixote does not fail just for circumstantial reasons (e.g., he is too old, or too weak, or has bad luck, or has hallucinations, etc.), he is trapped in self-inflicted failure right from the start. He has embarked on a course of action where no success will ever be convincing enough to him, compared to the success of his model, Amadís, to whom "real" success will always be felt to belong. Only the success of the radiant other and rival will appear in his eyes to be truly convincing.[2]

2. Tied to this existential failure, which isolates the individual from the reality around him and prevents him from learning from his own experience, there is another kind of failure, which might be better called sterility: the sterility of any action modeled on the fictional knightly model. Even when Don Quixote triumphs circumstantially, his triumph remains fruitless, it does not solve anything, it usually leaves things worse than they were before. In Part 1 the clearest example is that of Andrés, the boy momentarily saved by Don Quixote from the flogging he is getting at the hands of his master. This boy will eventually curse Don Quixote and ask him never again to help him. But the most painful case is that of Tosilos, Doña Rodríguez, and her daughter in Part 2 because in this case Cervantes leaves us with the impression that Don Quixote's action has resulted in something good for all concerned. We assume that Tosilos will marry the daughter, thereby solving everybody's problem. It is one of the most bitter and stunning moments of the entire novel when we find out later, in a totally unexpected way—in a scene unnecessary to the development of the novelistic action—that the whole episode left things much worse than they were before. Until that stunning moment, when a defeated Don Quixote is returning home, there was still a flicker of hope, but even that flicker is extinguished by Cervantes. Don Quixote will end his mad adventures without his madness having produced a single benefit to anybody: not a single *entuerto* straightened, not a single injustice eliminated, not a single widow or orphan remedied. The sterility of Don Quixote's madness is total. But this Cervantine intention gradually dawns on us, interestingly, as Cervantes's compassion becomes clearer also by the moment. It is not out of cruelty that Cervantes destroys the last remaining hope that Don Quixote may have ac-

Don Quixote the Snob

If Don Quixote were not so mad, if his insecurity before the triumphant other were not so intolerable, so inadmissible, if the radiance surrounding the God-like other were not so blinding, he would actually look like a snob. As a matter of fact, that is precisely what he looks like in Part 2, if only for a moment, when it appears to him that the knightly splendor of books of chivalry has been transplanted to the physical reality of the Duke's castle with all its attending pages and maidservants. All of a sudden that unexpected physical environment takes center stage, while the literary radiance of Amadís recedes into the background. Don Quixote acknowledges the impact:

> And this was the first time that he was positively certain of being a true and no imaginary knight errant, since he found himself treated just as he had read these knights were treated in past ages. (2.31.667)

This is another hopeful sign that Don Quixote might possibly be on the path to a cure for his madness. After all, being a snob is preferable to being insane. But what do the quoted words mean? Do they mean that he was just pretending before? Did he not believe that he was "a true knight errant"? Yes, he did believe it, but all the time he was struggling desperately with doubt. Those words reveal what he has always been most afraid of, what he has always tried desperately to hide from himself: Is he a real and true knight-errant, as real and true as Amadís most certainly is? In other words, the narrator's observation reveals a fundamental insecurity at the bottom of Don Quixote's madness, which the madness itself hides from view. A secret voice has always insinuated an intolerable truth in Don Quixote's heart: "You are not really a true knight-errant; you are not good enough to be one; your pretension to be like Amadís is laughable." It is the same voice that affirmed the undoubted genuineness of Amadís. These two voices are the two sides of the same communication. Madness is the price he pays for silencing the accusing side of that voice. The sudden impact of the new and physically real "chivalric" environment breaks the spell, as it were. For a moment it becomes possible to

---

complished something through his madness. This final realization is something like a purgation, intended to cleanse Don Quixote (and the reader) of any remaining knightly nostalgia. The moment is getting closer for his cure and his death.

hear the intolerable, the maddening, voice, but in a weakened state, so now less intolerable, less maddening. His madness relents a little, becomes less impenetrable, and we catch a glimpse of what lies behind it, the nature of the madness itself. And that is the moment when we see what we had never seen before: Don Quixote the snob. He becomes extremely anxious and fearful of being perceived as somebody who does not really belong in the company of these "chivalric" and noble people who are now attending to him with all the pomp and ceremony due to knights-errant. And he cringes and trembles at the thought that Sancho is going to show him up, is going to say something stupid, inappropriate, embarrassing in the presence of such noble company:

> In God's name, Sancho, control yourself. Do not show the yarn you are woven of, or let them see what gross and peasant stuff you are. . . . Do you not see, pitiful fellow that you are and unlucky me, that if they discover that you are a coarse boor or a funny idiot, they will take me for a charlatan or a fake knight?

If he feels that way in the presence of a duke, what would he feel like in the presence of Amadís himself! The thought of being seen as "a charlatan or a fake knight" in the eyes of Amadís would be too terrifying to contemplate. As I just said, being a snob is not the same thing as being insane. But there is no fundamental discontinuity between the desire of Don Quixote the snob and the desire of mad Don Quixote trying insanely to be like Amadís, to fit in with Amadís in the world of chivalry; there is no discontinuity between Don Quixote's trembling fear as he anxiously watches Sancho and the maddening need to silence the intolerable voice, the feeling, that tells him that he will never be a match for Amadís, that Amadís will always be beyond reach. It all depends on how strong the attraction of the model is. In this regard, the attraction of the Duke, the Duchess, and their castle is obviously no match for the blinding radiance of Amadís in the mind of Don Quixote. All they can produce is a fairly acute case of snobbery, nothing comparable to the devastating effect that books of chivalry can produce in Don Quixote the snob.

Chivalric Madness and Pastoral Madness

Don Quixote's doubt about himself is in direct relation to the attraction of the model of his desire. Contrary to what he imagines and yearns for, his faith in Amadís is ultimately incompatible with faith in himself. No amount of circumstantial success, therefore, will ever cure Don Quixote of his maddening snobbery, his devastating feelings of inadequacy, in the presence of his ultimate idol and rival, invincible Amadís. Success belongs to the idol-rival, the model-obstacle. Only the rival's idolized success will appear to be true and genuine in the eyes of the "unlucky" worshipper. But is this not another manifestation or aspect of the same existential logic that also condemns to perpetual frustration the desire of all those pastoral lovers we have just seen? Is Don Quixote's knightly desire any different from their pastoral desire? I do not think it is, insofar as neither one is governed by the reality of its object, and both are equally governed or mediated by a rival desire.

What we have seen in the love relationships of all those shepherds and shepherdesses is that everything is governed by the desire of the rival. This desire of the rival is more attractive in the eyes of the one in love than even the beloved's desire (remember Ismenia and her "joke" at the temple). They actually prefer the success of the rival to their own success. The defeat of the rival automatically deprives their own triumph of its meaning. The object of desire they snatch from the rival rapidly ceases to attract them. You may remember, for example, the case of Montano, who was only interested in whatever girl happened to be interested in his rival Alanio, that is, in whatever girl happened to find Alanio both irresistible and unreachable. You may remember how quickly he would lose interest in the girl if she defeated Alanio at the love game, and turned him, the unreachable little god of yesterday, into a suppliant pleading for mercy today. The only god they believe in is a prestigious and successful one, definitely not a defeated one, and most certainly not one on a cross. Both Montemayor and Gil Polo, as we saw, knew perfectly well that their characters were engaged in very unchristian maneuvers.

And so did Cervantes with regard to his own character Don Quixote. Let me beg the indulgence of those critics who are likely to be skeptical of what I am saying. I think there is sufficient reason to consider *Don Quixote* not only as a parodic and satiric critique of books of chivalry, but also as a very serious critique of the literary world of the pastoral. The object of Don Quixote's desire is, of course, a chivalric object, as defined by books of chivalry, but the psychological understanding and analysis of his desire owes much more to what had already been done with human desire in the pastoral novel than to anything found in books of chivalry. After all, we should not forget that Cervantes fine-tuned his novelistic capacity for analysis in the writing of *La*

Galatea. The internal logic of Don Quixote's insane and self-frustrating desire echoes the logic of the self-frustrating desire of pastoral characters. In Cervantes's novel, not only did the knights-errant of old come down from their enchanted fantasyland to the plains of La Mancha, so did the shepherds and shepherdesses of literary Arcadia.

All the interpolated stories involving lovers and friends that we find in *Don Quixote*, whether explicitly and formally related to the pastoral or not, are a continuation and development of themes already found in Montemayor and Gil Polo. We already saw in the strategies of the desire that kept Ismenia and Selvagia fascinated with each other a clear anticipation of what will happen in the story of *El curioso impertinente*. We should now pay some attention to the other two major love stories in Part 1, those involving Marcela and Grisóstomo in one, and Cardenio, Luscinda, Don Fernando, and Dorotea in the other.

The Story of Marcela and Grisóstomo

Today I do not think anybody can seriously doubt the fact that "shepherd" Grisóstomo's death was a suicide. Grisóstomo apparently hanged himself (he speaks of his impending death and "a hard knot") in utter despair of ever swaying Marcela's feelings toward him. Cervantes does not dwell on the physical details of the suicide. That's not what interests him. But there can be no doubt about the following: (1) Grisóstomo's death is meant to be real, (2) he is responsible for his own death, and (3) everything is a consequence of his frustrated relationship with Marcela.

The distinguished critic and poet Luis Rosales did not believe there was such a suicide. For one thing, he thought Cervantes was totally against suicide, which is undoubtedly true. But more to the point, he thought that Grisóstomo's "Song of Despair," read at his burial, in which he takes leave of Marcela and of life, is clearly related to the traditional "dying of love" metaphor of courtly lyrics, and therefore should not be taken literally, but in a purely poetic sense: "El estudiante se nos muere . . . , porque la obligación de un fino y derretido amante es morirse de amor. Ni más, ni menos. En realidad no tiene causa alguna para morir" (2.498–99; The student dies on us . . . because it is the obligation of a genteel and love-crazy lover to die of love. No more, no less. In reality he has no reason at all to die).

The logic of Rosales's argument leaves a lot to be desired. But that is not my point here. What I would like to say is that it is important to notice the connection between the real death of Grisóstomo and the poetic metaphor of traditional love lyrics. Because I think that is Cervantes's great discovery. When Cervantes brings down the old poetic metaphor to the plains of La Mancha, that old metaphor becomes harsh reality, real death. It is regrettable that, in his desire to defend Cervantes's clearly Christian attitude against Castro, the distinguished critic would feel compelled to separate the hell of the poets from true hell, whether existential or in the afterlife (which makes no difference here). Because what Cervantes discovers (as anticipated by the warnings of Gil Polo's Felicia) is the perfect correspondence between those two hells. The metaphorical delights of the traditional amorous frustrations of the poets could become literal and horrifying reality. They are far closer to the real thing than they, the lovers, had ever imagined. The poetic description was just as good for the real death as it had always been for the fictional one.

What appears to have confused the critic is that he saw no real reason for Grisóstomo to take his life, since it is true that Cervantes makes clear that "los celos y sospechas de Grisóstomo eran imaginarios, inventados y, en fin, cosa de fábula" (The jealousy and suspicions of Grisóstomo were imaginary, invented, and, in the end, something fictitious). This makes the critic wonder: "¿A qué carta quedamos? Si era difícil armonizar la conducta de Marcela con la conducta de la amada de la canción, es más difícil aún armonizar el suicidio de Grisóstomo con estos celos caprichosos y gratuítos" (2.498–99; So, what is it? If it was difficult to harmonize Marcela's behavior with the behavior of the beloved in [Grisóstomo's] song, it is even more difficult to harmonize his suicide with such a capricious and gratuitous jealousy). And it is indeed true that there is no objective, rational reason for the suicide other than the internal logic of a desire that turns upon itself in perpetual contradiction, thus turning its object exactly into "cosa de fábula," "inventada," "imaginaria." Has there ever been any other reason but the sick will of a free individual to go to hell? Nobody is pushed by external rational reasons to go to hell. Did Christian Luis Rosales not know that the doors of hell have been broken, and that there are no guards to prevent anybody from getting out of it, and that still nobody ever gets out? All the reasons to go to hell have always been "imaginary," "cosa de fábula," self-made. You do not have to go to hell if you do not want to. It's always up to you.

This suicide is Cervantes's way to introduce us to the pastoral world, which has now been transplanted to the historical reality of La Mancha. The reader may remember that this tragic and "pastoral" love story comes immediately after Don Quixote's grandiloquent speech on the mythical Golden Age, where we saw "the simple and lovely shepherdesses go from valley to valley and from hill to hill" practically naked but without the slightest fear of violence. Clearly these Golden Age shepherdesses seem to be an appropriate introduction to the Manchegan Arcadia we will visit immediately after, with Marcela and all the other girls roaming the fields, "communicating" with nature.

The mythical Golden Age, based on a poetic dream of spontaneous, "natural" desire, was a lyrical age in which, curiously, there was no lyrical poetic art because feelings came out of the soul "simply and plainly, exactly as they were conceived, without any search for artificial elaborations" (1.11.86). Everything was authentic and in perfect harmony with "Mother Nature." This is a vision of paradise on earth. But when the Golden Age Arcadia is transplanted to the reality of La Mancha, what looked like paradise all of a sudden becomes hell.

The voice of hell is indeed what Grisóstomo's "Song of Despair" conjures up: "haré que el mesmo infierno comunique / al triste pecho mío un son doliente" (I'll make hell itself my grieving heart to aid, / and in my breast infuse a tone of dole). And since this poem is the last one he wrote, a farewell to Marcela and the world, and is now being read at his burial, it is almost literally a voice from beyond the grave, from hell. In other words, Grisóstomo speaks already from the one place where hope, by definition, cannot enter, not because a superior power prevents it, but because those inside, consumed with bitterness and resentment, absolutely refuse to accept any hope. It is they who do their utmost to prevent even the slightest ray of hope from penetrating their place of darkness:

> [Y] entre tantos tormentos, nunca alcanza
> mi vista a ver en sombra a la esperanza,
> ni yo, desesperado, la procuro;
> antes, por estremarme en mi querella,
> estar sin ella eternamente juro.
>
> (1.14.148–49)

(And among all those pains have never scope
Once to behold the shadow of a hope,
Nor, thus despairing, will I hope allow;
But rather, to exacerbate my wrong,
To live forever hopeless here I vow. [104])

How did he get there? One thing should be immediately clear: Grisóstomo's hell was generated by the relationship he had with Marcela. Even before he went to the theological hell doctrinally demanded for suicides, his hopeless relationship with Marcela had become an existential hell for him, a self-frustrating, "no exit" enslavement to the other, to "divine" Marcela, almost a Sartrian kind of hell.

He tells us that he is there as a willing sacrifice to her tyranny, her "rigor":

Pues ya ves que te da notorias muestras
Esta del corazón profunda llaga,
De cómo alegre a tu rigor me ofrezco. . . .

(1.14.150)

(Since now by signs notorious from my heart's
deepest wound you can see how gladly I offer
myself to your rigor).

His sacrifice is a feast in her honor. His death is the proof, the visible sign, of her triumphant "glory":

Antes, con risa en la ocasión funesta
Descubre que el fin mío fue tu fiesta;
Mas gran simpleza es avisarte desto,
Pues se que está tu gloria conocida
En que mi vida llegue al fin tan presto.

(1.14.150)

(Rather, laughing on such terrible occasion,
reveal that my end has been your feast,
but it is folly to advise you of this,
because I know that your glory is recognized
as I hasten my life to its quick end.)[3]

3. The translation for these five lines is my own because, in my opinion, Cohen's translation here deviates too much from the original text.

Of course, Grisóstomo's words are not an accurate description of anything that Marcela has actually done to him, but they are a very profound and accurate description of his despair. The way he sees triumphant Marcela from the bottom of his despair is precisely how the "divine" human other must look in the eyes of the despairing one, the very one who has turned the human other into a god. Grisóstomo knows that the only thing that keeps him in hell is his obsessive, "obstinate" fascination with "Love's ancient tyranny," and its very embodiment, beautiful and cruel Marcela. He wants it that way. He insists in calling his living hell beautiful and being enslaved to the ancient love of so many beautiful and tragic love stories a higher form of freedom. That is also his hate-filled revenge on divine Marcela. Since his being in hell is the "proof" of her power and of everything his obsesive desire tells him that she is, he wants to remain there in order to prove that he is right about her, that he is right in desiring her. His revenge will be to want to be exactly where the divinity he has granted her places him. Not only that, but in order to confirm her place on her glorious pedestal, infinitely above him, and her cruelty as a sign of her divine nature, he will actually put the blame on himself:

> Yo muero, en fin; y porque nunca espere
> Buen suceso en la muerte ni en la vida,
> Pertinaz estaré en mi fantasía.
> Diré que va acertado el que bien quiere,
> Y que es más libre el alma más rendida
> A la de Amor antigua tiranía.
> Diré que la enemiga siempre mía
> Hermosa el alma como el cuerpo tiene,
> Y que su olvido de mi culpa nace,
> Y que en fe de los males que nos hace,
> Amor su imperio en justa paz mantiene.
>
> (And now I die, and so that never may I hope
> for a good outcome either in life or in death,
> obstinately will I persist in my fantasy,
> and say he does the best who loves the most,
> and that the soul most liberty doth know
> when most enslaved by Love's ancient tyranny.
> I will swear that my constant enemy
> in her fair body a fair soul contains

that her unkindness by my fault arose,
and only by the grievous hurt he does
can Love his empire in just peace maintain.

(106)

If there ever was a man absolutely determined not to learn from experience, Grisóstomo must be it. He surpasses even mad Don Quixote. Of course, that is why he is already in hell, while Don Quixote at the end of his story will step back from the abyss.

It would also be hard to find a clearer description of the working of hellish, self-destructive desire, the desire that clings obsessively to its own frustration, that remains fascinated by the obstacle in its path, by the rival desire that blocks its way, that prefers the triumph of the rival to its own triumph. And yet this is a concept not easily understood by most readers. Our quasi-instinctive tendency is to disassociate the object of desire from the obstacle in its path. We picture Grisóstomo's desire faithfully keeping in sight its object, beautiful Marcela, while something external to this desire of his (Marcela's own desire not to enter into a love relationship with anybody) blocks its way—a blockage which, in our naïve understanding, does not alter in any way the character of Grisóstomo's faithful desire, whose object does not change because of the blockage, and continues to be the obvious beauty of Marcela. In other words, we tend to think that what drives Grisóstomo's desire is one thing and what frustrates it is something else with a different origin, unrelated to his desire. Since Marcela appears so obviously attractive, we never question the logic, the rationality, of Grisóstomo's desire to possess her.

However, this kind of understanding cannot account for the self-contradictory nature of Grisóstomo's desire, for the logic of the process whereby Grisóstomo—as he tells us—creates his own hell and absolutely refuses to leave it. It is not the irresistible character of Marcela's attraction that sends him to hell, when it is blocked by her persistent refusal. If that were the case, he would either continue to hope forever that the obstacle would be removed and put out of the way, or he would simply give up his desire, for, as we will hear Marcela say in a moment, "desires are nourished on hope," and where there is no hope there should be no desire. But that is not the case with hell-bound Grisóstomo, for his desire for Marcela appears to feed on hopelessness itself. He does not desire Marcela directly, but indirectly, through her refusal, through the obstacle she throws in his path. In fact, his problem is that he can no longer separate the one from the other. He is attracted by what he hates to the same degree as he is attracted by what he loves. The two have become inextricably entangled in each other, they mirror each other, while desire oscillates between the two, unable to see one without the other, alternately attracted and repelled. In other words, the existential movement of desire is forced into an oscillation that tends of itself to accelerate. The more, the longer, Marcela refuses herself to Grisóstomo, the more beautifully attractive she becomes to him, even to the point where she will only attract him by refusing him, even to the point where the only thing that will trigger and drive his desire will be the obstacle in his path, her very refusal of his love, her opposing desire. At this point only "cruel" "tyrannical" Marcela appears irresistibly beautiful in his eyes. At this point a yielding or pleading Marcela would be utterly uninteresting to him. That is how he gets himself into hell, by actively seeking his own frustration, by preferring the utter darkness of hell to the smallest ray of hope. And all the while, as the attraction of her now cruel and tyrannical beauty increases exponentially in his eyes, so does the pain and suffering caused by her fascinating refusal, which he also hates and for which he seeks revenge. Existentially speaking, the consequences of the movement of this self-contradiction, if left to its own logic, can only be catastrophic: madness or suicide. We should also remember here that Don Quixote's unerring literary memory always portrays his lady Dulcinea as distant and indifferent to his suffering. For Cervantes can go without blinking, so to speak, from the most conventional metaphors of courtly love to a serious literary description of hell, to which the most demanding theologian of the time could not object. As Montero Díaz observed, "[T]oda la capacidad negadora que un teólogo del Siglo de Oro español podía suponer en un desesperado está centrada en esas dinámicas y poderosas estrofas" (All the negative power that a Golden Age Spanish theologian could suppose in human despair is concentrated in those dynamic and powerful stanzas).[4]

And what about Marcela? She shows up at Grisóstomo's burial site like a pagan goddess:

[Vivaldo] was going to read another of the papers . . . when he was prevented by a marvelous vision—for such it seemed—which suddenly appeared before their eyes.

4. Quoted in Rosales, *Obras completas*, 2.747.

For on the top of the rock in which they were digging the grave appeared the shepherdess Marcela, looking even more beautiful than she had been described. Those of them who knew her well were just as amazed. . . .

"I have come . . . to defend myself, and to prove how wrong are those who blame me for their own sufferings and for Grisóstomo's death. . . . I was born free, and to live free I chose the solitude of the fields. The trees of these mountains are my companions; the clear waters of these streams my mirrors; to the trees and the waters I disclose my thoughts and my beauty. . . . If desires are nourished on hope, as I never gave any to Grisóstomo or to any other, it may not justly be said that any man's end was my doing, since it was his persistence rather than my cruelties that killed him. . . . I told him that my will was to live in perpetual solitude, and that only the earth would enjoy the fruit of my chastity and the spoils of my beauty. . . . Let me not be called cruel or murderous by those whom I have never promised, deceived, lured on, or encouraged. Heaven has not yet fated me to love; and it is folly to think that I shall love out of choice."

This is an abridged version of Marcela's famous speech on the theme of individual freedom—a theme dear to Cervantes. But we must ask, What gave her the idea of displaying her inborn freedom so much out in the open, dressed as a shepherdess, tending her sheep in the fields, she being such a rich girl with enough money to pay for as many shepherds as she wanted? What gave her the idea of enjoying her freedom in "the solitude of the fields" followed by all the rich girls in town and surrounded by an equal number of young men, all of them also dressed as shepherds and pining away for her love? Clearly Marcela has been reading pastoral novels, and probably with the same intensity that Don Quixote had been reading books of chivalry. This may help explain her intense desire to remain virginal, "to live in perpetual solitude . . . that only the earth would enjoy the fruit of [her] chastity," her intense desire not to fall in love with anybody, to the point that it would be "folly to [even] think that [she] shall love." In other words, she wants to be a new and improved version of Diana, the goddess that presides over the Arcadian fields, and occupies the place of honor in the palace of wise Felicia in the two Spanish *Dianas*. It is precisely that inaccessible, goddesslike image, confirmed by her persistent refusal, that Grisóstomo is literally crazy about. This means that she is as fascinated with her poetic Diana role as he is. They are both attracted by the same fiction, and compete for the same "airy nothing," as Shakespeare would say, or, as I said in a previous chapter, the "illusion of autonomy." They compete for an illusory autonomy that has no reality beyond the convergence and reciprocal imitation of their competing desires. She sees it reflected in his desire and he sees it reflected in hers, that is to say, in her refusal. They both want the same thing. What happens is that the object of their desire cannot be shared. Divine Diana is divine because she is number one in the eyes of her fascinated worshippers. There is no other one like her. This is why she looks so self-sufficient and spontaneous. Her divinity cannot be shared. It is the same thing with Don Quixote and his knightly model. Don Quixote does not go out in search of adventures just to be another knight-errant. He is out to be number one, like Amadís.

The "pastoral" story of Marcela and Grisóstomo was cut short by his suicide. After her eloquent speech Marcela vanishes, and we never hear from her again. What would have happened if the story had continued? There is only one way for such stories to continue: at some unpredictable point Grisóstomo's obsessive love would have turned to hatred or disgust (the model/rival mechanism would have taken a turn); at that point, Marcela would have turned around and started pursuing the now distant and indifferent Grisóstomo with the same intensity and adoration as he had pursued her before. Just as Don Quixote reasoned, after discovering that his own story had just been published, that being the story of a knight-errant, "it must perforce be grandiloquent, lofty, remarkable, magnificent and true" (2.3), we must likewise conclude that being a story of shepherds and shepherdesses, that was the only way for it to continue. And it would have been a far from meaningless continuation, and fully within the logic of the desire that keeps the love story going, for it would have revealed how unstable and fragile such love relationships really are, and how easily the relative positions of god and miserable worshipper can be interchanged, for they are not based on anything except their mutual confirmation.

In fact, there is a sort of parodic continuation of the story of Marcela and Grisóstomo a little later on, in the story of the goatherder Lope Ruiz and the shepherdess Torralba, which Sancho narrates during the frightening night of the "batanes" (fulling mills), and of which I have spoken elsewhere. Lope Ruiz had been in love with Torralba, but she had paid little attention to him and had flirted with other boys. Then he got fed up with the situation and started hating her as much as he had loved her before. In fact, he decided to leave town in order not to have to see her again, at which point Torralba became crazy about him. She followed him out of town reverently, from a distance, barefoot, like a penitent pilgrim, in hopes of being forgiven by him.

I will not comment any further on this marvelous Sancho Pancescan version of the typical pastoral love story. Suffice it to say that the story is interrupted in a totally arbitrary way at the moment when Torralba is getting closer and closer to the escaping former lover, who is getting increasingly anxious by the minute, for he has to manage getting three hundred goats across an overflowing river and can only do it one goat at a time, while he knows she is getting closer. The listener is supposed to keep track of the number of goats, one by one, that make it across to the other side. Don Quixote loses track of the number of goats, and Sancho ipso facto forgets the rest of the story.

But what difference does it make, anyway, at what point the story is interrupted? We already know what is going to happen if the story continues: at some point the roles will be reversed again, the pursued will become the pursuer and vice versa, the god of yesterday will become the suppliant slave of today, and so on in endless alternating repetition (like the little boat crossing back and forth across the river, taking just one goat at a time).

At least that is the pattern that keeps typical pastoral love stories going and avid readers like Marcela and Grisóstomo as glued to them as Don Quixote was to his books of chivalry. For the endless reversals of the pastoral genre fulfill the same function as the endless adventures of the knights-errant in the romance of chivalry genre. The only important thing is to keep the avid reader's attention fixed on each of the moments of the alternating movement separately—on each of the goats, so to speak. What that avid reader does not see is that the alternating movement itself, the interchangeable roles of god and slave, are there from the beginning because they are inherent to the fictional model of desire. They are the two faces of the idol, the fascinating and the hateful.

The question is, as we anticipated in the last chapter, whether it is realistic to expect that such an alternating movement, predictable in a quasi-mathematical way, can be sustained indefinitely in real time, that is to say, in the real experience of the subject of desire. Grisóstomo's suicide is Cervantes's answer to that question. Moved to La Mancha, the typical alternating development of the pastoral love story soon reaches a devastating conclusion. Only in mythical Arcadia can one play with fire indefinitely without getting burnt. But the psychological violence that drives Grisóstomo to commit suicide does not enter Arcadia from outside. It is generated by the logic of the desire that keeps alive the interest in the pastoral love story. The internal dynamics of the desire that moves Grisóstomo to suicide is the same one that drives Don Quixote to madness: the fascination with the obstacle and all of its consequences. A couple of centuries later that same dynamics could have produced some of the complex and tortured characters of Dostoyevsky, for example, in whom we would have been able to feel the anguish firsthand, or to witness, with a chill, the fixed-eye look of madness. That was not Cervantes's style, or the style of his age. But let us make no mistake: Cervantes's clean smile, his compassionate irony, his lack of resentment, and his profound hope do not mean that he could not see as much or as well as the tortured Russian.

It could be argued, nevertheless, that Don Quixote does not seem at all suicidal, that the very idea of suicide seems incompatible with the image projected by Don Quixote. And that is correct. But there is a reason for that, as I have already suggested. Don Quixote is extremely lucky that he never found a flesh-and-blood incarnation of radiant Amadís on the plains of La Mancha, just as Grisóstomo found the image of divine Diana embodied in his neighbor Marcela, the daughter of rich Guillermo. What would Don Quixote do if confronted with the rejection or indifference of that possible Manchegan Amadís, an Amadís whose mythical attraction would be enhanced by that rejection or indifference? Contrary to what he may think, such an encounter would have been catastrophic for our knight. For there can only be one Amadís, not two. The question, once again, is the following: How realistic is it for Don Quixote to be so lucky indefinitely? How credible is it that the madman could maintain in his mind the fascinating image of literary Amadís, the knightly model, in its pure state, so to speak, hovering above the hard soil of La Mancha, in some sort of knightly heaven, without ever becoming incarnate in any human being? I believe that it is no more credible to keep mad Don Quixote indefinitely inmune to complete mental collapse or unbearable despair than it was to do it with the Arcadian shepherds. On the other hand, keeping Don Quixote always from reaching the breaking point confirms the fact that Cervantes did not invent him in order to destroy him, but in order to save him from his madness, even if that meant creating a character who borders on the implausible. Because if Don Quixote would not evolve toward his cure, he would have to evolve toward some sort of final breakdown (or the insane asylum, which was Avellaneda's solution). Cervantes's strategy is to lead Don Quixote toward his cure, but to leave behind many clear signs of the tragedy that he has been avoiding. Grisóstomo's tragedy is one of those signs.

Returning now to the theme of individual freedom, we should notice that it was not only the explicit theme of Marcela's speech. It is also reflected in another important detail, on which Cervantes placed special emphasis. Both Marcela and Grisóstomo are as free to make their own decisions as was conceivable or acceptable in their society. We are told in great detail that both are rich and orphaned—that is, they are not under the authority of parents. Marcela has a legal guardian, her uncle, a priest and parson in the village. But he is—we are told—a model Christian and would not try to impose his will on her. When she became of age, "he would have liked to marry her off soon [but] would not do so without her consent." In principle, Marcela and Grisóstomo are a perfect match. Whether they get married or not will only depend on what they freely decide. In other words, there is no external cause for the tragedy, nothing other than the free will of the two people concerned. They both chain themselves willingly to a mere fiction. I think we could say that, in Cervantes's eyes, this is the tragedy typical of free human beings. Nobody can lose what he or she does nor have. What distinguishes this tragedy is precisely a loss of freedom, which is the same thing as the infernal loss of hope, which is what happens to Grisóstomo.

We must further realize that when Cervantes transplanted the typical frustration of the love story from its conventional setting in the pastoral novel to the historical fields of La Mancha, he opened the floodgates, so to speak. He broke the barriers that contained the problem within the limits of the literary, and transformed the typical frustration of poetic love into human frustration pure and simple. If that sort of thing could happen among the people of La Mancha, it could happen anywhere. For there was nothing singularly Manchegan or unrepeatable in Marcela and Grisóstomo. It happened to them, ironically, because they were "born free." There was no particular predisposition in them or in La Mancha that can be blamed for the tragedy. What happened to them did not have to happen. When the problem came down from fantasyland into La Mancha, it came down into the world, it became a universal problem. As far as Cervantes the novelist was concerned, he was no longer simply imitating the pastoral, he was imitating human reality.

Montemayor and Gil Polo had seen the problem quite clearly, but they contained it within fairly rigid formal boundaries. Cervantes broke those boundaries. The problem could roam ominously over all kinds of situations, involving all kinds of people; no human relationship was in principle inmune to it, *as long as it could be poetically imitated, as long as it could be fictionalized*. In this regard, it should be pointed out that in Cervantes's society some relationships must have been felt to be more resistant to the problem than others. You may remember that the priest, for example, after reading the *Curioso*, was of the opinion that that sort of thing was believable between lovers, "but between husband and wife, there is something impossible about it." The priest's opinion speaks rather highly of his faith in the health and significance of marital relations, as befits an honest priest perhaps. But in the eyes of Cervantes obviously that sort of thing was indeed possible even between husband and wife, that is to say, even in the kind of situation that almost by definition was excluded from pastoral, poetic, love stories. For, as it is well known, marriage is always the end of the story, never the beginning. The priest's opinion is also a clear indication that Cervantes was well aware of the fact that he was taking the traditional tragedy of the love story beyond its traditional literary limits. There really is no limit to where Cervantes can go with his profound intuition of the problem of human self-made and utterly unnecesary frustration, with human self-induced madness.

The Story of Cardenio

So let us change the circumstances and the characters and see what happens. The story of Marcela and Grisóstomo is a classic story of unrequited love, so let's transform it into a story of mutual love and appreciation. Nothing could be more promising and propitious than the beginning of the story of Cardenio and Luscinda. They grew up together as children. Their families were of equal rank and means, and they loved each other tenderly. Everybody expected that they would get married some day and live happily ever after. Everything promised smooth sailing. But a little obstacle, not a big one, more like an irritating inconvenience, came up one day: Luscinda's father told Cardenio that neither he nor Luscinda were children any longer, and that he had to watch out for Luscinda's reputation. He could no longer allow Cardenio to visit freely with Luscinda as he had always done. Cardenio's reaction is most revealing, for he immediately seized on the poetic possibilities of this parental prohibition:

> Luscinda's father thought himself obliged, for prudence's sake, to deny me the house, in this closely imitating the parents of that Thisbe so much sung by the poets. Now this denial added flame to flame and desire to desire; for although they silenced our tongues, they could not stop our pens. . . . Heavens, how many letters I wrote her! What delicate and modest replies I received! How many poems and love songs I penned, in which my soul declared and revealed its feelings, painted its warm desires, went over its memories and refreshed its passion! (1.24.193–94)

Please notice that no sooner did the denial occur than he started living in his mind a beautiful love story in imitation of so many famous and poetic love stories. That is quite an imagination the young man had! And a very creative one too, capable of turning a little obstacle into a major poetic love story, a tragic one to boot! But we should know enough by now to realize that that in itself is an ominous sign, a clear anticipation of real danger. Fortunately at this stage he is still innocent enough, and his love for Luscinda is still healthy enough, to be able to do what he could have done as soon as the obstacle arose instead of embarking on an imaginary trip through fantasyland: ask her father for her hand in marriage.

> In the end, my patience exhausted and my heart consumed with desire to see her, I determined . . . to ask her father for her hand in lawful marriage, which I did.

Needless to say, Luscinda's father had no objection. In fact, he thanked Cardenio "for the honor I intended him, and for wishing to honor myself with his beloved treasure." But he also pointed out that Cardenio had to do things in the proper way. It was Cardenio's father's job to ask for Luscinda's hand on behalf of his son. Cardenio agreed, for he knew his father would be delighted to carry out this task: "My father would consent to my proposal as soon as I told him of it." So the road is clear, one would think. However, one never knows because we are dealing with somebody who has already proven himself quite capable of seeing a mountain in a molehill. At any rate, all he has to do now is to go and ask his father.

> Therefore I immediately went to inform him of my desires. But when I entered the room where he was, I found him with an open letter in his hand, which he passed on to me before I had uttered a word, saying: "You see from this letter, Cardenio, that Duke Richards wishes to do you a service."

Duke Richards wanted Cardenio to become a companion to his eldest son. This is a wonderful offer, coming from a grandee of Spain. Cardenio's father tells him that he must set out for his unexpected assignment in forty-eight hours. One might think that at that moment Cardenio would have felt the urgency of informing his father about his plans to marry Luscinda. But he says nothing. Instead, he goes back to Luscinda and her father, and, he continues, "begged her father to wait for a few days and postpone the settling of her marriage until I saw what Duke Richards wanted of me"—to which, of course, the father consents, although Luscinda did not like this new development at all and suffered some "fits of fainting."

To cut the story short, time passed and Cardenio never found the right moment to tell his father about his marriage plans. Meanwhile he and Don Fernando, the Duke's younger son, became extremely close friends. Cardenio told him everything about Luscinda in great detail. Don Fernando eagerly listened to Cardenio's descriptions of Luscinda's beauty. He never had enough of these conversations, to the point where Cardenio began to feel uneasy about it, but, as usual, did nothing. Actually it was worse than that:

> I told Don Fernando of her father's insistence that mine should make the request [of Luscinda's hand], and that I dared not mention the matter to my father for fear that he would not consent . . . because, as I understood, he did not wish me to marry before we knew what Duke Richards might do for me. To be brief, I told him that I dared not ask my father, not only because of this objection, but because of many others that unnerved me, without even knowing what they were, except that I had the feeling that nothing I desired would ever be realized. (1.27.227)

This was almost an open invitation for Don Fernando to intervene, which of course he did, telling Cardenio that he would do everything for him: "Don Fernando's reply was that he would speak to my father for me, and make him speak to Luscinda's." But what he actually did was to ask for Luscinda for himself. Luscinda's father could not reject such a tempting offer from the son of Duke Richards, and Luscinda herself was too weak to withstand the combined pressure of her new suitor and her father. After all, they had waited long enough for Cardenio, while he kept procrastinating for no valid reason. Luscinda's father accepted Don Fernando's proposal and she just went along. The marriage ceremony was carried out in private, and Cardenio, who had been warned at the last moment, arrived just in time to watch it from behind a curtain. After Luscinda said "Yes, I do," she fainted, and they found a note she had kept hidden in her chest, in which—we will find out much later—she declared she had already given her promise of marriage to Cardenio. In the commotion Cardenio, "burning all over with rage and jealousy," contemplated revealing himself and killing his treacherous friend and his unfaithful lover.

> But my fate ordained that, at that moment, I could have more than enough understanding [to know what I should do]. So, instead of taking vengeance on my greatest enemies, which would have been easy . . . I resolved to inflict on myself, and with my own hand, the punishment which they deserved—a punishment perhaps more severe than I should have inflicted on them by instant execution. For sudden death swiftly ends all pain, but death which is protracted by torture forever kills but never puts an end to life. (234)

These words sound a little like Grisóstomo's self-punishment in hell. In utter despair, caring nothing for his life, Cardenio runs out of the house and into the mountains. That is where Don Quixote and Sancho will find him, dressed in tatters, looking like a wild man. And that is where, during intervals of sanity, he will tell his story.

Apparently the flash of understanding he had at that crucial moment, when he decided to punish himself rather than his enemies, must have provided him with some clear and terrifying view, or suspicion, of what had really happened, and his active role in it, which would be reason enough to go insane: he tries desperately to hide such an understanding from himself while still following its implacable logic.

Some critics have noticed the glaringly obvious procrastination of Cardenio, and have wisely concluded that he is a very indecisive personality, which is of course the reason why he lost Luscinda to his treacherous friend Don Fernando—this is a clear warning, I suppose, to all lovers not to be so indecisive. All of this is undoubtedly correct, but also a little shortsighted.

My own conclusion is that we understand absolutely nothing of what is going on in this story if we do not understand the intimate connection that exists among the following things: (1) Cardenio's "creative" use of the original prohibition in order to turn it into the basis for a beautiful love story; (2) his paralysis before any kind of obstacle, no matter how insignificant; and (3) his incredibly irresponsible and even self-destructive behavior in the face of Don Fernando's increasingly obvious interest in Luscinda.

These are all aspects of the same phenomenon that we keep encountering in the most diverse circumstances: scandalized desire, that is to say, the desire that stumbles upon the obstacle, the *scandalon*, the biblical stumbling block,[5] *piedra de escándalo*, the Satanic obstacle, and remains scandalized, crippled by it, incapable of walking around the stumbling block and leaving it behind; this is another example of the desire that absorbs its own sustenance from the obstacle itself, and cannot live without it, desiring therefore through its own frustration.

I have said repeatedly that Cervantes is not interested in external or circumstantial obstacles, but rather in the obstacles that free individuals create for themselves, or willingly embrace wherever they can find them, which is the same thing. Cervantes focuses on obstacles before which individuals sacrifice their own freedom, driven by a desire whose object forever remains beyond their reach, that is to say, behind the obstacle, even to the point where obstacle and object of desire become undifferentiated, where every obstacle beckons as a sign of something desirable, promising what will never be obtained, promising therefore an illusion, a mirage, a fiction. Cervantes is very interested in the seduction of his characters by "external incitements," as A. Castro called them (see above), that will never deliver what they promised. When Cardenio's desire for Luscinda redoubled, adding "flame to flame and desire to desire" ("llama a llama y deseo a deseo"), after her father denied him access to her, turning their relationship into a fascinating and poetic love story, he was doing and feeling fundamentally the same thing Grisóstomo did and felt as soon as Marcela stepped into her poetic role of inaccessible Diana; for Grisóstomo, likewise, went from loving her to adoring her ("he no longer loved her, but adored her"). In other words, Cardenio's desire became as dependent on the obstacle in its path as Grisóstomo's desire had. The psychological mechanism that, as we saw, drove Grisóstomo to suicide, was the same one that paralyzed Cardenio before the slightest obstacle. For what we have to understand, once again, is that there is no objective, real difference between the poetic obstacle, that is, the obstacle that make things look poetic and incredibly attractive, and the obstacle that simply looks like

5. "He turned and said to Peter, 'Get behind me, Satan! You are an obstacle [*scandalum*] to me'" (Matthew 16.23). Peter is in the role of Satan at that moment, trying to "scandalize" Jesus. But Jesus will not stumble against such an obstacle, saying "Get behind me. Do not be a scandal to me!"

an obstacle, an impediment, a stumbling block on the path of desire. What we must understand, therefore, is that the fascination before the former and the anxious paralysis before the latter, though very different emotional experiences, are ruled by the same inner logic. They are the two sides of the same contradictory phenomenon, each one is implicit in the other. The obstacle paralyzes the will to go beyond it because it attracts as it impedes, it draws the anxious will toward itself.

There is perfect psychological coherence between the Cardenio who eventually went mad out of sheer self-contradiction and the one who had previosly said "I dared not ask my father, not only because of this objection, but because of many others that unnerved me, without even knowing what they were, except that I had the feeling that nothing I desired would ever be realized." These words clearly prove that, unlike most academic readers of this story, Cervantes understood with amazing precision why Cardenio was so indecisive, and the kind of tragedy that was brewing in his case, as in so many others, underneath such indecision.

But if Cardenio's potentially paralyzing transformation of the obstacle into the basis for a poetic love story points back in the novel toward Grisóstomo's tragic fate, his irresponsible attitude in the face of Don Fernando's increasing desire for Luscinda clearly anticipates the shameful desire that will become explicit a little later in the story of the *Curioso*, which is also, of course, the story of two close friends who become enemies.

There is no question about Cardenio's responsibility for arousing and sustaining Don Fernando's desire. The beginning may have been innocent enough: "I spoke of [my passion] to Don Fernando, for I thought that his great friendship for me forbade my keeping any secrets from him" (1.24.196). But it soon became clear to Cardenio that Don Fernando's constant praise of Luscinda was more than a little suspicious:

> It is true, as I confess now, that though I acknowledged the justice of Don Fernando's praise, it vexed me to hear those praises from his mouth, and I began to grow fearful and jealous of him; for there was not a moment when he did not want to talk of Luscinda, and he would start the conversation himself, even if he had to drag her in by the hair.

And yet Cardenio did nothing. Worse than that, as we have just seen, he managed to offer Don Fernando the role of becoming his representative, his mediator, in the affair, given the fact that he could not bring himself to do it, because, as he said, he could not shake off the irrational fear that his desire would always be thwarted. But that should come as no surprise at all to us, after we have seen him first fascinated by, then paralyzed by, an obstacle in both cases. For he is now facing a formidable living obstacle: Don Fernando and his rival desire. And he reacts to this new obstacle and rival desire in a totally predictable manner: he is both fascinated and paralyzed by it. He cannot get around it; that is to say, he cannot get to the object of his desire, Luscinda, except through Don Fernando's rival desire. He desires her through the rival's desire. It is the rival now who designates, who points to, what is desirable. Is it any surprise, therefore, if he maneuvers the situation in order to have Don Fernando act in his place? In other words, Don Fernando had already become Cardenio's mediator before he is even explicitly appointed to the job.

What we see in Cardenio now is what will become explicit in the Anselmo of the *Curioso*. At this point we do not yet see the subject of desire openly asking the friend to try and seduce his wife, as Anselmo will do. But we get as close to that as the particular circumstances of the story will allow. Cardenio, of course, does not have to convince his friend to show interest in his wife. The friend is already doing that in a obvious manner. He is just waiting for an opportunity, which is exactly what Cardenio will give him. But Cardenio still retains at least the semblance of an excuse, to which he will cling desperately: "Could I have foreseen this treachery? Could I even have imagined it? No, certainly not."

Cervantes, however, knows much more about Cardenio than Cardenio himself knows, and he is also much less prone to self-deception. Therefore, just as he proved capable of pulling the rug, as it were, from underneath Grisóstomo's excuse, by changing the circumstances and creating a new story where there was no inaccessible and cruel Marcela, but instead a loving and tender Luscinda, and yet the new version of Grisóstomo still manages to bring tragedy upon himself, in a similar manner the crafty author will now pull the rug from underneath Cardenio's excuse. He will once again change the circumstances and will transform the evil friend, the friend whose treason Cardenio "could not have even imagined," into an honest and honorable friend who could not even imagine a treason as awful as Don Fernando engineered. And still the new Cardenio, like the old one, will manage to turn his honest friend into a treacherous rival and bring upon himself the predictable tragedy. It seems, therefore, that there is no limit to human ingenuity when it comes to finding ways for self-destruction, or for a crafty author, in parallel, to give those ingenious ways the literary expression they so richly deserve.

In other words, there is a subjacent but easily detectable line of development running through the three stories. The outcome of the three, so far, is basically the same and equally tragic: Grisóstomo's suicide, Cardenio's madness, and Anselmo's death in the grip of intolerable anguish. The difference among the three is that, from one to the next the complicity of the grieving subject in his own demise becomes increasingly clear. To this end all external constraints on which the tragedy could be blamed have been progressively removed from the initial setting of the basic story. If Grisóstomo could blame his tragedy on the cruel and unyielding character of his beloved, that excuse will be taken away in the case of Cardenio. He cannot blame his tragedy on that. He will blame it on the treacherous character of his friend. But that excuse will also be taken away. Don Fernando will be replaced by honest and honorable Lothario, who will not only not impede his friend's wedding, but will happily arrange it himself, in sharp contrast to Don Fernando's behavior. As we reach this point, all the external obstacles have been removed. There is no excuse any longer: the desiring and grieving subject must acknowledge that he brought the tragedy on himself. And that is precisely what Anselmo will honestly recognize in the end. Contrary to Grisóstomo's "Song of Despair," his last will and testament, the following is Anselmo's last writing, which he could not finish. He died half-way through a sentence:

> "A foolish and ill-judged craving has cost me my life. If the news of my death should come to Camilla's ears, let her know that I pardon her. For she was not obliged to perform miracles nor did I need to ask her to. So, since I was the contriver of my own dishonor, there is no reason why. . . ."

The unfinished sentence is evidence that his death should not be considered a suicide. His grief must have been overpowering, but at that moment the open acknowledgment of his guilt and his pardon of Camilla prevents the grief from becoming hell-like, as opposed to the hellish, hopeless, self-feeding suffering of Grisóstomo, who refused to take Marcela off her hell-inflicting pedestal, where his suffering placed her. It is also the open acknowledgment and the pardon that save Anselmo from Cardenio's insanity, the existential anticipation of hell on earth.

In a certain sense, when we reach the story of the *Curioso*, at the end of the trajectory that may be said to begin with the story of Marcela and Grisóstomo, we reach bottom. From the point of view of shameful and inexcusable behavior, what Anselmo did surpasses anything that either Grisóstomo or Cardenio could have consciously admitted they would ever do. In this sense, Anselmo is the worst of them. And yet, it is precisely at this point of maximum degradation that a note of hope is sounded, as we have just seen, in Anselmo's recognition of his guilt and his pardon of unfaithful Camilla. The individual's guilt is clearer than ever, and yet, for Cervantes, that does not mean inevitable insanity and hell, even when it does mean unbearable anguish.

I am not trying to say that the three stories form some kind of indivisible whole, from which you cannot take any of the parts without loss of meaning. That is not the case; each of the stories is self-sufficient in the sense that none of them needs the others to convey its full meaning. But when you put them together, that meaning becomes clearer. Because in the final analysis they all mean the same thing. They just say it in different ways, from widely different circumstances, which is why they reinforce one another, and all together contribute to making the universal character of their ultimate meaning all the more clear.

For our purpose it does not make any difference whether or not the story of the *Curioso* stands "in a sense, separate" ("como separada") from the main story of *Don Quixote*, as opposed to the other two stories, which "concern the adventures that befell Don Quixote," as a mischievous narrator, obviously playing games with the reader, says in that famous passage at the beginning of chapter 44 of Part 2. For the same narrator also says there that "he has the skill, the knowledge and the capacity for dealing with the whole universe." Therefore we must assume that he has the capacity for traveling between very distant and separate things in a skillful and knowledgeable way, bringing together things that other people find difficult to connect. Otherwise, Cervantes would have undergone what happened to Avellaneda and the madman of Sevilla, who thought that adding stories or making something bigger was like blowing air into a dog. As Sancho said of "the son of a dog" who wrote the story of Don Quixote, he must have had no idea of what he was doing and ended up mixing "berzas con capachos" (a ridiculous hotchpotch). So, for the moment at least, I do not think we should worry about that.

There may be those who think I am trying to fabricate here something like a Procrustean bed, trying to reduce everything to a single measure, while ignoring the specifics of each situation. But what I am trying to do is precisely the opposite: to show the flexibility and fruitfulness of a basic idea and structure. The fact that Grisóstomo's suicide, Cardenio's madness and penitence in Sierra Morena, and Anselmo's death can be explained satisfactorily following the internal logic of what I have called the desire of the obstacle does not mean that we must ignore, for example, differences in individual personality among the different characters. Who knows, perhaps a Grisóstomo would have reacted differently in Cardenio's situation, when Luscinda's father denied him access to her. Maybe they would have decided to elope (if Luscinda had been more like Marcela), in order to follow even more closely the story of Pyramus and Thisbe. And heaven knows what Cervantes could have imagined from there on in order to make an interesting story. None of that would make it necessary to change the internal logic of the two lovers' desire, which is the same logic that governs the desire of the avid reader of poetical love stories. For every poetic love story would ultimately be the story of a desire, and that desire will have to multiply the obstacles in order to keep the interest of the story alive.

As further proof of what I am saying, let us examine in greater detail the behavior and personality of Cardenio's Nemesis, Don Fernando, who will undoubtedly appear in the eyes of many as candidate number one for the role of bad guy. After all, Grisóstomo, Cardenio, and Anselmo all did it to themselves, but Don Fernando did it to others, and, in addition, does not seem to feel any remorse for it.

Don Fernando

So we have to ask, Why did he do such a thing to his best friend? Or more precisely, How did he come to feel such an irresistible desire for Luscinda? And the answer is perfectly obvious: he caught such a desire from Cardenio himself. It was not destiny, as Cardenio said. It had nothing to do with the influence of the stars:

> But why do I complain miserable wretch that I am. For it is certain that when the stars in their courses bring disaster, rushing down with fury and violence, no power on earth can stop them, no human ingenuity avert them. Who could have thought that

Don Fernando, a noble and intelligent gentleman, indebted to me for my services and absolutely certain of success wherever his amorous fancy led him, would be bitten with the desire to take from me my one ewe-lamb, who was not even yet mine? (1.27.228)

To paraphrase Proteus's words in *The Two Gentlemen of Verona* that I had the occasion to quote before, "It was not his eye, but Cardenio's praise, not her true perfection, but his false transgression" that bit Don Fernando with the desire to take Luscinda. In fact, there is a history of similar "transgressions" behind this latest one.

In spite of the fact that, as Cardenio says, Don Fernando could have almost anyone his heart desired, he exhibits a clear preference for desiring what other people desire or have, for concentrating on what is not meant for him. In at least one respect Don Fernando deserves to be in the company of Don Quixote: he really likes a challenge—so much so, indeed, that we never see him desiring anything that is not a challenge. In other words, he has no interest in what he can get for free and without impediments. But he cannot tolerate that somebody could have something from which he is excluded. On his own, he has no desires, but he attaches himself like a parasite to other people's desires.

The first sign of the problem occurs as soon as Cardenio arrives at Duke Richards's house. You may remember that the duke "wanted [Cardenio] as a companion—not as a servant—for his eldest son," not for Don Fernando, who was the younger one. But as soon as he arrived, it was Don Fernando who became obsessed with him, for "although his elder brother liked me and was kind to me, he did not show me the same extreme affection and attention as did Don Fernando." It truly must have been "extreme" because everybody noticed it: "In a very short time he was so eager for my friendship that everyone noticed it." In other words, this new Cain could not just stand by and let his elder brother, the favored son, enjoy the company of the newcomer, from which he, the second son, had been excluded. He had to have what his brother had, and he practically stole it from him.

Then we find out that he was trying to have his way "with the daughter of a farmer, a tenant of his father's . . . so beautiful, so modest, so discreet, and so virtuous" that all his efforts had been in vain. Typically, he became so obsessed with this affair "that he decided to gratify his desires and overcome her virtue by a promise of marriage, knowing that it would be impossible to succeed by any other means." Cardenio, who knew about his friend's intrigue, became alarmed by such dishonorable behavior and tried in vain to dissuade his friend from carrying out his plan. Needless to say, as soon as Don Fernando had his way with the virtuous lady, by swearing under God to be her husband, his erotic desire cooled rather quickly: "As soon as Don Fernando had enjoyed the farmer's daughter his desires grew calm and his ardour cooled, so that if at first he had pretended that he wanted to go away in order to relieve his passion, now he was really anxious to go to avoid fulfilling his promise."

What happened to the beautiful and virtuous daughter of Duke Richards's tenant is, of course, the story of Dorotea, a rather determined young lady, who is not about to let Don Fernando get away with it, if she can help it. She will confirm in her own narration how quickly Don Fernando could go from irresistible desire before the obstacle to nothing once the obstacle has disappeared:

> Don Fernando repeated and confirmed his oaths, calling on yet more saints, and invoking innumerable curses on himself should he break his promise. The tears came once more to his eyes, and he sighed deeply. He clasped me more firmly in his arms, which had never let me go. Whereafter, when my maid had left the room, I ceased to be a maid and he became a perfidious traitor.
>
> Day followed on the night of my undoing, but not so fast, I think, as Don Fernando desired. . . . This I say because Don Fernando hurriedly departed . . . even before it was light in the streets. As he took his leave he promised me, though with less ardour than when he came in, that I could rely on his faith and on his oaths. (1.28.244)

Shortly after this Don Fernando turned his attention and his desire to that beautiful maiden of whom his friend Cardenio spoke to him in such glowing terms, with the results we already know.

As I said, Don Fernando would have to be candidate number one for the role of bad guy in all of these stories. One is struck in particular by the personality difference between him and his friend Cardenio, who is only one of his victims. Next to chronically indecisive Cardenio, forever procrastinating, we see a Don Fernando who rushes headlong from one object of desire to another, with no hesitation at all each time about what he wants at that particular moment. Not only is he willing to do whatever it takes to get it, he actually does it.

And yet what causes this frenetic activity is no different from what causes Cardenio's paralysis: the obstacle that either triggers or intensifies the desire, and simultaneously blocks its path. Logically speaking, it is impossible to separate the two contradictory sides of the obstacle, but it is also impossible to predict with certainty which side will predominate in the actual experience of the subject, toward which side he or she will incline. The internal logic that operates in both cases would be the same, but the actual experience will depend on individual characteristics or the specific circumstances of the situation.

In fact, taking into consideration the difference in the reaction to the obstacle of Cardenio and Don Fernando, an individualized diagnostic can be made for each of them. I think most readers will agree that Don Fernando's desire is much sicker, more pathological, and more unreal or without definite object than Cardenio's. Don Fernando's desire is entirely driven by, and totally dependent on, the obstacle: no obstacle, no desire. It is just as simple and drastic as that, and it is proven beyond doubt by his behavior with Dorotea. As soon as the obstacle disappeared, so immediately did the desire. In other words, the object of his desire has no reality of its own. There is nothing behind the obstacle that would attract his desire independently of the obstacle. Therefore, the object of his desire is pure appearance, an illusion created by the obstacle itself. He was never in love with the real Dorotea, never cared for the real Cardenio, or for the real Luscinda. However, it is precisely this complete absorption of his desire in and by the obstacle that, ironically, gives Don Fernando's behavior the appearance of somebody who stops at nothing, who does not hesitate before anything. Because, as far as his desire is concerned, there really is nothing beyond the obstacle, in reference to which the obstacle could reveal itself in his eyes as such, as what it really is, an obstacle, as something standing in the way of something else, capable of producing at least a moment of hesitation. *The truth is not that he does not allow any obstacle to stand in the way of what he wants, the truth is that he never goes beyond any obstacle that stands in his way.* Nothing stops him from embracing whatever stops him. Don Fernando never hesitates before the obstacle, he belongs to it, and since he never goes beyond it either, it may look from the outside as if he stopped at nothing. His desire having lost all sense of reality, Don Fernando actually lives on the border of criminality. If he were not the son of Duke Richards, I think he would be in jail already, or worse.

Cardenio, on the other hand, is not quite so sick. The reality of his Luscinda does not disappear completely behind the obstacle. His love for her is far more solid and real. They have loved each other since they were children. His fascination with the obstacle does terrible damage to the reality behind it, the reality of Luscinda and of his love for her, but does not destroy it completely. Accordingly, the obstacle, in his case, does reveal itself existentially as an obstacle, as something that impedes the movement toward some other reality that lies beyond it. He is thoroughly tempted by the poetic possibilities of the obstacle, but at the same time he is anxious about it, and feels very uneasy, "as if his desire would never be realized." He senses the emptiness, the disappearing of reality, that comes with the tempting attraction of the obstacle. In reference to Luscinda, every obstacle becomes for him both a powerful attraction and a deep source of anxiety.

In other words, no matter how vaguely or indistinctly, Cardenio still senses a difference between poetically glorious Luscinda, associated with the obstacle in his path, and the real Luscinda; and he feels rather deeply that when he waxes poetic and turns Luscinda into a beautiful and distant little goddess, he loses the real Luscinda whom he has always loved. But he does not know why, because he still sees only one Luscinda. All he knows is that the more deserving of poetic praise she appears to him, the more desirable she becomes, the deeper his anxious feeling that he will never reach her. Don Fernando, on the other hand, does not appear to feel such an anxiety. He overcomes the feeling of it with his criminal behavior.

By comparison with Don Fernando, Cardenio's anxious paralysis before the obstacle, although clearly a sympton of his sick desire, is also a sympton of remaining health. His anxiety is perfectly justified. It warns him about a loss that is quite real, although it does not have to happen. This comparative situation is similar to what we found in the case of Don Quixote the snob versus Don Quixote the madman: Don Quixote's snobbery rises to the surface and becomes visible as his madness relents a little, as his absorption in and by the model-rival, the fascinating obstacle, Amadís, relaxes. As I said then, comparatively speaking, Don Quixote's snobbery is a good sign, a sign of possible recovery. And it is also helpful in understanding what lies at the bottom of Don Quixote's madness, which the madness itself hides from us. Don Fernando and Cardenio both suffer from the same existential disease, but the severity of the disease is greater in the former than in the latter, while the visible symptons vary accordingly.

In fact, this is the disease that has caused all the troubles in the three interpolated stories we have examined, as it is also the disease that relates these stories to Don Quixote's madness. It is a disease ultimately rooted in the fundamental instability of human desire, in its inherent potential to come in conflict with itself, because it is never one with itself, it always involves another.

Further Reflections on the Desire of the Obstacle

The desire of the obstacle, the transformation of the obstacle into an object of desire, is an unavoidable possibility of the internal logic that governs the development of mimetic desire, the theory of which has been developed and explained in numerous ways by René Girard, whose pioneering thought is the basis of my own reflections.[6]

The desire of the obstacle is human desire blind to its own mimetic pursuit of the other's desire. It is blind because it mistakes the effect for the cause, seeing the model or mediating desire, which it follows, as outside interference, an obstacle in its path, and also as the proof that what it seeks is indeed desirable. Because—it reasons to itself—if it were not desirable, the other (the unrecognized model) would not desire it. And once human desire becomes existentially constituted that way, it tends to perpetuate itself that way. The subject of such a desire will tend to desire only if the obstacle is there. And if an obstacle, whether real or imagined, blocks his path, the subject will assume the existence of an opposing intention, a rival desire, a desire that "proves" the value, the desirability, of the object.

The desire of the obstacle is the literary desire par excellence, the desire of the knightly challenge as well as of the love affair forever frustrated. It is

6. In his recent book, *Para entender el Quijote*, Ciriaco Morón argues that the *Quixote* "no es un libro de rivalidad mimética," and seems to believe that the "doctrine" on which René Girard and myself base our view of Cervantes's novel "might find a foundation in Luther or Freud, but not in Catholic theology" (329). As I have had the pleasure of subsequently explaining to him in person, his statement is based on a seriously deficient understanding of Girard's mimetic theory of desire and the origins of human culture in general. I trust he is now fully aware of the fact that the greatest interest by far generated by Girard's theory has been among Catholic theologians in particular, including some at the highest levels of Vatican authority, closest to the late Pope John Paul II. They should know.

the desire that keeps literary fiction alive, looking like the real thing. Obstacles and frustrated desires keep our interest going. Aristotle said that we like the mimetic representation of things that, in themselves, are unpleasant or unattractive because we learn from such mimetic representations, and it is natural for humans to like learning. But even if we accept his argument, it does not explain our *preference* for such imitations, the overwhelming *preponderance* of such unpleasant things in the annals of mimetic representations. Cervantes knows that it is not an intense desire for learning that drives a fascinated Don Quixote in search of adventures or an equally fascinated Marcela into artificial pastoral surroundings.

Literature does not do violence to reality, does not fictionalize reality, by imitating, by representing, something that is purely imaginary. *It is not exactly the power of the imagination as such that fictionalizes reality, but rather the power of desire.* Literature fictionalizes reality when it turns it into an object of mimetic, rivalrous desire. At such a moment literary fiction violently constrains reality, puts it, as it were, into a straitjacket. For a reality fictionalized is a reality reduced, constrained, not expanded, not liberated, as the old romantics and their descendants have been saying forever. Reality loses its openness, and therefore its relative though irreducible unpredictability, when it is seen through the lens of mimetic desire. Because mimetic desire, left to its own devices, can become quite predictable, not in reference to its object, which can be anything at all, but in its relationship with the inevitable model, on which the choice of object will ultimately depend. To paraphrase something that Marcela says in her famous speech on individual freedom, the number of objectively desirable things is practically infinite, and yet not every desirable thing is actually desired. The question must therefore be why only certain things, and not others, become subjectively desirable.

The choice, as well as the interindividual rules of the choice, is what really interests the great literary masters. And they are in an ideal position to wonder and meditate on the fact that through the ages the choice of human beings has been clearly for poetic objects that imitate primarily, more than anything else, misfortunes and disasters. All poets know that conflicts sell.

It could be said that all the frustrated or heroically challenged characters invented by the great literary masters are nothing but so many manifestations of that fascinated reader or spectator who keeps coming back for more of the same poetic object, in which impeded desires are imitated. It was Oscar Wilde who said that "it is the spectator, and not life, that art really mirrors" (2), and I think that was a profoundly accurate observation.

In Calderón's famous play *La vida es sueño* (*Life Is a Dream*), the jester, Clarín, addresses the spectators with the following words:

> There is no better window on the play
> than the one which, without pleading
> with a ticket agent, a man brings with himself,
> for at every spectacle he peeps, in the nude,
> at his own shamelessness.
>
> (2.2.1171–77)

In other words, the spectator sees on the stage what he brings with himself as a spectator, which is himself in the nude. The desire that draws him to the spectacle denudes him, reveals his own indigence, his vulnerability, his shame, and that is what is being presented to him on the stage. But if this is so, the poet, the fiction maker, is just as indigent. He has no desire of his own either. He must conform to and catch the desire of the spectator or reader. For, as Kierkegaard said, he is not a prophet or an apostle proclaiming the truth to a deluded spectator. In fact, the poet, the imitator par excellence, is in as much danger of being deluded by the fiction he has created as the spectator himself. The poet is deluded, that is, into thinking that the desire he has created is independent of the desire on which he feeds as a poet, as an imitator. This is why Don Quixote is the emblematic figure not only of the fascinated spectator or reader, but also of the fascinated fiction writer. Cervantes knows that when he is talking about Don Quixote, he is also talking about himself.

The great poets know all this, and this knowledge becomes for them an inexhaustible source of irony. The desire of the poet, qua poet, and the desire of the spectator, qua spectator, meet each other on equal ground and feed on each other. The fictional object, the poetic icon, deflects their symmetrical looks into each other's eyes together with the danger structurally inherent in such an encounter. The fictional object becomes something of a sacrificial substitute for the possibility of a real conflict. It represents within itself the conflict that has been averted and from which it takes its meaning. All poets know that conflicts sell, but only the great ones also know that the reason why they sell and the reason why there are conflicts to begin with is frequently one and the same.

The internal dynamics or logic of the mimetic conflict, whether it is real or a fictional substitute, are the same. And that means that the very thing, the fictional substitute, that can detour and avert the real conflict may also become its triggering mechanism, its conduit. One possibility cannot be separated from the other. Every real conflict is a priviledged potential piece of poetic fiction, and every poetic fictional conflict carries with it the possibility of becoming real, that is to say, of being taken for real, of being imitated in real life. But that also means that the real mimetic conflict, with real violence and real casualties, carries within itself a process of derealization, of fictionalization, of the very reality it destroys. And the greater the violence is, the more intense the mimetic attraction and mutual dependence becomes, and, as a result, also the more unreal and irrelevant the object of the violence is rendered. It does not matter what the beginning object of contention may have been, or the beginning justice or injustice of the cause. The inherent mimetism of the violence itself will eventually take over. *An apocalyptic human conflict that would destroy the entire planet would also be, more than any other thing, about nothing because it would have turned everything into some kind of universal fiction.*

Of course, we can only talk about real human violence fictionalizing the reality it destroys so long as we can conceive of reality itself as something that stands outside the internal dynamics of the mimetic conflict and its violence, beyond the grasp of rivalry and competition; as long, therefore, as we conceive of reality as such as something that rivalry and competition inevitably miss, no matter what the object of the rivalry happens to be. But the historical possibility of conceiving reality that way has not always been there. As anthropology has taught us, there was a time when there was no such conception, when nobody saw any fundamental incompatibility between reality as such and violence, whether human or otherwise. Then, the decisive question was not whether violence fictionalized reality, but whether violent destruction was real or only fictional. And it was something of a sacred duty to fictionalize violence in order to drain it of its destructive power, to prevent it from causing real harm. In such a context, to speak, as we are doing here, of these two things, real and fictional violence, as sharing the same internal dynamics, as being structurally the same thing, with the possibility of sliding easily from one to the other, would have been taboo, perhaps a horrendous sacrilege. For everything was at stake then, including survival itself, in being able to separate one from the other, or to turn the real thing with real blood and real casualties into its imitated representation. To be able to produce an accurate imitation of the real thing, but without real effects—that is, without real blood—was about the only way to protect oneself from the real conflict.

Clearly, today nobody attaches such ritual and momentous responsibility to the poetic fictionalization of violence. This is why we can treat it with unprecedented freedom. Because, in spite of some romantic outbursts, nobody can seriously think today that fictionalizing and ritualizing violence can prevent real violent destruction from occurring. Poetic fiction, the direct heir to the old rituals, cannot save us from our own mimetic violence. The desacralization process has taken that possibility away from it. But the fact that it cannot save us does not mean that it has lost its ancient link with real violence. Quite the contrary: if it can no longer save us, it is precisely because it itself has been discovered to be a form of violence, not a break with violence, or a denunciation of it, but a way of playing with it, both hiding it and hiding from it, which is, once again, what Calderón's famous jester, the spectator, the peeping tom, tries to do in *La vida es sueño*, but to no avail.

A great poet like Cervantes is profoundly aware of the two sides of this new situation. He knows of the radical irrelevance of poetic fiction as an instrument of salvation, but he also knows that behind fiction's apparent playful façade, behind its claim to innocence, there is real violence. In fact the new great poet is far more clearly aware of that than the old ritual man could ever be precisely because his salvation from violence no longer depends on fictionalizing and ritualizing it. The fictionalizing of the mimetic conflict has lost its capacity for salvation, but not its capacity to turn into real violence. That is what Cervantes is talking about when he brings both knights-errant and pastoral lovers down to earth.

CHAPTER XI

Juan Palomeque's Inn

They all gazed at one another in silence, Dorotea at Don Fernando, Don Fernando at Cardenio, Cardenio at Luscinda, Luscinda at Cardenio. But the first to break the silence was Luscinda, who addressed Don Fernando:

"Leave me, Don Fernando, out of regard for yourself if for no other reason. . . . See how Heaven, by ways strange and mysterious to us, has brought me to my true husband. . . ."

Then . . . Dorotea summoned up all the strength she could, got up, and threw herself on her knees at his feet. . . . "Think, my lord, . . . you cannot be the fair Luscinda's, because you are mine; nor can she be yours, because she is Cardenio's. It will be easier, if you will think for a moment, to make your heart love the woman who loves you, than to force into loving you a woman who loathes you." . . .

They begged him to reflect that it was not by chance, as it appeared, but by a special providence of Heaven, that they had all come together in such an unexpected place.

(1.36.327–330)

Providential Coincidences

We have already alluded to the functional similarity—first noticed years ago by J. B. Avalle Arce—between the magical solutions that occur at sage Felicia's palace in the pastoral *Dianas*, especially Montemayor's *Diana*, and the accumulation of providential coincidences that occur in Juan Palomeque's inn in the *Quixote*. These coincidences will provide the opportunity for the happy resolution of the problems in which Cervantes's lovers Cardenio, Luscinda, Don Fernando, and Dorotea have become entangled. It could even be said that we are dealing with a deliberate response by Cervantes to that part of Montemayor's *Diana* that he did not like. For, as the priest says of Montemayor's novel during the scrutiny of Don Quixote's library, "I am of the opinion that it should not be burnt, but all the part dealing with sage Felicia and the enchanted water should be taken out."

The problem with the priest's opinion is that if you take out "all the part dealing with sage Felicia and the enchanted water," you leave Montemayor's perennially frustrated lovers without a solution to their problems. And we must assume that Cervantes, the novelist, would not like that either. He would not leave his own lovers going nowhere, endlessly repeating the same mistakes back and forth—especially since he has also shown us that such endless repetition is not realistic, that what eventually happens in the absence of a solution is complete disaster: lives broken, unbearable anguish, madness, and suicide. Cervantes must have thought that such terrible consequences from such entanglements required a more credible and trustworthy solution than the power of a magic potion.

He trusts in God's providence, in those "ways strange and mysterious to us." This is neither magic nor a miracle. The most obvious difference between a magical solution and God's providence at the inn is that the latter does not impinge at all on the individual responsibility and freedom of the people involved. Quite the contrary, God's providence is a call for them to return to and to acknowledge such freedom and responsibility. God's "mysterious ways" offer them a second chance. It is both a warning and a sign of hope: not everything is lost. There is still hope because there is still freedom. The four lovers have not reached yet the suicidal stage of a Grisóstomo, for example.

And it is not a miracle either. God's mysterious ways are an integral part of an external and historical reality disenchanted, desacralized, just recently discovered or rediscovered in Cervantes's age to be far richer and more complex than anybody had previously imagined. This modern reality was open to unlimited scientific exploration without fear of sacred taboos. But it was also a reality that was always bigger and extended further than the rational reach of science—hence its mysterious quality. This modern reality and scientific (or philosophical) reason still did not coincide completely. Divine providence was more than the ground that sustained reason, contrary to what Hegel came to think, for whom trust in reason was the same as trust in Providence.[1] Cervantes's conception of providential reality, at least in this instance, is closer to the views of his contemporary Francis Bacon, the great defender of "natural philosophy"—the immediate precursor of modern science—as well as of the separation between "divinity" and philosophy: "[Let] no man upon a weak conceit of sobriety or an ill-applied moderation think or maintain, that a man can search too far or be too well studied in the book of God's word [the Bible], or in the book of God's works [nature]; divinity or philosophy: but rather let men endeavour an endless progress or proficiency in both" (*The Advancement of Learning*, 1.3.8). The progress in the knowledge of God's works is endless, but it never gets to penetrate "the mysteries of God": "For the contemplation of God's creatures and works produceth knowledge . . . , but having regard to God, no perfect knowledge, but wonder, which is broken knowledge" (*The Advancement of Learning*, 1.3.9). If Cervantes were a philosopher, I think he would have agreed with what Bacon said in approval of some of the pre-Socratic philosophers and in criticism of Aristotle: "[In] my opinion both Empedocles and Democritus, who complain, the first madly enough, but the second very soberly, that all things are hidden away from us . . . that truth is drowned in deep wells, that the true and the false are strangely joined and twisted together . . . are more to be approved than the school of Aristotle so confident and dogmatical" (*Essays*, 272). These words are significant here not for what they tell us about pre-Socratic philosophy, but for what they reveal about the new spirit of inquiry and its sense of the mystery that lies at the bottom of reality, God's reality, begging to be explored without fear of the truth, but never to be exhausted.

The ultimate mystery of God-sustained reality is inseparable from God's providential action in the world. It is a witness to God's freedom, as it were. And, in this sense, it is also inseparable from a certain degree of uncertainty, an uncertainty that scientific reason will not only never eliminate, but that is in fact essential to the possibility of science itself. Furthermore, it is not only

1. "The great assumption that what has taken place in the world has also done so in conformity with reason—which is what first gives the history of philosophy its true interest—is nothing else than trust in Providence, only in another form"; quoted in Susan Neiman, *Evil in Modern Thought*; emblematic reference preceding "Table of Contents."

essential to science, but essential to the possibility of individual human freedom. In other words, God's freedom, the ultimate mystery of reality itself, is the very ground on which individual human freedom rests. If any attempt to scientifically eliminate, or to try to ignore, that ultimate uncertainty is not only unscientific, but an illusory Promethean attempt to become God, any attempt to eliminate that ultimate degree of uncertainty in human relations becomes an intolerable act of tyranny, strictly forbidden by God, "*che tal certezza ha Dio più proibita, ch'al primo padre l'arbor de la vita*" (my emphasis; for God has forbidden such certainty more than he forbade [our] first father the Tree of Life), as we can read in Ariosto's story of the magic goblet, to which Lothario refers in the *Curioso* to support his argument that what Anselmo wants is against the will of God. Or as we also read at the end of *El celoso extremeño*. That ultimate uncertainty, both in the external world of nature and history, and inside the human individual, bears God's signature, and it cannot be tampered with without devastating consequences.

What we now have to understand is that the logic of the providential intervention at the inn corresponds exactly to the logic or the nature of the human problem it is meant to address. The silent voice of Providence calling the characters *from beyond themselves*, from circumstances they do not control, to their responsibility as free individuals worthy of their freedom, is not a deus ex machina. It is what their problem demands. Because their problem has involved a significant loss of inner freedom, as their individual desires became mimetically entangled with, and mediated by, one another's desires. This loss of freedom is also, as we saw, a loss of contact with reality, a fictionalization of the real, in particular a fictional transformation of what they are in one another's eyes—in other words, a fictionalization of their relationships. Seen through the lenses of their mimetically mediated desire, reality has shrunk, as it were; it has certainly lost its unfathomable richness, and, as reflected in their relationships, is rapidly becoming quite predictable, as predictable as the typical relationships in all those pastoral stories that some of them have been reading. Loss of inner freedom and loss of contact with reality are the two Cervantine sides of the same danger, constantly present in the mimetic dynamics governing human relationships: the danger posed by loss of transcendance, by the turning of the human other into an absolute point of reference. Don Quixote's madness is the paradigmatic example of such a loss of inner freedom and of contact with reality.

Providence does not intervene to fulfill their desires, but rather to correct them, cure them, bring them back to reality, that is to say, Providence restores the reality of the other in their eyes, breaking the spell of fiction. Providence operates here, at the inn, in exactly the same way that it will also operate at the end of the novel in the cure of Don Quixote's madness. That cure at the end will not be any more of a miracle than this one is, unless, of course, we want to call the benevolent divine activity of sustaining reality itself a miracle—in other words, unless we want to call God's love "L'Amor che move il sole e l'altre stelle" (the Love that moves the sun and the stars), a miracle, which Cervantes undoubtedly would.

In other words, the explicitly providential coincidence of all these characters showing up at Juan Palomeque's inn, unexpected and perhaps improbable as it is, but not totally beyond the realm of possibility, is meant to represent, within the fictional parameters of the novel, an irruption of the real, of freedom's space, of God's space, into the fictionalizing predictability of the lovers' relationships with one another.

Of course, this also proves, once more, that Cervantes is no romantic. He does not think that novelistic fiction is a hymn to human freedom, an expansion of reality, a breaking through the limitations of a real world viewed as narrow, confining, routine-bound, repetitive, as romantic readers have been repeating endlessly to this day, while ignoring the fact that Don Quixote's madness is the very opposite of an expansion of reality, that it is instead an agonistic shrinking of it. Of course, Don Quixote is the first romantic reader of himself. He is precisely in search of such an expansion of reality. He wants to get out of oppressive routine and into the open space of freedom, which is in itself an admirable project, to be sure. But everything crumbles because of his fascination with the chivalric model, radiant Amadís. All his projected expansion, all his flight toward freedom, will turn out to be pure fiction, a mirage, a hiding of the truth. And the truth is that a false and deceiving expansion, a fictitious freedom, is, in fact, an oppressive constraint, a repetitive, infernal monotony.

In Cervantes authentic freedom is inseparable from that which is real, insofar as it is real. It belongs not in the world of fiction, but in the real world. The novelistic fiction is true to itself and tells the truth when it acknowledges its estrangement from authentic freedom by representing it as coming from the outside, as the unpredictable. Cervantes's realism goes well beyond stylistic concerns and questions of artistic verisimilitude (important though these concerns really are to him). It is also of a kind utterly unknown to Aristotle, and therefore not properly comprehended by the Aristotelian distinction between poetry and history.[2] Cervantes's realism is obviously felt as part of his Christian faith. And that faith in what is real that guides the entire novel is what rises to the surface at some privileged moments.

Perhaps we, readers of *Don Quixote*, have not meditated enough on the implications of what we have generally acknowledged to be characteristically Cervantine: its realism. Do we fully understand the fact that the encounter of Don Fernando, Cardenio, Luscinda, and Dorotea with God's reality at the inn follows the same logic that inspires the very conception of *Don Quixote* as the first modern novel? *Don Quixote*, the novel, is the narrative space where not only the Manchegan hidalgo, but all previous fictional characters, knights-errant and pastoral lovers, meet historical reality head-on. Out of such an encounter with reality their fictitious character, their artificiality, their predictability, was exposed, brought out into the open for everybody to see, together with the terrible consequences that had been hidden from readers by the artificiality and the fiction. For the fictional environment in which they lived was by no means a neutral or purely formal space. But they also became so much more human, so much more truthful. They were transformed into the characters of a new kind of novel inspired by the spirit of truth. The realism that exposed them also offered them the possibility of a new life. The same realism that guided Cervantes's hand through the internal logic of Grisóstomo's suicide, for example, will also offer the four lovers an opportunity to save themselves at the inn. The realism that exposed the madness of Don Quixote's knightly and pastoral fiction also saved Don Quixote and became the foundation of the realistic novel *Don Quixote*. What can save the character from his or her self-made fiction within the novel also saves the novel historically. The hope of the character is also the hope of the novel.

Cervantes's Christian providential realism sets him apart from the romantic. Likewise, it sets him apart from pagan providentialism. Given Cervantes's admiration for Heliodorus, one might be tempted to see in the providential

2. Cf. Toffanin's view of the *Quixote* as "la risposta più profonda . . . al questionario aristotelico"; see above, Introduction. Also note Forcione's opinion of Toffanin: "Toffanin [saw] Cervantes's great achievement in discovering the poetic possibilities of historical reality" (1970, p. 4). This is true as long as we consider such possibilities as belonging to historical reality as such, qua reality.

coincidences at Juan Palomeque's inn an echo of the many providential occurrences in Heliodorus's influential *Ethiopian Romance*. I think that would be a mistake. But it may be useful to examine the difference between the two briefly.

Heliodorus's romance, the story of the love and long travails of Theagenes, reputed descendant of Achilles, and Charicleia, a young virgin devoted to Artemis, is probably the best among the romances of the Hellenistic period. It is also the one most overtly religious. Fleeing from Delphi and Greece, the lovers will eventually end up in Ethiopia, where they are destined to be sacrificed to the gods, until it is revealed that Charicleia is in fact the daughter of the reigning monarchs, who was exposed at birth. The ending will be a happy one, and not only for the lovers: from that day on no more human sacrifices will be allowed in the kingdom.

The incredible and constant changes of fortune the two perfectly virtuous and chaste lovers undergo become an explicit theme in the novel. Time and again the narrator or the characters themselves reflect on the fact that they are relentlessly tossed in every direction by circumstances beyond their control. They feel deeply that they are playthings of the gods, as Plato would have said. Hardly anything ever happens that is not "providential," but more often than not they believe such "providence" to be malignant. The general feeling conveyed is that you never know what awaits you, but there's a better than even chance that it will be bad. Here are a couple of examples among the countless that could be quoted:

> [Theagenes and Charicleia] had just approached the lake . . . when they saw a group of armed men moving towards the island.
>
> The sight made them dizzy . . . as if the repeated assaults of fortune had deprived them of sensation. . . . Charicleia proposed that they run back to the cave. . . . But Theagenes held her back and said: "How long shall we keep fleeing from a fate which is everywhere pursuing us? . . . Flight will only gain us futile wandering, a vagabond life, and the incessant asaults of our hostile deity. . . . A little while ago he made us captive, but then left us deserted; he held out prospect of deliverance and flight to freedom, and now sends ruffians to destroy us. It is a game of war he is playing against his victims; he has staged our drama like a play in the theater." (115)

At one point in the story Calasiris, an Egyptian priest of Isis and a fatherly figure, who engineered the lovers' escape from Delphi, then lost them, and is concerned about their fate, arrives in Memphis precisely at the moment when his two sons, in rivalry for the position of high priest, are engaged in combat to the death:

> It was then that some divinity or fortune which is the arbiter of human destiny introduced a novel episode into the tragedy being enacted, as if to prevent the opening of a new drama to compete with the old. At that very day and hour it prepared an entry for Calasiris, like a *deus ex machina*, and made him an unhappy witness to the mortal struggle of his sons. (164–65)

Sometimes it is called a god or a demon, other times fortune, destiny, fate, or even just human nature, but whatever it is called, it does not allow you to have pure happiness and must always mix bad things with the good. Whatever it is, the characters are at its mercy. No matter what they do, they cannot control it. Even if they are suffering the consequences of their own acts, it is still the god or destiny that is pursuing them for what they did.

In the end the two virtuous lovers will inherit a kingdom and be happy. So we must assume everything they suffered was a test of their virtue. But the test itself is conceived as something purely external. What tests the inner virtue of the lovers assails them from the outside. The inner virtue resists those assaults and remains always itself, untainted. Their relationship is determined by that inner virtue. It is simply an expression of it. Therefore, since that inner virtue never changes, the relationship itself is never in danger of internal collapse. And that is a fundamental difference from the way realistic human relationships are conceived by Cervantes.

In Cervantes, we might say that things are the other way around. The relationship is primary. Whether one is good or bad, virtuous or vicious, depends on the kind of relationship one maintains with the human other, the lover, the neighbor, or whomever. There is no such thing as unchanging virtue apart from the relationship itself. One can go to hell with the best of intentions, because the best of intentions can be transformed into something bad and destructive within the internal dynamics of the human relationship. Therefore the real testing ground in Cervantes is the intersubjective relationship itself, and the threat to it originates within its own evolving dynamism.

The specifically Cervantine test of the virtuous character comes at the end of all the external meanderings of circumstancial fortune. When the Hellenistic author has finished with all the tests that either destiny or the gods have devised for a virtuous character, he or she still has not reached the typical Cervantine test, which comes precisely at that moment, that is, at the end of the journey. Witness, for example, the end of the journey in the *Persiles*, of which I have spoken elsewhere.[3] It is then that the relationship between Persiles and Segismunda is most intimately tested from inside the relationship itself. The same thing could be said of the end in *El amante liberal*, the most "Byzantine" of the *Exemplary Novels*, where the liberality or generosity of the lover is tested: How can he be generous by giving away what does not belong to him, namely, his beloved, a free human individual? ("How can I offer [to another] what is so far from being mine?"). That is to say, the object of this final test is the relationship itself: What is she to him? How does he view his relationship with her?

Together with the transfer of the danger from outside forces to the internal dynamics of the human relationship between the self and the other, the guilt of the outside world, of the reality beyond the relationship, recedes or disappears. There will no longer be some kind of deity, a god or a demon, pulling the strings of human beings for his or her own amusement; there will no longer be a deity whose capricious power one must appease by piously playing along with him or her, by rolling with the punches, so to speak, turning the unpredictable ups and downs of one's life into a religious offering, a sacred dance, no matter how painful:

> "On! [said Charicleia] I too will dance after the fashion appropriate to the demon that holds me in sway. To him I will chant dirges and writhe in a dance of lamentation." (149)

In Cervantes God does not manipulate the characters. God's modus operandi is not that of the poet.[4] Cervantes's novelistic fiction can no longer be a sacred game, a propitiating dance. For it is not God who turned the characters' lives into a novel. They did it themselves in and through their relationships. And as they did, they allowed themselves increasingly to become like predictable puppets in a web of relationships that no one controls, least of all a transcendant hand beyond the web itself. Cervantes's providential intervention is no more than an appeal for the restoration of that which is in danger of collapse, individual responsibility and freedom on the one hand, and real-

3. See my *Mímesis conflictiva*, 126–32.

4. Cf. Forcione, "The Cervantine Figure of the Poet: Impostor or God?," 305ff.

ity and truth, on the other. For it is important to emphasize once more that Cervantes's solution is radically different from the purely mythical solution of the magic potion. Cervantes's solution is not a solution unless the individual believes in it and willingly accepts it.

Above all there is something that differentiates Cervantes's providential intervention from the traditional one, whether pagan or not. The traditional poetic divine intervention is either to punish the guilty or to reward the virtuous. Who ever heard of a divine intervention to help the guilty, to give the guilty a second chance before it is too late! But that is precisely what this whole episode at the inn is all about. Cervantes is not trying to satisfy some sense of poetic justice, or the reader's desire, by satisfying the desire of all these lovers. He wants to save his characters from themselves and teach them and us a lesson. In this Cervantes is the direct heir to Gil Polo, but with a greater and deeper understanding of the problem.

The circumstances of the intrigue are such that, if we had to pick one "bad guy" in particular on whom to put the blame for all the suffering of the lovers, that "bad guy" would undoubtedly be Don Fernando. He is indeed at the center of the episode. He is clearly the kind of individual that a less generous and intelligent author would love to turn into the vehicle for a punishing "example," the kind of scapegoat whose demise everybody would find extremely cathartic. One could easily imagine, for example, a determined woman like Dorotea—who has already demonstrated that she is quite capable of taking care of herself—taking revenge on her unfaithful fiancé by killing Don Fernando in the presence of everybody, especially when she sees him holding Luscinda in his arms. Honor and jealousy intertwined have always been a powerful motive for vengeful action, of which we can see an example in the case of Claudia Jerónima, who kills her fiancé, in Part 2 of the novel (although it is also important to notice that it turned out to be a mistake on her part). In fact, Dorotea herself makes an indirect reference to such a possibility when, after presenting the facts of her just grievance against Don Fernando, she tells him:

> Pero, con todo esto, no querría que cayese en tu imaginación pensar que he venido aquí con pasos de mi deshonra, habiéndome traído sólo los del dolor y sentimiento de verme de ti olvidada.
>
> (But, for all that, I would not have you think for one moment that I have come here on the steps of my dishonor; grief alone has brought me here, and sorrow at seeing myself forgotten by you.)

In other words, it would have been quite natural for Don Fernando and everybody else to think that she was there to see her honor restored or to kill the man who stole it from her, like the Rosaura of *La vida es sueño*. Clearly that was not what Cervantes intended. For it is precisely to the "bad guy," Don Ferdando in this case, that God's providential second chance is more directly offered.

What Cervantes intended was to appeal to the basic human dignity of this clearly guilty man, and to call him out of the trap in which he had imprisoned himself, to look inside himself and hear the voice of his conscience, which will not fall silent or stop pursuing him until he does what he knows he ought to do:

> Y cuando todo esto falte, tu misma conciencia no ha de faltar de dar voces callando en mitad de tus alegrías, volviendo por esta verdad que te he dicho, y turbando tus mejores gustos y contentos.
>
> (Should all these [reasons] fail, your own conscience will not fail to cry out silently in the midst of your joys, upholding the truth I have just spoken to disturb your greatest pleasures and delights.)

It is also by no means irrelevant that the voice telling the guilty one that he is indeed guilty and will not be able to hide from his guilt is the voice of the victim, a victim who is telling the truth, but who is also willing to forgive.

The tension is extremely high in this scene. Even after Don Fernando, "overwhelmed with shame and horror" by Dorotea's words, lets Luscinda go, he turns pale with anger and jealousy and reaches for his sword as he sees her take refuge in Cardenio's arms. It is brave and resourceful Dorotea, once again, who saves the situation. But for a moment, as the two old friends turned rivals look at each other, everything hangs in the balance and things can go either way with equal ease. This is also the moment in which the inner freedom of the individual is itself at stake, because it is also the moment in which inner responsibility is either accepted or rejected. And it is clearly Cervantes's way of showing how central and how fragile that freedom is.

However, in my opinion, we would misunderstand everything if we saw this providential intervention and the appropriate Christian response of the characters as no more than a pious gesture on the part of Cervantes. It is indeed a pious gesture—there is no denying that. But such Cervantine piety is backed by, and intimately connected to, one of the most profound insights into the workings of human desire that literary fiction has ever produced. He knows that to turn Don Fernando into the one "bad guy," and his victims into righteous executioners would be to make a mockery of the truth. As we saw in the last chapter, Don Fernando's pathological desire is only an aggravated case of the same pathology that affects Cardenio and to a lesser degree Luscinda and even Dorotea, all of whom are quite capable of fictionalizing their respective objects of desire. Ultimately Don Fernando's pathology is only one more manifestation of the dynamics of that typically human desire of the obstacle that is at work in all the interpolated stories and in the overall framing one, the story of Don Quixote's madness. To repeat, the divine intervention that saves all these characters is no different from the divine intervention that will save Don Quixote on his deathbed.

It is all part of the same rich intuition. If Cervantes finds it necessary to appeal to divine providence in order to offer his characters the possibility of solving the problems in which they are all involved, it would not be logical for him to leave in their hands the possibility for justice and punishment. And that means that their problem is much deeper than what the summary execution of poetic and cathartic justice would be capable of solving. Both the possibility of a solution and the possibility of just punishment involve appealing to a reality that transcends not only the limits of the individual actions of the characters, but the limits of literary fiction itself. If in Heliodorus's novel, as we have just seen, reference to the action of the gods or of fortune is also reference to the internal dynamics of the literary work (tragedy and/or comedy), in Cervantes it is the opposite: providential action sets the limit beyond which individual human action cannot go on its own, and consequently also the limit of literary fiction, since there is nothing specifically human which, left to its own devices, could not be fictionalized, that is to say, trapped in the loss of transcendance generated by mimetic desire.

The Story of the Christian Captive[5]

If we had any doubts that when Cervantes thinks of divine providence, he thinks of something that transcends novelistic fiction, operating in and through reality, historical reality, the reality from which the entangled char-

5. I consider my excessively brief comments on this story in *Mímesis conflictiva*, some thirty years ago, totally inadequate and misleading. I simply did not pay the story the attention it truly deserves.

acter has become separated, the sudden appearance of the Christian captive and his story at the inn ought to dispel such doubts.

The story certainly fits the moment. Almost immediately after the four characters have been providentially reconciled, "a traveller entered the inn . . . , a man who by his dress seemed to be a Christian newly arrived from the land of the Moors. . . . Behind him on an ass came a woman dressed in Moorish fashion, with her face covered and a veil on her head. . . . On entering he asked for a room, and seemed annoyed when he heard that there was not one to be had in the inn; but going up to his companion . . . he lifted her down" (1.37).

Needless to say, the sudden arrival of these newcomers, whose appearance and clothing are described meticulously, silenced everybody ("a todo puso silencio"), and incited everybody's curiosity. Everybody except Don Quixote apparently. For at that moment it is as if Cervantes had forgotten that Don Quixote is there. That is something so astonishing, so strange, so totally out of character that it must leave the reader perplexed. Can anybody familiar with Don Quixote conceive that he would be in this inn, faced with the sudden arrival of these attention-grabbing strangers, and not say a word, not ask a single question, not offer his services immediately (as Luscinda and Dorotea do)? The fact is he does nothing, not even offer some minimum sign of courtesy. This untiring scout of anything that even remotely looks like an adventure, curious of anything that may stand out, this perennial seeker of differences, sniffing in the wind anything that smells of poetic fiction, this man does not say a word. He is there—we know he is there—but he might as well not be there. It is as if, all of a sudden, Don Quixote disappeared from view, became invisible, at the entrance of these newcomers. There is not the slightest communication between the Christian captive and Don Quixote, not at that moment, or at any other time during the stay of both of them at the inn through some eight chapters. However, it is not as if Don Quixote's presence goes unnoticed by the other characters. They all sit at the same table, and they ask Don Quixote to sit at its head. This is the moment when Don Quixote will deliver his famous speech on "arms and letters," which is clearly inspired by the story of the Christian captive. The Christian captive and Zoraida also sit at that table, but it is as if an invisible barrier separated them from the Manchegan knight. I do not recall any such situation with any other character in the entire novel. As if to make this lack of communication even more obvious, the reader may recall that as soon as the captive finishes telling his story, the *oidor*, the judge, who will turn out to be the captive's brother, and his beautiful daughter, Doña Clara, arrive at the inn, and no sooner have they entered than Don Quixote resumes his typical behavior: he will be the first to approach and greet them, and to compliment the young girl. The situation demands some comment.

When, at the beginning of chapter 44 in Part 2, we are told that both the story of the *Curioso impertinente* and that of "The Captive Captain" are "in a sense, separate from the [main] story," as opposed to the other interpolated stories, "which are cases that befell Don Quixote himself, and could not be omitted," we must ask in what sense is the story of "The Captive Captain "separate from the main story," that is to say, different from the other stories that befell Don Quixote. Because, in a purely literal sense, the story of the captive "befalls" Don Quixote quite as much as, or even more than, the story of Marcela and Grisóstomo, or that of Cardenio, Luscinda, Don Fernando, and Dorotea, since it was all told in his presence by the captive himself. But he, Don Quixote, is kept consistently away from the story and its narrator. He has nothing to say about it. There seems to be something about this story which, in Cervantes's mind, resists, even repels, intervention on the part of Don Quixote. It is as if Don Quixote were forbidden to step over that line. Apparently something about this story would be spoiled, altered, misinterpreted, if Don Quixote were to intervene, in the way he intervenes in the story of Marcela, for example, or in that of Cardenio and the others.

I do not think, of course, that this should be taken in the sense that the purity of the story, as it were, would be compromised by Don Quixote's intervention, as if he were the carrier of a disease. And yet there seems to be something sacred about it, not formally, not qua story, but about its meaning. For it must be out of respect and reverence for the truth of the story, deeply, personally, felt by Cervantes, that Don Quixote is kept at bay. The meaning of the story would run the risk of being compromised, perhaps obscured, if made to accommodate the interference of Don Quixote's madness. And I think the reason is that Don Quixote's madness cannot differentiate between reality and fiction, which prevents him from understanding the most profound meaning of the story of the captive. Even though the story is told literally in front of Don Quixote, its meaning remains beyond his field of vision. In the deepest sense, he does not see it. The story of the Christian captive that Cervantes wants to tell (at least its most important part) is meaningless to Don Quixote. It is as if he were not there. There is no meaningful contact between the two.

But if the story of the Christian captive marks the upper limit beyond which mad Don Quixote does not see or understand, the story of "Foolish Curiosity," the other story mentioned by the ironic narrator of Part 2 as being "in a sense, separate," marks the lower limit, so to speak. Of course, in this case the story is not just separate "in a sense," it is indeed formally separate; it is presented as a *novela* found among other papers at the inn that is read aloud to everybody's enjoyment. It did not "befall" Don Quixote or anybody else participating in the main action of the *Quixote*. But that cannot be the reason why it gets paired with the story of the Christian captive, in the mind of Cervantes, as being "in a sense, separate" from the main story of *Don Quixote*. What may have some significance in the pairing of the two stories is the fact that Don Quixote is literally absent from the reading of the *novela*. While it is being read, he is sleeping in a different room and dreaming of giants. In fact, he will interrupt the reading with his shouting, as if to indicate, perhaps, that he is not too far away from it. He is not literally absent from the story of the captive captain, but he is deliberately kept out of it. Thus, in different ways, both stories are outside Don Quixote's field of vision. If mad Don Quixote could not, by definition, understand the meaning of the story of the Christian captive, I suggest he would remain equally blind, equally impervious, to the meaning of the story of "Foolish Curiosity," even if he were physically present during its reading. Indeed, Don Quixote would be as blind and impervious to its meaning as anybody who would take up the defense of Don Quixote's madness as the criterion to interpret Cervantes's novel, which is what happened to Unamuno, as we have already seen. Had Don Quixote been prompted to react to either one of these two stories, his reaction would have been the same: What in the world does that have to do with me or anything that has happened to me?

This is another way of saying that, in spite of literal and formal differences in the presentation of the two stories, there is a deeper reason for the pairing of the two as "separate" from the quixotic action of the novel: they are deeply related to each other as polar opposites. They are clearly not just two stories among all the interpolated stories of Part 1: they are *the two stories* that stand in sharpest contrast with each other. One exemplifies faith and hope, the other exemplifies utter degradation, anguish, and despair. And the hope of the one is offered precisely to those suffering from the moral and existential disease represented by the other. Don Quixote's madness could be defined as blindness before those two things: he does not understand the hope because he does not understand the inner workings of the disease. Mad Don Quixote's vision and understanding moves within the upper and lower limits marked out by the two opposite stories. That is not necessarily a narrow space. It certainly gives Don Quixote enough freedom of movement and thought to argue his case, and to convince countless generations of readers and critics to come to his defense. But that is not enough for Cervantes. He sees more than Don Quixote. He sees the story that could cure him, as well as the story that could destroy him completely. How could it be otherwise? Given the extraordinary depth and scope of Cervantes's view of humanity through the figure of Don Quixote, how could he write any story at all, particularly in the vicinity of Don Quixote, without also writing directly or indirectly about Don Quixote himself? Could Freud become interested in anything psychological that would have nothing to do with his theory of psychoanalysis? Could Marx think seriously about anything important in economics that would have nothing to do with his theory of capital formation or historical class struggle?

I am by no means the first to see the sharp contrast between these two stories. Pierre Ullman, for example, thought that the real antihero in *Don Quixote* was not Don Quixote but Anselmo, while the real hero was the captive, and that Don Quixote himself was simply a burlesque hero. I am not sure that the traditional category of the heroic would be the appropriate one to characterize Captain Ruy Pérez de Viedma. He certainly did his duty as a soldier. We are told he advanced to the rank of captain on his merits, and he showed bravery at Lepanto. But he did not have much of an opportunity to become a hero. He was captured almost immediately. In other words, I do not think that heroism, at least traditional warrior heroism, is Cervantes's main focus. The captive's story is not the story of the heroic deeds of Ruy Pérez de Viedma. It is the story of his extraordinary providential liberation from captivity. And his liberation from captivity is, of course, inseparable from his relationship with this beautiful woman, "so surpassingly lovely that she seemed to me the most perfect creature I had ever seen; and more than that, when I remembered my indebtness to her, she seemed to me a heavenly goddess come down to earth to bring me happiness and relief" (1.41.366).

The basic story may have been written by Cervantes even before he started writing the *Quixote*,[6] and it could be detached from the novel without any major changes (of course, the same thing could be said of the other interpolated stories). It would fit perfectly, for example, among Cervantes's collection of *Exemplary Stories*, published between Part 1 and Part 2 of the *Quixote*. For it is clearly meant to be exemplary in every respect. Nevertheless, whenever it was written, the story fits perfectly at the point where Cervantes inserted it in his famous novel, and it is there, within the *Quixote*, that the story acquires the full extent of its meaning.

Its most striking feature is its link to real history, which goes far beyond any novelistic need. It is the first thing that most *cervantistas* notice about it. Because of that, it has even been considered the beginning of the modern historical novel. Be that as it may, the fact is that the historical character of the events in the context of which Cervantes places the story is truly amazing. In the words of John J. Allen, one of its most attentive readers: "La segunda parte [de la historia del cautivo] . . . está llena de fechas, de batallas, de acontecimientos políticos; da detalles de la participación de más de veinte personajes históricos en los sucesos de Europa y el norte de Africa durante los años de 1567 a 1575" (1976, 150; The second part [of the story of the captive] . . . is full of dates, battles, political events; it gives details about the participation of more than twenty historical personages in the events of Europe and North Africa between 1567 and 1575). And what is perhaps even more significant, much of the military life of the captive coincides with the military life of Cervantes himself: "En la historia de la carrera militar del cautivo resalta la correspondencia con la de Cervantes. En 1589 [the year in which the captive arrives at the inn and tells his story] Cervantes tenía la misma edad que el cautivo ('poco más de cuarenta años'), llegaron los dos a Italia en 1569, pelearon los dos en Lepanto en 1571, se encontraron en Navarino (1572), en Túnez (1573), y la Goleta (1574), y terminan juntos en Argel en 1575" (1976, 151; There is a striking parallel between the military career of the captive and that of Cervantes. In 1589 Cervantes was of the same age as the captive ["a little over forty years"], they both arrived in Italy in 1569, they both fought at Lepanto in 1571, they were at Navarino [1572], at Tunis [1573], and at La Goleta [1574], and they ended up together in Algiers in 1575). The reader

6. See Murillo (1981), 47.

should remember also that the captive speaks of a soldier, Saavedra, a captive too, whom he met in Algiers—in other words, Cervantes himself, who was there at that time.

It seems that even the Moorish girl, who offered the captive enough money to ransom himself, if he would only promise to take her along to Spain and marry her, was also based on a historical figure, the daughter of Agi Morato, a powerful Christian renegade, who lived close to where Cervantes (and the narrator-captive) was kept as a prisoner for ransom.[7] It has also been pointed out that the action of this woman rescuer, in its general outline, is reminiscent, to some extent, of a well-known legend that, in different ways, tells the story of a Christian captive liberated by a Moslem woman who has fallen in love with him.

All of this has sparked controversy among Cervantes scholars concerning the relative value of the novelistic or legendary elements versus the historical elements in the autobiographical story of this Cervantine captive, Captain Ruy Pérez de Viedma, born in an unnamed location in the mountains of León, not far from the town called Cervantes, which, according to Emilio González López (180), was ruled in the Middle Ages by the family of the Saavedras.

Some believe that the emphasis should be on the novelistic elements of the story,[8] since it is for a novelistic purpose that the historical elements are included. Others feel that Cervantes is really going out of his way to include the historical elements in the story, that he is placing special emphasis on them, and therefore that the historical elements should not be considered less important than the novelistic elements. Still others have found a middle way. The story of the captive, they argue, is neither history nor pure novelistic fiction, but something in between: a tale rooted in folklore in which specific historical elements merge with universal folkloric patterns.[9]

I think there is an element of truth in all of these positions. Clearly, the captive story is much more than a series of historical events presented in the form of a short story. The historical elements are there to serve a fictional function, and not the other way around. They acquire their meaning within the framework of a fictional form. However, the fact that all those elements

7. See Garcés, 207ff.

8. The leading critic of this persuasion is Francisco Márquez Villanueva; see his *Personajes y temas del Quijote*, 100ff.

9. See Murillo (1983) and Rodríguez.

are undoubtedly historical is by no means a matter of indifference. They do not acquire their meaning within the novelistic fiction simply as facts, but as historical facts; their historicity is clearly intentional. Perhaps, as some critics have suggested, we should call the autobiographical story of the captive a tale, an orally transmitted legend generally accepted as true. But I really think what we call it is unimportant. What is important is that Cervantes openly relishes the idea of connecting such a story at every turn, whenever he can, to historical reality, God's providential reality, God's providential story. And, needless to say, God's story can more than compete with fiction in terms of marvelous and unpredictable events:

> "Listen, then, gentlemen, and you will hear a true story, and I doubt whether you will find its equal in the most detailed and careful fiction ever written." (1.38.345)

In addition to its connection with real history, the story is also special because of the quality of the relationship among the main characters in the story. The Moorish girl must pick out a Christian captive to trust with her plans for escape and also with her money. And her trusting attitude seems to spread to the other characters. She inspires enormous respect and selfless love. In the words of L. A. Murillo, "Under her influence the tale becomes an account of ideal harmony and love between Ruy and Zoraida, ideal Christian devotion and trust and loyalty between the Captive and the renegade on whom all depend, as they surmount each obstacle to freedom" (1983, 236). Nothing could stand in sharper contrast with the "antiheroic" story of Anselmo, who, in his foolish curiosity, seeks an impossible and forbidden certainty.

At the same time, we must not forget that the story of the *Curioso* is but the lowest point of a trajectory that begins with the story of the relationship between Marcela and Grisóstomo, and includes the relationships among the other four lovers up to the point of their Christian response to the providential meeting at the inn. In other words, the exemplary story of the liberation of the Christian captive and the woman he has promised to marry stands in sharp contrast not only to the story of the *Curioso*, but to all the other love stories in *Don Quixote*.

The fundamental difference between those other stories and this one is the following: those stories are stories of self-inflicted misfortune and tragedy. The obstacles to the fulfillment of the lovers' desires were put in their paths, whether knowingly or not, by the lovers themselves. On purely objective grounds there was no reason for the terrible suffering and the despair endured by those lovers. For example, the way Marcela and Grisóstomo are introduced to us, one would think that they are a perfect match, for they really look like they are made for each other. That kind of situation becomes explicitly thematic in the case of Cardenio and Luscinda, who are openly promised to each other. Tragedy did not have to happen. And yet they all manage to bring it about. One or both of the lovers were attracted to it, thus echoing the destiny of so many poetic lovers before them, whose tragedies also did not have to happen, but were, nevertheless, quite predictable, because, as we all know, that is the very stuff poetic, fictional love is made of ("The course of true love never did run smooth"). That is to say, they all managed to fictionalize their relationships by generating obstacles out of the very relationship that should have made them happy, and placing those fascinating and frustrating obstacles in their own paths, right in front of the very objects of their desire. They unwittingly preferred what robbed them of their happiness to the happiness itself.

What could be more contrary to that than the story of the relationship between the captive and Zoraida? It is, indeed, as if Cervantes had turned the stories of those other lovers inside out. Here the obstacles are not of their own making. They are external to their relationship, completely real, and quite formidable. Neither the captive nor Zoraida put them there. Real human history put them there, even if that human history is still full of fictionalizing desires. And these two people are not attracted to the obstacles at all. They are not looking for quixotic challenges. And neither is Cervantes, who does not treat the obstacles as a series of interesting adventures. In this case the obstacles are meant to be nothing but obstacles. The two friends and betrotheds fervently hope and trust that they can overcome their problems with the help of God. They have a clear goal beyond all the obstacles and they never lose sight of it: to get to Christian Spain where she will be baptized and they will be married. This is another reason why they are also quite different from Heliodorus's lovers. Likewise, because of their trust in God, they do not think that they are entirely at the mercy of circumstances beyond their control. The obstacles and dangers they encounter may test their trust in God, but they never feel that God is playing cruel games with them.

In other words, the captive and Zoraida are not caught in any kind of reciprocal mimetic entanglement because their relationship has a transcendent point of reference, a divine mediator who is not a rival or a stumbling block. Thus their relationship is not at all like the relationship at the center of the typical love story, where feelings and desires move in the realm of pure immanence, with each partner being the mediator and potential rival of the other's feelings and desires—that is, the kind of purely immanent relationship that, regardless of the psychological quality of the feelings involved, is always in danger of generating its own obstacles. The mutual trust and profound respect that characterizes the relationship between the captive and Zoraida is not, in Cervantes's eyes, the result of their being very nice people (most of Cervantes's lovers are very nice people), but the result of their trust in God, which is also the basis for their hope-filled realism. They are not presented formally as saints, but they are examples of unshaken faith.

But are they really in love? The question has been asked occasionally of these two exemplary betrotheds. It seems to be a logical question. After all, if their story is supposed to stand in contrast to the other love stories, it seems logical to make sure that we are comparing apples with apples. But one must be careful, for the question sounds a little like the one that every adolescent (at least in our modern Western culture) has always asked of his or her own feelings: Is it really, really love? What if it is not? What if it is only infatuation, or only friendship, or maybe only a feeling of compassion, or something else? What are the signs of true love? How can I know for sure? What if I make a mistake, thinking it is love now, and later I discover it is not?

The hesitating adolescent has every reason in the world to be hesitant. But he or she is a little confused. The real object of his or her fearful hesitation is not his or her feelings, but the stability of the human relationship in which he or she is engaged. Will it last? Will there be harmony, mutual care, selfless concern, understanding, and other positive things, or the opposite? If it lasts, if there is harmony, mutual care, and so on, it is love; if the opposite, then it is not love. Our typical adolescent is the victim of a common delusion in our "sentimental education." There is no such thing as a specific feeling so genuinely, so undoubtedly, love that if you have it you have the guarantee of a successful relationship. Furthermore, our analysis of the four love relationships shows that even the presence or absence of an erotic component does not change the nature of the risk that threatens the relationship. With or without eroticism, the human relationships that interest Cervantes are always at risk of generating their own internal destruction.

Cervantes is not in the business of analyzing and categorizing feelings. For example, we know that Alonso Quijano had some tender feelings for Aldonza Lorenzo, but how does that apply to Dulcinea? Is Don Quixote in love with Dulcinea in the same way that he was in love with Aldonza? Does it matter to him, or to Cervantes, whether or not a real Aldonza still exists somewhere beyond fantastic Dulcinea? And what about Grisóstomo? Is he really in love with Marcela when he kills himself "for love"? What of Cardenio? Does he go crazy out of love for Luscinda? Does Don Fernando love Dorotea, or Dorotea Don Fernando, or could it be something else here too? Quite frankly, I do not think that Cervantes, the novelist, the author of *Don Quixote*, ever worried about such questions. What is perfectly clear is that howsoever we choose to define and categorize those feelings and desires, none of those definitions or categorizations would give us the slightest clue as to why all those people were headed for disaster. Feelings and emotions, all by themselves, no matter how tender and pure they may be, do not guarantee the stability of a human relationship. In fact, it seems more likely that the feelings and emotions are a result of the relationship than the other way around.

The text gives us enough clues (e.g., the way the captive looks at, and describes, the physical beauty of Zoraida, or the way she looks at, and worries about, him) for us to be sure that they love each other with the kind of love that contemplates a marital union and living together for the rest of their lives. After all, the captive is described as a handome man in his early forties, and Zoraida is described as an incredibly beautiful young woman. But their love story does not look at all like the other love stories. We have no problem recognizing the other love stories as such, as love stories, because we have seen many similar stories before in the fictions of the poets, to use Cervantes's phrase. Indeed, as our analyses of the Grisóstomo-Marcela and Cardenio-Luscinda stories have shown, this formal similarity with the fictions of the poets can be much more than just formal: it may play a decisive and explicit role in the internal development of the stories themselves. In other words, in one way or another, all of these stories reflect a process whereby reality is willfully ignored, misrepresented, or fictionalized, for fear of facing the truth, because the truth is too painful to face. The stories that we hear from these characters, whether it be Grisóstomo's "Song of Despair" or Cardenio's easily interrupted story, are self-deceiving and self-serving. The autobiographical narrator is not telling the whole truth. Fear and anxiety govern those autobiographical stories, not the spirit of truth.

The story of the captive and Zoraida, on the other hand, is a *discurso verdadero*, a true discourse, or perhaps we should say a discourse of the truth. It is a discourse that believes in the truth of what it says because it has faith and a profound confidence in the existence of the truth and believes that what it says is in accordance with the truth. It is ultimately meant to be something like a hymn to the truth. It says everything that, in good faith, ought to be said about the events it narrates and about the relationship between the protagonists. It is not a defensive discourse because the narrator has no anxious need for self-justification. Everything is clear and open. Everything can be seen, there is nothing that the narrator would want to hide from himself.

By its content, the story of the captive does not look at all like the typical fictional stories of friends and lovers, but if we take into account its formal presentation in the *Quixote*, its most immediate and clearest contrast is with the story of the *Curioso*. Formally, this story is the most fictitious of all, in the sense that it is formally presented as something poetically invented, a *novela*, which probably did not happen in the real world anywhere. Indeed, we should remember that the priest is not at all convinced that such a thing could ever really happen. In other words, just as there is a clear correspondence between the real historical framework, in which the story of the captive is situated, and the faith in the truth that characterizes its protagonists and their actions, we should also consider a similar correspondence between the fictional framework of the *Curioso*, and the falsehood, the lying, the hiding of the truth in which the protagonists are involved. In other words, I do not think it is accidental that a story about "foolish curiosity" is formally presented as a *novela*, while the story of the captive is offered as a *discurso verdadero* deliberately placed in a real historical context and evidently related to Cervantes's life experience.

In an excellent study on "The Pertinence of El *curioso impertinente*," Wardropper noticed the formal difference between *Don Quixote*'s main story and the interpolated love stories, in particular the *Curioso*:

> *Don Quixote* treats of natural truth, which includes verisimilitude and psychological observation, the truth of Cervantes' world of *experiencia*; *El curioso impertinente* treats of artistic or artificial truth, truth in the abstract. . . .The short stories are artificial compositions in contrast to the natural main plot. They serve, I believe, to present similar themes to those of the *historia* under a different guise. (593)

If this formal difference between "natural truth" and "artistic or artificial truth" is visible in the comparison between the *Curioso* and the main plot, I submit it must be even more visible and striking in the comparison between the *Curioso* and the story of the captive and Zoraida. For "the truth of Cervantes' world of *experiencia*" becomes even more central and decisive in this case.

But Wardropper also notices something else of great significance: "Cervantes identifies literary creation with lie: characters in *Don Quixote* repeatedly assert that books of fiction—chivalric and pastoral—are lies, *mentiras*. . . . This firmly maintained position implies that life is true and art is false—a view consonant with Cervantes' views on arms and letters" (599). This must mean, therefore, that on the truth scale that goes from the *Curioso* to the story of the captive, the former, which is the most formally artificial, is also the most fictitious, the most distant from the truth, the most lying, while the latter must be the least fictitious, the closest to the truth. The form reflects the content, and vice versa. If the deliberate historical background of the story of the captive and Zoraida is inseparable from its Christian content and the kind of harmonious human relationship created between the two protagonists, then it is only logical to assume a similar connection between the deliberate formal literariness of the *Curioso* and the needless and utterly self-created tragedy of its narrative content.

This intimate Cervantine connection between form and content has not escaped the attention of the critic. Wardropper sees the comedy in which Anselmo, Lothario, and Camila have entangled themselves as some sort of artificial puppet show (with Cervantes pulling the strings). It is all a lie, an unnecessary lie, or distortion of the truth:

> The initial truth from which the lie emerges in this spectacle is that Lotario is a good friend of Anselmo . . . and that Camila is as good and faithful a wife as Anselmo thinks she is. Unnecessarily he submits these two truths . . . to a test, not realizing that certain truths, if tested, cease to be truths. (599)

There is no question that the critic sees the connection between the artificiality of the form and the arbitrariness of the disastrous content. But it seems that the reason behind it is not fully comprehended. The quoted passage inevitably raises more questions than it answers. What "certain truths" are those that cannot be tested, and why? How is it that the truth, if it really is the truth, cannot be put to the test? Can the truth be something like the cardboard visor on Alonso Quijano's helmet, the strength of which should be accepted on faith?

I think the problem has not been properly formulated. The problem is not with the truth as such, but with Anselmo's test, which is not a true and honest test of anything, but already a lie, a rationalization designed both as a trap and as a way of deceiving himself. It is a devil's test. We cannot trust such a test to give an honest answer, to tell the truth. It would be like using the devil to test the goodness of God. This is why Christ did not allow himself to be "tested" by the devil. The real test that interests Cervantes is not the one formulated by Anselmo, namely, a test of the truth, for it is he, Anselmo, who is being tested by the truth instead. The real test is the following: Can he accept the truth, the truth of Lothario's friendship and Camila's fidelity? Can he live with it? And if not, why not? What has he already done to himself that he can no longer trust the truth? How can he be cured by the truth if he cannot put his faith in it? For the truth he wants to test cannot be separated from faith and trust. In other words, what has already happened within his double relationship with Lotario and Camila that has turned the truth of their friendship and love into a source of anxiety and insecurity, into an obstacle, a Satanic stumbling block? This is the question raised by the *Curioso*, one for which we have already attempted to give an answer.

Together with the destruction of Lothario's friendship and Camila's love, what has also disappeared from their relationship is truth, or rather, faith and trust in the truth. And when the relationship is no longer governed by faith in truth, there is no possible test that will restore such faith. You have to have trust in the objectivity of the truth beyond the interpersonal relationship, before you can test anything. But the problem with Anselmo is that he did not have such a faith. For, if he did, he would not have doubted Camila, since there was nothing beyond his own insecurity, beyond his own already sickened relationship, to justify the test. Anselmo's doubt is a witness to the fact that faith in the truth had already disappeared from his relationship with Lothario and Camila, that all sense of transcendance had vanished, and everything had become pure mimetic inmanence. And, as the disease spread, they all started to move in a world of their own making, a world devoid of truth and reality, a world of pure fiction. The story of the *Curioso*, a work of artifice and fiction, a *novela*, as opposed to the captive's "true discourse," tells the story of some human beings who transformed their lives into a work of artifice and fiction.

We must remember, therefore, that the story of the fictionalization of the real, of the truth, is not the story of a single individual before the world, but the story of a relationship between individuals. That is to say, it is the story of the relationship between the self and the other, or of the self before the other, not the story of the isolated self before the world. There is always an *other* between the self and the reality that has disappeared, that has ceased to be relevant.

The funny story of the two braying aldermen looking for a donkey that is no longer there, and running into each other repeatedly as each one follows the braying of the other, is a perfect comical symbol of the process we are talking about, which can easily turn from comedy to tragedy. Indeed, that is what would have happened in this case, as the two neighboring towns were caught up in their own joke, if the two warring parties had not diverted their violence from each other onto poor Sancho and Don Quixote, who had to flee the scene in a hurry, thereby demonstrating how useful a diverting scapegoat can be, when there is really no reason, no objective reality, for the confrontation, except the confrontation itself.

In the case of the two braying aldermen, the disappearence of the donkey was purely accidental: it was eaten by wolves. In the fictionalizing process, there are no wolves. The disappearence of the "donkey," of reality, which is the reason they keep converging toward each other, is a result of the convergence itself. There is no need for wolves. The mutually attracting parties do the job themselves. They eat up the very reality that should mediate and bridge their relationship. Each one, then, becomes the absolute mediator of the other, as they sink deeper and deeper into a world of fiction.

Cervantes enjoys this kind of situation, in which a given relationship between people seems to take on a life of its own in complete detachment from the reality of its circumstances, feeding on an increasingly mimetic reciprocity. One of the best-known examples happens at Juan Palomeque's inn shortly after the events we have been analyzing.

"Donde se prosiguen los inauditos sucesos de la venta" (The extraordinary happenings at the inn continue)

Events at the inn can occur rather abruptly and at a very fast pace. We go from the terrible tragedy of the *Curioso* to the hope-filled story of the captive in little more than a transitional chapter—the chapter, of course, in which the transition from predictable bad consequences to providential resolution of the interpolated love stories is effected. But, as usual, Cervantes is deeply aware of how fragile any human relationship can be, and how vulnerable its peace and stability. The inn becomes a comical showcase of such fragility. There is peace this moment and utter confusion and violence the next. It certainly looks like Don Quixote is right: a thing can change into its oppposite almost by magic. The inn appears to be enchanted.

For example, there was peace and quiet for a moment right after the innkeeper and some guests who wanted to leave without paying had stopped fighting and settled their differences. Nobody was punching or wrestling anybody,

> when the devil, who never sleeps, ordained the sudden arrival at the inn of that barber from whom Don Quixote had taken Mambrino's helmet, and Sancho Panza the ass's harness which he had exchanged for his own. As the barber was taking his ass to the stable, he saw Sancho Panza mending some part of the pack-saddle; and as soon as he recognized him, he attacked him boldly, crying: "I've got you now, master thief! Give me back my basin and my saddle with all the harness you robbed me of." (1.44.402)

Needless to say, Sancho is not the least inclined to give up what he is more than willing to believe are his rightful spoils from the knightly battle his master had won fair and square. So the two fight for the possesion of the ass's harness. The fight is, of course, meant to be a comical spectacle. But at least, at this stage of the fight, the object of contention, the harness, appears to be solid and well defined. No matter how insignificant as a justification for the fight the harness may be, the two men are fighting over something, not over nothing. But as readers of this famous episode will remember, the situation deteriorates very quickly. Soon almost everybody at the inn joins in a real fight far less comical, and much more absurd, over nothing, or in the terms of its absurd logic, over the definition of what they are fighting about: Is it a barber's basin or Mambrino's helmet?

In other words, the barber, the priest, and others in Don Quixote's party, most prominently Don Fernando, have been caught in their own game. It was all a joke *to* them, but now the joke is *on* them, and it is no longer a joke. The violence is quite real: "So the whole inn was full of tears, shouts, screams, amazement, fear, alarm, dismay, slashings, punches, blows, kicks and effusion of blood." Once again, this is literally a fight about nothing. The original reality of its object has already disappeared. There is no reason for the violence except the violence itself. The contending parties are mimetically trapped in their own violent reciprocity. Each one fights the other because the other is fighting back. They converge toward each other, like the braying aldermen, because the "donkey" is no longer there, reality has disappeared.

If there is some kind of moral lesson to be derived from the absurdity of this objectless fight, it is probably something like this: it is dangerous to play with accepted reality. For as soon as we turn it into a fiction, a joke, something to play with, we are no longer just playing with it, we are in fact also playing with the *other*. If the reality that is supposed to mediate between the self and the other, so that they can understand each other and coexist peacefully, weakens or vanishes, then the self and the other must face each other in the raw, as it were, unprotected, and this is a very volatile and dangerous situation because each one is really at the mercy of the mimetic response of the other. Without an external point of reference, neither one can be sure of what the other intends.

In order for there to be a play with a minimum of stability and mutual understanding, the players would have to create their own ad hoc reality, a ludic ground and/or a *plaything*, a completely separate entity in which none of the players would have any individual interest whatsoever, a neutral ground or object, equidistant from all contenders, that would mediate their relations *externally*, from the outside. For it is crucial that this ad hoc reality, this *plaything*, be declared without intrinsic value to anybody—something like a ball, for example—before it can acquire its absolutely unique mediating value. In some places, one hears, it could be the carcass of a previously sacrificed goat. . . . In fact, the *plaything* must be previously expelled by all the players in order to acquire its uniqueness, a uniqueness that is not granted to it by its materiality, but strictly by a social, a collective, process. This collective process that gives meaning and value to the materially valueless *plaything* is fundamentally no different, I think, from the process described in great detail by Karl Marx, whereby one commodity is expelled from the company of all other commodities and becomes money, something without material or use value that becomes the measure, the mediator, of all commodity value. Marx understood perfectly the error of traditional economists, who looked for the origin of money in the material value of precious metals, in gold, for example.[10]

In other words, if violence is to be avoided, something must come be-

10. See "A Marxian Epilogue" in my *The Sacred Game*.

tween the self and the other that will mediate their relationship from outside the relationship itself. Otherwise, they will become their own reciprocal mediators, they will converge mimetically toward each other, and that is the very source of all human-made trouble. In that sense, the function of the *plaything* is no different from the function of true reality, God's reality. God is simply the absolutely transcendant mediator. Somebody said that if He did not exist, we would have to create Him. And, in a certain sense, we do it all the time, even as we play with a ball or with the carcass of a sacrificed goat. Furthermore, we Christians have been told that the God that sustains the entire reality of the world is precisely the one that was despised, declared worthless, expelled. The fundamental difference with the *plaything* situation is that the Christian God also revealed that He was expelled without cause, without deserving it, for He was innocent. This means that the expulsion had no justification, our violence was unnecessary, we did not have to kill, to expel, anybody in order to keep reality in place and God as a transcendant mediator. Because the innocence of the Christian God means that He is absolutely transcendant precisely because He has nothing to do with our own violence. At the root of our modern scientific faith in the objective reality, the impartiality, and the intrinsic rationality of the world lies the innocence of God, a God who does not take sides when humans are fighting, but allows Himself to be expelled, victimized, if that is what it takes to bring about the reconciliation of the fighters, to provide them with the victim they have always needed to keep the peace and the objective meaning of the world around, to keep an ass's harness being an ass's harness and a barber's basin a barber's basin.

Naturally, from this Christian perspective, all human violence is in the final analysis, in its ultimate reference to God's transcendant innocence, without ultimate foundation. All human violence is always, in and of itself, at the very least, a little bit absurd, a little bit without real object. And I think it is this underlying, deep, Christian awareness and feeling that is at work in Cervantes's characteristic delight in presenting so many absurd battles in the *Quixote*, so many absurd battles all around Don Quixote's madness. The absurdly chaotic melée at the inn over the "baciyelmo" is just one of them, one in which the absurdity becomes particularly obvious because it involves all kinds of people, including some perfectly reasonable and rational human beings.

The *Baciyelmo*

The ridiculous absurdity of the fight is so striking that it becomes hard to understand how illustrious *cervantistas* could have ignored it to interpret it as something like a difference of opinion: some thought it was a barber's basin, others thought it was Mambrino's helmet. Thus—they tell us—Cervantes, with his characteristic ambiguity, his all-inclusive *perspectivismo*, and so on, will settle the dispute by calling it, in Sancho's words, a *baciyelmo*.

But, of course, calling it a "baciyelmo" does not solve anything at all. Nobody knows what a *baciyelmo* is. There is no commonly accepted reference. It does not bring peace between the defenders of the "bacía" and the defenders of the "yelmo." Calling it a "baciyelmo" is a clear indication that it does not make any difference what you call it. It is not as if the thing has acquired a new identity. It has, instead, in the course of the fight, lost the one it had. "Baciyelmo" is a purely fictitious entity. The thing has become just a word, whether "bacía" or "yelmo," that the contenders throw at each other. "Bacía" and "yelmo" have become enemy twins, echoing each other, mirroring each other on either side of the battle. "Baciyelmo" only refers to the violent process whereby a "bacía" is no longer a real "bacía" or a "yelmo" a real "yelmo." "Baciyelmo" could also be a way to call attention to the absurdity of the fight, a way to cry to the contenders, "Please stop the fight, it doesn't matter what you call it, just stop the nonsense."

They have all become quixotified. It is therefore ironically appropriate for Don Quixote to be the one to put a stop to this absurd fight:

> Did I not tell you, gentlemen, that this castle is enchanted, and must be inhabited by some legion of demons? Behold the confirmation of my words, and gaze upon the discord in Agramante's camp transferred here and performed in our midst. See here they are fighting for the sword, yonder for the horse, here for the eagle, there for the helmet; we are all fighting and all at odds. Come then, Sir Judge, and you, Sir Priest; let one of you stand for King Agramante, the other for King Sobrino, and make peace amongst us. For, by God Almighty, it is a great villainy that people of such quality as we are here should slay one another for such trivial causes. (1.45.407)

There is, indeed, a lot in common between the discord in Agramante's field, or any other fictional discord, and the objectless discord over the "baciyelmo."

CHAPTER XII

Tricksters Tricked

The *baciyelmo* episode is part of a larger pattern in the novel that becomes especially conspicuous in Part 2. As Don Quixote parades his peculiar kind of madness in the most diverse settings, it becomes increasingly clear that people who are attracted to him not as a person full of good sense in everything unrelated to knight-errantry, but as a madman, become contaminated by his madness. As "a certain Castilian" shouts at Don Quixote in the streets of Barcelona, "You're a madman. . . . But you have the knack of turning everyone who has to do with you into madmen and dolts. Just look at these gentlemen riding with you!" (2.62.871).

The Castilian's words are not entirely correct. Not everyone who becomes involved with Don Quixote becomes contaminated by his madness. We have already seen the most notable exception to this rule, Don Diego de Miranda, the "gentleman in green." It is important to remember that exception so that we know what it means not to become contaminated. Also, it is not true that Don Quixote has "a knack for turning everyone . . . into madmen." The people whom he meets do it to themselves by the way they choose to relate to him. Think, for example, of the Duke, the Duchess, and their entire household, whose tricks take up so much space in Part 2. I have already mentioned Cidi Hamete's opinion on the subject: "In fact Cidi Hamete says that he considers the mockers as mad as their victims, and the Duke and Duchess within a hair's breath of appearing fools themselves for taking such pains to play tricks on a pair of fools" (2.70.916). It is clear, then, that this idea of the contagious character of Don Quixote's madness or foolishness becomes an important one throughout Part 2.

From Part 1 to Part 2

However, even though the idea becomes particularly obvious in Part 2, that does not mean that it is entirely unrelated to what goes on in Part 1. The main formal difference between the two parts seems to be the fact that the author "decided not to insert any tales, either detached or connected, in this Second Part" (2.44.746). But a moment's reflection will make us realize that the idea of the contagious character of Don Quixote's madness is intimately related to the role or function the interpolated stories had in Part 1. As my analyses of the main stories have shown, the problems that assail the human relationships portrayed in them have the same fundamental structure, are of the same nature, as the intersubjective process that drives Don Quixote's madness. We begin to understand the scope of what is at stake in the madness that Don Quixote represents for Cervantes when we see people like Marcela, or Cardenio, or Anselmo suffering from the same psychological disease, but in widely different circumstances. All the interpolated love stories of Part 1 are essential for a proper understanding of the universal character of the madness of which Don Quixote is only the most visible, the most emblematic, victim. In reference to those stories we begin to understand the purely rhetorical character of Don Quixote's uniqueness. In truth, the uniqueness or singularity of Don Quixote's madness is more apparent than real. But this conclusion, the notion that Don Quixote's madness is not unique, is obviously related to the idea that keeps recurring in the closely knit Part 2 about the contagious character of his madness. It could be argued that, in this regard, Part 2 is a logical sequel to Part 1. *One way to show that Don Quixote's madness is not unique is to show that it is contagious.* Besides, is that not precisely what tricks the tricksters of Part 2, namely, their perception that they are not at all like mad Don Quixote? Is that erroneous perception not what breeds in them an unwarranted sense of security? In the face of Don Quixote, they feel much safer than they ought to. In other words, the role that literary tinsel and excitement played in the lives of many of the characters in the interpolated stories of Part 1 is now played by the already published story of Don Quixote in the lives of the tricksters of Part 2.

At a more obvious and literal level, however, the cases of the tricksters tricked in Part 2 bring to mind situations like that of the absurd fight over the *baciyelmo* in Part 1. In the case of the *baciyelmo* we saw the reality of the object at stake disappear as it was caught in the violent mimetic reciprocity of the parties involved. As the reciprocal violence fed on itself, the object of the dispute, the external point of reference, became utterly irrelevant, a mere word without objective content, a fiction sustained by nothing but the violent convergence of the disputants on each other. Now we are going to see the same phenomenon, but from a reverse angle. Instead of seeing something real disintegrate into complete irrelevance, a fiction, we will see a mere appearance, a fiction, violently acquire the status of something real and important in the eyes of those who made it up. Intersubjective human violence works its "magic" both ways: it can turn reality violently into a fiction, or it can turn a mere fiction into the object of real violence. In truth, of course, the only thing that such a violence really does is to ignore reality completely, and to replace it with some sort of play of mirrors, a mimetic play, in which violence itself looks like reality on one side and fiction on the other. In this mimetic play there is no difference between one thing and the other because such a difference is no more than an optical effect, so to speak, of the violence itself; it is an illusory difference between reality and fiction, whose only function is to keep alive the violence that creates it.

This equivalence, this equilibrium, between fiction and reality, the work of human violence, places tricksters and tricked on the same level. But this is precisely the equivalence with which the tricksters play, as they imitate Don Quixote, as they quixotify themselves in jest. They either do not know or remain willfully blind to the fact that what they do in jest is what violence does even better, more thoroughly, in earnest. Knowingly or not, the model that the tricksters imitate in their trick is the mimetic reciprocity of human violence. They play with this reciprocity, the breeding ground of violence itself. *They play with violence in the false belief that they can avoid it through the play itself, through the imitation.* They imitate violence and believe they protect themselves from it by imitating it, which is something like playing with fire while using a highly flammable instrument. All it takes is a spark in the form of a slightly harder blow, or a minute act of uncontrolled violence, no matter how small or accidental, to turn the play, the joke, into real violence. To go from feigned or implicit violence to the real thing is much easier than the trickster thinks, because it is precisely in the context of real violence where the difference disappears between reality and fiction.

In other words, the mocking imitators of Don Quixote's madness are much closer than they imagine to the madness they mock. Just how close depends on the intensity of their mocking desire. It is "the pains" they take to mock a fool that turn the Duke and Duchess into fools. For the mocking desire imitates the desire of the mocked. They mock Don Quixote by imitating Don Quixote's desire. And in such a situation the mockery will only remain just mockery, fiction, so long as the mocker, the trickster, stays in control of his or her own imitative desire. As soon as he or she loses control, the difference between trickster and tricked disappears, and both will be on the same level.

The Obstacle Once More

And, lo and behold, that loss of control, that turning of the fiction into violent reality, occurs precisely against the obstacle. As soon as the mocked one resists the mocker in earnest, opposes him or her, becomes an obstacle in his or her path, the mocker loses control over his or her mocking desire, and the jest is no longer a jest. The stumbling against the obstacle is the determining factor in the transformation of the jest into something violently real. But, if we pause for a moment, isn't the obstacle also what quixotifies Don Quixote? Is Don Quixote not, as we have already seen, the prototype of all the seekers of obstacles, that is to say, of challenges, of literary adventures? It does not matter at all that Don Quixote adheres to the obstacle with fascinated eyes, while the frustrated trickster does so in anger and resentment. It is adherence to the obstacle in both cases; it is dependence on, and servitude to, the obstacle, the model-rival, the stumbling block, the Satan of the Gospels. The obstacle is the great test of human desire. To fail the test, to allow oneself to be dominated by the obstacle, is to turn the obstacle into an object of desire. This object, as we have seen repeatedly, is ambivalent in it self: attractive on one side, hateful on the other. As soon as the trickster fails this test, his or her similarity to mad Don Quixote is much deeper than he or she imagines.

We do not have to search very far to find revealing cases. They are all over Part 2. They involve the Duke, for example, when his game is interrupted by his vassal Tosilos, and the Duchess, for example, when she spies on Doña Rodríguez and Don Quixote. But perhaps the two most famous are those of the defeated Sampson Carrasco, as the Knight of the Mirrors, in chapters 12 through 15, and the one with Altisidora feigning to be hopelessly in love with Don Quixote, when Don Quixote rejects her declaration of love and tells her "to retreat within the limits of [her] chastity" (2.70).

The Trickster Samson Carrasco

Here are Sampson Carrasco's words to his "squire," following his unexpected and humiliating defeat at the hands of Don Quixote:

> "It is all right for you [to go home] . . . but it would be folly to think that I shall go back home till I have thrashed Don Quixote to a pulp [hasta haber molido a palos a Don Quijote]. And it will not be the desire to restore him to his senses that will drive me after him, but the desire for revenge; for the pain in my ribs will not allow me to entertain a more charitable purpose." (2.15.561)

Obviously a lot more than his ribs is hurting. His squire asks him the following question:

> "Don Quixote's mad, and we're sane. Yet he gets off sound and smiling, while your worship comes out bruised and sorrowful. So . . . which is the madder, the man who is mad because he can't help it, or the man who's mad by choice?"
>
> To which Sampson replies: "The difference between these two is that the madman of necessity will be so forever, but the madman by choice will cease to be so when he will."
>
> "Very well then," said Thomas Cecial, "I was mad by choice when I consented to be your worship's squire, and now, using the same power of choice, I want to stop being your squire and go back home."

That is exactly correct: all that Sampson Carrasco has to do to stop being mad in the same way as Don Quixote is to give up his plan to challenge the madman on the madman's own ground. But that is precisely what he angrily refuses to do at that moment. In fact, he is now more serious than ever about that challenge. As he says, we are crazy if we think he is going to give it up. And that is the point at which he becomes truly quixotified, the point at which overcoming the obstacle becomes an end in itself and not just a means. That is the moment when the important thing is not the goal that may have existed beyond the obstacle, but the obstacle itself. At that point, reassuring himself before the triumphant other becomes an urgent need. To ask him then to give up the challenge is just as useless as to ask Don Quixote to give up his knightly adventures, and for the same reason. The urgent need for vengeance is the need to restore one's own image to oneself because that image is now entirely in the hands of the other. The desire for vengeance is also the expression of an intolerable servitude.

What is important to understand is that such a need for vengeance, such a submission and dependence on the obstacle in anger and hatred, is a phenomenon whose internal structure of meaning, whose logic, is the same as that which produces the quixotic fascination with the obstacle, the challenge, the adventure. If it were true that the object and goal of Don Quixote's desire were justice or charity, he would not be mad. But that is not what he desires in his madness. If Alonso Quijano ever had that desire, his avid reading of knightly fiction has diverted it toward the obstacle. Radiant Amadís is not the one who brings peace and justice; instead, he is the one who overcomes all kinds of obstacles in his way. In like manner Don Quixote goes out in the world in search of evil creatures and obstacles. That is what defines him as a knight-errant, which is what he needs urgently, that is, with an urgency testifying to his need for a triumph before idolized and invincible Amadís. Whether the triumphant other is seen as a fascinating demigod or as something odious does not change anything regarding the dependence of the subject on it. The difference between Sampson Carrasco's angry search for vengeance and Don Quixote's madness, as developed in Cervante's novel, is not so much a matter of essence as of degree.

Altisidora

The ease with which the resentful desire for vengeance can turn around and become its opposite can be seen with greater clarity in the case of Altisidora. Her circumstances do not allow her to follow Don Quixote, but it is not difficult to imagine that she would if she could. Here is her angry reaction when Don Quixote rejects her feigned amorous advances:

The knight addressed her: "I have told you many times, lady, how distressed I am that you have fixed your affections on me. . . . I was born to belong to Dulcinea del Toboso . . . , and to think that any other beauty can occupy the place she holds in my heart is to imagine the impossible. This should be sufficient to make you retreat within the limits of your chastity, for no one can be bound to perform the impossible."

Hearing this, Altisidora, showing signs of being angry and upset, said to him: "My God, Don Stock-fish, Brazen Soul, Date Stone, more obstinate and hard-hearted than a peasant courted when he is aiming at the butts, I'll tear your eyes out if I get at you. Do you really imagine, Don Vanquished, Don Cudgelled, that I died for you? All you've seen tonight has been pretence. I'm not the sort of woman to let myself grieve by so much as the dirt in one finger-nail for such a camel, much less to die for one!" (2.70.918–19)

As an ironic Duke remarks, when he hears Altisidora's violent reaction, "That . . . reminds me of the saying: He that flings insults will soon forgive." I think that Altisidora was lucky that Don Quixote left so soon. For, in all likelihood, she would have tried very seriously and in earnest to seduce such a hard-hearted fellow, so faithful to Dulcinea. And in such an attempt, fueled by resentment, her feigned attraction to the knight could have become existentially quite real. The idea that disdain is a powerful attraction is all over the theater of the Golden Age. And is that not the very idea we have studied in the two *Dianas*?

Unamuno's Reaction

Unamuno understood that to some extent:

Este rasgo debía bastar para convencernos de cuán real y verdadera es la historia que estoy explicando y comentando, porque esto de acabar por tomar en veras las burlas la desdeñada doncella es de las cosas que no se inventan ni pueden inventarse. Y tengo para mí que si Don Quijote flaquea y cede y la requiere, se le entrega ella en cuerpo y alma, aunque sólo fuera para poder decir luego que fue poseída por un loco cuya fama llenaba el mundo entero. (*Vida*, 212)

(These remarks should suffice to convince us of how real and true this story is that I am explaining and commenting on. For the fact that the disdained damsel ended by taking the jest in earnest is the sort of thing that is not invented nor could be invented. And I am convinced that if Don Quixote had weakened and yielded and courted her, she would have given herself to him in body and soul, if only to be able to say later that she had been possessed by a madman whose fame filled the entire world.)[1]

He saw that the trickster could easily be caught in her own trick. But if this is so, Altisidora would not have given herself to Don Quixote "if only to be able to say later that she had been possessed by a madman whose fame filled the entire world." Her "love" would have been only the other side of her resentment and her anger. Perhaps Unamuno senses that it is damaging to the literary soul of his hero to reveal resentment and rejection as something involved in the mechanism whereby literary fiction puts on the appearance of reality, operates as something real. Because if that is the case, Don Quixote's sublime heroism, so obviously literary, would all of a sudden lose much of its sublimity.

But there is another lesson to be learned through the logic of the trickster who is tricked, in other words, through the logic whereby the mocker of yesterday may become the admirer, the worshipper, of today. Modern readers in the style of Unamuno, who are the majority today, are not the descendants of Don Diego de Miranda, but the heirs to the old mockers. The heroic Don Quixote of today is the heir to the antiheroic one of yesterday. Don Quixote, fascinated seeker of obstacles, continually scandalized, possessed by the obstacle, scandalizes in turn. We, readers, stumble against him. And to this stumbling both the mockers and the passionate defenders are witness.

The Author and His Work

But what about Cervantes himself, the novelist, the great trickster? How did he escape the historical contamination, the contagion? The answer is already implied in everything I have been saying about the relationship between Cervantes and his creation: he managed to resist the scandalizing temptation, the undeniable literary attraction of his Don Quixote. Because—I must insist—this literary attraction is one thing, and the extraordinary depth of the novel, which is what has given it its enduring relevance through the cen-

1. I use Kerrigan's translation with some modifications; see *Our Lord Don Quixote*, 301.

turies, is another. These two things are by no means unrelated, but they are not the same. The literary attraction derives from the scandal, it is linked to the desire of the obstacle, the literary desire par excellence. The depth, the historical relevance, the truth of the novel, derives precisely from being a process, an evolving structure, guided by the author's desire to overcome the scandal, to save Don Quixote from his alienation in and by the obstacle, to restore to him his vision of reality, to which the attraction of the obstacle is the great impediment. And that is also what keeps the author from siding with either the mockers or the glorifiers, from being tricked, or seduced, by his own novel.

It is not a question of removing Don Quixote from his pedestal in order to replace him with Cervantes. The depth of the novel does not come from Cervantes's unfathomable depth, superior intelligence, or anything of the sort. The desire that guides the novel toward saving Don Quixote from his alienation, as I said at the beginning of this book, is a simple compassionate desire. It is a compassion of extraordinary simplicity, which means that it is not cathartic, not literary, not caught and sustained by contagion—in other words, it is a genuine compassion, guided, of course, by an uncommon clarity of vision. This compassion is the opposite of scandal. Compassionate Cervantes is not scandalized by Don Quixote, he does not contest with him, which means he does not relate to him in a duplicitous, ambivalent manner, in the manner in which one relates to the stumbling block. In his compassion for Don Quixote, Cervantes, literary inventor of Don Quixote, does not relate to him in a literary manner. He invents him in a literary manner, of course. Don Quixote is a literary fictional character and, as such, he is inevitably ambiguous. But Cervantes's compassion is not a response to, nor is it prompted by, such an ambiguity. The Cervantes who judges his character compassionately is not exactly the same one who invents him, even though his compassionate judgment exerts a powerful influence on the development of his invention, and in ways not always immediately obvious. It is this compassion from beyond the fiction that gives the fictional character his characteristic independence, his amazing realism—a kind of independence and realism that cannot be invented, that cannot be conferred by means exclusively literary. Contrary to what Unamuno said, Altisidora's reaction is eminently literary. What is not literary is Cervantes's compassion. The depth of the novel comes from that which is least attractive, literarily, poetically, within the novel. Cervantes's compassionate simplicity is what neither the mockers, on the one hand, nor the defenders, on the other hand, have ever been interested in.

As I noted in Chapter II on *Guzmán de Alfarache*, Saint Augustine did not think that the tears he shed when reciting Virgil's lines describing the death of Dido could be described as tears of true compassion because what kind of compassion—said the saint—can exist for a fictional character, whose misfortune entertains us? Such a compassion is as purely apparent and fictional as its object. For the saint, his tears were tears in imitation of tears, purely mimetic, triggered by contagion. That is not the kind of compassion we attribute to Cervantes here. Cervantes never forgets for a moment that Don Quixote is pure fiction. It is not, therefore, that he feels sorry for the things that happen to Don Quixote at the hands of others, the beatings he suffers, or the mockery he undergoes. After all, it is he, Cervantes, who exposes his character to public ridicule. He is behind all the beatings and the mockery. Thus, when he speaks of tricksters tricked by their own mockery, he knows he is talking about himself. Therefore, if he feels true compassion, he ought to feel it for himself, for what he does as he writes his novel. In other words, this kind of compassion, true compassion, is not an apology to Don Quixote. What could such an apology be except another literary invention? It is, rather, an apology before God, that is to say, an act of repentance. The cure and salvation of Don Quixote at the end of the novel is the final expression of that act of repentance, a structural form of repentance, because it is an integral part of the novel, inseparable from its meaning. The novel is not complete, it has not said everything it has to say, until it reaches that end. When Cervantes saves Don Quixote from his madness, he saves him from the novel as well, takes him beyond fiction, takes him to a point where he is no longer Don Quixote, a novelistic character, because it is the point at which Cervantes returns to himself at the end of his quixotic journey.

Cervantine repentance could either lead to a complete abandonment of the novelistic enterprise, in which case we would not have the *Quixote* today, or to the acceptance of his own role as a witness to the presence of reality in the very heart of fiction—to the presence of reality standing precisely between the author and his character, acting as a mediator, or perhaps a filter, between the two, a constant reminder that he is writing fiction and nothing but fiction. The fact that Cervantes chose this second option means two things: one, that he still had faith in the possibility of literary fiction to tell the truth in spite ot itself, and, two, that the object of his repentance was not simply the formal and abstract fact that he was writing a novel, but the meaning of what he was actually doing as a man, as a responsible human individual, in the writing of that novel. He understood with extraordinary clarity the ways in which that human individual, answerable to God, was using and manipulating the hands of the artist who was creating Don Quixote. And he understood that what he, the man, was doing through the medium of his art (and, in a sense, while hiding behind his art) was not, in the final analysis, so different from what his character Don Quixote was doing, or what the mockers of Don Quixote were doing.

The repentance with which we are dealing is not the episodic kind we found in Avellaneda's *Quixote*, when Alvaro Tarfe decided to pay all the expenses at the insane asylum where they locked up Don Quixote. It is a continuing way of relating to his novel. It is not a way to wash his hands of what he is doing (which is what Avellaneda tried to do), or of begging for our pardon, but a repentance born out of a deep and thorough understanding of what he is doing. This repentance is a measure of the depth of his vision, a vision that goes beyond the formal limits of this artist, this master novelist. Cervantine repentance is a way of bringing God into the picture as a mediator between him and his literary creation, as an antidote, perhaps, or as a warning, against the temptation of playing God with his creature, which would actually be an indication of weakness and dependence on fiction. Cervantine repentance liberates Don Quixote from the hands of an all-absorbing, overbearing author as much as it liberates Cervantes from dependence on his fiction.

An Example of the Opposite: Unamuno's *Niebla*

For an illustration of what happens (or what it means) when you leave God, that is, reality, transcendance beyond the intersubjective relationship, out of that picture, we may go, once more, to Unamuno, whose attitude regarding his own literary creation is the opposite of Cervantes's humility. In this case we are talking about his novel (or *nivola*) *Niebla*, published a few years before *Abel Sánchez*, of which I have already spoken. The reader of *Niebla* may remember that, toward the end of the novel, Augusto Pérez, its protagonist, whose fiancée has just run away with another fellow, is thinking about suicide:

He wanted to put an end to himself, who was the source of all his misery. But before carrying out his plan it occurred to him, like a drowning sailor who grasps at a straw, to come and talk it over with me, the author of this whole story. . . . Accordingly, he came here to Salamanca, where I have been living for twenty years past, to pay me a visit. (Warner Fite translation, 291)

Thus the fictional character confronts the author. He talks to him face to face in Salamanca, where Professor Miguel de Unamuno used to teach. And his author tells him that he cannot commit suicide because in order to kill oneself one has to exist:

The poor man shook like a drop of mercury and looked at me with the stare of one possessed. He tried to rise, perhaps with the idea of flight, but he could not. He could not summon the strength. . . .

"The truth is, my dear Augusto," I spoke to him in the softest of tones, "you can't kill yourself because you are not alive; and you are not alive—or dead either—because you do not exist."

"I don't exist! What do you mean by that?"

"No, you do not exist except as a fictitious entity, a character of fiction. My poor Augusto, you are only a product of my fantasy and of the fantasy of those of my readers who read this story." . . .

Upon hearing this the poor man continued to look at me with one of those perforating looks that seem to pierce your own gaze and go beyond; presently he glanced for a moment at my portrait in oil which presides over my books, then his colour returned and his breathing became easier, and gradually recovering, he was again master of himself. . . .

"Listen to me, Don Miguel—could it be that you are mistaken, and that what is happening is precisely the contrary of what you think and of what you have told me?"

"And what do you mean by the contrary?" I asked, rather alarmed to see him regaining his self-possession.

"May it not be, my dear Don Miguel," he continued, "that it is you and not I who are the fictitious entity, the one that does not really exist, who is neither living nor dead? May it not be that you are nothing more than a pretext for bringing my history into the world?"

"Really this is too much!" I cried, now becoming irritated.

"Please don't get so excited, Señor de Unamuno," he replied. "Keep calm. You have expressed doubts about my existence . . . then please don't be disturbed if I in turn doubt your existence rather than my own. Let us come to the point. Are you not the person who has said, not once but several times, that Don Quixote and Sancho are not only real persons but more real than Cervantes himself?" (293–95)

The first thing that strikes the reader of this passage is the confrontational, the violent, manner in which the meeting between author and character is conceived. They do not meet for mutual comfort or understanding. It is a tug of war between the two of them. They sound as if they could not share existence on the same level. They cannot coexist peacefully. In fact, it seems to be a question of survival, of life and death: "I am afraid," says the author, "that if I do not kill you soon, you will end by killing me" (303). Each one accuses the other of being nothing but a fiction, or a mere "pretext," an instrument, in the service of the other. Whoever controls the fiction controls the other. Existing, being the author, means being in control of the other, and, conversely, being a fictional entity is being entirely dependent on the other, entirely at his mercy.

Unamuno's author will not allow his character to commit suicide, not out of compassion, but because suicide would mean the ultimate rebellion of the character by taking his life in his own hands. A fictitious entity cannot commit suicide not because he does not really exist, but because his fictitious existence does not belong to him. It is in somebody else's hands. That is why it is not real. The real Unamunian question is not directly about existing. It is about being oneself or not being oneself. If one is not oneself, that means one cannot differentiate oneself from the other, one is in the power of the other, in which case one does not truly exist. Fiction equals total dependence on the other.

According to this logic, Unamuno's author (or Unamuno as author) needs or requires a completely submisive character, one that is totally subjected to him. Any sign of independence, of "self-possession," on the part of the character "alarms" him. On the other hand, it is also clear that such a need for complete submission of the other is in itself, in turn, a profound form of dependence. Such an author, who will not, or cannot, settle for anything short of absolute dominion over his fictitious character, is as dependent on his fiction as his fiction is on him. One could also say that such an author creates his fictional character in order to exorcise, to get rid of, his own fiction.

The problem, of course, is that Unamuno's author knows that. He knows too much for his own good. And this second or reflective knowledge is what speaks through Augusto Pérez in the famous encounter, a variation on the old psychomachia technique.

Nothing could be more contrary than this to Cervantes's attitude with Don Quixote. Cervantes does not need the complete submission of his character, a substitute for the human other, the neighbor, the *proximus*. He does not need to turn the other into a fiction (as he tells us mad Don Quixote does) in order to be himself. And the reason he does not need it is that he is not helpless, naked, before the other, as Unamuno's author seems to be. That is to say, Cervantes *is* in ways that transcend, that are not determined by, his authorial relationship with Don Quixote. Cervantes *is* much more than the inventor of Don Quixote. And all that reality that extends far beyond the author-character relationship is God's reality; it does not belong to either the author or the character. God, or God-supported reality, stands between Cervantes and Don Quixote. And that changes everything. One may be fiction before the other, but one is not fiction before God, that is, in the eyes of God, unless, of course, one turns God Himself into a fiction, the human other in disguise, in which case we are back in the hopeless struggle between the I and the other. It seems, however, that Unamuno, in some way, in some embittered way, knows this too. He must know of the hopeless struggle without God, of the impossibility within such a struggle to differentiate reliably between reality and fiction. Otherwise, why would he feel the anxious need to confuse the two, to confuse everything:

> "Ah, but it is necessary to corrode. And to confound. Above all else to confound; and to confound everything. Dream with waking, fiction with reality, the true with the false; to confound all in one homogeneous mist." (282)

The anxious hope is that, if the "mist," *la niebla*, the fog, is thick enough, the lacerating and hopeless need to differentiate between reality and fiction in the struggle with the other will disappear, it will stop making sense. God Himself will stop making sense. At least the God that says that there is enmity between reality and fiction, that fiction undermines reality, and vice versa. I think this is the God that Unamuno was trying to do without, without succeeding completely in his attempt. And he knows of that failure too:

Poor Domingo, now thoroughly terrified, put his master [Augusto Pérez] to bed [his deathbed].

"And now, Domingo, I want you to be repeating in my ear, slowly, the *Pater Noster*, the *Ave Maria* and the *Salve*. That's the way—a little at a time . . . : Now listen, take hold of my right hand and pull at it. It does not seem to be mine, just as if I had lost it—and help me to make the sign of the cross—that's the way. This arm must be dead." (314)

However, what is really surprising is that at no time during the encounter between author and character in Salamanca is there any mention of the reasons why Augusto Pérez, the fictional character, was driven to thoughts of suicide. One would think that would be a major topic of their discussion. It would have been logical for the character to ask the author: If I only exist in your fantasy, what about the pain and the anguish that has led me to consider taking my own life? They certainly felt very real. How does one invent pain and anguish to make them look like the real thing?

As it turns out, the cause of all the pain and the anguish is one of the oldest in the book of literary fiction: the humiliating failure of a typical story of love and jealousy. In fact, Augusto Pérez's existence before he got involved in that story was totally uninteresting, not the sort of thing that would make for an exciting piece of literature. But then everything changed:

"I began, Victor, by being a kind of shadow, a fiction. For years I have wandered about like a spectre, like a manikin formed out of mist, not believing in my own existence, imagining myself to be a sort of fanciful character which some hidden genius had created for his own consolation or relief. But now, after what has happened, after what they have done to me, after this mockery, this cruelty of jest—now, now I do feel my own existence, now I can actually touch myself. Now I no longer doubt that I am real!" (288)

"After what has happened to me . . . I no longer doubt that I am real." But what has happened to him is the very stuff of which literary fiction is made. Why, then, does it feel so singularly, uniquely real? How does such a standard literary pain become his pain? Let us listen again to that conversation between Augusto Pérez and his friend Victor before he goes to Salamanca to meet Unamuno:

Victor found Augusto, who had collapsed in a corner of the sofa, looking down at the floor and through it.

"What's the matter?" he asked. . . .

"You ask me what is the matter? Don't you know what has happened to me?"

"Yes, I know what has happened to you externally. . . . What I don't know is what is going on inside of you. In other words, I don't know why you are taking it in this fashion."

. . . .

"What hurts me most is not the lost love. It's the ridicule! the scorn! the mockery! the mockery! They have mocked at me and made a laughing stock of me! They have made me out ridiculous and contemptible! They wanted to demonstrate—I don't know what—that I do not exist."

"What luck!"

"Don't joke about it, Victor."

"But why shouldn't I joke about it? You set out to make an experiment and they have made you the experiment. You wanted to make her the frog and she has made you the frog. Jump into the pool, then, and croak for your living!"

"I ask you again . . ."

"Not to jest, eh? Well, I am going to jest. Jests were made for such occasions as this." (281–82)

Well, now we know why the pain felt so real, why he took it "in this fashion." He stumbled against the obstacle, against the other, the woman who triggered and encouraged his desire, and then rejected him, becoming an obstacle to that same desire. *The experimenter has become himself the experiment, the trickster has been tricked*, and that is no longer a joke. It is one thing to feel oneself "a kind of shadow, a fiction [wandering] about like a spectre, like a manikin formed out of mist, not believing in my own existence," and quite another to be treated as such by the other, to see one's own emptiness through the eyes of the rejecting other. In such a situation the emptiness becomes intolerable. The wandering "fiction," the "shadow," feels real pain at the hands of the other: "Now I do feel my own existence," he says. However, he owes that painful existence to the other. He has come to life chained to the other, entirely at the mercy of the other. Before he stumbled he felt he was "a sort of fanciful character" invented by somebody, "a manikin," a puppet in the hands of "some hidden genius." Now that the other has "demonstrated" to him that "[he does] not exist," he believes he really exists, but he is no more in command of this new existence than he was of the old one. Regarding his radical dependence on somebody else, nothing has changed. The only difference is that such a dependence can no longer be ignored. It has become a source of unbearable anguish.

And yet, therein lies the solution! says the friend: They have demonstrated to you that you do not really exist, that you are a dream, a fiction. "What luck!" Do not fight it! You are a fiction. "You wanted to make her the frog, she has made a frog of you. Accept the situation, then, and make a frog of yourself." There is no difference between reality and fiction, continues the friend: "Confound everything . . . confound them all in one homogenous mist," and you will not feel the pain.

In other words, the very same thing that turns your life into a living hell, an intolerable emptiness at the mercy of another, against which you rebel, feeling alive through your rebellion, gives you the clue to the solution, to protecting yourself from such a living hell: the emptiness itself. Fiction is the clue. Fiction is the antidote to fiction. For fiction is a formidable weapon in the hands of the other, as long as you are terrified of becoming a fiction. But if you recognize yourself as nothing but "a shadow, a fiction," perhaps like Calderonian Segismundo in *Life Is a Dream* ("una sombra, una ficción"; 2.5.2184), you disarm the other, there is no longer a reason to fear. When the other treats you as a nonentity, turn yourself into a fictional character and your life into a novel or a comedy. After all, isn't the world a stage, *un gran teatro?*

Yes, that seems to be true, but the reasoning is misleading. It is not really fiction that terrifies you, but only fiction in the hands of the rejecting other, the stumbling block, as he looks at you. Augusto Pérez had no problem "not believing in [his] own existence," living like a shadow, until he felt treated as such by the woman he wanted to marry. You are not really trying to protect yourself from fiction, but from the fictionalizing, victimizing violence of the other. You are trying to defend yourself from a violence that turns you into an embittered slave of that other, a violence that scandalizes you. Because the secret of the power, the Satanic power, that the scandalizing other wields over you is your desperate need to be something real, to be somebody, *before him*. For you do not want simply to be real, you want to be real before him, in his eyes. Scandalized as you are, glued to the obstacle, to the other as obstacle, reality means nothing to you, unless the other acknowledges it (just as Don Quixote, as we saw, could not care less whether Dulcinea was real or not, as long as it was the sort of thing demanded by the chivalric model). Augusto Pérez wanted to commit suicide, but he became terrified when the author told him he was going to kill him or cause him to die because he was nothing but a fiction of his, and he had nothing more to do with him. Everything ties you to the other. However, the other is caught in the same double-bind. He will not acknowledge your reality, except in the same manner as you do his, violently, that is to say, in a negative way, as he is treated like fiction by you, and feels the same desperate need to be real before you, his other. This is the confrontational, the violent, situation between the I and the other, with each one striving to dominate, to fictionalize, the other, in which the difference between reality and fiction becomes an illusion. For they are only the two sides of the same violence that keeps the rival parties mimetically dependent on each other, two opposites mirroring each other and perfectly interchangeable. This is indeed the Calderonian power play, the dream of life, from which there is only one way to escape, "*acudir a lo eterno*," to appeal to the eternal, to God, as Segismundo said. It is also before the eyes of God, not the other's eyes, that Calderón's "great theater of the world" is played out.

Given the fact that Unamuno's novel provides no way to go beyond itself, to question itself as fiction and nothing but fiction—in other words, given the fact that Unamuno's novel proclaims that there is no such thing as reality beyond the limits or the power of fiction (except, perhaps as a pious wish)—the dispute between Unamuno and Pérez about who is real and who is fiction is not only endless, it is also a definition of the novel itself: the space where the difference between reality and fiction is defined as the power struggle between the I and the other locked in endless combat. Reality is, by definition, excluded from such a struggle. Reality and fiction cannot be separated violently, because it is violence itself that erases the difference between the two. Reality can only be identified as such in peace. The violence between the I and the other has to stop. One way for it to stop obviously is for one to kill the other ("I am afraid that if I do not kill you soon, you will end by killing me"). But that is a rather precarious peace, and much too short lived. A collective process must come into play, not one against one, but, by contagion, all against one, in other words, the scapegoat or victimizing mechanism, of which we have already spoken, by means of which a transcendant point of reference, a transcendant mediator, is established beyond the violent relationship between the I and the other. That mediator, the point of reference beyond the violence, is the basis of external reality as perceived by human beings. Christians believe that Christ, the sacrificial victim, is the one "through whom all things were made." That belief expresses a universal anthropological fact: the collective victim, the bringer of peace, is the one through whom everything stands in place.

Of course, not all victims, and therefore not all transcendant mediators, are equally reliable when it comes to grounding reality beyond the fictionalizing power of human violence. Pre-Christian primitive mediators were just as violent as their human counterparts, but they were sacred, that is to say, they sacralized violence, made it untouchable, thereby taking it out of human hands. As René Girard has been saying for the last several decades, sacred violence was human violence removed, made distant, thereby creating a peaceful space, surrounded by the sacred, by the untouchable, within which reality could be apprehended and human life could function. The primitive solution, therefore, was a metamorphosis, a transformation of the destructive mimetic violence between the I and the other into the protecting violence of the distant gods. These gods, once they were established, demanded the sacrifice of the victim, on whose shoulders violence became sacred, in order to keep the metamorphosis going. And this metamorphosis had a diachronic dimension as well, a ritual one: original destructive violence was imitated, represented, ritualized, in order to bring about the desired transformation from bad to good.

But we have to understand that the mentality, the mind-set, bred by the primitive solution is still alive, in spite of all the historical adjustments it has undergone, in particular under the formidable pressure of the Christian text, which says that the founding victim is innocent, and the violence that kills him strictly human, not required (although allowed for love of humanity) by God, and therefore not sacred. It is still alive as the internal logic of the solution proposed in *Niebla* for the endless violent confrontation between reality and fiction, between the I and the other. The "nebulous" or misty solution proposed by Victor is a transformation of violence from bad to good (or at least, harmless, which is good enough), using the power of violence itself: since violence fictionalizes everything, erases all the differences, let us use the power of fiction to fictionalize violence itself. Violence "confounds" everything into a "homogeneous mist"; therefore, let us use the mist itself to confound violence, to render it harmless. If violence produces fiction, fiction can produce violence, but this violence will only be fictional, not real; at the very least, the reality of violence will be diffused, "nebulized," so to speak. In the old days, such a nebula would have been terrifying and sacred, and as such, propitiated and kept at a distance. Today, for Unamuno, and the rest of us, the nebula, desacralized by the power of the Christian word, has lost its terrifying capacity, and has become somewhat of an intellectual exercise. Nevertheless, it still keeps enough suggestive power to give us the feeling that we are in fact dealing with more than words and concepts.

However, the proposed "nebulous" solution amounts to burying your head in the sand. It is a cover-up, a hiding of the truth. Or to be more precise, it is a mimetic cover-up: hiding the problem behind an imitation of it, hiding it by imitating it, by deliberately fabricating an appearance of it from which the violence has been drained as in a sleight of hand, as if to say, "Look, you can take it, there is nothing to it, it doesn't hurt." This mere appearance, this mimetic fiction, is indeed inspired, driven, by the real problem, by the violent mimetic confrontation inside of which reality does vanish from the eyes of the contenders, becomes irrelevant, unperceived, but it is nonetheless a ruse, a strategic lie, designed to hide real violence, not to reveal it. It is indeed the oldest ruse in the history of humanity, the oldest kind of knowledge, the *mêtis* of the Greeks, of Odysseus in particular. Unfortunately, such a ruse no longer works. It worked before, when the threat of violence was a sacred threat hanging over the community, when the ritual imitation of violence was a way of appeasing and placating the sacred source of violence, a way of playing along with the gods, while actually avoiding them, getting out of their way, cheating them of their prey, but it doesn't work now.

Did the real Unamuno really believe in such a solution, in the saving power of the mist, in fiction? I do not know. But he was certainly aware of the fact that such a solution was not Christian. For, in the end, he knew that Augusto Pérez's problem was indicated in the symbolic fact that he did not have the strength to lift his right hand to make the sign of the cross at the moment of his death. Domingo, his servant, had to help him. And I do not think that Unamuno suggests at any time that the "nebulous," the fictional, solution could be a valid substitute for Christian faith. It seems far more likely that the old solution is precisely proportional to the weakening of Augusto Pérez's Christian faith—just a measure of that weakness, not a substitute for it.

But if this is so, we have to ask:

What happened to Unamuno's *quijotismo*? Where is his Don Quixote when he is most needed? Is Don Quixote not Unamuno's prototype of the fictional character who is more real than his author? Could he not say with as much reason as Augusto Pérez, "They have mocked at me and made a laughing stock of me! They have made me out ridiculous and contemptible"? If Augusto Pérez needed a savior within the nebula itself, the very embodiment of the confounding of reality and fiction, it seems it had to be Don Quixote. Has Unamuno lost faith in Don Quixote, just as his character lost the strength of his Christian faith?

I think that, quietly, Unamuno knows that his Don Quixote is not the proper savior for the occasion. He cannot take Augusto Pérez out of the "niebla." It is not a hero that this dying man needs, having been fictionalized, and reduced to the status of a nonentity by scorn. Compassion is not exactly a heroic quality. There is a crucial difference between fighting heroically against the mist, struggling to be oneself through the struggle itself against the mist, to be oneself in reference and in opposition to the nebulous background, and, on the other hand, to save the individual from the mist, to rescue him from the power of the mist without having to look back. For in order to do this the saving lifeline must be anchored beyond the mist, outside the mist. This is why the absence of the heroic from *Niebla* is particularly significant.

Unamuno's Don Quixote is a fighter against the mist, but he is made of the very same stuff as the mist—his madness is made of the same undifferentiated confusion. *Unamuno's Don Quixote is not the one who rescues the individual from the mist. On the contrary, his Don Quixote is portrayed as the one who saves the mist itself, by transforming it, by turning it into the stuff of heroes.* Our Lord Don Quixote, as Unamuno called him, is the Lord of the Mist, the one who dignifies it. This heroic Don Quixote is an exceptional witness to the transformation of destructive violence into protecting violence, of poison into antidote. He is the closest that Christian Unamuno could come to the old sacralizing process, to the old transformation of the terrifying nebula, the violent undifferentiation, confounding, of everything, into sacred, heroic, gods. But how could Unamuno, "the man with the sign of the cross on his chest," as Machado called him, truly believe in the saving power of such a hero?

Unamuno called Don Quixote *un loco divino*, "a divine madman," but he was quick to add, "not the most divine of all. The most divine of all madmen was and continues to be Jesus, the Christ" (*Cómo se hace una novela*, 117). He never confused Don Quixote and Christ; a proof of that is in the absence of the quixotic solution from *Niebla*. It never occurred to Unamuno to fill the vacuum left by the weakness of Augusto Pérez's Christian faith with quixotic faith. But he never knew how to differentiate properly between the two. As I have said from the beginning, the basic blindness in Unamuno's *quijotismo* consists of his inability to see any fundamental contradiction between his faith in Don Quixote and his faith in Christ. He never saw the radical incompatibility between the Christian victim, Christ, and the heroic victim that his admired Kierkegaard, for example, clearly saw.

Cervantes never made that mistake. He had no intention of saving or dignifying the mist through Don Quixote, but quite the opposite: he intended to save Don Quixote from the mist: "My judgment is now clear and free from the misty shadows of ignorance with which my ill-starred and continuous reading of those detestable books of chivalry had obscured it." Cervantes knew what those dense or misty shadows, *sombras caliginosas*, obscured, made very difficult to see: to put it once again in the words of mad Cardenio's sonnet, "the struggle of the primeval discordant confusion," a world from which reality has disappeared ("ascended to its empyrean halls"), leaving behind a deceitful semblance of it. As we discovered in Chapter IV, madness has a "cosmic" dimension in Cervantes, an apocalyptic one. Cervantes wants to save Don Quixote and himself from confusion. He strives for clarity, and he does it in the only way possible, without violence, compassionately.

Transparent Depth

The most extraordinary thing about the *Quixote* may be its transparent quality, the transparency of its depth. As I said at the beginning, the depth is there for all to see, up front, in the humble story of the madman who has become alienated, become an other to himself, because he has been strangely seduced by literary fiction. As we see and laugh at all the crazy things the madman does, we keep hearing also the voice that tells us that it is indeed a pity that such a fine person is so estranged from himself, and that the decent thing to do is to try and cure him, to bring him back home and to himself, to a view of his own reality without the lens of fiction. That is all. A child can understand that.

And yet it is so difficult to see with the eyes of a child! It is so difficult to believe what is there before us in plain view! It is especially difficult in a novel, for a novel's attraction lies in complicating things that appear to be simple. Cervantes's merit consists in maintaining the simplicity throughout all the complications, resisting the easy temptation posed by something like Unamuno's mist. He could do it because he had faith in reality, in the independent existence of reality and truth, which are ultimately the same thing. He had faith, which is the opposite of believing that one has the truth, that one possesses it. To have faith in the truth is to let the truth exist on its own, beyond the I-other relationship. Reality and truth demand confidence, trust, in exactly the same manner as interpersonal relations require trust in order to be truthful, sustained by reality—in other words, in order to prevent them from becoming fictional. Because, as soon as one of the parties tries to possess the truth of the relationship, to fix it in place, to control it, what happens is what we saw in the story of jealous Anselmo, the *Curioso*, who aspired to a kind of Satanic certainty forbidden by God; or what happens to a jealous Carrizales of El celoso extremeño (*The Jealous Extremaduran*), who also searched for a certainty without faith or trust, and ended up, like Anselmo, recognizing his disastrous mistake.

Reality and truth are matters of faith and simplicity of vision, the opposite of duplicity, which is always linked to the deterioration of the interpersonal relationship, to the scandal, to rivalry. If one does not believe in reality, in the truth of reality, that is a sign that one is putting too much faith negatively, violently, in the other; that one has placed the other between oneself and the truth (instead of the truth between oneself and the other); that one has turned the other into a scandal, a stumbling block. If one does not have faith in the truth, in the independent existence of the truth, it is probably because one believes the other has taken possession of the truth, has taken the truth violently from oneself. Not to believe in the truth is to envy the truth, to look at it with evil eyes through the eyes of the other. Loss of faith does not destroy the truth, but it does turn it into a source of conflict, into a poison. One cannot be saved without the truth, but neither can one be condemned without it.

The transparent simplicity of the *Quixote* is an invitation to read it in the same manner. This is a difficult task, to be sure, but one quite easy to understand. The basis for such an ideal reading can only be the recognition of a Cervantes and a Don Quixote finally reconciled, through the overcoming of the power play and the rivalry between author and character accurately diagnosed by Unamuno, even though he could not achieve it himself. The *Quixote* must be read from the standpoint of Don Quixote's final cure and salvation, and that requires taking Don Quixote's fictionalizing madness seriously, the madness that turns him into a fictional character, and his life into a novel. Fortunately for him and for us, that novel was unprecedented, it was a modern novel, that is to say, a novel without heroes or antiheroes. But to maintain such an ideal reading, one has to begin by trusting Cervantes, by believing that his ultimate goal is to tell us the truth, by believing that, in spite of his occasionally mischievous irony, and his evident "delight in pulling the wool over his readers's eyes," as Wardropper said, he does not want to deceive us, or himself.

Bibliography

Cervantes's Works

The Adventures of Don Quixote. Trans. J. M. Cohen. London: Penguin Classics, 1950.

Don Quijote de la Mancha. Instituto Cervantes. Ed. Francisco Rico. Barcelona: Crítica, 1998.

Exemplary Stories. Trans. C. A. Jones. London: Penguin Classics, 1972.

La Galatea. Ed. Juan Bautista Avalle-Arce. Clásicos Castellanos. Madrid: Espasa-Calpe, 1968.

Obras completas. 2 vols. 17th ed. Ed. Ángel Valbuena Prat. Madrid: Aguilar, 1970.

Secondary Works

Adamson Hoebel, E. *The Law of Primitive Man: A Study in Comparative Legal Dynamics*. Cambridge, Mass.: Harvard University Press, 1964.

Alemán, Mateo. *Guzmán de Alfarache*. Ed. Francisco Rico. Barcelona, Spain: Planeta, 1983.

Allen, John J. "Autobiografía y ficción: El relato del capitán cautivo (*Don Quijote* I, 39–41)." *Anales cervantinos* 15 (1976): 149–55.

———. "*El celoso extremeño* y *El curioso impertinente*." In *Studies in the Spanish Golden Age: Cervantes and Lope de Vega*, ed. Dana B. Drake and José A. Madrigal. Miami, Fla.: Universal, 1978.

———. "The Providential World of Cervantes' Fiction." *Thought* 55, no. 217 (1980): 184–95.

Alter, Robert. *Rogue's Progress: Studies in the Picaresque Novel*. Cambridge, Mass.: Harvard University Press, 1964.

Álvarez Amell, Diana. *El discurso de los prólogos del Siglo de Oro: La retórica de la representación*. Potomac, Md.: Scripta Humanistica, 1999.

Arellano, Ignacio. Ed. F. de Quevedo. *Historia de la vida del Buscón*. Madrid: Colección Austral, 1997.

Arias, Joan. *Guzmán de Alfarache: The Unrepentant Narrator*. London: Támesis, 1977.

Asensio, Eugenio. *Itinerario del entremés. Desde Lope de Rueda a Quiñones de Benavente*. Madrid: Gredos, 1965.

Auden, W. H. *The Enchafèd Flood*. New York: Random House, 1950.

Augustine, Saint. *Confessions*. Trans. William Watts. Cambridge, Mass.: Harvard University Press, 1912.

Avalle-Arce, Juan Bautista. *Deslindes cervantinos*. Madrid: Edhigar, 1961.

———. *La novela pastoril española*. Madrid: Ediciones Istmo, 1974.

Avellaneda, Alonso Fernández de. *Don Quijote de la Mancha*. 3 vols. Ed. Martín de Riquer. Madrid: Espasa Calpe, 1972.

———. *Don Quixote de la Mancha (Part II). Being the Spurious Continuation of Miguel de Cervantes' Part I*. Trans. and ed. Alberta Wilson Server and John Esten Keller. Newark, Del.: Juan de la Cuesta, 1980.

Ayala, Francisco. *Cervantes y Quevedo*. Barcelona: Seix Barral, 1974.

———. *El Lazarillo: Nuevo examen de algunos aspectos*. Madrid: Taurus, 1971.

Bacon, Francis. The Advancement of Learning *and* The New Atlantis. London: Oxford University Press, 1906.

———. *The Essays*. Ed. John Pitcher. Harmondsworth, Middlesex, U.K.: Penguin Books, 1985.

Bakhtin, M. M. *The Dialogic Imagination*. Ed. Michael Holquist. Trans. Caryl Emerson and Michael Holquist. Austin: University of Texas Press, 1981.

Balthasar, Hans Urs von. *Tragedy under Grace: Reinhold Schneider on the Experience of the West*. Trans. Brian McNeil, C.R.V. San Francisco: Ignatius Press, 1997.

Bandera, Cesáreo. *Mímesis conflictiva. Ficción literaria y violencia en Cervantes y Calderón*. Madrid: Gredos, 1975.

———. *The Sacred Game: The Role of the Sacred in the Genesis of Modern Literary Fiction*. University Park: Pennsylvania State University Press, 1994.

Barish, Jonas. *The Antitheatrical Prejudice*. Berkeley and Los Angeles: University of California Press, 1981.

Barrick, Mac E. "The Form and Function of Folktales in *Don Quijote*." *Journal of Medieval and Renaissance Studies* 6 (1976): 101–38.

Bateson, Gregory. *Steps to an Ecology of the Mind*. San Francisco: Chandler, 1972.

Bellinger, Charles K. *The Genealogy of Violence: Reflections on Creation, Freedom, and Evil*. Oxford, U.K.: Oxford University Press, 2001.

Bembo, Pietro. *Prose e rime*. Ed. Carlo Dionisotti. Turin, Italy: Unione Tipografico-Editrice Torinese, 1966.

Bercé, Ives-Marie. *Fête et révolte. Des mentalités populaires du XVIe au XVIIIe siècle*. Paris: Hachette, 1976.

Bigeard, Martine. *La folie et les fous littéraires en Espagne 1500–1650*. Paris: Centre de Recherches Hispaniques, 1972.

Bjornson, Richard. "*El Buscón*: Quevedo's Annihilation of the Picaro." *Iberomania* 4 (1976): 41–66.

Blackburn, Alexander. *The Myth of the Picaro: Continuity and Transformation of the Picaresque Novel, 1554–1954*. Chapel Hill: University of North Carolina Press, 1979.

Bloom, Harold. *The Western Canon: The Books and School of the Ages*. New York: Harcourt Brace & Co., 1994.

Brancaforte, Benito. *Guzmán de Alfarache: ¿Conversión o proceso de degradación?* Madison: Hispanic Seminary of Medieval Studies, 1980.

Calasso, Roberto. *La ruine de Kasch*. Paris: Gallimard, 1987. (Original title: *La rovina di Kasch*. Milan, Italy: Adelphi, 1983.)

Calderón de la Barca, Pedro. *Obras completas*. 3 vols. Ed. Ángel Valbuena Briones. Madrid: Aguilar, 1973.

Caro Baroja, Julio. *El carnaval (Análisis histórico-cultural)*. Madrid: Taurus, 1965.

Castro, Américo. *Hacia Cervantes*. 3rd ed. Madrid: Taurus, 1967.

Cavillac, Michel. "Mateo Alemán et la modernité." *Bulletin Hispanique* 82 (1980): 380–401.

Cavillac, Michel, and Cécile Cavillac. "A propos du *Buscón*, et de *Guzmán de Alfarache*." *Bulletin Hispanique* 75 (1973): 114–31.

Clement of Alexandria. *Exhortation to the Greeks: The Rich Man's Salvation. To the Newly Baptized*. Trans. G. W. Butterworth. 1919; reprint, Cambridge, Mass.: Loeb Classical Library, Harvard University Press, 1999.

Close, Anthony. *Cervantes and the Comic Mind of His Age*. Oxford, U.K.: Oxford University Press, 2000.

Combet, Louis. *Cervantès ou les incertitudes du désir. Une approche psychostructural de l'oeuvre de Cervantès*. Lyon, France: Presses Universitaires de Lyon, 1980.

Cros, Edmond. *L'aristocrate et le carnaval des gueux. Étude sur le Buscón de Quevedo*. Montpellier, France: Université Paul Valéry, 1975.

———. "Lectura sacrificial de la muerte de Cristo y rivalidad mimética en *El Buscón*." In *Homenaje a Quevedo*, ed. Victor García de la Concha, 339–46. Salamanca, Spain: Ediciones Universidad de Salamanca, 1982.

———, ed. *Historia de la vida del Buscón*, by Francisco de Quevedo. Madrid: Taurus, 1995.

Darbord, Michel. *La poésie religieuse espagnole des rois catholiques à Philippe II*. Paris: Centre de Recherche de l'Institut d'Études Hispaniques, 1965.

Dostoyevski, F. M. *The Devils*. Trans. David Magarshack. Penguin Classics, 1953.

Dudley, Edward. "Don Quijote as Magus: The Rhetoric of Interpolation." *Bulletin of Hispanic Studies* 49, no. 4 (1972): 355–68.

———. *The Endless Text: Don Quixote and the Hermeneutics of Romance*. Albany: State University of New York Press, 1997.

Dunn, Peter N. *Spanish Picaresque Fiction: A New Literary History*. Ithaca, N.Y.: Cornell University Press, 1993.

Dupuy, Jean-Pierre, ed. *Self-Deception and Paradoxes of Rationality*. Stanford, Calif.: CSLI Publications, 1998.

Egido, Aurora. "Retablo carnavalesco del Buscón Don Pablos." *Hispanic Review* 46 (1978): 173–97.

Epicurus. In Diogenes Laertius, *Lives of Eminent Philosophers*, vol. 2. Trans. R. D. Hicks. 1931; reprint, Cambridge, Mass.: Loeb Classical Library, Harvard University Press, 1995.

Festugière, A. J. *Epicurus and His Gods*. Trans. C. W. Chilton. Cambridge, Mass.: Harvard University Press, 1956.

Forcione, Alban K. *Cervantes, Aristotle, and the Persiles*. Princeton, N.J.: Princeton University Press, 1970.

———. *Cervantes' Christian Romance. A Study of Persiles y Sigismunda*. Princeton, N.J.: Princeton University Press, 1972.

Foucault, Michel. *Folie et déraison. Histoire de la folie à l'âge classique*. Paris: Plon, 1961.

———. *Madness and Civilization: A History of Insanity in the Age of Reason*. Trans. Richard Howard. New York: Pantheon Books, 1965.

Fribourg, Jeanine. "La fête patronale en Espagne: Substitut du carnaval." In *Le Carnaval, la Fête et la Communication. Actes des Premières Rencontres Internationales. Nice, 8 au 10 mars 1984*, 41–53. Nice, France: Editions Serre, 1985.

Friedman, Edward H. *The Antiheroine's Voice: Narrative Discourse and Transformations of the Picaresque*. Columbia: University of Missouri Press, 1987.

Garcés, María Antonia. *Cervantes in Algiers: A Captive's Tale*. Nashville, Tenn.: Vanderbilt University Press, 2002.

Gauchet, Marcel. *Le désenchantement du monde: Une histoire politique de la religion*. Paris: Gallimard, 1985.

Gilman, Stephen. *The Novel According to Cervantes*. Berkeley and Los Angeles: University of California Press, 1989.

Gil Polo, Gaspar. *Diana enamorada*. Ed. Francisco López Estrada. Madrid: Castalia, 1987.

Girard, René. *Le bouc émissaire*. Paris: Grasset, 1982.

———. *A Theater of Envy: William Shakespeare*. Oxford, U.K.: Oxford University Press, 1991.

———. *Violence and the Sacred*. Trans. Patrick Gregory. Baltimore: Johns Hopkins University Press, 1977.

Goodhart, Sandor. *Sacrificing Commentary: Reading the End of Literature*. Baltimore: Johns Hopkins University Press, 1996.

Grivois, Henri. "Adolescence, Indifferentiation, and the Onset of Psychosis." *Contagion* 6 (1999): 104–21.

———. *Le fou et le mouvement du monde*. Paris: Bernard Grasset, 1995.

———. *Tu ne sera pas schizophrène*. Paris: Les Empêcheurs de penser en rond / Le Seuil, 2001.

Grivois, Henri, and J.-P. Dupuy, eds. *Mécanismes mentaux, mécanismes sociaux. De la psychose à la panique*. Paris: La Découverte, 1995.

Heliodorus. *An Ethiopan Romance*. Trans. Moses Hadas. Ann Arbor: University of Michigan Press, 1957.

Hicks, R. D. *Stoic and Epicurean*. New York: Russell & Russell, 1962.

Ife, B. W. *Reading and Fiction in Golden Age Spain*. Cambridge, U.K.: Cambridge University Press, 1985.

Jameson, Fredric. *The Political Unconscious: Narrative as a Socially Symbolic Act*. Ithaca, N.Y.: Cornell University Press, 1981.

Jewers, Caroline A. *Chivalric Fiction and the History of the Novel*. Gainesville: University Press of Florida, 2000.

Kennedy, Judith M., ed. *A Critical Edition of Yong's Translation of George of Montemayor's Diana and Gil Polo's Enamoured Diana*. Oxford, U.K.: Clarendon Press, 1968.

Kierkegaard, Soren. *Either/Or. Part I* and *Either/Or. Part II*. Ed. and trans. Howard V. Hong and Edna H. Hong. Princeton, N.J.: Princeton University Press, 1987.

———. Fear and Trembling *and* The Sickness unto Death. Trans. Walter Lowrie. Princeton, N.J.: Princeton University Press, 1968.

———. *Journals and Papers*. Vols. 1 and 2. Ed. Howard V. Hong and Edna H. Hong. Bloomington: Indiana University Press, 1970.

Krist, Ernst. *Psychoanalytic Explorations in Art*. New York: Schocken Books, 1964.

La picaresca. Orígenes, textos y estructuras. Actas del I Congreso Internacional sobre la Picaresca. Madrid: Fundación Universitaria Española, 1979.

Lázaro Carreter, F. "Estudio preliminar." In F. de Quevedo, *La vida del Buscón*. Ed. Fernando Cabo Aseguinolaza. Barcelona, Spain: Crítica, 1993.

Leupin, Alexandre. *Fiction et incarnation. Littérature et théologie au Moyen Age*. Paris: Flammarion, 1993.

Lope de Vega. *Obras escogidas. Tomo II*. Ed. Federico Carlos Sainz de Robles. Madrid: Aguilar, 1964.

Lynch, William F., S.J. *Christ and Apollo: The Dimensions of the Literary Imagination*. New York: Sheed & Ward, 1960.

Machado, Antonio. *Juan de Mairena*. 2 vols. Madrid: Cátedra, 1998.

———. *Prosas completas*. Ed. Oreste Macrí. Madrid: Espasa Calpe, 1989.

Márquez Villanueva, Francisco. *Personajes y temas del* Quijote. Madrid: Taurus, 1975.

———. *Trabajos y días cervantinos*. Alcalá de Henares, Spain: Centro de Estudios Cervantinos, 1995.

Marx, Karl, and Friedrich Engels. *The German Ideology: Part I*. Ed. C. J. Arthur. New York: International Publishers, 1970.

Masterpieces of the Spanish Golden Age. Ed. Angel Flores. New York: Holt, Rinehart, and Winston, 1957.

May, Terence E. "Good and Evil in the *Buscón*: A Survey." *Modern Language Review* 45 (1950): 319–35.

———. "A Narrative Conceit in *La vida del Buscón*." *Modern Language Review* 64 (1969): 327–33.

Molho, Maurice. *Introducción al pensamiento picaresco*. Salamanca, Spain: Anaya, 1972.

Montemayor, Jorge de. *La Diana*. Ed. Juan Montero. Barcelona, Spain: Crítica, 1996.

Moreno Villa, José. *Locos, enanos, negros y niños palaciegos. Gente de placer que tuvieron los Austrias en la Corte Española desde 1563 a 1700*. Mexico City: Editorial Presencia, 1939.

Morón, Ciriaco. *Para entender el* Quijote. Madrid: Rialp, 2005.

Murillo, L. A. ."Cervantes' *Tale of the Captive Captain*." In *Florilegium Hispanicum: Medieval and Golden Age Studies Presented to Dorothy Clotelle Clarke*, ed. John S. Geary. Madison, Wis.: Hispanic Seminary of Medieval Studies, 1983.

———. "El *Ur-Quijote*, nueva hipótesis." *Cervantes* 1 (1981): 43–50.

Nagy, Gregory. *The Best of the Acheans: Concepts of the Hero in Archaic Greek Poetry*. Baltimore: Johns Hopkins University Press, 1979.

Niebuhr, Reinhold. *Beyond Tragedy: Essays on the Christian Interpretation of History*. New York: Charles Scribner's Sons, 1937.

Ortega y Gasset, José. "Ideas sobre la novela." In *Teoría de la novela*, ed. Agnes y Germán Gullón, 29–64. Madrid: Taurus, 1974.

Parker, Alexander A. *Los pícaros en la literatura. La novela picaresca en España y Europa (1599–1753).* Madrid: Gredos, 1971.

Peirce, Charles S. *Selected Writings.* Ed. Philip P. Wiener. Reprint; New York: Dover Publications, 1966.

Perrot, Danielle, ed. *Don Quichotte au XXe siècle. Réceptions d'une figure mythique dans la littérature et les arts.* Clermont-Ferrand, France: Presses Universitaires Blaise Pascal, 2003.

Pinel, Philippe. *Traité médico-philosophique sur l'aliénation mentale.* Reprint; New York: Arno Press, 1976.

Preminger, Alex, O. B. Hardison Jr., and Kevin Kerrane. *Classical and Medieval Literary Criticism.* New York: Frederick Ungar, 1974.

Presberg, Charles D. *Adventures in Paradox:* Don Quixote *and the Western Tradition.* University Park: Pennsylvania State University Press, 2001.

Quevedo, Don Francisco de. *Obras completas.* 6th ed. Vol. I. Ed. Felicidad Buendía. Madrid: Aguilar, 1974.

Reed, Walter L. *An Exemplary History of the Novel: The Quixotic versus the Picaresque.* Chicago: University of Chicago Press, 1981.

Rico, Francisco. *The Spanish Picaresque Novel and the Point of View.* Trans. Charles Davis. Cambridge, U.K.: Cambridge University Press, 1984.

Riley, E. C. *Don Quixote.* London: Allen & Unwin, 1986.

———. "Whatever Happened to Heroes? Cervantes and Some Major European Novels of the Twentieth Century." In *Cervantes and the Modernists,* ed. Edith Williamson, 73–84. London: Támesis, 1994.

Robert, Marthe. *The Old and the New:* From Don Quixote *to* Kafka. Foreword by Robert Alter. Berkeley and Los Angeles: University of California Press, 1977.

Rodríguez, Alfred, and Ángela Irwin. "*El capitán cautivo* de Cervantes: ¿Barroca hibridización de historia y folklore?" *Anales cervantinos* 32 (1994): 259–63.

Rodríguez Matos, Carlos Antonio. *El narrador pícaro: Guzmán de Alfarache.* Madison, Wis.: Hispanic Seminary of Medieval Studies, 1985.

Rosales, Luis. *Obras completas.* Vol. 2, *Cervantes y la libertad.* Madrid: Editorial Trotta, 1996.

Rosen, George. *Madness in Society: Chapters in the Historical Sociology of Mental Illness.* Chicago: University of Chicago Press, 1968.

Russell, Peter E. *Cervantes.* Oxford, U.K.: Oxford University Press, 1985.

Sánchez y Escribano, F. "Un tema erasmiano en el *Quijote,* I, xxii." *Revista Hispánica Moderna* 19 (1953): 88–93.

Saward, John. *Perfect Fools: Folly for Christ's Sake in Catholic and Orthodox Spirituality.* Oxford, U.K.: Oxford University Press, 1980.

Schoeck, Helmut. *Envy: A Theory of Social Behaviour.* New York: Harcourt, Brace & World, 1969.

Schwager, Raymund. *Jesus in the Drama of Salvation: Toward a Biblical Doctrine of Redemption.* New York: Crossroad Publishing Co., 1999.

Serres, Michel. *La naissance de la physique dans le texte de Lucrèce.* Paris: Les Editions de Minuit, 1977.

Solé-Leris, Amadeu. "Psychological Realism in the Pastoral Novel: Gil Polo's *Diana enamorada.*" *Bulletin of Hispanic Studies* 39 (1962): 43–47.

———. *The Spanish Pastoral Novel*. Boston: Twayne Publishers, 1980.

Stegman, André. "Sur quelques aspects des fous en titre d'office dans la France du XVe siècle." In *Folie et déraison à la Renaissance*, 53–73. Bruxelles: Editions de l'Université de Bruxelles, 1976.

Sullivan, H. W. *Grotesque Purgatory: A Study of* Don Quixote, *Part II*. University Park: Pennsylvania State University Press, 1996.

Swain, Barbara. *Fools and Folly during the Middle Ages and the Renaissance*. New York: Columbia University Press, 1932.

Swain, Gladys. *Le sujet de la folie. Naissance de la psychiatrie*. Toulouse, France: Privat, 1977.

Thomas à Kempis. *The Imitation of Christ*. Ed. Paul M. Bechtel. Chicago: Moody, 1980.

Toffanin, Giuseppe. *La fine dell'umanesimo*. Milan, Turin, Rome: Fratelli Bocca Editori, 1920.

Trilling, Lionel. *The Liberal Imagination: Essays on Literature and Society*. New York: Charles Scribner's Sons, 1976.

Ullman, Pierre L. "Cervantes y el antihéroe." In *La picaresca. Orígenes, textos y estructuras. Actas del I Congreso Internacional sobre la Picaresca*, 547–52. Madrid: Fundación Universitaria Española, 1979.

Unamuno, Miguel de. *Abel Sánchez. Una historia de pasión*. Ed. Isabel Criado. Madrid: Austral, 1997. (English translation: *Novela / Nivola*. Trans. Anthony Kerrigan. Bollingen Series, vol. 6. Princeton, N.J.: Princeton University Press, 1976.)

———. *Del sentimiento trágico de la vida. La agonía del cristianismo*. Madrid: Akal, 1983. (English translation: *The Tragic Sense of Life in Men and Nations*. Trans. Anthony Kerrigan. Bollingen Series, vol. 4. Princeton, N.J.: Princeton University Press, 1967.)

———. *Niebla*. Ed. Francisco Fernández Turienzo. Madrid: Alhambra, 1986. (English translation: Mist. Trans. Warner Fite. New York: Howard Fertig, 1973.)

———. *Obras completas*. 16 vols. Madrid: Afrodisio Aguado, 1950–1964.

———. *San Manuel Bueno, mártir. Cómo se hace una novela*. Madrid: Alianza Editorial, 1968.

———. *Vida de Don Quijote y Sancho*. Madrid: Austral, 1964. (English translation: *Our Lord Don Quixote: The Life of Don Quixote and Sancho with Related Essays*. Trans. A. Kerrigan. Introduction by Walter Starkie. Bollingen Series, vol. 3. Princeton, N.J.: Princeton University Press, 1976.)

Vaillo, Carlos. "El *Buscón*, la novela picaresca y la sátira: nueva aproximación." In *Estudios sobre Quevedo*, ed. Santiago Fernández Mosquera, 261–79. Santiago de Compostela, Spain: Universidad de Santiago de Compostela, 1995.

Wardropper, Bruce W. "The Pertinence of 'El curioso impertinente.'" *PMLA* 72 (1957): 587–600.

Weiger, John G. *The Individuated Self: Cervantes and the Emergence of the Individual*. Athens: Ohio University Press, 1979.

———. *In the Margins of Cervantes*. Hanover, N.H.: University Press of New England, 1988.

Welsford, Enid. *The Fool: His Social and Literary History*. London: Faber & Faber, 1935.

Whitenack, Judith A. *The Impenitent Confession of Guzmán de Alfarache*. Madison, Wis.: Hispanic Seminary of Medieval Studies, 1985.

Wilde, Oscar. *The Picture of Dorian Gray*. New York: Barnes & Noble Classics, 2003.

Willeford, William. *The Fool and His Scepter*. Evanston, Ill.: Northwestern University Press, 1969.

Zambrano, María. *El hombre y lo divino*. Mexico City: Fondo de Cultura Económica, 1993.

Zijderveld, Anton C. *Reality in a Looking-Glass: Rationality through an Analysis of Traditional Folly*. London: Routledge & Kegan Paul, 1982.

Ziolkowski, Eric J. "Don Quixote and Kierkegaard's Understanding of the Single Individual in Society." In *Foundations of Kierkegaard's Vision of Community: Religion, Ethics, and Politics in Kierkegaard*, ed. George B. Connell and C. Stephen Evans, 130–43. Atlantic Highlands, N.J., and London: Humanities Press, 1992.

———. *The Sanctification of Don Quixote: From Hidalgo to Priest*. University Park: Pennsylvania State University Press, 1991.

Index

www.ingramcontent.com/pod-product-compliance
Lightning Source LLC
LaVergne TN
LVHW090151080826
844660LV00013B/756/J
9780813214528